Business Storytelling FOR DUMMIES® A Wiley Brand

by Karen Dietz, PhD and Lori L. Silverman

FOR DUMMIES® A Wiley Brand

Business Storytelling For Dummies®

Published by: **John Wiley & Sons, Inc.,** 111 River Street, Hoboken, NJ 07030-5774, www.wiley.com

Copyright © 2014 by John Wiley & Sons, Inc., Hoboken, New Jersey

Published simultaneously in Canada

For general information on our other products and services, please contact our Customer Care Department within the U.S. at 877-762-2974, outside the U.S. at 317-572-3993, or fax 317-572-4002. For technical support, please visit www.wiley.com/techsupport.

Wiley publishes in a variety of print and electronic formats and by print-on-demand. Some material included with standard print versions of this book may not be included in e-books or in print-on-demand. If this book refers to media such as a CD or DVD that is not included in the version you purchased, you may download this material at http://booksupport.wiley.com. For more information about Wiley products, visit www.wiley.com.

Library of Congress Control Number: 2013949562

ISBN 978-1-118-66121-5 (pbk); ISBN 978-1-118-73017-1 (ebk);
ISBN 978-1-118-73019-5 (ebk); ISBN 978-1-118-73028-7 (ebk)

Manufactured in the United States of America

10 9 8 7 6 5 4 3 2 1

Contents at a Glance

Table of Contents

Part II: Moving People to Action: Creating Compelling Stories 97

Chapter 6: Crafting a Story 99

Introduction

Welcome to *Business Storytelling For Dummies*! We guarantee if you choose to read this book, your work life will change for the better.

What makes us say this? We believe that business storytelling is the most critical skill set to hit the business arena in ages. You're probably asking, "Well, if that's the case, why isn't everybody doing it already?" Ah. What looks really simple on first blush isn't. That's why you now have this resource in your hands. Although it takes a little time to put the strategies, tools, and techniques of story into action, the results are striking.

We'd love to give you a magic wand and have everything you touch turn into golden stories but alas, that talented we are not — yet! What we *can* do is remind you that you already tell stories, and with this book in hand you can become an awesome business storyteller. Then you can dazzle your co-workers, stand out in your career, and run rings around your competition. Woo-hoo!

About This Book

For years, we've wanted to write a pragmatic book on business storytelling. And voila! We now have this book to share with you. We didn't want you to just grasp concepts associated with storytelling; we wanted you to be able to take action after reading each chapter. So we've spent a lot of time documenting "how-to" steps. This was hard for us. Storytelling is as much an art form as it is a science. It's not linear. We know those who are advanced in the subject will appreciate the value of reducing complex topics to a series of step-by-step bullet points that cover the basics. At the same time, we recognize that there's more than one way to skin a cat. Yet we wanted to give you a clear-cut place to start. We hope those new to storytelling will benefit from our efforts.

We also had a personal agenda. We wanted to give you the latest, greatest information and tips we had on the subject. This means there are topics here that you may not find anywhere else.

There are two different audience slants for this book. The first has to do with your role. The second has to do with the type of organization you're affiliated with. With that in mind, this book is for you if

- ✔ You're an individual who needs to make a compelling point in a presentation or a meeting in order to get people to take action.
- ✔ You're an account manager or sales professional wanting to enhance customer relationships and increase your closing rate.
- ✔ You're a supervisor who needs to get your staff on board with changes and motivate them to continually produce high-quality work.
- ✔ You're a project or program manager who needs to garner commitment, communicate progress more effectively, and capture best practices.
- ✔ You're a mid-level manager who needs to build a collaborative work environment and drive innovation and creativity.
- ✔ You're a senior leader who needs to rally and align large groups of people around a common vision to achieve new goals.
- ✔ You're an entrepreneur who wants to grow your business in unique and cost-effective ways.

We did our best to cover these organizational types throughout the book. You'll find the content valuable if you

- ✔ Work in a startup that's looking for more funding and visibility in the marketplace.
- ✔ Are a small or microbusiness that wants to use stories to attract and retain customers and expand into new markets.
- ✔ Are attached to a nonprofit seeking to build a community and spread your cause.
- ✔ Are in a creative field and want to bring storytelling into your design and production work.
- ✔ Are employed in a public sector organization seeking cost-effective ways to effectively communicate with employees and constituents and shift their thinking and behaviors.
- ✔ Work for a privately held or publicly owned enterprise that desires increased brand awareness, more market share, and more compelling corporate communications.

What was our overall goal for this book? To get you to benefit from the active use of storytelling techniques and processes in your daily work and your daily life. *Business Storytelling For Dummies* shows you how to drive your organization to new heights and become a force for change yourself.

We used the following conventions throughout the book:

- ✔ Websites appear in monofont to help them stand out — like this: www.dummies.com. Some addresses may need to break across two lines. Just type exactly what you see in this book, pretending the line break doesn't exist.

- ✔ Any information that's helpful or interesting but not essential to the topic at hand appears in *sidebars*, which are the gray-shaded boxes sprinkled throughout the book.

- ✔ Whenever we introduce a new term, it's italicized.

You'll see three additional conventions in the book:

- ✔ Any time a story or other type of narrative example is used, we indented it so you can easily identify it.

- ✔ We've put several stories that we reference into the Appendix.

- ✔ We've noted cross-references throughout the chapters so you can easily find information.

We made several assumptions about you:

- ✔ You want practical advice. We provide our own personal experiences and those of others — as well as steps for doing whatever we suggest.

- ✔ You want examples of what we consider to be well-constructed, compelling stories. So we give you several.

- ✔ You want to read more than what's here. We provide numerous links to articles, blog postings, books, and other resources we've found to be of interest.

- ✔ You most likely define *story* differently than we do. We make sure that every story we present or refer to is consistent with our definition. When it isn't, we mention that.

- ✔ We use the words *storytelling, storifying,* and *story work* in this book to include finding stories, evoking them from others, digging into them for meaning, crafting them, using story triggers as memory devices, and telling them.

Throughout this book are a variety of examples of story use and actual stories that people gave us permission to use. Please respect the copyright notices in the front matter of this book.

Icons Used in This Book

Look for the following symbols to find valuable information in the book:

This icon indicates helpful advice, tips, how-tos, and steps to doing whatever we encourage you to do.

This icon points out pitfalls and mistakes to avoid. Read them!

This icon points out important information you should try to remember and details we want to embed in your brain.

This icon links you to a website, book, blog posting, video, audio, or article that we encourage you to check out.

This icon highlights what we and/or others have done related to the discussion point. To the best of our knowledge, these real-life examples are valid.

Beyond the Book

You'll find free articles and a cheat sheet for the book on the Dummies website (www.dummies.com/extras/businessstorytelling/). One article gives advice on how to title a story. Because we know how hard it is to turn data into a story, the second article provides another example of how to successfully do so. Two additional articles discuss how to use stories with virtual teams and ten things you should always do when working with stories (the opposite of Chapter 17).

We've created three cheat sheets to help you use the content in this book. First, we summarize beyond Chapter 4 all the types of stories we mention in the book. The second cheat sheet is about crafting a storyboard. The final one summarizes all the story structures we present in the book.

Where to Go from Here

If you want help in a specific subject area, search for it either in the table of contents or the index. If we want you to know something prior to this material, we provide a cross-reference to this information. Feel free to jump to any topic of the book and get what you need right when you need it. Or take a more traditional approach and start with Chapter 1.

Take the time to delve more deeply into various topics by going online to check out the links we provide throughout the book. This extra information will help take you to the next level. It certainly has expanded our thinking.

We hope this book empowers you to do more than you've ever thought possible — to get your voice heard, get people to take action based on what you share, and achieve results you thought were out of reach. Story on!

Part I

Getting Started with Business Storytelling

In this part . . .

- ✔ Highlight the role of storytelling in business and its impact on individuals.

- ✔ Identify the ultimate goal of business storytelling and the results that can come through its use in organizations.

- ✔ Identify the core elements of a story and what distinguishes it from anecdotes, case studies, examples, and other forms of narrative.

- ✔ Outline seven types of personal and organizational stories to have in your hip pocket at all times.

- ✔ Evoke, listen to, and capture stories from others in a way that empowers and honors these individuals.

Chapter 1

The Scoop on Business Storytelling

In This Chapter

▶ Highlighting the role of story in the new economy

▶ Identifying the best definition of a story

▶ Connecting story to the physical, mental, emotional, and spiritual

*I*s storytelling a tool, a technique, or a core competence and a business strategy? We believe it's all of the above. More and more businesses are recognizing that storytelling is more than giving presentation skills to managers and staff. They're acknowledging it's a critical capability in effectively leading an organization. That working with stories requires an overall strategy that addresses *why* and *what*, in addition to building skills that speak to *how*. That storytelling in marketing, branding, and sales is about engagement, listening, and creating storied experiences to sustain customer loyalty and profits. That stories provide deep, rich, and meaningful experiences for people if crafted and told well. And that stories can be the wellspring for change and help unite a community around an organization.

Storytelling's Role in Business

For years, businesses have realized that story can mean big money. In the 1995 article, "One Quarter of GDP Is Persuasion," economists Deirdre McClosky and Arjo Klamer calculated that persuasion activities (advertising, public relations, sales, editing, writing, art making, and so on) accounted for 25 percent of the U.S. gross domestic product (*American Economic Review*, vol. 85, No. 2). Author Steven Denning, formerly of the World Bank, conjectures in *The Leader's Guide To Storytelling: Mastering the Art and Discipline of Business Narrative* (Jossey-Bass, 2011), that if half of that amount is devoted to story, then storytelling is worth $2.25 trillion annually (www.stevedenning.com/Documents/Leader-Foreword.pdf). A 2013 review of literature relating to McClosky and Klamer's research suggests this persuasion number is closer to 30 percent of the U.S. gross domestic product, which equates to $4.5 trillion annually (`www.treasury.gov.au/PublicationsAndMedia/Publications/2013/Economic-Roundup-Issue-1/Report/Persuasion-is-now-30-per-cent-of-US-GDP`). These numbers alone are enough to pay attention to storytelling!

Getting in on the storytelling action

How does this mountain of money that's being spent on persuasive communications — which could be devoted to business storytelling — translate to organizational work? Dan Pink, the author of the *New York Times* best-seller *A Whole New Mind: Why Right Brainers Will Rule the Future* (Berkley Publishing Group, 2006) says business is entering a new age marked by the need to do the following:

✔ Use synthesis to detect patterns and opportunities for new innovations

✔ Create artistic and emotional beauty (think Apple)

✔ Craft a meaningful satisfying narrative through story

✔ Empathize with others

✔ Provide purpose and meaning in both work and the products and services consumed

✔ Replace seriousness with play

He goes on to state that desktop PCs and automated business processes have heightened the value of two types of skills. In *expert thinking*, new problems are solved for which routine solutions do not exist. In *complex communication*, interpreting information, explaining, persuading, and influencing becomes essential to success. Storytelling builds competency in both skills.

Futurist Rolf Jensen also explores this need. In his book *The Dream Society: How the Coming Shift from Information to Imagination Will Transform Your Business* (McGraw-Hill, 1999), he states, "The successful employee of the future is a virtuoso at acquiring and conveying knowledge, and coalescing and improving the work environment. The employee who, through telling stories about the organization's results, manages to strengthen corporate culture will be considered a valuable asset. Nothing so inspires an organization as an enlivening story relating how the whopping contract was finally won, despite adversity and horrendous odds. The storyteller creates corporate culture." He goes on to say, "Anyone seeking success in the market of the future will have to be a storyteller. The story is the heart of the matter."

When it comes to business offerings, story is front and center for Rolf Jensen. He talks about a shift from generating products or services and then telling a story about them to *first* focusing on the story that will *then* generate the product or service. For him, the next generation of experience is when a company and its customers are selling the story together as co-storytellers, with engagement driving sales.

Jensen cites Harley-Davidson as an example. In 1999, the Harley story was about transportation. Today, the Harley Owners Group (HOG), a collection of more than 1,400 groups, encourages its members to tell a much broader lifestyle story around the theme "born to be wild." This broader story serves as the background to video anecdotes (these don't contain all the elements of a story as explained in Chapter 3) about individual women riders who have created one-of-a-kind H-D motorcycles. You can view them at www.harley-davidson.com/en_US/Content/Pages/women-riders/the-right-bike.html.

How storytelling can help your business

In *The Experience Economy: Work Is Theater & Every Business a Stage* (Harvard Business School Press, 1999), Joseph Pine and James Gilmore reinforce this shift with its emphasis on story when they say, "Every business competing for the future is customer centric, customer driven, customer focused, customer-yadda-yadda-yadda. So what's new? This is new: Experiences represent an existing but previously unarticulated *genre of economic output* (author emphasis)."

Stories are experiences. When you share a story, you relive an experience and invite others to share in it with you. In this way, you move people from focusing on the tangible and intangible qualities of products and services to memorableness. And today's customers want memorable experiences. They want to engage with organizations that reveal themselves. Buyers perceive greater value when the experience lingers in their memory.

There's also a second outcome: Stories, when crafted well, can be transformational. Over time, as customers interact with your product or service, their lives will change — perhaps even transform — hopefully for the better. This happens when your enterprise helps each of them aspire to a happier place. We talk more about this transformation later in this chapter and in Chapter 14 when we cover using story in marketing. For an enterprise to help customers in this new way implies moving the organization from a mindset of sparking sales to embodying qualities connected to these stories that all parties can share — which has lasting consequence beyond the immediate consumption of a product or service.

Nutritious stories versus junk food stories

Every day, you're surrounded by entertaining junk food stories that leave you wanting more. Think of the latest zombie or vampire movies, reality TV shows, or other stuff on TV or the cinema that excite you or make you laugh.

Notice that they don't make you say, "A-ha!" or, "Oh, now I get it," or "Ahhh, that's deep." Like soda and potato chips, junk food stories briefly satisfy an immediate craving. Don't get us wrong — a little junk food is fine. But you're usually hungry again later on.

Junk food doesn't build health; it can lead to a host of maladies. In the same way, junk food stories also create maladies, which can include narrow thinking, distorted views of reality, exploitation, arrested development, and even stereotyping (more on this topic at `http://uxstorytellers.blogspot.fr/2012/06/danger-of-single-story.html`).

Good nutrition nourishes your body, making you feel energized, alive, and happy. Similarly, *sustaining stories* are those that feed you well. They nourish and sustain your psyche, spirit, and relationships with others, leading to higher levels of aspiration, and more energy, aliveness, meaning, and satisfaction.

One of the goals of this book is to steer you away from junk food stories toward sustaining stories. We want to help you craft and tell deeply satisfying, meaningful stories to sustain your organization over the long haul. Storytelling isn't merely a tool or device to use once in a while. It's an essential strategy and competence for all organizations to survive and thrive. The age of storytelling has arrived.

How We Define Story

There are many definitions of story in the field, which often leads to confusion. To bring clarity about what we mean by story and why we use the definition that we do, let's review a few definitions. The *Merriam-Webster Online Dictionary* defines story as follows:

> *1: a history such as a: an account of incidents or events; b: a statement regarding the facts pertinent to a situation in question; c: anecdote especially and amusing one; 2a: a fictional narrative shorter than a novel; b: the intrigue or plot of a narrative or dramatic work; 3a: a widely circulated rumor; 4: a lie or falsehood; 5: legend or romance; 6: a news article or broadcast.*

his definition doesn't tell us too much that's helpful. It includes several narrative forms like anecdotes and works of fiction, genres like legends, romance, and news articles, and a statement of facts or an accounting of an event. This is a descriptive definition — it describes various types of stories. But it doesn't help us understand what a story really is and what it does.

Not everything is a story

It's popular in some circles to say that *everything* is a story. That's simply not true. Most of your daily life isn't a story. Many of your conversations aren't stories. A lot of what you read isn't a story. And they don't have to be. But if you want to turn a human event into a story, then you need to pay attention to the specific process for creating a story. Story is simply a way of structuring information in order to create context and relevance, engage listeners, be memorable, and generate some nugget of meaning.

In today's business world, as you'll see in Chapter 2, without a story you get diminished results. But telling a story is only half the equation. You also need to be listening for stories. As you'll find out in Chapter 5, you need to listen to the stories your colleagues, prospects, and customers share with you so you can discover their needs and then meet them.

TIn his book *Story Proof: The Science Behind the Startling Power of Story* (Libraries Unlimited, 2007), Kendall Haven offers another definition of story:

> *Story: n.: A detailed, character-based narration of a character's struggles to overcome obstacles and reach an important goal.*

This is a structural definition — it's about the elements that create a story. Quite often, you'll see definitions of this type. They say for a story to be a story it must have a plot, characters, emotion, a problem, and a resolution. Even though this helps us get closer to understanding what a story is, structural definitions only focus on what comprises a story — its elements. These types of definitions often become a laundry list of ingredients that don't help you craft and tell better stories and don't help you understand what a story really is and what it does.

Here's our definition of story that we use throughout this book:

> *"A story provides packets of sensory language presented in a particular way that allows the listener to quickly and easily internalize the material, comprehend it, and create meaning from it."*

This is a dynamic definition of story. When you focus on the results that occur from telling stories, then you understand what the story is supposed to do for you — which is why you tell them in the first place. Why do we prefer this definition? It focuses on what a storyteller is actually trying to achieve. When you know why you want to share stories, you have the context for understanding the elements of a story and can construct them with more confidence.

How Stories Impact People

Every day, you're bombarded with tons of so-called stories. Not all are worth attending to — poorly crafted stories are a dime a dozen. If you want your stories to stand out from the crowd, upping your storytelling game is essential. Upping your game means crafting stories that impact people in four ways simultaneously: physically, intellectually, emotionally, and spiritually.

The physical impact

In *Wake Me Up When the Data Is Over: How Organizations Use Stories to Drive Results* (Jossey-Bass, 2006), Arthur L. Major, director of System Safety at Lockheed Martin Space Systems, describes the physical behavior he observed in senior leaders when he wove stories throughout a presentation on what he planned to do to reduce mishaps and near misses. "I saw executives lean forward, put their pens down, look at me and listen." He goes on to say, "Their behavior changed because I changed the way I presented."

These executives settled in to listen. They were attentive because they wanted to know where his stories were going. At the same time, their behavior demonstrated that they were open and receptive to the experience and what they were hearing. Sure enough: These executives approved his approach for another year.

As story coaches, speakers, and trainers, we as authors have been privileged to present a number of compelling stories to audiences and to watch groups of people as they listen to a compelling story. Listeners noticeably shift their physical behavior. They may lean in or sit back. They stop what they're doing — they stop taking notes, put down electronic devices, and cease having conversations. They often stare directly at the person who's telling them a story. Sometimes the room becomes very quiet. Other audiences may mutter things like "Wow," "That's unbelievable," or, "Really?" They may laugh — or cry. In any case, all their physical behaviors point to a deeper kind of listening in the moment.

The mental impact

What are these listeners processing? Here's what Princeton University neuroscientists Greg Stephens and Uri Hasson (*Proceedings of the National Academy of Sciences*, July 27, 2010) found when they took brain scans of a graduate student telling a 15-minute unrehearsed story and those listening to a recording of it (www.pnas.org/content/107/32/14425). Although speaking and listening are known to invoke different brain functions, "On average, the listener's brain responses mirrored the speaker's brain responses with some time delays. The delays matched the flow of [the] information." They also found that an additional area of the listener's brain is lit up — the part that anticipates what's next. That didn't happen in the teller's brain.

What does this mean? The speaker's words actually shape how the listener's brain responds to what's said. This is groundbreaking! It implies that stories create an immediate connection between people.

Citing evidence from more than 350 studies in fields such as cognitive science, neural psychology, and brain development, in *Story Proof* Kendall Haven says our reliance on story through the ages has caused a rewiring of the human brain such that it's predisposed to think in terms of story. Story is how the brain creates meaning. This predisposition is strengthened through hearing and telling stories in childhood.

Think about it. If listeners' brain responses are mirroring the teller's brain responses almost instantaneously — like a mind meld — and the human brain is predisposed to think in terms of story, that implies that you pay closer attention when you hear a story. Once you connect to and link the story to your memories and past experiences, meaning-making occurs. Imagine the influences that this revelation can have in a business setting.

The emotional impact

Where does this meaning-making happen? Let's take a look at the brain.

The left side of your brain is your data center. It processes information in a linear fashion, focuses on language and logic, and is attentive to reasoning. But the left brain also tends to be more skeptical and loves numbers and facts. Because it's emotionally neutral, it's always seeking more information. Whenever people are engaged in ongoing debates about information, you know the left side of the brain is in full swing.

The right side of your brain is the fountain of creativity. This part processes information through the imagination. It's where symbols, images, music, metaphors, dreams, and emotions are. It's more focused on sensory material (what you can hear, feel, taste, smell, and see), tends to fill in information gaps, and is more accepting. Instead of seeking more information for debates, the right brain's curiosity leads you to want resolution. And here's a huge surprise: The right side of the brain is the path to the limbic (emotional) system and quickly becomes emotionally engaged if it is stimulated.

Why is this important? According to Michael Gazzaniga, author of *Who's in Charge? Free Will and the Science of the Brain* (HarperCollins, 2011), the emotional brain is where feelings of trust, loyalty, and hope are activated and where unconscious emotional decisions are made. In his book *How Customers*

Think: Essential Insights into the Mind of the Market (Harvard Business Review Press, 2003), Gerald Zaltman says that 95 percent of the time our minds are on autopilot, which means that *most* of our decisions are made unconsciously.

Now consider this: Geoff Kaufman and Lisa Libby found that stories are perceived as *truer* than facts because we identify with and internalize the characters (`www.tiltfactor.org/wp-content/uploads2/Kaufman_Libby2012_JPSPadvanceonlinepublication.pdf`). When you can see yourself in the story, it becomes more real than facts.

Let's now put these pieces of the puzzle together. If it's true that the left brain is emotionally neutral, is always seeking more information, and tends to be more skeptical, why would you only want to *solely* speak to it? And, if it's true that stories are perceived as truer than facts because we identify with the characters, why would you want to rely on business speak to influence behavior? Especially if the right side of the brain, which is emotional in nature, is where decisions are unconsciously made before facts and data come into the picture? What makes storytelling different is that it's a *whole brain* and *whole body* experience.

Paul Zak, director of the Center for Neuroeconomics Studies and Professor of Economics, Psychology and Management at Claremont Graduate University, conducted a series of research studies that focus on a story a dad tells about his two-and-a-half year old son, Ben, who's dying of brain cancer (`www.youtube.com/watch?v=q1a7tiA1Qzo&sns=tw`). The dad expresses that it's hard to play with Ben knowing he's dying, especially because Ben is so happy. Zak demonstrates that two primary emotions — distress and empathy — were elicited in those who heard the story. He found that cortisol is released in the listener when the main character of a story is distressed (due to a problem, challenge, struggle, and so on). Cortisol helps you focus your attention on something of importance. Oxytocin is also released, which prompts feelings of care, connection, and empathy.

Zak concluded that for a story to cause these physical changes, it must have dramatic arc structure — capturing tension with a problem or struggle and a climax. When a story does this, it changes a listener's brain chemistry.

What's the bottom line? When you're impacted emotionally by listening to a compelling story, two things are occurring simultaneously: You're both *imagining* what's happening and *analyzing* the story for content, information, and key messages. As a result, you're more prone to remember, recall, and internalize the story and take action on it.

The human spirit impact

In the field of story work, almost everyone says evoking emotions is good enough. We don't. We believe that for a story to truly compel people to action — the ultimate goal of any story in business — it must touch the human spirit. Every day you're bombarded by messages via TV, podcasts, articles, blog postings, billboards, and other media that try to tug on your heartstrings — to the point where you may have become somewhat immune to emotional appeal. That means any messages you and your company send out have to stand out above all this noise in order to be heard and acted on.

Reflect back on stories you've heard over your lifetime. Have any given you goose bumps? Or made the hair stand up on your arms or neck? Such a story strikes you to your core. There's a special quality about it that makes it unforgettable. You feel compelled to share it and can't stop thinking about it. You might even say to yourself, "I need to do something. Like, right now." Can business stories do this? Absolutely. Can you tell these types of unforgettable stories? Yep. That's why we wrote this book.

Touching the human spirit also includes stories that are the ultimate embodiment of good. They transcend our personal view of the world and offer an expanded way of being and living that supports our own aliveness and the aliveness of others. Mrs. Meyer's Clean Day, owned by Caldrea, is one company that plays in this realm. In describing "Who We Are," Caldrea says, "Each day, we look for ways to inspire everyone on the planet to breathe in, smile, and live beautifully. This philosophy is the glue that connects what we do every day to the larger impact we want to make on the world and the little ways we want to help you love your home and your life in it. We're committed to using earth-friendly practices and have instituted programs at our office to protect and care for the environment, and our employees (www.caldrea.com/who-we-are).

At Mrs. Meyer's Clean Day, this embodiment of good philosophy is depicted through a film series: short video anecdotes (these don't contain all the elements of a story as explained in Chapter 3). These videos are stated to be "A celebration of individuals whose generosity, hard work and connection with nature inspire us every day." You can check them out at www.mrsmeyers.com/film-series.

Dispelling the Myths of Storytelling

Used judiciously and properly, stories can make a marked difference for all types of organizations. However, you may need to overcome some of the following myths about storytelling. We raise them here and address them throughout the book in more detail:

✔ **Stop wasting my time — this is taking too long.** Stories are how people convey meaning. It's true that no one has time today to listen to information that isn't meaningful. That means no one has time for bad storytelling. Stories are one of the quickest ways to make a point. Stories engage and inspire action. Sharing a story first allows people to make decisions and take action much more quickly later on. Just because a story may need eight minutes to be told in exactly the way it needs to be shared, don't let that deter you from using it. People will spend the time to listen to well-constructed compelling stories, which means structuring them well is your issue.

✔ **Stories are false and are make-believe.** Authentic and genuine storytelling is one of the best ways to share who you are and what your organization is all about. Real-life stories, when chosen, told, and crafted well, transmit cultural values, make the complex simple to understand, and convey both knowledge and wisdom. In addition, storytelling and story listening build empathy. Empathy allows you to experience the product or service from the mind of the user and understand their true needs. Empathy makes us human; there's nothing false about that. We all want to connect, inspire, and influence on purpose. These are crucial roles that stories can fulfill.

✔ **Just give us the facts.** You may wonder, "Wouldn't it just be easier to skip stories altogether and simply deliver the facts?" Nope — it may be simpler, but it's not easier. Remember our discussion of left and right brains? If you don't engage their right brain through story, people shut down when faced with too many facts and data. You'll have to remind them later of the information. You'll have to follow up with them to make sure they understood its significance. You'll need to continually link the data to daily work, and so on. Ugh, what a boatload of work.

✔ **Numbers are simply abstractions.** And, bullet points are merely summaries. Both only *reflect* reality. A story, however, *becomes* reality because people immediately engage with and internalize it. Remember, no one ever waged a filibuster or staged a takeover because of charts, graphs, or bullet points.

✔ **I shouldn't — or don't know how to — talk about myself.** People want the human face behind the enterprise. Customers want human relationships, not a faceless organization. People want to hear your personal stories, delivered humbly, authentically, and with respect. No one can argue with the truth of your experience. It's simply a matter of learning how to select, craft, and tell your personal stories. Storytelling and story listening skills can be learned. Armed with knowledge about what works and what doesn't through this book, your abilities to influence and move people will become easier and more natural.

Chapter 2

The Why, What, How, and Who of Business Storytelling

• •

In This Chapter

▶ Showcasing results from storytelling initiatives

▶ Demonstrating how business storytelling is different

▶ Applying stories at work

• •

 When we first met in 2003, we chatted for hours about what needed to happen next in the field of story in business and where exciting story research was happening. That conversation led to ideas that culminated in Lori's book *Wake Me Up When the Data Is Over: How Organizations Use Stories to Get Results* (Jossey-Bass, 2006).

For that book, Lori, Karen, and other story practitioners interviewed more than 70 organizations worldwide about their use of story in business applications such as customer service, financial management, leadership development, human resources, project management, and more. The book documents specific story practices and the results achieved from them.

Because the field of story work in business was still fledgling, many people only had anecdotal qualitative feedback to share. Yet all interviewees experienced positive results through their story efforts. Many enterprises reported more than one type of impact, such as Kimpton Hotel and Restaurant Group. It reported three outcomes from its storytelling efforts:

✔ Doubling the number of its hotels to 40 in the five years prior to the book being published and readying to double in size again.

✔ Returning guests were 55 percent of customers compared to an average rate in the service industry of 20 to 25 percent.

✔ Turnover was lower than any other major hotel company in the United States when compared to industry standards, as demonstrated through independent survey results.

Here are the summarized results across all organizations, as first reported by Lori in the article "There Are Five Sides to Every Story: Which Are You Missing?" in *Communication World* (IABC, January–February 2007):

- ✔ 36 percent have experienced positive financial impact to the bottom line through increased growth, profitability, and/or increased funding.

- ✔ 18 percent have noted that story use has moved them closer to furthering specific organizational goals.

- ✔ 17 percent have reported increased levels of engagement between people and the organization and/or higher levels of teamwork.

- ✔ 17 percent are able to show a positive impact on the amount and type of customer feedback, improved customer satisfaction, and/or improved customer perceptions of the brand.

- ✔ 11 percent have experienced decreased workflow cycle time, improved speed of message delivery or time to market, and increased efficiencies.

- ✔ 10 percent reported an impact on training feedback and effectiveness, including transfer of skills and knowledge to the workplace.

- ✔ 8 percent noted positive cultural changes.

- ✔ Other results include closing more deals with clients, increased visibility through media or industry awards and rankings, improved staff retention, practical problem solving, bringing core values to life, overcoming issues, and improved employee satisfaction and decreased absenteeism.

Would these sorts of results make a difference in your organization? Then keep reading. This chapter covers all sorts of ways that story significantly impacts what each and every one of us does in our daily work.

It's a Proven Fact: Storytelling Works

Karen picked up where Lori's last book left off. Each day she powers up her computer, straps on her reading glasses, caffeinates her bloodstream (yes, she's aware of the health effects), and scans the web, hunting for the best articles on business storytelling. Each month, she processes hundreds of articles, throws out all the fluff and the junk, and then reviews and comments on the gems she unearths. If you'd like to follow along, check out `www.scoop.it/t/just-story-it`.

Here's one important piece she found: the Significant Objects Project (`http://significantobjects.com`), the brainchild of journalist Rob Walker. It ran from July to November 2009 as a quasi-anthropological experiment.

Talented writers were invited to invent a story about an object purchased from a thrift store. On average, these items cost $1.25. The premise was that if a story were attached to an object, it would be perceived as more valuable. The stories were fictional, meaning great care was taken to avoid giving the impression that the story was true; creating a hoax wasn't the goal.

This was put to the test by selling the objects, complete with story and photo (but no item description), on eBay. The result? The project sold $128.74 worth of thrift-store junk for $3,612.51. Clearly, stories attached to almost worthless items made them more valuable. People wanted them and were willing to pay much higher prices for them.

What does this example have to do with *your* organization? Simply put, we're all seeking one of the secrets of the universe: how to create the right conditions for someone to reach into their pocket, open up their wallet, and hand us money, whether it be for a project, a new offering, or a new venture. Stories are the key to unlocking this secret.

Karen also uncovered a study put together by the folks at co:collective about the impact of storytelling on corporate growth and share price. The research distinguished between *storytelling* and *storydoing* businesses (check it out at `www.storydoing.com/idea`). In their words:

> Storytelling companies convey the story of their brand, business, or product by telling that story, usually through PR or paid advertising; storydoing companies consciously convey their story through direct action. Storydoing companies use their core story as an organizing principle for activities throughout the company: new product development, recruiting, compensation, partnerships, as well as any communication that they create. Our hypothesis is that storydoing companies spend fewer dollars on paid media, and the dollars they do spend work harder, which makes storydoing companies more efficient.

Co:collective identified 42 companies, which they divided up as best they could into storytelling and storydoing companies. Some of the methodology is problematic. First, this is a small sample. Second, the degree to which storytelling is embedded in the DNA of a storydoing company is still evolving; some on the list embody story better than others. None has fully embraced storytelling in all aspects of their businesses as we talk about in Chapter 12 based on our story research and hands-on experiences. Third, the research only requires that a company have *a story*. In Chapter 4, we show that organizations need to have many kinds of stories. Even with these challenges, we're encouraged by this research effort and the attempt to show the difference that embodying stories can make in a business. Here are the results:

✔ Revenue growth over a 4-year period for storytelling companies was 6.1 percent, but for storydoing companies it was 10.4 percent — a significant difference.

✔ Annual operating income growth was 7.1 percent for storytelling companies versus 16.1 percent for storydoing companies.

> ✔ Annual share price growth difference was significant. Storytelling companies actually lost 4.4 percent in share price. Storydoing companies' share price increased by 5.6 percent.

We believe that if you follow the approaches outlined in this book, your organization has a heightened ability to achieve these results. In addition, storytelling can create a huge distinction if you think of it as a core business activity like this research suggests, instead of merely a communication strategy.

What's been learned about the impact of story in individuals who hear and tell them? Not only do people remember *compelling* stories, they share them. They remember these stories much better than they remember facts and information. Over and over again, it's been demonstrated that compelling stories

- ✔ Are relaxing to listen to and engage all of the senses.
- ✔ Reflect and connect with people's needs and emotional states.
- ✔ Captivate people's interest and make them more attentive listeners.
- ✔ Are "sticky" and embed themselves in people's subconscious.
- ✔ Communicate information quickly.
- ✔ Swiftly and successfully convey the meaning of complex concepts.
- ✔ Show how people solved real problems by making the abstract concrete.
- ✔ Foster creativity.
- ✔ Act as catalysts and spark relevant conversations.
- ✔ Are frequently shared with others.
- ✔ Enhance individual and organizational learning.
- ✔ Make information more believable.
- ✔ Provide a way for listeners to draw their own conclusions.
- ✔ Convey and demonstrate your values and passions.
- ✔ Help people imagine a future that's achievable and worth achieving.
- ✔ Stimulate action.
- ✔ Create unique, collaborative connections with customers and prospects.
- ✔ Create engagement and trust with employees, customers, prospects, and funders.
- ✔ Build and strengthen relationships instead of having one-off transactions.
- ✔ Differentiate your company from its competition.
- ✔ Generate a return on engagement, emotion, and connection.
- ✔ Establish economic value.

Professor Howard Gardner of Harvard University says, "Stories are the most powerful weapon in a leader's arsenal." We agree. We would even venture to say that stories are *the* most powerful core competence for both you and your organization in the 21st century.

What Makes Business Storytelling Different?

It's likely you were raised on fairy tales and kids' books and movies. And you're still surrounded by all sorts of story-based TV shows, films, and books, including fiction, biographies, autobiographies, and so on. Even video games are stories nowadays. In business, there's everything from the "ain't it awful" stories shared around the water cooler to educational fables about penguins, to help us make sense of chaotic organizational life.

When we talk about business storytelling, we're talking about your personal stories and those of your organization that are constructed and shared in authentic and compelling ways so that they instantly connect to others, including employees, leaders, prospects, customers, consumers, and vendors, to name a few.

Several years ago, Lori was asked to speak to communications professionals at a regional International Association of Business Communicators (IABC) conference on the use of organizational stories. When she mentioned that these stories differed from anecdotes, examples, case studies, and the like, she saw puzzled looks. She stopped and asked, "What's going on?" What she heard surprised her. "You're making a distinction we're not familiar with. What would a business story look like as an anecdote or description?" That interaction led her to approach Karen about creating a document that displayed the differences between narrative forms (covered in Chapter 3).

A story for business use is different. It has special elements and structures. Many books in the field don't make the distinctions that we make. So why should you? Answer this question: Is your ultimate goal to move people to action? If so, then only a story as we've outlined it in this book will do the trick. The other narrative forms, because they're merely information-based, may help you relay knowledge, but they won't guarantee that people will be moved to do anything other than say, "Oh, that's nice."

Hollywood: What to take and toss

Hollywood stories are designed to entertain. However, although also important in business, entertainment isn't sufficient in an organizational setting. You must design your stories to help people, and ultimately entire organizations, change their behavior.

So take the drama, the visual power of cinema, good scriptwriting, and strong characters from Hollywood to heart. We'll show you how to integrate these elements into stories that engage, influence, and move people to action, which is what we want all business stories to do.

Move people to action: The ultimate goal

Consider this scenario based on an old joke:

> The CEO of a large company brought all of his employees together for an annual meeting. He and his staff had toiled for days on preparing his material. His PowerPoint presentation was magnificent. It contained beautiful graphics, and the company's vision statement was in big bold letters. Sales charts, projections, and project lists were plentiful.
>
> When it was all said and done, an attending employee wandered home and mentioned the meeting to his wife. "Who spoke?" she asked. He answered, "The CEO." She then asked, "What was his presentation about?" And he answered, "Well, he didn't say."

It's obvious this employee wasn't moved to action — or even engaged.

What kinds of actions can stories inspire? Here are a few:

- **Increasing website traffic:** Stories are keyword rich, making it easier for people to find your site through web searches. Smart organizations use stories on their websites and blogs to tease. They link them to social media sites like Twitter, Facebook, and LinkedIn.

- **Generating leads:** Sharing stories often leads to people having a keener understanding of how your organization's products and services address their needs, sparking them to contact you.

- **Creating a unique selling proposition:** Stories provide real-world examples of how your organization differs from its competitors.

- **Increasing sales:** Stories help prospects more readily identify with your solutions and see themselves being successful.

- **Generating donations and investments:** Sharing stories gives people a reason to donate or invest — and a sense of the vision for the future they're helping to create.

- **Deepening customer relationships:** Tell a great story, and customers will share it with their own tribes, leading to increased interest and increased sales. Allowing customers to co-create stories can build significant loyalty.

- **Solidifying staff engagement:** Sharing stories with staff builds a strong culture, creates shared realities, operationalizes both vision and values, and helps guide positive behaviors.

✔ **Accelerating project work:** Using stories to help set expectations and outline why and what needs to be done helps staff realize the meaningfulness of their contributions, which can heighten productivity.

✔ **Getting change to stick:** Stories can help staff at all levels become clear on why and what needs to change and how to make it happen.

Using Stories at Work

People often assume stories reside primarily in corporate communications, advertising, branding, and marketing. But these aren't the only applications for stories in your organization. In addition to what we've just mentioned, we've seen stories successfully used in the following ways:

✔ External applications

- Developing new business opportunities

- Sales meetings and presentations

- Public relations including press releases, media relations, crisis management

- Year-end reports

- Planning and executing mergers and acquisitions

- Forging partnerships and strategic alliances

- Venture capital and philanthropy

- Market and consumer research

- Customer service

- Advocacy

✔ Internal applications

- Developing leaders and engaging employees

- Interviewing job prospects

- Strategic planning and implementing change

- Enhancing teamwork and training

- Knowledge transfer through best practices and lessons learned

- Managing projects

- Strengthening corporate culture: vision, mission, core values

- Developing a business case and soliciting internal funding

In our experience, organizations tend to use stories for one or more of these applications. But we've yet to find an organization where story resides within *all* of these internal and external applications — where story is truly embedded in the DNA of the enterprise. Perhaps your organization could be the first to do so. We talk about how to make that happen in Chapter 12.

Know when not to tell a story

You might think we want you to use stories all the time. Well, that's not quite true. We recognize there are times when you don't need to share a story. For example, if you've just witnessed an accident on the highway, you need to hop on the phone and dial 911 and report the facts. You aren't going to chat with the dispatcher and say, "Let me tell you about this accident I just saw. . . ."

So don't go crazy. Share stories judiciously. Some work-related situations where you don't want to use story include:

- ✔ When it's more appropriate to issue a directive.
- ✔ When people have heard enough stories during a meeting.
- ✔ When you need to show somebody something.
- ✔ When you need to listen first before saying anything.

Pull people versus push messages

If you've been in the work world for any period of time, you've probably been to a conference or lengthy workshop where hour after hour, you're bombarded with information. Even though you may have taken short breaks in the morning and afternoon, along with lunch, you barely had time to process what was pushed at you, much less creatively figure out how to use it.

If you attended in person, you may have walked in and out of the room a few times, read material on your notebook tablet or phone, or worked while half listening to the speaker. Those few times when stories were shared, you saw people become riveted.

The point? There are two ways to share knowledge: You can *push* information out to people or you can *pull* them in with a story. Pushing messages out to the marketplace or internally to staff is a bad habit. The new habit you should form is to share stories that pull people into your world. That's the cornerstone of engagement. Isn't that what you want — customers and staff who are engaged with you on an ongoing basis?

Everyone is born a storyteller

The famous anthropologist Gregory Bateson in his book *Steps to an Ecology of Mind: A Revolutionary Approach to Man's Understanding of Himself* (Chandler Publishing, 1972) shares an anecdote. He's asked a question about how organizations would know when they had made a computer that worked like the human brain. His reply was "When the computer replies to a question with, 'Let me tell you a story . . .'"

You may be thinking to yourself, "Well, I don't tell stories." Or, "I'm not a good storyteller." We believe just the opposite. You already have an innate ability to share stories. How do we know? Spend some time at a park or playground or in your neighborhood around young children. They all create and tell stories (granted, some true and some not).

It's been said that you master the ability to tell stories by age three. But you don't master analytical and conceptual language until around age eight. As you go through formal schooling and start working, you get caught up in thinking that spouting facts and figures and using lots of PowerPoint slides will do all your influencing for you. But they don't. Why? As we discuss in Chapter 1, your brain is hard-wired for stories. We all think and talk in stories. Stories are what people share, day in and day out.

We realize you may feel uncomfortable telling stories. Or you may think using stories at work isn't very *professional*. As we tell every single client we work with, you're a natural born storyteller. You have what it takes. We're here to reawaken and remind you of your innate story skills.

Storytelling Principles in Business

Woven throughout this book are core principles about business storytelling. You've gotten the first: Move people to action. Here are several others:

- ✔ **All stories need to be treated with respect:** Know that story has the power to transform, harm, or heal. Whether you recognize it now or not, your personal stories carry great wisdom. Treat your stories well and they will treat you well.

- ✔ **Be authentic and ethical with your storytelling:** This is far more important than being polished.

- ✔ **When you share a story, you spark a story:** The most magical and highest value of storytelling is in sharing stories face to face.

✔ **Real stories, real people:** Whose stories are you going to tell? People want to hear about you and your organization, not fables like the tortoise and the hare. Our rule of thumb is personal stories first, tales later.

✔ **Transcend information:** Stories convey complex ideas and impart meaning to them far better than any facts or figures.

✔ **Life is tough:** Which means you need to sometimes tell tough stories. If those you share lead to an "ahhh" moment or an "a-ha, I get it" insight or an "Oh, I see" realization, you're doing a good job.

✔ **Move beyond the transaction:** Stories are a rich source of meaning, understanding, personal insight, and wonder that go far beyond mere transactions (such as a sale).

✔ **Walk the talk:** Stories model behaviors, social norms, and ways of being that make it easier for others to do the same. Live by the lessons you share.

✔ **Storytelling is fun, energizing, and a form of deep play:** Sharing stories can be both deeply satisfying and personally stimulating. It's also a creative act and an enjoyable activity. Learn the fun side of storytelling while respecting the stories that are told.

LOTS: The language of the senses

Storytelling has its own kind of language. And it's definitely not the language of acronyms, definitions, science, data, and information. What is it? Simply put, it's using LOTS: the *language of the senses*. Stories go far beyond the sharing of experience. They need to be communicated in a conversational manner, such that people can re-imagine in their own minds what you saw, smelled, felt, tasted, heard, and intuited. When you use sensory language or lots of LOTS, people's brains, emotions, and senses all become immediately engaged. And what could be more powerful than that?

Chapter 3

What Makes a Story a Story

In This Chapter

▶ Identifying the core elements of a story

▶ Distinguishing between describing a situation and telling a story

▶ Recognizing and using narrative forms that aren't a story

Almost everywhere you look today, authors of websites, blogs, magazines, newspapers, advertisements, marketing promotional materials, and the like declare they're sharing a story. All too frequently they aren't. These "stories" often sound like, "We have an awesome product. Here's a customer that says so. You should buy it. You'll think it's awesome too." There's no beautifully crafted visual language, no gripping conflicts to be resolved, no interesting characters to relate to, and nothing meaningful to gain. You might even wonder why they wasted your time with such hollow declarative proclamations.

When we're asked to present business storytelling workshops, one of the first things we do is share a well-crafted story — to both model storytelling and to help people recognize a story when they hear one. Then we debrief what made that story work.

In this chapter, we do the same thing. Through the first story, we reveal the core characteristics of a story and tease out the difference between *telling* and *describing* a story. Through a second story, we demonstrate how stories differ from nine other forms of narrative we find used in business: anecdotes, case studies, descriptions, examples, news reports, profiles, scenarios, testimonials, and vignettes.

Recognizing a Story Based on Its Core Elements

Here's a business story. What do you think makes this story a story? What do you think makes it a compelling one?

Making Her Mark

Story contributed by Cristi Kanenwischer

It was a Friday — June 4th, 2009 to be exact. Cristi Kanenwischer, the business manager for Wolfe Architectural Group, was putting the final touches on a simple two-sided brochure she'd just made. It had pictures of three signature projects on it along with a list of services and project experiences. Her early morning work wasn't complete until she'd adhered a brightly colored piece of ChapStick with her firm's logo on it to the brochures and put them into little re-sealable bags.

She couldn't help but recall Louise's words from a class she'd taken from her the week before at the Procurement Technical Assistance Center: "Hey, there's gonna be a seminar on the 4th of June at the Mirabeau Hotel by various state government staff from the west side of the state on the ins and outs of getting work. I think it would be really helpful if you attended."

In April, Cristi's firm had turned in a proposal to the General Administration Office for on-call architectural services in response to a statewide request for proposals. Soon the GAO was going to select three firms to provide services for the entire state of Washington on projects valued at $300,000 dollars or less. Three times over the last seven years her firm had tried the same thing without success. Since no one in her company knew anybody in the GAO, and the selection was going to be made soon, she wasn't feeling optimistic.

"We need all the help we can get." Cristi thought to herself. "The economy's not getting better any time soon. We've got to find government work to replace the work we've lost. Maybe it'll give me a chance to learn about these agencies and their policies and procedures. . . . But you know, if I do get an opportunity to meet someone of influence, I'd better be prepared."

Cristi got to the hotel a few minutes before the start of the first seminar session in the grand ballroom. She found an open chair at a table with people she knew well. She noticed all the agency people were seated at raised tables at the front of the room. As they were being introduced, she quickly scoped out the place, looking for Louise.

She found Louise sitting on the panel. Next to her was Mr. Dixon, the Assistant Deputy Director of the General Administration Office. "This must be my lucky day!" Cristi thought. "I'm praying I still have a chance to make an impression. Now, all I have to do is figure out how to meet him without raising too many eyebrows."

It didn't feel right to call attention to herself by asking a question in the first Q&A session. Plus, several of the folks who went up to the microphone seemed openly angry about why they hadn't been considered for certain projects and how all the decent contracts got awarded to the Seattle area. That didn't feel good either.

The aroma of chicken soon permeated the room. When lunchtime came, Cristi decided to make her move. Before she got her meal, she excused herself and went to the bathroom to freshen up. Then, with a big ol' smile on her face, she made her way to where Louise and Mr. Dixon were seated.

Among the clattering of plates and silverware, she caught Louise's eye. "Louise. It's so good to see you again. Thank you for suggesting I attend today. I'm really looking forward to hearing all the different speakers." Then she turned slightly. "Hello Mr. Dixon. I'm Cristi Kanenwisher with Wolfe Architectural Group. I'm looking forward to listening to your presentation after lunch."

Without missing a beat, she quickly handed him a brochure. "Here's a sampling of our work. If you check out our website, we've got more examples there. . . . Oh, it looks like your meals have arrived. It's a pleasure meeting you, Mr. Dixon. Good to see you again, Louise. Enjoy your lunch."

Mr. Dixon's presentation was the first one after lunch. Cristi made it a point to sit as close to the front of the room as possible. She wanted to make good eye contact with him. When he walked in, he gave her a nod of recognition. She thought, "Oh, that's so cool. He remembers me!"

As he went through his talk, Cristi noticed most of the people in the room looked really tired. They weren't even looking at him. But none of this mattered matter to her. She focused on listening really well and taking good notes and asking appropriate questions. She wanted him to know that she appreciated him being there. Her sole mission was to connect.

She waited for him after he was finished. He motioned for her to walk with him to the hotel lobby. So she did.

Cristi took the chance to speak first. "Thanks for taking the time out of your busy schedule to come and educate us about what you do and what you expect."

Mr. Dixon responded, "You're welcome. How did it sound? I wasn't supposed to be here today. The man who made the slides and was supposed to be here got sick."

"Oh, I'm sorry to hear that. I learned a lot from your talk. It was very well organized." Cristi said. She still remembers her parting words to him as she shook his hand. "I hope every time you use the ChapStick, you think of WAG Company and remember me, the ChapStick Girl."

And with that, Dixon took the brochure with the ChapStick on it out of his briefcase, looked at it again and said, "Yep!" And then he walked away.

The following Monday, Cristi checked the GAO website to see if results were posted for the RFP. Nothing. She checked again on Tuesday. Nothing. Wednesday. Still nothing, Thursday. More nothing. Friday. Nothing again. The following Monday. Oy — nothing. Tuesday. Nothing. Wednesday: "What? Is this right? Where's Russ? Russ . . . you gotta see this. We got selected by the GAO. We did it!" Russ — her boss and the principal of the firm — almost fell off his chair. He was convinced it was because of the connection that Cristi made with Mr. Dixon.

Since 2009, WAG has received eight projects from the state and was selected for a second, two-year contract in 2011. Given this track record, there's no doubt that Cristi truly made a meaningful connection.

Think about your own work. How critical is it that you "make a meaningful connection?" And with whom? If it's indeed important, then you need to take some immediate steps, just as Cristi did on behalf of her company. Before the end of the day, identify these steps, jot them down, and make a plan to go do them. *Used with permission. Copyright © 2010 by Cristi Kanenwischer, as crafted by Lori L. Silverman. All rights reserved.*

Flesh out the plot/conflict

"Readers search for meaning not through successes and achievements, but through conflict and struggle. Conflict is energy. It is tension."

— Kendall Haven in *Story Proof* (Libraries Unlimited, 2007)

In order for narrative to be labeled a story, it must by definition include some sort of plot. A plot can involve a problem, issue, concern, challenge, dilemma, or paradox, with specific obstacles to overcome.

There are two reasons why conflict is critical in a story. First, our brains are hooked on struggle and trouble. This attraction to trouble is how we know to pay attention to something in particular when we're constantly bombarded by volumes of information being pushed to us. Your mind sifts through this material and asks, "Is this something I need to pay attention to? If so, how exactly does this relate to me? What's the personal context I can place this information in? What exactly does it mean to me? And should I bother to remember it?"

You filter information at the speed of light. Almost instantaneously, you evaluate it, decide if it's worth your attention, interpret it, find personal memories to connect with it, tag it for later retrieval, and determine whether you need to take action on it. Without conflict, struggle, or trouble in a conversation, your brain just passes it by because there is little of consequence to pay attention to.

The other reason conflict is critical is because conflict is the engine that drives excitement and engagement in a story. In her book *A Writer's Guide to Nonfiction* (Perigee, 2003), Elizabeth Lyon says, "The universality of human suffering and struggle compels your reader-stranger to invest in your story." A character earns our respect and admiration when he struggles. As he tries to overcome those challenges, we come to care for that person and empathize with his concerns and issues.

Let's flash back to Cristi's story for a moment. In it, we quickly hear about the drop in business and the need to gain government contracts to recover those losses. But the firm has failed to do so three times in the past seven years. Tension mounts as we ask ourselves, "What needs to happen this time for the company to achieve a successful outcome?" The beauty of this conflict is that each and every one of us can identify in some way with this challenge in our own organizations.

As she works through this conflict, Cristi experiences other obstacles. Would she meet someone of influence by attending the seminar? What's the best way to approach Mr. Dixon? How can she position her company in a favorable light? As Cristi's situation demonstrates, it's not unusual for other obstacles to be present in a story; these twists and turns serve to keep our attention and bond us to the main character. "Oohh, ooohh, ooohh," we think to ourselves. "What's going to happen next?"

Real people in real stories

When using stories in business settings, we encourage you to focus on *real people in real stories* rather than made-up stories. These can include your personal stories in addition to stories from others.

Cristi's story satisfies this story element. It's about Cristi sharing her real-life experience — one that was a milestone for her and her firm.

For the most part, it's best to avoid telling fairy tales or Aesop's fables. Why? Fables don't enable you to build a credible relationship with another person(s). Other people want to know about you: What makes you tick, why they should trust you, and what makes you an expert no matter your role within a company. Only your personal stories will do that kind of work.

If you want to achieve impact with your stories, follow two additional guidelines:

- ✔ Name your characters.
- ✔ Focus on one main character.

Why name your characters? People don't relate as well when you substitute words such as friend, coworker, mother, or boss for names.

Case in point. Imagine hearing the following sentence in a story: "One day Susan was at her desk when the phone rang . . ." Chances are, your brain starts searching its memory banks for all the Susan's you've encountered in life. Once it finds one, your brain immediately latches onto her. In that moment, an instantaneous connection is made. You listen to the rest of the story having already begun to internalize it.

Research on building compassion and empathy shows that greater compassion and empathy are present when the main person in the story has a name. A name allows you to more closely identify with this individual. As Rule and Wheeler conclude in their book *Creating the Story: Guides for Writers* (Heinemann, 1993), "A story is about people. About people in trouble or conflict. Caring about the main character makes readers care about the story."

There's another reason characters need to have a name. "Whether a story is believable depends on the believability and reliability of the character," states W. Fisher in his book *Human Communications as Narration: Toward a Philosophy of Reason, Value, and Action* (University of South Carolina Press, 1987). When characters are believable, their viewpoints and the story become believable, which allows us to appraise and judge the events of the story and learn how to act ourselves.

Focus on one main character. As soon as that number doubles to two, psychologist Paul Slovic of the University of Oregon has found, compassion fatigue sets in (http://articles.washingtonpost.com/2010-01-17/newd/36838772_1_insiko-hawaiian-society-pamela-burns).

Without a main character, your story loses its focus and the ability to connect, which dilutes empathy. The story loses its impact. Although the brain may comprehend large numbers, the listener finds it hard to feel this magnitude because their brain can't tell the difference between one child dying of hunger and ten thousand of them experiencing the same thing.

Express inner and outer dialogue

A way to express emotion and breathe life into your characters — whether you're talking about yourself or someone else — is to use inner and outer dialogue.

Inner dialogue is the internal monologue you have within yourself. It's what a character is thinking or feeling but not outwardly expressing. Sharing inner dialogue in a story is like sharing a secret with the world. You're revealing more about the character.

In Cristi's story, she shares her inner dialogue in this paragraph:

> "We need all the help we can get." Cristi thought to herself. "The economy's not getting better any time soon. We've got to find government work to replace the work we've lost. Maybe it will give me a chance to learn about these agencies and their policies and procedures. . . . But you know, if I do get an opportunity to meet someone of influence, I'd better be prepared."

Cristi's story also has her sharing a prior conversation she had with Louise. This is also considered inner dialogue.

How can you do this? When you share a personal story, use phrases such as "Now what was I thinking?" or "George thought to himself . . ."

Outer dialogue is what a character openly discloses to another person. It adds spice and variety to a story and cements people's interest. When telling a story, because we often paraphrase dialogue or point to dialogue, listeners might not expect to hear it. It happens like this: We say, "Tom said he was going to the mall but . . ." Instead, if we used outer dialogue, we'd parody Tom's voice: "Tom said, 'I'm going to the mall but . . .'"

We hear outer dialogue in Cristi's story when she approaches Louise and Mr. Dixon at the head table. "Louise. It's so good to see you again. Thank you for suggesting I attend today. I'm really looking forward to hearing all the different speakers." Then she turns slightly. "Hello Mr. Dixon. I'm Cristi Kanenwisher with Wolfe Architectural Group. I'm looking forward to listening to your presentation after lunch."

Although one of the distinctions between describing a situation and telling a story is the use of inner and outer dialogue, keep it brief and to the point. Don't go wandering off sharing irrelevant dialogue just because you think dialogue is good. Sprinkle dialogue judiciously through the story but don't go overboard.

LOTS: Tap into words that touch the senses

Stories must contain lots of LOTS. As mentioned in Chapter 2, *LOTS* stands for *language of the senses*. The best-crafted stories activate at least two of our five senses: hearing, seeing, smelling, tasting, and touching.

When you use sensory language, you create an immediate connection to your audience. Instantly, both their imaginations and physical bodies become engaged. This makes it easier for them to remember the story and brings them viscerally into the situation. It also makes it more fun for you to tell.

For example, you could say, "I sat down at my desk and started answering my e-mail." Or you could say, "I sat down in my creaky chair in front of my well-worn desk to check the fire hose of e-mails in my inbox, rapidly clicking away in response at the keys on my well-worn keyboard." Which sentence captures you more?

When you provide sensory language in your stories, you automatically trigger a variety of reactions in people. If you're sharing a story and give visual cues about the environment, mention a smell, refer to a sound, allude to a taste, touch an object, or express how something felt, each person who hears or reads the story will connect to different input. Some will hear the sound and not smell the smell. Some will see certain visual images that differ from what others see.

This is okay. It means that people are connecting to your story in ways that create meaning for them — and to specific images and experiences in their personal mental databanks. That's the beauty of storytelling: As you share your story, people are internalizing it in their own unique and particular ways.

Now go back and re-read Cristi's story. This time notice the following sensory triggers as you review it:

✔ What did you see?

✔ What did you hear?

✔ What did you smell?

✔ What did you taste?

✔ What did you touch?

Let's take a minute to chat about your answers:

✔ **What did you see?** Did you visualize what Cristi looks like? Were you able to envision the ballroom in great detail — tables, chairs, dais, projection screen, name badges, and the like? How about Cristi's workplace: Were you able to imagine her chair, desk, computer, and office? You may have gotten a picture of how Mr. Dixon appears and how he's dressed. Did he have a beard or was he clean-shaven? Was he wearing a suit and/or eyeglasses? Was he pudgy or thin? What color was his hair, and did he have a receding hairline? Maybe there's someone from your past that felt a lot like Mr. Dixon or Cristi and that's the person you saw in your mind's eye. All of these options are correct.

✔ **What did you hear?** Some folks hear things in stories, some don't. In Cristi's story, perhaps you heard the voices of Cristi and/or Mr. Dixon. Perhaps you heard the plates and silverware clanking during lunch. Maybe you heard the words and the tone of voices used by those who were asking challenging questions in the Q&A. You may have even heard words or sounds that weren't even mentioned in the story. Because most people tend to be more visually oriented than auditory, maybe you ignored all the sounds and focused on other sensory triggers.

✔ **What did you smell?** Did you smell the chicken or the ballroom? Maybe Cristi's perfume? Or the scent of the ChapStick?

✔ **What did you taste?** Did you taste the chicken? Or the flavor of the ChapStick?

✔ **What did you touch?** Were you holding the brochure in your hand? Did you pull out the chair that Cristi sat in within the ballroom? Were your hands taking notes? Were your fingers typing away at the keyboard with her as she checked the website?

If it's critical that a particular person or item or scene needs to be visualized, heard, smelled, tasted, or felt in a specific manner, then you'll have to provide the necessary details for that to happen. At least provide enough sensory language so that people can attach to something familiar. With stories, if you don't provide much detail, the listener's mind provides it based on their personal memory bank.

There's one more aspect to sensory information that's important: emotions. As you read Cristi's story, what emotions did you feel? All kinds of emotions were present in it — from disappointment to anxiety, confidence, joy, and surprise, to name a few. Did you feel any of these or other emotions as you read the story?

Sharing emotions in stories is good — but a word of caution here. Due to your storytelling, people may feel bad, guilty, hopeless, or afraid. Leaving them wallowing in these feelings is a big no-no. Touch lightly on these emotions and ensure your story transforms them into hope, respect, or relief. If you don't, they won't listen to you anymore because they'll feel bad in your presence. That's the last thing you want.

> *"Our experiences — the ones we remember, anyway — are those that have both sensory and emotional dimensions. In some respects the emotional side is the more important for it allows us to structure our world."*
>
> — Valerie G. Hardcastle in "The Development of Self," from *Narrative and Consciousness: Literature, Psychology and the Brain*, by G. Firemen, T.E. McVay, and O.J. Flanagan (Oxford University Press, 2003)

Use contrast

Contrast is a very powerful and often unrecognized element in creating a compelling story. It creates both tension and interest.

What do we mean by contrast? Contrasts are simple binary oppositions between hot and cold, young and old, light and dark, happy and sad, good and evil, rich and poor, beautiful and ugly, tall and short, and so on. There is significant research to demonstrate, as outlined in Kendall Haven's book *Story Proof* (Libraries Unlimited, 2007), that opposing relationships, like hot and cold, are an essential element in helping people to create meaning from a story.

Contrast is also how your brain sorts out what's important and what to pay attention to. It's no different than when you look at a painting and say, "Oooh, I love the artist's use of blue against that yellow." Or, "Wow, see how the light of the sky shows through those dark clouds." Visual painters know how to use contrast to grab attention and draw people into their canvases. The same applies to storytelling. No contrast? Snorseville.

What sorts of contrasts are you able to identify in Cristi's story? To start with, there's the contrast between losing work and winning a contract, between the known and the unknown, between male and female, between authority and non-authority, and between fear and joy.

It's not unusual for a raw story (the original version of it) not to contain much contrast. This means you'll need to add contrast into the story. It's easy to do and doesn't take much time. Scan your story and mark the several places where you could add contrast or beef them up. Then jot down the contrasts you want to add or change. This will make the story much crisper, more interesting, and more meaningful. We talk more about contrast in Chapter 7.

Employ drama and intrigue

To engage deeply, we, as humans, crave twists and turns, interesting characters, and drama and intrigue. *Drama* is an exciting, emotional, and/or unexpected event or set of circumstances.

Intrigue arouses our curiosity and interest. It might come from a secret plan to do something detrimental to someone or it could be the fascinating and mysterious elements in your story. Intrigue can also be sparked through the element of surprise. In a story, you could simply say, "The husband died and then the wife died." Or you could say, "The husband died and then the wife died from laughing so hard." The latter well-known example tickles the funny bone and leaves you more curious, wanting to know more.

Here's the challenge you face in making your stories compelling: You hardly notice when the people around you, the environments you inhabit, and the situations you find yourself in match your expectations. Your mind cuts down on clutter by ignoring them. When the story you share falls within the realms of the expected, your audience has no reason to be interested.

If you want somebody to pay attention to your story, make sure you include the unexpected. Even babies perk up, stop what they're doing, stare longer, or look surprised when something unexpected happens in their world.

Take another look at Cristi's story. Where do drama and intrigue come into play? They show up when she first notices that Mr. Dixon is at the seminar and are enhanced when she plots how to approach him and wonders to herself what the outcome will be. Drama and intrigue are also evident toward the end of the story when day after day after day she finds nothing on the GAO website about her firm's proposal. Is there a surprise or something unexpected? Yep. The ChapStick.

Using dialogue is one of the best ways to create drama and intrigue in the minds of your readers or listeners. So is elongating time (for example, "day after day after day" versus "two weeks later") when telling the story orally. This sort of emphatic language stimulates audiences to keep paying attention so they can discover what's going to happen next. Given that you want them to hang on your next word, this is one way to make that happen.

Identifying layers of meaning

As you reflect on Cristi's story, what meaning does it hold for you? Was there a moral that stood out? Or a specific lesson that you learned? For you, the story may be about creativity. For someone else, it could be about perseverance. For others, it could be about taking a chance. Some readers might find it validates what they already do. Then again, you may see it as an example of bureaucracy, exemplifying power and control.

To create an even richer story that people continue to mull and learn from over time, you may want to strategically embed multiple meanings within it. Think of it this way: Characters could embody different meanings because of how they act and transform. The problem/challenge could convey different meanings depending on how many obstacles are included and how they're overcome. What a personal story means to you (which you share with others at the end of the telling) could shift and change over time. How people perceive you as the teller adds other shades of meaning to the story.

Depending on the specifics of the story and how long you have to tell it, these components are all intertwined. If this sounds complicated, don't worry. Most of this happens naturally as you share your story. We raise the topic here so you can begin to have more conscious control over your storytelling. In Chapter 6 on crafting stories, we provide more specific techniques for meaning-making.

Layering meanings into a story also has an implication. Make sure that none of the meanings a story holds has the potential to offend anyone. You can avoid this scenario by sharing the story one-on-one and asking people what meaning the story holds for them. This danger doesn't happen often, yet it's good to check in with someone else just to make sure. Is there anything insulting in the story I just shared? Is there anything that someone could object to? Getting answers to both questions can keep you on the straight and narrow — and out of trouble.

Find the key message: The most important point

All stories, as we've defined a story, have a resolution where the problem is solved or the challenge is overcome or the struggle is transformed into victory. Only, that's not the end of the story — at least not in business.

Ultimately, you want to move people to action. So identifying the key message of a story is critically important. The *key message* is the *most* important point embodied in a story. It's the one layer of meaning that resonates on a universal level. It's the one layer of meaning that you for sure want to convey. It's the entire point of the story.

In Cristi's story, the most important point is *make a meaningful connection.* It's the singular lesson that captures both the essence of the story and inspires people to do something different. How was it derived? Cristi alludes to the desire to connect when, early in the story, she says to herself, "But you know, if I do get an opportunity to meet someone of influence, I'd better be prepared." Her behavior reinforces this key point when she reaches out to Mr. Dixon before lunch, takes the time to attend his session, and extends herself afterward.

In Chapter 6, when we cover how to craft a story, we outline several ways to figure out its key message. As you tell your stories, the more you hone in on the most important point, the more likely this message will be received, considered, remembered, and then shared with others via word of mouth.

Describing isn't telling

When working with clients on storytelling, we always ask to review stories they're currently using. Time and time again we're amazed when they give us lots of material that contains very little story. It's mostly descriptions of situations. Even when we ask people to tell us a story about an accomplishment they're most proud of, in order to get a sense of their storytelling skills, 90 percent of the time they *never* share a story. What we hear instead is something akin to, "I decided to take on this project. It took six months, but we finally got it done and I'm really proud of the work I did."

It's easy to get confused about what a story is, because some people in the marketplace think everything is a story. However, "describing" a situation is not the same as "telling" a story. Although describing a situation can deliver a lot of information and data, emotional reactions and sensory details are often lacking or missing altogether.

Allow us to illustrate. Here's a narration of events:

"I went to work. I made some sales calls. Then I went home."

That's not much of a story, is it? We doubt you'd walk into a bookstore to pay money to read that story. Or go to a movie to watch it.

Describing a situation is a lackluster second cousin to a full-fledged story. Consequently, mere description usually gets you lackluster results.

Now consider this narrative:

"Going to work this morning, I wasn't feeling particularly great. I sell office machines. The end of the month was coming and I hadn't made my sales goals. Hoping today would be a better day, I decided to do something different. What the heck did I have to lose? When I got to my desk I pulled out my contact list and started to make a few calls. Instead of telling people about our great service, I started to ask them if they'd share with me one of the most frustrating experiences with their office equipment. Boy, did I get an earful! One office manager's copier had just broken down — right when she needed to make copies of some critical documents for a board meeting later that day. I offered her a loner from our warehouse and promised I'd get it to her and have it set up right away. I arrived at her company within the hour and got everything set up to her unending delight and disbelief. After she made the copies, I sat down with her and said that if she contracted with our company, because of our quality machines and outstanding customer service, this situation could be avoided, or we'd remedy the situation immediately just like I did today. Guess what? I walked away with a sale! That taught me a valuable lesson about listening, and I experienced new ways to reach my sales goals. By the time I got home that evening, I was feeling on top of the world."

The more you transform a description of events into the telling of a story by adding emotions and a variety of sensory details, the more impact you'll have.

 The absolute best stories you can share in business are those you can relive in the telling. As you recall the story and relive it in your mind, your audience gets to experience it too. And you come across as real and authentic. When you talk about an event in the third person, or from 20,000 feet, people can't connect and can't experience what you did themselves. So keep your own stories in the first person using lots of *I* words.

Defining Different Types of Narrative

Everything people say is considered narrative. However, not all narrative is a story. As we share in Chapter 1, a story provides packets of sensory material presented in a particular way that allows the listener to quickly and easily internalize the information, comprehend it, and create meaning from it.

Because people seem to have difficulty distinguishing between a story and other forms of narrative, we've identified ten different types of narrative. They are: story, anecdote, case study, description, example, news report, profile, scenario, testimonial, and vignette. To help you visualize these distinctions, we've provided a well-crafted story in the appendix from Robert (Bob) McIlree called "The Price We Pay to Get Results." Go ahead and go read that story now. We'll wait for you.

In this section, we transform this story into the nine other types of narrative to illustrate the different forms narrative can take. Because all narrative forms have a place in business, we also suggest situations when they may accomplish your objectives.

Anecdotes

An *anecdote* is a short personal account (your personal take on a situation). It tends to leave out sensory information and dialogue as well as context and setting. Here's Bob's story as an anecdote:

> One time I was being denied viewing access to several databases so I could fix a customized software application. In asking for permissions, I couldn't get anywhere. As a last resort, I filed a Freedom of Information Act request to get my access reinstated. That got my boss's attention. The database administrator and I both got chewed out, but I got my access.

Anecdotes are very handy, especially when time is short. They're very popular for just this reason. But only having a repertoire full of anecdotes means you're missing out on the real power of sharing fuller, richer stories. So keep a few anecdotes around to share, but don't get suckered into thinking anecdotes are the backbone of business storytelling.

Here are some situations where anecdotes may be useful:

- ✔ You're in an elevator with only a moment to share a situation.

- ✔ You're at a networking event and want to spark a conversation where you can share richer stories.

- ✔ People are distracted and have little bandwidth to spare to hear a full story, and an anecdote will make your point without frustrating them.

- ✔ You're giving a full presentation and you suddenly remember something to share that will help you make your point but not derail the topic.

- ✔ You're listening to someone else's story and something that's said sparks an anecdote within you. While still keeping the focus on the other person, the original story, and the topic at hand, you find a way to quickly share your anecdote to convey understanding/connection.

Case studies

A *case study* is an analysis of a particular event or situation that can be used as a basis for drawing conclusions in similar situations. It's also a record of somebody's problems and how they were dealt with. Case studies are usually presented in sections: situation, solution, result, and analysis. It's not unusual for a case study to follow story structure and have a beginning, a middle, and an end. In other situations, they're hybrids of descriptions and stories.

Here's Bob's story as a case study:

> **Bob's Situation:** Bob received a call from the support staff in the information systems area. A customized software application that he'd developed as a consultant to a federal government agency had stopped functioning. This application makes extensive use of internal databases and is very useful and popular with agency staff charged with controlling budget dollars. Lots of money would be lost if this application were shut down for long periods of time.

> Bob is properly and officially credentialed with this agency. He has a badge to enter its facilities, complete access to the computer systems that he supports, and a small office where he's required to work onsite

due to federal computer security restrictions. When Bob began to work on the problem, he kept getting error messages that said he didn't have permission to view the databases. Somehow his security level had been altered. The only way this could've happened was if the database administrator had removed his clearance. The person who could give him access gave him the runaround. Bob called his boss. Even though she said she'd take care of it, nothing happened. He was stuck.

Bob's Solution: Not one to give up, Bob started mulling over strategies to work around, through, or over the problem. He quickly hit upon an idea. Though risky and long-winded in process, it would send a clear message that something was seriously amiss. He decided to file a request to access the data under the Freedom of Information Act — what is typically called FOIA. This meant working through the "front door" of the agency — the one the general public must use to get information. By law, the agency must allow or deny the request within a limited period of time. He figured none of the data he needed was sensitive or secret. Even if it were, the FOIA request would be routed to the proper department and eventually to his manager for decision and disposition.

The Result: The next week Bob's request landed like an F-16 fighter jet on his manager's desk — which prompted her to come and see him. She asked what was going on. Bob replied that the database administrator had ignored his request and basically blown him off. Without saying a word, she picked up his phone, called the database administrator, and told him to fix the problem. As she hung up, she looked straight at Bob and politely asked him not do that again. They agreed that to bring closure to the situation, he would withdraw his request. The next day, Bob did so. The database administrator quickly corrected the situation, and Bob was able to proceed with his work.

Analysis: What lesson or meaning do you take away from this case study? How does what Bob experienced apply to what you do in your work? What causes situations like this to take place in an organization?

Situations where case studies may be useful include the following:

- ✔ Teaching critical-thinking skills.
- ✔ When highlighting how you work with customers to solve their problems.
- ✔ Stimulating the creation of ideas in training sessions.
- ✔ Explaining how other companies have managed similar situations to add credibility to your solution(s).

Descriptions

A *description* gives a brief explanation of a situation. It's a simple, high-level narration of events that uses a brief timeline to represent what was experienced instead of conveying the totality of the experience. This form of narrative is similar to "examples," in that descriptions are often used when "talking about" a story instead of telling one. Here's Bob's story as a description:

> Bob, an IT consultant, was denied access to a critical database he had been hired to work on. He repeatedly asked various managers and supervisors for the access but was denied. So Bob bent the rules and found a way around the denied requests so he could complete his work.

Because a description is presented in the third person, it's not about you. It's about someone removed from you. That makes it harder to emotionally connect to it.

Situations where descriptions may be useful include the following:

- ✔ When you want to see whether a situation is worthy of being developed into a full-blown story.
- ✔ When you're testing the waters to see if someone wants to hear the real story.
- ✔ When you're writing an executive summary for a report.

Examples

An *example* is a particular single item, fact, incident or aspect that serves to "illustrate" an opinion, theory, principle, rule, guideline, or concept. Examples are similar to "descriptions" in that they're often used when "talking about" a story instead of telling one. They lack most story elements. Here's Bob's story as an example:

> Sometimes in organizations, following traditional protocol does not work. One day, Bob learned this as an IT consultant when his viewing access was denied to critical databases so he could repair a customized software application. Even though Bob's boss asked Bob's coworker to grant him access, he could not get the approvals. So Bob found a creative way to gain approval access that still fit the rules but was outside of the normal flow of events.

Use examples when you want to quickly point to what other companies have done as a way to add credibility to you. For example: "XYZ company did this; ABC company did it too; and JKL company accomplished the same thing by. . . ." You're not sharing a story; you're merely pointing out examples to back your claims.

Here are a few situations where examples may be useful:

- ✔ You want to reference what someone else has done.
- ✔ You want to make a quick point without derailing a story.
- ✔ You don't have much time and need to add validity to a concept you're sharing.
- ✔ When print or online space hasn't been allocated for a full story.

News reports

A *news report* is an accounting of recent events or developments. It telegraphs the end of the story at the very beginning of it. The tip of the iceberg is the first line or two: Who, what, when, where, how, and why are usually in the opening sentence or paragraph. Then additional details are expanded on as the report is written, with the least important ones at the bottom so an editor can cut the end of it to fit the available print/online space.

News reports follow an inverted pyramid rather than a traditional story arc (see Chapter 6). In a news report, up front you get the broad setting and context for the story, an introduction to the main character, and the problem/challenge or opportunity. Here's Bob's story as a news report:

> For 14 days, tens of thousands of taxpayer dollars were at risk through several critical federal government databases, which deal with a key agency's budgeting process. It took the filing of a Freedom of Information Act (FOIA) to get enterprise architecture consultant Robert McIlree the right to use and repair them. Previously McIlree, an expert in repairing the databases, always had access. Significant amounts of money are lost if the application McIlree was hired to repair is shut down for long periods of time. But new homeland security rules and bureaucratic turf wars made the database inaccessible to him. Two weeks after McIlree's filing of the FOIA, it got the agency's attention. He was finally granted access and was able to repair the databases. In an interview, McIlree and an agency representative reported all was fine and back in top working order without harm to the agency. For the full story, see our online version.

Situations where news reports may be useful include the following:

- ✔ When relaying information in an annual or financial report.
- ✔ In press releases.
- ✔ When writing news articles about your company.
- ✔ When sharing news internally in your organization.

Profiles

A *profile* is a concise biographical sketch. Profiles are informational descriptions that create very little emotional connection for the audience and typically don't include a problem or its resolution. Profiles are often promotional pieces that are mistaken for stories. Here's Bob's story as a profile:

> Bob has been working as an enterprise data architect in the information technology industry since the early 1990s. His claim to fame is the ability to come into organizations and tackle tough problems quickly. His work is widely known in the financial services, insurance, consumer products, energy/utilities, telecommunications, and transportation industries where he is valued as a provider of innovative solutions.
>
> Bob started working for a federal government agency as a consultant in 2002. He encountered some initial hiccups but was eventually able to smooth things out with some original thinking, successfully resolving the issues. Today he continues to go beyond his current client's expectations as he did at this agency.

We've found that companies often share customer profiles under the guise of customer stories. How boring. To highlight or promote a customer, find a way to share their story. Why waste time and effort writing profiles that won't make an impression or get you the results you need when you could spend that same time and energy crafting a compelling story about them?

Here are three situations where profiles may be useful:

- ✔ Internal project proposals.
- ✔ At the end of a written presentation document.
- ✔ When requested as part of an RFP.

Scenarios

A *scenario* is an imagined sequence of possible events designed to help people consider its implications or generate new ideas. Scenarios may show up as stories (we provide examples of these in Chapter 4), but more frequently they are descriptions. They tend to be crafted in the third person, so they aren't as compelling as stories that are told in the first person. You can also craft them so you or others can place yourselves in the situation, as we've done here. Similar to case studies, scenarios are often used in training and educational settings to stimulate thinking and creative ideas. Here's Bob's story as a scenario:

> Imagine you've received a call from the support staff in the information systems area. A customized software application that you developed as a consultant to a federal government agency has stopped functioning. This particular application makes extensive use of internal databases and is very useful and popular with agency staff charged with controlling budget dollars. Lots of money is lost if this application is shut down for long periods of time.
>
> Now, you're properly and officially credentialed with this agency. You have a badge to enter their facilities, complete access to the computer systems that you support, and a small office where you're required to work onsite due to federal computer security restrictions. When you begin to work the problem, you keep getting error messages that say you don't have permission to view the databases. Somehow your security level has been altered. The only way this could've happened was if Jim, the database administrator, had removed your clearance. This doesn't surprise you. Jim is known to have an insatiable thirst for power and control over his domain.
>
> You immediately place a call to him. "Jim, "I'm having trouble looking at a couple of databases. I keep getting error messages that tell me I don't have access." Jim replies, "Oh. We've just implemented our new 'cyber security' scheme. It's a requirement of Homeland Security." You say, "Well, I have a problem — a real live support issue that needs to be addressed right now." Jim counters with, "You'll have to get me some sort of documentation for the permission. Then it'll have go through the proper channels and be approved by a committee. You know, I really don't have the time to deal with this right now. You say, "Thanks." And hang up. Right then and there you know you'll have to go around Jim. All you've been given by him are excuses. As far as you're concerned, Jim has arbitrarily and without notice removed your permission to access the databases.
>
> What will you do? Provide three different options.

Situations where scenarios may be useful include the following:

✔ When imagining possible futures as part of strategic planning.

✔ When you want to stimulate new thinking and creative ideas.

✔ When considering the implications of an imagined event for disaster preparedness.

✔ To present a case or situation that's so emotionally loaded that listeners become overwhelmed and freeze. Stories of severe trauma can fall into this category. When presented as a scenario, listeners are able to detach somewhat from the personal trauma involved and pay more attention to the scenario.

Testimonials

A *testimonial* is a favorable report or statement about the qualities or virtues of somebody or something. A testimonial can also be an expression of appreciation, a statement testifying to benefits, or a character reference or letter of recommendation. Testimonials are often mistaken for stories. Here are two different types of testimonials about Bob's story:

Version 1: I loved Bob's story. It really helped me get unstuck about my own problem with my needs being met.

Version 2: For the last 18 months I've been having a lot of problems with one of my coworkers who appears to continually undermine my efforts. I've bought a number of books, talked to some people, but nothing has worked. In a workshop I had the opportunity to read your story and in 30 minutes of discussion about it, I realized that the reason my actions weren't working is because I was misinterpreting my coworker's behavior. He was just abiding by the mandatory rules. Thank you for allowing me the opportunity to have this insight and to craft different action steps.

Here are a few situations where testimonials may be useful:

✔ In a proposal.

✔ On a website.

✔ In a brochure.

✔ On the back of a business card.

Vignettes

A *vignette* is a brief, often elegant incident or scene, depicted as in a play or movie. It may also be a short descriptive piece (rendered in third person). A vignette is often an episode that's part of a larger story. Sometimes it can stand by itself, but it's often used to stoke the audience's curiosity and desire to hear the full story. The aim of a vignette is simply to capture a revealing slice of life. Here's a vignette from within Bob's story:

> "Jim, I'm having trouble looking at a couple of databases. I keep getting error messages that tell me I don't have access." Jim replies, "Oh. We've just implemented our new 'cyber security' scheme. It's a requirement of Homeland Security." I say, "Well, I have a problem — a real live support issue that needs to be addressed right now." Jim counters with, "You'll have to get me some sort of documentation for the permission. Then it'll have to go through the proper channels and be approved by a committee. You know, I really don't have the time to deal with this right now." I say, "Thanks." And hang up. Right then and there I know I'll have to go around Jim.

You can create a story by stringing together a series of related vignettes. Each one should build toward the key message at the end and have a nugget of meaning that supports the main point of the larger story. Think of vignettes as interchangeable pearls on a string that when put together add up to a beautiful necklace.

Situations where vignettes may be useful include these:

- ✔ To capture someone's interest.
- ✔ When a point the vignette captures needs to be made.

Putting It All Together

So what's the bottom line here? Well, what we're clear on is that stories come in all shapes and sizes and that many people and organizations naturally confuse stories with other narrative forms.

All the narrative forms listed in this chapter are missing one or more story elements. The elements most commonly excluded are sensory language, inner and outer dialogue, and the key message — any one of which can make a story significantly less effective. Our goal is to make you really smart about stories so you can avoid the mistakes others have made. And to help you avoid wasting your time and energy with narrative forms that won't get you or your company the results you desire.

Use the other forms when appropriate, but whenever you can share a story, make that your first choice.

Chapter 4

Stories to Have in Your Hip Pocket

In This Chapter

▶ Identifying seven story types to have ready in a pinch, personally and organizationally
▶ Obtaining each type of story
▶ Pinpointing types of stories to stay away from

*B*eth's in charge of business development and marketing for her firm. Karen (your author) phoned Beth because Beth had signed up for an association-sponsored workshop on story techniques. As the instructor, Karen wanted to make sure the workshop would meet her expectations.

No more than 20 minutes into the interview, Beth asked, "Where do I start? My organization has lots of stories. And I have several of my own. Which ones should I focus my attention on? Where should I go to find these stories?" Karen responded, "Great questions, Beth. I'll make sure to cover them."

We suspect you have the same need as Beth. Here's what we know: Stories come in all different shapes and sizes. They also come in different types.

The ultimate goal is to match 1) the type of story and 2) the strength of its key message to 3) the appropriate situation. The more overlap there is between these three elements, the more effective you'll be at moving people to action.

Having Stories Ready to Go

There are two buckets of stories you need: stories about yourself and stories about your organization. Yes, we realize you can also tell other people's stories or those of other enterprises. We spend time covering how to do that in Chapters 5 and 12. For now, we'll stick with yours and those about your enterprise.

On a personal level, why have stories about yourself in your hip pocket?

- ✔ An interviewer may want to know how you got to where you are, how you learned what you know, and what you aspire to in life.

- ✔ You may want to share with your colleagues how you do what you do or how you did something successfully in the past.

- ✔ It may help a coworker who's facing myriad challenges to hear about your struggles and the persistence you displayed in overcoming them.

- ✔ A team you're working with may find it useful to learn what you value in life and how that relates to the project you're working on together.

- ✔ As part of new hire and/or employee training, you may want to share an amazing customer experience you had to demonstrate appropriate customer behavior.

On an organizational level, what sorts of stories need to be readily available?

- ✔ Potential customers may be curious about the inception of the firm and how that defines what the organization does today — in addition to what the future holds.

- ✔ Because customers have already invested time and money in your company, they may want to know the inside scoop on how products are made or what's involved in providing a specific service.

- ✔ Business partners may need to understand what your organization stands for, what drives employees, and the ethics behind everything that's done so they know what they can depend on.

- ✔ Your customers and prospects could find it fascinating to learn about what you consider mundane, such as back stories of what makes your organization tick and challenges it's faced and overcome.

- ✔ Sharing customer stories can help reinforce the *know, like, trust* process that's vital to growing your business.

In this chapter, we present seven different types of stories. You'll get at least one example of each along with a few ideas on how to identify them in your personal life and in your workplace. This is your core list. A few additional story types for specific applications are discussed in upcoming chapters.

We have one observation that's key as you read through this chapter. Not all story examples depicted here are complete stories as we define them in Chapter 3. Although they have a few of the elements, they all have room for refinement. Looks like there's still a lot of work to be done in this arena!

"Founding" Stories

You as an individual have a *founding* story and so does the organization you're a part of. It's not unusual for these stories of origin to morph over time as you or your firm evolves.

Your founding stories

Your stories of origin are those moments in your life that made a huge difference in who you are today. Sometimes people talk about these as *I finally realized who I am* or *Here's when I began to feel comfortable in my own skin* situations. Although these significant milestones may be separated by time, they're interconnected because they all define "you" as a person.

Here's an example of an individual founding story. In the 2005 commencement address that Steve Jobs gave at Stanford (http://news.stanford.edu/news/2005/june15/jobs-061505.html), he shared three stories: one about connecting the dots, a second about love and loss, and a third about death. His love and loss story is about how he got let go from Apple by the board of directors at age 30. He talks about feeling like a "beginner" after this significant turning point.

How did he go about finding himself in the midst of this difficult situation? He stayed grounded by doing what he loved. His work defined him. Being fired allowed him to be rebirthed when he began working for NeXT and Pixar and fell in love with the woman who eventually became his wife.

What can you do to uncover these sorts of milestones or turning points in your life that encapsulate your founding stories? Ponder these story prompts:

- ✔ An event surrounding your birth may be of huge significance to you. Enlighten me about a time like this.
- ✔ Share with me a memory about an early childhood situation that defines you to this day.
- ✔ Tell me about an event that has profoundly shaped you as a person.
- ✔ Tell me about that moment when you just knew you needed to pursue the career or business you have today.

You may wonder, "Where would I tell such stories at work?" And, "Who would be interested in hearing them in the workplace?" Your challenge when you use any kind of personal story at work is to demonstrate its relationship to the business situation and/or topic at hand.

Any time you interview for a new job or assignment, the interviewer may be interested in knowing these things about you. When you're building a relationship with business prospects, they may want to hear one of these stories. Once you join a new organization, team, or project, your coworkers may want you to disclose these experiences, depending on their importance to the organization's work. In one-on-one conversations, it may be valuable to share a founding story of yours as a way of forging deeper bonds with others.

The organization's founding story

Every organization has a unique founding story about its inception and which problem it originally was focused on solving. For Facebook founder Mark Zuckerberg, it started in a dorm room. For Hewlett-Packard, it started in a garage. For Microsoft, it began in a computer user's group. For Scott Heiferman, co-founder and CEO of Meetup, it began with 9/11.

Whether it's an entrepreneurial venture or a large corporation, the beginnings of most organizations are typically humble. A humble origins story can have great power, as illustrated by Geil Browning in a blog post for Inc.com titled "Tell Stories & You'll Boost Sales (Because of How Human Brains Are Wired)," available online at www.inc.com/geil-browning/tell-stories-boost-sales-human-brain.html.

Browning reflects on people at a networking event asking her what she does at Emergenetics International. She could say, "I own a human capital consulting firm that provides assessments for employee development, recruitment, and retention." But she doesn't. Instead, she tells about how she grew up at her family's kitchen table, listening to her mother and grandmother trade tales about their classroom experiences as teachers. These stories inspired her to become a teacher, where she quickly built up her own repertoire of stories.

One boy, 11-year-old Randy, was a handful — and often boisterous. Because at the time she was a teacher, schools weren't designed to help kids like Randy, working with him made her want to discover *how* students learned, so she left to pursue her doctorate. She studied left-brain/right-brain thinking, an area where she felt she could make a difference.

Before she returned to teaching, she met the CEO of a large bank who wanted help getting his dysfunctional team to perform better. She says, "A lightbulb went off! I discovered a calling to both learning and business. It encouraged me to create a way for people to clearly see who they are, and how they think, behave, and communicate — and what all that means at work."

The birth and almost death of Tide

Founding stories can be about the inception of a product or service. There's a three-minute video about the birth of the laundry detergent Tide on YouTube that's worth watching: www.you tube.com/watch?feature=player_ embedded&v=xfU8LH0onPI#! It shares how the laundry soap was created and then almost canceled into oblivion, but for the persistence of one man. It's a great example of how an origin story about a product (or service or firm) can be told quickly and easily, leaving people inspired, educated, and emotionally connected to it.

Geil's personal story is the founding story of her company, Emergenetics — the story reveals its reason for being. Where and when could Geil use this story? To promote her firm, in proposals and proposal presentations, when going for funding, and when asked how she got into this line of work. The same is true for you if you're an entrepreneur or small business owner.

Here are ways to identify founding stories about some aspect of the business:

- ✔ **Ask the founder(s):** Tell me about that moment in time that motivated you to start the organization. Or about a problem that you couldn't solve that led you to start this organization. Or about an experience that compelled you to conceive this organization.

- ✔ **If it's your own company:** Tell me about that moment when you clearly knew you had to open your own business. Or about an experience you had earlier in life that led you to create this organization.

- ✔ **If your organization has been around for a long time:** If no one recalls how it started, dig into archives and old newspaper clippings.

- ✔ **If you work for a government agency:** The founding story may be buried in legislative materials or the creation of a law. Go find that stuff and piece together the story. If you can, interview those who may have been involved at the time.

- ✔ **If the company has completely reinvented itself:** One vivid example is when the Joban Coal Mining Company in Japan became the Spa Resort Hawaiians. To capture this rebirth, consider asking, "Tell me about the event or situation that was a key turning point in the organization."

- ✔ **For existing products and services:** Figure out who was responsible for their creation and (if possible) ask them: "Tell me about the situation, or series of situations, that caused you to invent XYZ."

- ✔ **If you're working on a new offering or innovation:** Keep track of what sparked the effort. Then craft a story about it.

"What We Stand For" Stories

What we stand for stories are about core values and the work ethics that surround them. These stories relay non-negotiable principles that guide how you or the organization choose to lead your life and/or conduct business.

Stories about what you stand for

Stories about what you personally stand for communicate what you value and prize the most. These stories may come from experiences in your personal life or within a work setting unrelated to where you're employed today.

Consider this "raw" story from Jean Peelen that she shared at a 2003 session on Core Value Storytelling at the Smithsonian Associates Program (www. creatingthe21stcentury.org/Values.html). This story was sparked in an activity in which trios of attendees were asked to tell a story to each other that connected them to what is most essential to their being:

> I was in a coaching group with about fifteen people and we were coaching each other. One person in the group was named Kathy and she was about forty-five years old, an African-American. She was financially in dire straits. She had essentially no money.
>
> In the middle of the group, or in the time allowed for the group, Kathy developed liver cancer. She had a very, very bad prognosis.
>
> I wasn't Kathy's coach. A friend was Kathy's coach. After her surgery and in the middle of chemotherapy and Kathy was clearly wasting away, her body was wasting away, she told her coach that she had decided to become an actress. Not just an actress but an Academy-award winning actress. I don't know what I would have said, if I had been Kathy's coach at that time. I'm grateful that I was not.
>
> What my friend — her coach — said was: "Great! What a great idea! Go for it!" So Kathy started taking acting classes. Kathy died two months later on the way to her dream. The symbol that I drew for this story was an Academy Award, which Kathy won. My core value lesson from this story is that I will never, ever, ever close down possibility for another human being.

Jean shared with us that she uses this story in a variety of ways. She's done all of the following:

✔ Repeated the story many times in the context of speaking to groups or in workshops on the topic of "Reinventing Your Life."

✔ Used it as an example of not putting limitations on your dreams or of not thinking that you know in advance what's possible.

✔ Applied it to individuals in the decision-making process or vision-seeking process.

✔ Used it with organizations when inspiring vision.

We all have situations in our lives that help us define what we stand for at the core of our being. Here are a few ways to identify your stories:

✔ Tell me about a situation that caused you to realize you hold strongly to a specific value in life.

✔ Paint for me a picture of a time in your life where you were very clear about what's essential to your ethical well-being.

✔ Enlighten me about a time when a principle you hold became non-negotiable for you.

Like Jean, you too can relay these experiences in the workplace. As before, you may be asked to convey them in interviews for a new job or assignment and/or once you join a team or project. These stories are also invaluable when coaching and mentoring others and when providing performance feedback.

"What the organization stands for" stories

Here's what a lot of organizations do. They list single words or a set of phrases as their values, such as these:

✔ We empower each other to do the right thing.

✔ Service before self.

✔ We do what we say we're going to do when we say we're going to do it.

✔ The customer comes first.

✔ We strive to be kind and caring in our interactions with each other.

Then they define each one by a sentence or a paragraph description. In a blog article or newsletter, they might even recognize people who demonstrate these behaviors: "Susan stayed late three nights to get a critical project out the door for our client. Not only did she stay late, she went above and beyond what the client originally asked for, which was rewarded by our getting another piece of business." This is a description, not a story (see Chapter 3 for a lot more about the difference between a story and other kinds of narrative). As such, it doesn't suffice to change behavior.

What's needed are stories — stories that depict how the values are *embodied* in your workplace. Not stories to say that your organization has values. What's most important to convey is what's done to actualize these values.

To demonstrate, here's a synopsis of a favorite story from Ed Fuller (http://management.fortune.cnn.com/tag/ed-fuller/). In 1985, Ed was a general manager at the Boston Marriott Copley Place, where a month after opening, catering was $300,000 below budget. "My career is lost," Fuller recalls thinking after a senior executive called and said, "I can't believe it. Bill Marriott is beside himself." The executive said he was flying to Boston and asked Fuller to dinner after "we deal with the problem."

It turns out that a Marriott family member had ordered clam chowder, and it had arrived cold. Another onsite manager hadn't handled it well. "If [the family] is treated badly, we assume the customer is treated worse," said Fuller, who has since retired from Marriott and is author of a book of workplace stories, *You Can't Lead With Your Feet on the Desk* (Wiley, 2011).

When he was president and managing director of Marriott Lodging International, Fuller shared this story with new managers to convey why it's important to follow one of Marriott's priorities (what we call a core value): serving the customer well — which means serving hot, not cold chowder. This focus on food tackles a potential cause of being under budget.

Customers and clients also want to hear this type of story. Sixty-four percent of more than 7,000 consumers stated that "shared values build relationships" in a study by Karen Freeman, Patrick Spenner, and Anna Bird. According to the study: "A shared value is a belief that both the company and the consumer have about a brand's higher purpose or a broad philosophy." This runs counter to the belief that "interactions build relationships" (http://blogs.hbr.org/cs/2012/05/three_myths_about_customer_eng.html).

This is why TOMS Shoes is so successful and popular. Consumers are drawn to the stories of how the business is operated and how kids benefit because the company lives its values by giving away shoes and restoring eyesight through the Seva Foundation. Here's one to check out: "A Student Leader in Cambodia: Ream's Story," available online at www.toms.com/our-movement/1#A-Student-Leader-in-Cambodia-Reams-Story.

Here are some ways to flesh out stories about what the organization stands for and how people in your organization embody these espoused values:

> ✔ **If you're an entrepreneur wanting to distill what your firm stands for:** Identify up to ten values that are critically important to how you want to run your firm. Then systematically collect stories of how your organization embodies them.

✔ **If you have feedback from customers, members, patients, clients, and so on:** Pull out situations that appear to exemplify the values that these individuals feel are important in how your organization interfaces with them. Craft stories around these experiences.

✔ **If your organization has been around for several years:** Ask long-tenured employees: "Tell me about a time when the business operated in such a way that what's highly prized came to the surface." Or, "Tell me about a time when qualities we most prize came through in our interactions with customers." Or, "Tell me about a time when what we most prize about our business products or services was clearly demonstrated."

"What We Do" Stories

What you do. What I do. What we do. All are important stories to have in your hip pocket for those moments when you're asked about them.

Stories about what you do

What you do stories are memorable moments in your work life that define how you spend your time. Telling stories about that isn't as easy as it may seem. Why? Because many people tend to *describe* what they do — they don't tell stories that allow others to *experience* what they do as an individual.

Here's an example. When asked what kind of work she does as a consultant, Lori could easily say, "I'm a strategist." Followed by, "I help organizations develop long-range breakthrough-oriented scenario-based strategic plans and implement large, messy changes." But how boring. And what a mouthful of words. Instead she often relates this story:

> One of the exciting parts of my work is I get to meet and talk with business leaders in a whole variety of industries. One day, I was to interview a board president to gain some insights so I could facilitate scenario development with the entire board and the organization's most senior leaders. Before I could ask him the questions I'd prepared, he said, "There are a few things I'd like to ask you first. I'm interested in knowing exactly what you do and how you got here." I replied, "Do you want to know the actual situation or might I provide another response?" He answered, "I'd like to hear both."
>
> I said, "My client contact attended a workshop I gave three weeks ago on strategic thinking. She left mid-afternoon to meet with her CEO. An hour later, while I was still teaching, she called, texted, and e-mailed to

say her CEO wanted my help with this board retreat. Several of us spoke by phone about how to best use the morning of the retreat in light of the organization's desire to create a new strategic plan. Based on what I learned in that call, I suggested we do scenario planning. That's how I got here."

"Now, for what I really do. I'd like you to meet Mary Poppins. A need appeared and I showed up. I'm just beginning to learn about the organization and how to approach the retreat." He laughed, and we proceeded with the interview. At the end of the meeting, before we departed, he said, "I have one thing to ask of you. I'd like you to consider folding up your umbrella and staying awhile, Mary Poppins."

Like Mary Poppins, I often get asked to show up, without much notice, and without a lot of fanfare. When I sense my work is done, which means the organization has gotten what it needs and is able to proceed on its own, I fold up my umbrella and go elsewhere.

Do you see how this story allows you to experience what Lori does as a consultant? Not only does it offer an example of what she does, it also employs the Mary Poppins metaphor which adds another dimension to the conversation. She excels at meeting last-minute demands.

Here's how you can identify stories so others can experience what you do:

- ✔ Tell me about a time when you were influenced by a mentor or coach and how that shaped the way you view your work.

- ✔ Paint me a picture of a memorable moment in your career that has impacted your perception of the work that you do.

- ✔ Enlighten me about an event that has profoundly impacted you as a person and how this is reflected in your work.

- ✔ Tell me about the personal legacy that you're leaving through the work that you do.

- ✔ Tell me a story about your work that reflects its ultimate importance.

Stories about what the enterprise does

In his 2009 TEDx talk, "Start With Why" (www.youtube.com/watch?v=u4ZoJKF_VuA&feature=player_embedded), advertising professional Simon Sinek says sharing what you do falls into three circles:

- ✔ **The outermost circle:** This is the *what* — what you do.

- ✔ **The middle circle:** This is the *how* — how you do it.

- ✔ **The innermost circle:** This is the *why* — why you do what you do.

He finds that few businesses know this. Instead, they reveal what they do by talking about the *what*. You'll hear something like: "We make great phones. They're easy to use and simply designed. Want to buy one?"

The *why* of what your enterprise does isn't to make a profit. That's the result. The *why* is what it believes in. People want to do business with organizations that believe in what they do. It all starts with having a passion for something: to change the world in some way, to expand horizons, make people safe, enlighten, serve, entertain, bring comfort or joy — or solve a problem.

Here's how one organization connects in this manner through story. Since 1979, Mercy Corps has been "helping people in the world's toughest places survive crises they confront and turn them into opportunities to thrive." When you visit the nonprofit's home page at www.mercycorps.org, you'll see a link to Top Stories. On the day we visited this site, we found 309 stories, including "Mothers Coping with War," by Sumaya Agha (www.mercycorps.org/articles/jordan-syria/mothers-coping-war-i-embrace-them-and-tell-them-not-fear). These stories are authored by field staff, in narrative form or as photo essays. They're first-hand accounts of what they learn when assisting individuals, families, and entire communities.

What can your organization do to have publically visible stories in its hip pocket like Mercy Corps? Try the following:

- ✔ Tell a story about the *why* behind what you, as staff, are collectively paid to do as an organization.

- ✔ Talk about a customer challenge that demonstrates what drives your business.

- ✔ Enlighten someone about a situation that demonstrates the impact your organization has on the lives of individuals or the community at large.

- ✔ Visualize and tell me about a specific moment in time that revealed to you and your colleagues the importance of the work you all do.

"Future" Stories

A *future* story revolves around an image of a possible, attractive, and desirable state not yet realized. Articulating the future in a tangible manner, as if it's already happened, makes it more real and can help to overcome the inertia that people experience when asked to change. Although there are many kinds of future stories, we cover vision and scenario stories here.

Personal vision stories

How does a personal vision story come to be? And can it spark one's future work? Here's how it revealed itself to Carrie Severson:

"In early 2009 I felt this big void in my life. This happens about every two years after settling into a new job. This time I was working in the advertising industry. One day after work I came home, sat on my floor, and surrounded myself with magazines. I had my notebook in one hand and a pen in the other and I prepared myself to finally figure out what I was supposed to do with my life. I wrote down questions I didn't have answers to: 'What was I supposed to do with my life? What can I see myself doing for the rest of my life? What am I passionate about?' The last question was the easiest. I knew what I was passionate about. I just didn't know how to do that at that point in time. Every day after work for months on end I would repeat this scene.'

"On April 7, I wrote: 'Dear God: I want the job of my dreams. Are you waiting for me to tell you what that looks like? Because I don't know. Are you waiting for me to tell you what company I want to work for? Because I don't know. I know I want to talk about health in a well-rounded sense and I want to be surrounded with people who are living with their mind, body, and soul as one.'

"On July 30, I wrote: 'I'm going to give to girls the understanding that each of them are unique. I'm going to launch a nonprofit and impact the lives of girls and their parents. I'll learn how to write a business plan. I'll talk to community leaders to figure out how to run a business. I'm going to utilize my powerful and positive life intentions I've created for myself and I'll give what I can to girls so they grow up in light.'

"By November, I was writing daily in my journal for a nonprofit career to manifest itself. One day, I wrote: 'Dear Spirit: I welcome a career in the nonprofit sector so I can learn how to best manage one when I am ready to launch one. I deserve to serve Phoenix and girls here. Thank you for gracefully guiding me to my career move now. I am about love, respect, and acceptance and I welcome the opportunity to be true to my authentic self. Thank you for guiding me to my next career move so that I can fully be a fit for me and my life purpose.'

"In December 2009 I was clear on what I wanted to do with my life— sisterhoods and self-esteem. I knew I was supposed to empower girls and help them understand how to be better to one another. Ellen DeGeneres was on the cover of *O* magazine. I ripped off the cover, and put it on my mantel in a picture frame — knowing one day I'd write for *O* magazine and be on *Ellen*. But I hadn't yet started learning how I'd get there.'

"Finally on December 6, 2010 I wrote: 'I will resign from my current job this month. My heart belongs to shine brighter on the pathways for girls in town. It is my life purpose to help them see, grow, and learn from one another. My soul is fulfilled with this move. I want to enter 2011 as an employee of a profitable nonprofit that changes the lives of individuals.'

"I launched Severson Sisters (`http://seversonsisters.org`) on January 21, 2011."

Carrie's personal vision story emerges and unfolds over time. She didn't force this vision into place. Instead she allowed it the space and time it needed to present itself. During those two years, each time Carrie told her story, it enlarged itself and became clearer. The gift this story gave to Carrie is what she states best: "I created my daily job out of my personal passions. As a result, that void I always felt in my heart is nowhere to be felt."

How does Carrie use this story? She says: "I share my vision for my life whenever I'm asked how I came up with the concept of Severson Sisters — speaking in public, media interviews, meetings with corporate partners, volunteers, or when accepting awards."

You, too, can use your personal vision story in several ways. You may want to tell it to your boss in your annual performance review when discussing growth opportunities. Sharing it when exploring other career options can also be fruitful. If you're getting help from a small business development center or SCORE to start a business, communicate it to your counselor.

Keep in mind that personal vision stories shift and change over time. As you go about implementing yours, you may gain additional insights and feedback that cause you to become clearer on what you seek and to tweak it a bit.

There's a second type of individual future story: the scenario.

Personal scenario stories

Imagine the following situation. You're a leader of a staff of 100. One of them — a well-educated, high-level individual contributor — has continually been a challenge. You've consistently provided excellent performance feedback, but some behaviors you've commented on still persist. You're not clear about what to do. You call a colleague, and the person says, "Close your eyes. Let me take you through three different possible scenarios that could occur. As I share each one, pay attention to how you feel." Your colleague then provides a story around each possibility:

1. You do nothing, and the behaviors persist and worsen.

2. You continue to provide feedback, and the behaviors may or may not get better, but they don't get worse.

3. You take more formal disciplinary action with the employee, and she's eventually dismissed.

When your colleague gets to the third story, you know in your gut that it's the right one.

As this example shows, everyone crafts scenarios regularly in their personal lives. Whenever you have a decision to make, you roll through multiple options. We suggest you craft stories around these scenarios when the issue is complex, has significant consequences, or is fuzzy somehow.

Flesh out your personal future stories and decision scenario stories through . . .

- ✓ **Personal future story:** Consider journaling stories related to the following prompts. Then, step back and observe what they're telling you in sum total: Tell yourself about a time when you truly expressed your passions. Or . . . Paint a picture of what you see yourself doing for the rest of your life. Or . . . Create in your mind's eye a story about what you envision your legacy is to be in this lifetime.

- ✓ **Personal scenario stories:** Select a complex decision that you need to make. One that's unclear. Brainstorm at least three options. For each option, craft the story of what the outcome would look like if it were to be realized. Then step back and figure out which story best depicts the outcome that best suits the situation.

Your organization's future stories

An organization's future story is the story of the future that you and your business's customers, by being in relationship with each other, create to bring about a difference in the world. It's a story of the better future that you're advancing together, along with what you're doing now to achieve it.

Here's how Karen's future story for her firm Just Story It came to be:

> For many years I've helped individuals and companies find, craft, and tell their future story. But I kept asking myself, "Hey, Karen, what's your future story? What's the future that you and your clients are creating together?"

> For close to two years, I kept asking clients, "What's the future that we're creating by doing this work together?" And then I'd ask myself, "And what are you so passionate about in this work?"

I'd try my thoughts out on friends and colleagues. They'd share their thoughts and give me feedback, until finally one day I was sitting at my desk working on a client report when out of the blue, my future story came to me. My thoughts were so strong and coming so fast that I immediately stopped what I was doing for the rest of the day and furiously began writing down all the images that were flooding my brain, resonating in my body, and getting me very excited.

In the end, I created a document called "My Manifesto: The Future We Create Together" (available on Karen's website at `www.juststoryit.com/my-manifesto.htm`).

When clients call me it's because they want to make a difference — at work, as leaders, with customers, and within their businesses. They want to influence others and change the world in some way. But they're frustrated time and again because they only seem to get so far. My clients and I work together on their stories. Like archeologists, we have to find them first, so we go on a hunt to find the treasures. We bring the treasures we've unearthed into our lab where we hone them, craft them, and polish them up.

As we shape these jewels, we continuously discover the wisdom in our personal stories that help us navigate the world and do the human dance a bit better. Our understanding of each other and the world becomes greater than the sum of the parts through this process. By the end of our journey we've created a world where people are so authentic and engaging that the stories they share automatically pull other people in.

But that's not the end of the story! We also listen to people's stories in return in an ongoing dynamic conversation that we hope touches hearts and builds strong relationships. Leaders engage with stories dynamically, inspiring staff and stakeholders to achieve incredible goals — where businesses or nonprofits engage through stories and customers fall in love with them to achieve amazing results. Strangers become friends; aliens become customers; barriers continue to break down. And throughout this journey, we're able to experience and witness each other's magnificence. In the end the world, not just the organization, becomes a better place to live in. This is what I do every day, and this is the future we build together.

Sharing your firm's future story helps people collectively imagine a future that's both achievable and worth achieving. It helps staff, customers, and prospects understand what you're working toward — and that they could be working with you on it now to collectively realize it.

Here's how Karen relays hers: "When I share my future story, I include the story of how it came to be. Otherwise it's a manifesto, not a story. I also tell them that I can see excitement in other people's eyes when they hear it. This excitement sparks a conversation about what storytelling work means to them personally or to their organization, and how it all ties into the future they're creating." Karen also states that when she adds the ending about how other prospects react, she quickly finds out whether a new prospect is a potential client who wants to make the same kind of difference she does.

Some organizations portray a vision story via video. In "Corporate Vision Videos: Telling the Story of the Future," Jim Kalbach states that "the intent [of vision videos] is to demonstrate a concrete *hypothesis of the future* that not only drives initiatives and investments, but also provides inspiration. . . . They explicitly describe a proposed future *experience* for humans. . . . [and] provide a common view of a future that teams *and* entire companies can rally around." You can view several corporate vision videos at http://uxtogo.useeds. de/2012/04/06/corporate-vision-videos-telling-a-story-of-the-future/.

Zingerman's Community of Businesses in Ann Arbor, Michigan routinely crafts future stories for specific initiatives or projects. In his article for Inc. com "Creating a Company Vision," available online at www.inc.com/ magazine/20110201/creating-a-company-vision.html, Ari Weinzweig gives an example of a project vision story. The organization helped create the story in 2005 for the Thursday evening farmers' market it hosts in the parking lot of Zingerman's Roadhouse. It represented the vision for the market in 2008, which has since come to fruition.

Both of the preceding examples showcase using vision stories to aspire and align stakeholders. In this way, they can accelerate goal attainment.

Given that the world we live in is fraught with uncertainties, it also behooves organizations to explore a variety of scenario stories around issues that are critical to their future existence. A collaboration among Ontario, Canada's creative media cluster, the Strategic Innovation Lab (sLab) at OCAD University, their project funder Ontario Media Development Corporation (OMDC), and their corporate sponsors explored four possible scenarios associated with the question, "What will our media and entertainment be like in 2020?" For each scenario, they wrote a story from the perspective of a single character, named Apti Riel, a woman in her late 30s. You can view a summary of the scenario development process and the four scenario stories, along with relevant contextual information, at http://2020mediafutures.ca/Scenarios.

You may wonder why these groups came together to write these scenario stories. They wanted to help multiple, related organizations to "future-proof" themselves — to anticipate possible shifts and changes and prepare for them by making informed strategic decisions and fostering new initiatives and types of relationships. Maybe you need to "future-proof" your organization too. Using stories within the scenario-planning process can help make alternate future realities real and tangible, which makes them memorable and actionable. For more information on this process, check out `www.well.com/~mb/scenario_planning/`.

What can you do to craft organizational or project-based future stories, or scenario stories? Here are some ideas:

- **Organizational future story:** This story is based on the organization's vision, strategies, and goals coming to fruition at some future specified date in time. It expands a vision statement into a full-blown situation, with characters and conflicts that are overcome. To aid in doing this, you may want to conduct interviews with future-thinking customers, vendors, and others who know your organization, and the difference your products and services are making and could make in people's lives. We give you ideas on how to create this story in Chapter 16.

- **Project-specific future story:** Similar to an organizational future story, a project-specific future story is based on what life will be like when the vision and project plan are fully implemented and operationalized. See Chapter 16 for more information.

- **Organizationally based scenario stories:** We like the approach that the 2020 Media Futures Project used. You can download several reports that outline their approach at `http://2020mediafutures.ca/Reports`.

"Success" Stories

The good news is, we all have *success* stories to tell. These appear to be the most prevalent type of stories found in hip pockets. However, quite often success stories are authored as profiles or testimonials rather than stories. Many of them don't have the heightened level of impact that they could. This section talks about some personal and organizational success stories that we like for business use.

Your personal success stories

There are many kinds of personal success stories. Here's an example:

The year 2008 was filled with milestones for Rena Huber. It marked the year of her 50th birthday, the year her husband Jack turned 65, and the year of their 25th wedding anniversary. To celebrate and renew their wedding vows, they embarked on a three-week cruise to Bermuda, then across the Atlantic to places like France, Spain, and Rome, before returning to the United States On this trip, Jack told her, "When you turn 55, we're taking an around-the-world trip." Little had Rena known this was an item on Jack's bucket list:

> Although 2008 was full of celebrations, for Rena 2009 began with changes at work. And she saw friends losing their jobs and their homes. Rena took stock of what was around her. At that time, she and Jack lived in a retirement community. Although she wasn't on meds like so many of their friends, nor was she regularly traipsing off to the doctor like several of them, she knew it was just a matter of time before her lifelong weight issue spawned a problem like diabetes. She also knew some changes were needed if they were going to take an extended round-the-world cruise. Three years and nine months before her 55th birthday, she asked herself, "Have I done everything I could do to optimize my options and choices?" The answer: "I need to make a lifestyle change." This triggered two immediate shifts: adding strength, flexibility, and cardio exercises to her already active schedule and what Rena affectionately calls *decrap and declutter.*

> Because she wanted to have options and choices at age 55, she went a step further and researched a variety of diets, which eventually helped her lose 95 pounds naturally over a period of nine months, under medical supervision. Never having thought she could do that, she asked herself, "What else have I been thinking I could never do?" That sparked running. Not just ordinary running. Running half-marathons all across the country. Her first was at Disneyland in Anaheim in 2010. For her, it's about the inner satisfaction. "People tell me I'm grinning from ear-to-ear as I run. It's addictive," she says.

> Rena is now thinking about taking on full marathons. Why? "My last mile is always my strongest mile. I now wonder, 'What else am I holding back?' I'm obviously not depleted at the end of a race."

In her dual roles as the Director of the AAAME Program (the APS Academy for the Advancement of Small, Minority- and Women-Owned Enterprises) at APS and the President of the Greater Phoenix SCORE Chapter in Phoenix, Arizona, Rena shares an expanded version of her success story in women's mentoring groups, with SCORE volunteers, and with business owners to help them set goals, remove limitations, and become inspired to be more than they think they are. "My story helps with credibility and by providing examples — 'If she can do it, then I can too.' By exposing my vulnerability and offering details of my journey, I can help lead others to their greatness."

Like Rena, sometimes when you're surrounded by challenges at work, a success in your personal life can garner you recognition. Take the case of Art Fry, the inventor of Post-it Notes for 3M, which has become a common story. For five years he talked about his new invention within the company. But it wasn't until a fateful night when he used what was to become Post-it Notes instead of bookmarks in his hymnal to mark the songs on that evening's church program that he saw the true possibilities of this product. That success didn't translate into success for IBM overnight. It took another five years before the product was perfected and brought to market. Art Fry's personal story is frequently told when companies are seeking to innovate and want their employees to know that their efforts might not transfer into immediate successes on a broader scale.

Not all successes in life are planned. Nor is success defined only by monetary gain. This means you need to think more broadly in your personal life about what success means. What are some ways to identify personal success stories that would add value if told in the workplace? Try reflecting on these story prompts:

✔ Share with me a memory about a time when as a child (or teenager or adult) you achieved a major personal success that was unexpected.

✔ Tell me about a time when you set out to do something as a child (or teenager or adult) and you found success beyond your wildest dreams.

✔ Enlighten me about a time in your personal life when you stumbled into a wildly successful situation.

✔ Tell me about a time when you consciously decided to become successful at something and, beyond all odds, reached your goal.

Where might these stories be useful at work? Are there situations where your colleagues or teammates believe that success is out of reach? What about circumstances where motivation toward a goal is waning and people need a boost? Are you coaching or mentoring someone who needs to be inspired?

Your organization's success stories

Remember Cristi's story from Chapter 3? She's the ChapStick girl. Her situation is an organizational success story sparked by her actions toward a desired organizational goal. Especially because the contract was renewed beyond the original agreement.

To obtain success stories like this, carefully nurture and craft them within your organization and its supply chain — vendors, strategic business partners, customers, consumers, and the like — and then give them voice. If done well, sharing these stories will help these same individuals become more passionate about what they do and strengthen their relationship to your enterprise.

Every time someone leaves for another job or retires, you lose valuable experience. Sharing employee success stories —not just what they did but how they did it—facilitates knowledge transfer and acknowledgment of the success. Success stories help staff perform better and respond more quickly and effectively when they encounter a similar situation.

So, how do you unearth success stories in your enterprise?

- ✔ **If you're an entrepreneur:** Talk to your customers. Pull the stories out of them by saying, "Tell me about a significant success you were able to achieve with the assistance that you received."

- ✔ **If you have customers, members, patients, clients, and so on:** Draw out testimonials and thank yous and turn them into success stories. You may need to re-contact these individuals for more input.

- ✔ **If your organization has been around for several years:** Go back into the archives and search for past successes that no one is talking about anymore. They are timeless. Craft stories around them and make them visible. They may be just the spark that's needed internally to motivate a stalled team and externally boost sales.

- ✔ **If you have long-tenured employees:** Have them tell you about a memorable success that they helped create. Or a situation that was highly successful that didn't get enough air time. Or about a rock star employee who sparked a significant business success.

- ✔ **If you have sales professionals:** Ask for their favorite success stories — the ones that turn prospects into buyers.

"Overcoming Barriers" Stories

Why do some people persevere and others give up? What is it that makes some organizations succeed against all odds and others fail? These are stories of overcoming barriers and obstacles. People love to feast on this type of story because they give us courage, hope, and heart to do the same ourselves.

Your stories of overcoming barriers

On September 2, 2010, the *New York Times* reported the story of Ms. Cha: `www.nytimes.com/2010/09/04/world/asia/04driver.html?_r=2&scp=1&sq=at%20first%20she%20didn%27t%20succeed&st=cse&.`

In her 60s, Mrs. Cha's envy of people who could drive led her to get a license in the small county of Wanju, south of Seoul, South Korea. She took hundreds of driving tests, five days a week, investing more than five years of her life in achieving this goal. It cost her five dollars every time she took a test. Not only did she study constantly and receive tutoring, she got up at 4 a.m. to take three different buses to the testing center.

Mrs. Cha wanted a driver's license so bad she retook the written portion of the exam 950 times. She still had to pass two driving skill and road tests — she failed at each of them four times, taking her to a total of 960 tries to get her license, achieving her goal at age 69. Why did she persevere? She wanted to take her grandchildren to the zoo and not wait hours for buses. Her steadfast desire and stubbornness gave her strength to overcome all obstacles. Ultimately, not only was Mrs. Cha awarded a license, Hyundai, South Korea's leading carmaker, presented her with a $16,800 car after hosting an online congratulatory campaign. She's also appeared in a Hyundai commercial.

You may not be Mrs. Cha, but you have personal stories like hers. Stories of times when you overcame a challenge. Perhaps you didn't have to persist as much as she did — or maybe yours were even more difficult.

An example of this type of story and its relationship to business is at the end of the March 5, 2013 *New York Times* article "Y Combinator, Silicon Valley's Start-Up Machine," by Nathaniel Rich which can be found online at www. nytimes.com/2013/05/05/magazine/y-combinator-silicon-valleys-start-up-machine.html?pagewanted=all&_r=0. He reflects on the last thing Paul Graham told him on Demo Day, a day when 47 firms pitched investors for money. Graham is the director of a camp called Y Combinator, which helps create startup companies. Rich tells the story of the amazing things Graham did to overcome his fear of flying to help the reader understand what fuels Graham's enthusiasm for the work that he does.

Like Graham, your personal stories of how you persevered to overcome trials and tribulations have a place at work. Use them when you coach or mentor others, when giving performance feedback, and when inspiring individuals and groups to achieve an audacious target. In fact, these stories are how some professional speakers get started. A significant obstacle is put in their path, they find a way overcome it, and they're hired to talk about it as motivational speakers to sales organizations, leaders, or groups of employees.

To identify this type of story in your past, try these on for size:

- ✔ Share with me a memory about a time when you overcame a major life hurdle.

- ✔ Tell me about about a time in your life when you found yourself surrounded by so many obstacles that you thought you'd never be able to dig yourself out — but you did.

- ✔ Enlighten me about a time in your personal life when you stumbled into a wildly successful situation.

- ✔ Tell me about a time when you consciously decided to become successful at something and against all odds reached your goal.

Your organization's stories of overcoming barriers

Go back to Bob McIlree's story in the appendix. It's an example of Bob as contractor overcoming an organizational barrier. You have employees just like Bob. They're constantly overcoming obstacles in their daily work and project initiatives. Sharing these stories internally can help identify fixes to problems and redesign work processes. Don't forget to also find and share stories about employees who've accomplished Herculean feats on behalf of customers:

If you're an entrepreneur or small business, periodically share the obstacles you've overcome in your business journey when the right situations presented themselves. If your firm has had a major scare — as Johnson & Johnson did back in 1982, when seven people died in Chicago suburbs after taking poisoned Tylenol — it's important to tell stories throughout the experience. As Johnson & Johnson learned, stories about overcoming obstacles — the immediate recall, the reward offered for the murderer, and so on — can enhance your reputation and build customer loyalty.

People like to be reminded that we're all fallible, that we all make mistakes. It's one thing to tell a client that you maintain quality parts; it's another when they hear and experience how your quality has really been tested. Learning from the failures or mistakes and the wisdom of others is psychologically satisfying. We appreciate and respect those who've grown from their mistakes and can share the lessons they've learned.

Here are a few ways to find these organizational stories:

- ✔ Tell me about a time when an employee saved the day.

- ✔ Tell me about a major obstacle on a project and how it was resolved.

- ✔ Enlighten me about a situation where a group went the extra mile to satisfy a customer.

- ✔ Build me a story about a huge, unexpected challenge that arose and what was done to rectify it.

- ✔ Go back through the organization's archives and find situations where the entire firm or a single brand offering was compromised and what was done to overcome them. Then craft stories to help others appreciate these situations.

"Memorable Customer" Stories

We've all been in situations where we're an in-person or online customer: the grocery store, the dentist, when doing financial transactions. The opposite is also true: We're often in situations where others are our customers, whether they're internal or external to the organization. And guess what? We all talk about these situations. So it's in your best interest to figure out which are the very best to have in your hip pocket.

Your customer stories

Here's a customer story from Lori:

> Imagine being called in Arizona on a Tuesday afternoon by a company to ask you to be "feet on the ground" for a client project in Massachusetts the following Tuesday morning. Not only did all the contracts have to be written and approved beforehand, I also needed to find temporary housing because of limited dollars for air travel to and from Phoenix. It needed a kitchen so I could cook because of my allergy to eggs. After a few phone calls, I found a great deal at the Marriott TownPlace Suites in Tewksbury, Massachusetts.
>
> Wanting to avoid as many hassles as possible, I flew red-eye Sunday – Monday into Manchester, New Hampshire and drove an hour to the hotel property. Arriving around noon, I made her way to the room after a friendly check-in with the hotel manager. I soon identified a problem. "Oy! There's no wireless here. And this network cord is only a few feet long. How am I going to work from the sofa?", I muttered to myself. I called the front desk to ask for a longer one. Before I could say more than a few words, I heard, "Consider it done." And voila, just like that, there was a knock on the door with what I needed.
>
> It didn't matter what request I had, nor how quickly I needed some-thing done: A package has arrived. A light bulb needs replacing. What about a snow scraper for the blizzard that hit the end of October? Every time I called the front desk, I heard the same words: "Consider it done." In fact, I didn't even have to dig my rental car out from under that snow; a staff member had already done so for me.

Lori has shared this story that uses the key message *consider it done* numerous times, first with all her friends and colleagues via social media to remark on how refreshing it was to find this level of service. The story has made its way into training workshops on persuasion and influence. She also shares it with prospective clients when she's asked how she responds to client requests. And, not surprisingly, she's told it to staff at other Marriott properties.

We all know great customer service experiences travel fast. So does the opposite kind of experiences. Here are some ways to identify the most memorable experiences you've had so they can be crafted for retelling:

✔ Share with me a memory about an experience that made you say, "Wow. That was awesome service."

✔ Tell me about a time in your life when you were shocked at how a customer issue that you were having was resolved.

✔ Enlighten me about a situation in your personal life when an employee went above and beyond the call of duty to delight you.

Your organization's customer stories

Some of the easiest and best customer stories are those about people you work with, day in and day out. How they solved a customer's problem, went the extra mile, overcame an obstacle to meet a customer need, and the like. One would think these stories would be easy to collect — but they aren't. Often people say, in response to being asked to document what they did for an internal recognition award, "Oh, I was just doing my job." That's why it's so important to share the entire story about what you observed they did and not just heap praise on them. Doing that gives the story legs. Customer stories can be used to showcase a best practice, for training, and to redesign a document or process.

What about your customers? Customers are most likely to talk about what other customers and prospects really want to know. In her blog article "How to Help Your Customers Help You by Sharing Their Stories" (http://contentmarketinginstitute.com/2012/09/how-to-help-your-customers-help-you-by-sharing-their-stories/), Manya Chylinki shares how Deana Goldasich, CEO of Well Planned Web, turned a single customer interview with stories into 38 pieces of content: 1 internal customer e-mail, 2 white papers, 2 infographics, 3 case studies, 9 blog posts, 10-plus external drip e-mails, and 11 testimonial quotes.

Customer experience stories can infuse the day-to-day work of your employees with meaning and purpose, because they can more easily see the difference their work makes in the lives of others. These stories can promote performance, perseverance, and passion. They also create a more intimate connection with the customer, beyond just an intellectual understanding. Plus, depending on the story, they can be used to educate both staff and customers on how best to use your organization's products and services.

Interviewing customers and prospects and evoking their stories will gain you rich material to guide product development and service delivery — and help you more closely connect with your prospects as you carry out marketing and advertising activities. These stories also provide insight into the psychology, unmet needs, and underlying values of these individuals, if you take the time to ferret them out. Knowing what story your customers live can help you build a long-lasting, profitable relationship with them. Check out more on this topic in Chapter 14.

Here's a dilemma: Listening to customer stories can require extra effort because your brain is operating on several levels. You're not only hearing the story, you're trying to comprehend, analyze, evaluate, and remember that content. Something else to watch out for is the instinct, in sharing a customer's story, to make yourself or your company the hero, when the real hero is the customer. Your challenge is to maintain the correct point of view. You may think the thing — the product you're selling — is the star. You may think the process you use is the star. But that would be like making a movie about the Batmobile instead of Batman.

The goal is to have the story be about the people who are using your product or service. And they'll love you for it. Customers share stories when it's about them, not when it's about you or your company.

Every story has a villain, and every story has a person you cheer for. Your customers stories need to embody both hope and empowerment that others can solve the same challenges they had by working with you.

Here's the synopsis of a story from Southwest Airlines that demonstrates this:

> A man was en route from L.A. to Denver to see his [young] grandson for the last time. The boy was being taken off life support. . . . The man's wife called Southwest to arrange the flight and explained the emergency. Unfortunately, the man was held up by traffic and long lines at LAX. . . . He finally made it, 12 minutes after the plane was to leave. . . . The pilot waiting for him said, "They can't go anywhere without me and I wasn't going anywhere without you. Now relax. We'll get you there. And again, I'm so sorry."

You can find this story and other examples of customer stories that are crafted with the customer as the hero at http://mentalfloss.com/article/30198/11-best-customer-service-stories-ever. We also talk more about this focus in Chapter 14.

Memorable customer experience stories aren't always positive, success stories. They can also identify issues and gaps in your organization. To start capturing those, here are a few ideas:

✔ **From employees:** Tell me about a time when a customer used our product or service and had a huge win. Or a situation where a customer used our product or service and saved the day in their company. Or a situation where a customer used our product or service and was able to overcome a significant obstacle.

✔ **From customers:** Tell me about a time when you used our product or service and had a huge win. Or a situation where you used our product or service and saved the day in your company. Or a situation where you used our product or service and were able to overcome a significant obstacle.

Stories to Avoid

As we've already said, avoid stories that make you sound arrogant or self-serving. Offer your story as a gift — share a lesson learned, offer an insight, or provide a decision that you made about that experience.

Stories focused on perfection should end up on the cutting-room floor too. Perfection negates authenticity. It's okay to be vulnerable and show people the mistakes you've made and the lessons you've learned.

As great as it is to vent about customers that drive you nuts, don't put those experiences into stories. Put yourself in the listener's shoes. They might commiserate with you; they might share an awful customer story in return. But at some level, when they walk away, they're going to wonder, "Is this how he talks about customers all the time?" And: "Is this how he might talk about me when I'm not around?"

Don't badmouth the competition in stories either. In the end, *you* look bad, not them. It's a game of one-upmanship that you won't win; you're trying to make yourself look good at the expense of someone else.

The same goes for stories of rotten employees. Leave them at home or in your therapist's office. You'll only make yourself look inept, petty, or out of control. Instead, for more traction, collect stories of great employees.

At all costs, ignore stories about guilting somebody into making a purchase. It may bring a short-term sale, but it'll boomerang in the long term because the guilt will be remembered. Make people feel great in your presence and excited and inspired to purchase what you and your company have to offer.

 In the end, your stories are more than just entertainment — they're your authentic voice. Strive to have all kinds in your hip pocket for that very moment when you need to pull one out and use it. And avoid those that don't suit you or your organization well.

Chapter 5

Listening: Hearing What Others Have to Say and Capturing It

*W*e have a secret to share. One that'll bring you more benefits than you can imagine. In business storytelling, telling stories is only half the equation. It'll only get you some of the results that you desire. So what's the other half? You need to listen for and deliberately evoke stories from others. Why? Asking people for their stories and acknowledging what they have to share says, "I care." *I care about you as a person. I care about what you think. I care about your feelings.* All this helps build strong, trusting relationships.

Although that seems simple at first, it's actually a little more involved. We often ask questions to get at what happened in a situation. But the most popular questions we ask don't elicit stories — at best, they only draw out the information that was requested, and barely that if you're asking a teenager.

In this chapter, you'll learn why your favorite questions won't work to draw out usable stories (even though the brain remembers situations in the form of story narrative). We introduce three techniques that *do* work to evoke stories: story prompts, story modeling (there's more on this topic in Chapter 12), and story triggers. You'll also gain skills on how to listen in a very specific manner so that you create engagement with the other person, draw meaning from the story, and openly acknowledge the vulnerability of the person who's sharing it. This chapter ends with a variety of ways to capture the original rendition of a story as the first step in polishing it to perfection.

Improving Storytelling by Listening

There's one thing you can do right away to improve your storytelling skills. It's the most important quality in being able to be a fabulous storyteller. That single most important element is to *listen*.

The word *storytelling* is really inaccurate when talking about applying stories to your professional life. *Storytelling* creates a picture in our minds of someone standing up in front of a group of people in a presentation or meeting setting and telling a story. Or it may conjure up images of a small group of people standing around the break room or someone's desk and listening to a person share a story about what happened the day before. But telling a story is only half the equation. The other half is learning how to listen — and then doing it on a regular basis.

The beauty of storytelling is that it's a co-created experience between the teller and the listener. Both are equally involved in the story, even in a large group setting. When you listen to a story, you aren't passively hearing it. You're actively internalizing the story and making sense of it in real time. Chances are, after you hear a story from someone else, it'll spark a memory of a story in you, one that you'll want to share in return.

When President Lyndon B. Johnson was a junior senator from Texas, he kept a sign on his office wall that read: *You ain't learnin' nothing when you're doin' all the talkin'*. He knew the secret: Listen for stories far more often than you tell them. When working with stories in your organization, the first important principle to embrace is to avoid being solely a storyteller and become much more of a story listener. Deliberately asking for and consciously listening for stories should be your main focus. That's how you build relationships that weather the test of time, figure out how best to relay information to people, learn more about your internal and external customers' needs and preferences, pick up on competitive intelligence information, and build loyalty.

People who feel deeply listened to and appreciated are the ones that move toward us; they want to sit in our radius and be nearer to us. Imagine what your department or organization would be like if it had customers who moved toward you, wanting to be in your sphere of influence (read more about this in Chapter 14).

Be in service to the story and storyteller

You're probably asking, "How do I ready myself to listen?" Take the position of being in total service to the storyteller. You want to *listen* the best story out of them as is humanly possible. You don't want to hear a half-baked story. You want to listen in such a way that the listener freely shares a story that is deep, rich, and satisfying.

Because storytelling is a joint activity, listening means stopping what you're doing and giving your total attention to the other person for as long as it takes for them to tell the story. In today's overly busy workplaces, where everyone is running around at a million miles an hour, this kind of listening isn't as easy as it sounds. If you don't have that much time, it's okay to tell people you have exactly three minutes to hear their story.

You should also be in total service to the story itself. That means not interrupting the teller as the story is being shared. Be silent. Yes, we realize this advice is contrary to most listening techniques (such as *active listening*, which involves paraphrasing what you heard and adding what you think the person is feeling at that moment in time).

Stories have a particular flow to them. When you interrupt the teller, two things happen:

- ✔ You take over control of the conversation.
- ✔ You stop the inherent flow of the story.

Don't be concerned if the person is telling you the story out of order or seems to be skipping details you believe you need. Later in this chapter when we teach you how to listen delightedly, we'll provide specific ways to address these points.

When people get this kind of deep, appreciative listening, they freely open up. You might be amazed by the experience. We've had people tell us after a story listening exercise that they suddenly realized they'd never been truly listened to before. Wow! That's powerful. And a tremendous service — to them and to their story. No doubt they'll remember that encounter and us as listeners for a long time to come.

Reveal what's in people's hearts

Something unique happens when you deliberately listen for stories. People share information they never intended to reveal. They provide details you never knew to ask for. Along with this, they may tell you what moved them, their deepest thoughts and feelings, and what the situation meant to them. In this way you learn their emotional state, their need states, their values and mental models, and much more. This allows you to quickly get to the heart of the matter.

Why is this? When you request a story, and people share it with you, they relive the experience. When they relive it, they can't help but attach once again to all the emotions they felt while the situation was unfolding in front of them. Now imagine what sort of impact this can have in building trust, working through difficult issues, and engaging others in change.

Uncover market, customer, and employee intelligence

When you're listening for stories, all kinds of meaningful material will emerge. Asking for certain kinds of stories from specific people and market segments will gain you a wealth of information about your marketplace, your customers, your employees, and your own work. You'll find out what makes your customers/prospects tick and discover the answers to *who*, *what*, *why*, *where*, *when*, and *how* questions without ever having to ask them. Guesswork is removed because you'll have a heightened understanding of competitor reputations, the motivations behind consumer behavior, and the real problems people are seeking to solve. All this material will inform both your business strategy and the tactical steps you need to put it into action.

Discover new ideas for products/services

Most companies think they need to conduct focus groups to learn about customer satisfaction, gain ideas about new products/services, or understand incremental improvements they can make to their products/services. But people in focus groups are seldom asked for stories, says Gerald Zaltman, the top guy in the field, and the author of *How Customers Think: Essential Insights Into the Mind of the Market* (Harvard Business Review Press, 2003) and *Marketing Metaphoria: What Deep Metaphors Reveal About the Minds of Consumers* (Harvard Business School Press, 2008).

Zaltman's approach takes a handful of people and individually spends time evoking and listening to their stories about a company's product or service through a technique called the Zaltman Metaphor Elicitation Technique (ZMET). Out of these sessions bubble up a wealth of ideas. The organization discovers what people really think, how they live their lives, the images and metaphors that guide them, and what they're really seeking. These folks will even share ideas they get on their own for improvements. Listening to these stories and the metaphors associated with them generates all kinds of creative ideas you can use in your work. For example, the metaphor that people have used to describe the Nestle Crunch bar has to do with a cue about time, "whether an hourglass or a clock" (for more on this subject see www.fast company.com/33672/metaphor-marketing).

Organizations that don't have an appreciation and a way to listen to customer stories end up shooting themselves in the foot and wondering why customers aren't engaging with them. It's because they don't understand that the dynamics of storytelling requires a unique form of listening in return.

Deciding on Perspective

You've likely heard the idioms *There are two sides to every story* and *There are two sides to every question.* Some people suggest there are actually three sides: Yours, theirs, and the truth. When it comes to stories, there are as many sides as the number of people who've been touched by the situation — which in some cases, means a seemingly limitless number of perspectives.

So what? What does that mean to storytelling? It means you need to determine which side(s) of the story you need to hear. If you elect to formally capture the story for use in a presentation, in a document, or for placement into a *story bank*, you need to be especially strategic in figuring out which perspective will be of most value to the most people in the long term.

Identify who has story and perspective

Imagine you just read a Facebook posting from your friend. Dave says he was in a biking accident earlier in the day. His post says a car hit him as he was turning the corner while riding his bike on a major thoroughfare. He broke his wrist and got some nasty bruises and a gash on his knee. The bike is totaled. How many stories exist in this situation? There's Dave's story about what it was like to be hit and his thoughts on how the situation could have been prevented. In addition, there are multiple stories associated with all the bike rides he's taken with his bike and what it's like for him to lose such a beloved vehicle.

Is that it? No, there's the car driver's perspective on what she experienced and why, and what's lacking to alert drivers to bikers at the intersection. Imagine all the people who observed the situation. Each of them has their own take on what happened, the lesson they each took away from the situation, and what they believe could have mitigated the accident.

Which story do you listen to? Which story do you pay most attention to? Which story do you choose to capture, if you elect to share it with others? One? Some? All? These questions aren't trivial in the field of business storytelling. Whichever stories get listened to, captured, transmitted, and promoted to others have the ability to influence decisions and actions.

When a problem arises, you may elect to listen to several perspectives to get a feel for the totality of the situation. In a staff meeting, for example, you may hear multiple stories about what's happened in the past when a specific change was made.

If you want to tell stories in a presentation to make a point, capture stories to share with others in a deliberate manner, or find compelling stories to place into a story bank for anyone to use, then your first consideration in choosing them has to do with listening for the key message in it. Figure that out first and then ask yourself who has the story that best supports what you want to convey. See Chapter 6 for more on how to identify this key message.

Identify the myriad uses of the story

Before we get into the uses you might make of a story, there's something you need to consider: Was the story meant for your ears only? If so, then you don't have the right to pass it on in any manner. You can ask for permission to do so, but chances are good that you won't get it.

Assuming it's okay to use the story, identify and consider all the ways you might use it. There are many: You could use the story in oral presentations, in a blog or newsletter article, in a press release, in a report, grant proposal, or business case, in tours of your facility, new hire orientations, customer proposals, in marketing materials … the list is endless. Once you have a feel for the potential uses, ask yourself which perspective on the story would be most fruitful.

The customer's perspective on a story is not always the best one to capture as we discuss in Chapters 13 and 14. Especially if you're advocating for additional funding for your organization, group, or project. Instead, tell the story about what's been compromised in the past or the problem in your group that resulted from lack of funds. These will have far more impact than relaying a specific customer problem you've already solved that could increase in magnitude. Why? In the latter case, you're demonstrating how you effectively overcame the issue without funding.

Deciding which stories to listen to and capture brings us full circle to the need to learn how to evoke stories.

Evoking a Story

Evoking stories is the deliberate process of sparking specific stories in others that you have a hunch will be beneficial to hear because of the perspective and message they convey and their multiple potential uses. In our experience, we've found that asking simple questions rarely, if ever, provokes a story. This means you need to spend a little time consciously planning out the words you use so that you actually get what you're seeking.

Stay away from questions

One of the biggest mistakes people make when trying to evoke stories is asking for information or descriptions. For example, in an interview for a project team role or new position, they pose the following sorts of questions or statements:

- What drew you to this organization?
- What situations or circumstances cemented your loyalty to us as a company?
- When was the last time you felt that you received exceptional mentoring?
- How do you stay energized and inspired?
- Describe a time when you've observed a corporate value in action.
- Describe a situation in which you used new ideas to resolve an issue.

This is what they hear in response:

- **What drew you to this organization?** I like the fast pace and ability to get things done. I also like how innovative this company is.

- **What situations or circumstances cemented your loyalty to us as a company?** When my dad died they gave me extended family leave. I'll always appreciate my boss and the company for the way they handled my situation.

- **When was the last time you felt that you received exceptional mentoring?** When I first came here, I knew very little about the industry. John stepped in and really helped me a lot. Without his mentoring, I'm sure I would've been long gone.

- **How do you stay energized and inspired?** By seeing my progress, even the little steps. And by seeing my staff really blossom and get better at what they do.

- **Describe a time when you've observed a corporate value in action.** One of our values is customer service. One of my staff stayed late and went the extra mile to help a customer overcome a problem they were having that she knew our company could solve. She could've waited to the next day, but she stayed late just so we wouldn't lose the customer.

- **Describe a situation in which you used new ideas to resolve an issue.** Our supply of widgets was drying up because a hurricane in the Pacific was holding up our shipment. So one of my staff reached out through a variety of social media and found a supply to keep us going until our regular shipment came in.

As you can tell from these typical responses, framing questions using *what*, *when*, and *how do you* leads to information and opinions. Starting off a statement with *describe* gets you just that: descriptions. In both cases, people "talk about" the story instead of "telling" you one. Each answer now requires additional probing — more questions and more answers — to get to the meat of the matter. It's inefficient. And who has time to waste?

Sure, there are those rare occasions where you might hear a story — if the person intuitively tells stories or is skilled enough in storytelling to know to provide one. But how often is that the case?

Here's the bottom line: Using a questioning approach may eventually get you where you want to go, but it's time-consuming and hard to do. Chances are high that you'll get spotty results because you always run the risk of missing the immediate connections and relationships that stories create.

Spark the story you want: Story prompts

As we mention in Chapter 1, given that the human brain stores memories in the form of story narrative, it's in your best interest to steer clear of questions and find ways to evoke stories out of people when you want or need to hear the totality of a situation. Story prompts are one way to do this.

Story prompts have two parts: the front end of the statement and the closing to the statement. The front end starts with a phrase such as *Tell me about.* . . . With certain individuals, it may help to say, *Tell me a story about.* . . . The word *about* is key in this statement. If you leave it out, all you're doing is turning a question into a statement (as in *Tell me how you* . . . or *Tell me what you* . . .).

Variations on *tell me about* include these phrases:

- ✔ Enlighten me about a time when . . .
- ✔ Convey to me . . .
- ✔ Visualize a time for me when . . .
- ✔ Build me a story about . . .
- ✔ Create in my mind's eye . . .
- ✔ Paint the full picture for me about . . .
- ✔ Craft for me the scenario . . .
- ✔ Share with me a memory about . . .

Avoid the following openings to your prompts. We can guarantee they'll rarely get you a story in return:

- Describe for me . . .
- Explain to me . . .
- Illustrate for me . . .
- Clarify . . .
- Give me the details . . .
- Put in plain words . . .
- Account for . . .
- Help me to understand why . . .
- Demonstrate to me . . .
- Present . . .

The closing portion of a story prompt is as critical as the front piece of the statement. Avoid being general. Phrase it in such a way that the person recollects only one or a few memories. This will make it easier for the person to select a story to share with you. For example, instead of saying, *Tell me about that new project you're working on*, rephrase it as *Tell me about an unforgettable situation that happened to you recently on that new project you're working on.*

Here's a variation you can also use: Include a sentence before the front end of the statement that adds specificity. For example: *I heard you just had a really bad customer experience. Tell me about what happened.*

Okay. You get the picture. Now let's go back to the questions that were posed earlier and reword them into story prompts:

- **What drew you to this organization?** *Story prompt:* Tell me about a specific event that crystallized your decision to work for this firm. *Possible response:* Oh, I just thought they were like any other company until one day, as I was heading into my second interview . . .

- **What situations or circumstances cemented your loyalty to us as a company?** *Story prompt:* Enlighten me about a time when your loyalty to the company was permanently cemented. *Possible response:* I'd been here about a year, so I was still the newbie. It was a Wednesday and I was in a meeting when my boss's assistant came in and pulled me out. She had a message that said my dad had just had a stroke. I flew home right away and called my boss twice a day with updates. When I learned how much rehab dad needed, the firm worked out a deal for me even though I didn't have a whole lot of benefits. They . . .

✔ **When was the last time you felt that you received exceptional mentoring?** *Story prompt:* Paint me the picture of a time when you said to yourself, "Wow. That was the best mentoring I've ever experienced." *Possible response:* I was hired in from a different industry. It seemed like a good fit. Still, I knew very little about our marketplace. Talk about a steep learning curve. I met John from XYZ department and he saw how I was struggling. Without me asking, he stepped in and really helped me get on solid ground by . . .

✔ **How do you stay energized and inspired?** *Story prompt:* We all need to stay energized and inspired. Tell me about the best thing you've ever done for yourself. *Possible response:* Oh, it's little things. Sometimes I'll go for a walk; sometimes I'll give myself a treat for meeting a deadline. But the best time was when I . . .

✔ **Describe a time when you've observed a corporate value in action.** *Story prompt:* Pick a corporate value that holds a lot of meaning for you. Enlighten me about a time when you saw it demonstrated in an amazing way. *Possible response:* That's easy. It's customer service. It was the end of the day and I was heading home. As I passed by a bunch of cubicles, I heard my staff talking excitedly on speakerphone with Harold, who also reports to me. I asked what was going on, and they said Harold was on his cellphone with the police in Florida. Seems robbers had grabbed a woman at an ATM. They were taking her to other ATMs at our branches to get more cash. The police wanted to know if we could predict which machine they'd hit next. We could. We did. The woman was rescued. We were in the office until nine that night. Talk about living our values!

✔ **Describe a situation in which you used new ideas to resolve an issue.** *Story prompt:* Tell me about the most memorable time when you came up with a new idea to resolve an immediate issue. *Possible response:* We had two weeks to come up with a name for a new product. Being we were on a shoestring budget, we decided to give it a go ourselves. I did a few hours of research on how to come up with creative ideas and put together a workshop of completely zany things. We did stuff like . . .

As these examples demonstrate, story prompts tend to generate real memories and experiences from people. You'll gain a much richer understanding of the situation in less time when you use them instead of traditional questions.

Prime the pump: Story modeling

One way to get the full story with your story prompt is to tell a story before you ask for one in return. By doing so, you demonstrate how to open up, show willingness to tell something about yourself, and give others permission to do the same. This makes them comfortable and relaxed. And more often than not, you'll spontaneously spark a story in your listener that they'll want to share with you in return. Stories are truly like viruses. Think about your daily conversations. Someone shares a story with you, and a similar experience pops into your head that you want to share. If the conversation is mutually satisfying, you end up swapping stories back and forth.

There are times when you'll begin to model a story, and someone will jump in and start telling you a similar story in return. What do you do? Stop talking. Let the person talk. Isn't that what you wanted in the first place?

Whether you're with one person or a group, prime the pump by sharing a short, well-thought-out story first. Follow it by asking for a story via a story prompt. Be prepared. The floodgates will open. Lack of stories to listen to will never be your problem.

Evoke a story with memories, props, and more: Story triggers

Want one more way to get stories from people? Try using story triggers.

How does this work? Imagine holding up a photo or image and asking for a story about a memory it triggers. "As you look at this photo, tell me about a time when . . . ." Alternatively, you could share a photo and ask people to identify all the sounds, emotions, and tastes that come to mind. This is useful when you need to capture creative ideas and sensory images to use in conjunction with stories in marketing materials.

Here are a few more ideas. Play a piece of music or an audio file and ask people to communicate the very first story that comes to mind. Or share a metaphor and ask for a story. For example, you could say, "Tell me about a time when the saying *have your cake and eat it too* held true for you."

Be creative. Almost anything can be used as a story trigger. When one company wanted to introduce a major transformation, a crystal pyramid was created with various symbols (such as the Chinese symbol for change) and quotations about change on each side of it. All executive team members received one and were asked to put the pyramid in a visible location in their office. It sparked a lot of conversation about the current change that was underway in the organization.

Be careful about showing a photo or image and having people make up a story about it to use in decision-making. This will catapult you into the land of getting stories about what others *think* they need. Unknowingly, you'll cloud the issue. Only when you use people's past memories and experiences in the form of stories will you get true clarity.

Apply these approaches in everyday work

Here are several kinds of situations that lend themselves to evoking stories from people through prompts, triggers, and modeling. How many of these relate to you?

✔ When interviewing for open positions.

✔ When you want to learn about new staff during onboarding.

✔ When assessing knowledge transfer.

✔ When seeking to gain new product and service ideas.

✔ When figuring out what to change in existing processes.

✔ When you want to learn more about existing customers or prospects.

✔ When you want to validate brand value.

✔ When seeking input about your company's reputation.

✔ When you want to learn more about the underpinnings of your company's culture.

✔ When bringing together a team for the first time.

✔ When generating creative/innovative ideas about chronic problems.

✔ When training staff on core values.

✔ When gathering feedback in a performance review.

✔ When generating best practices or discussing lessons learned at the close-out of a project.

Listening to Stories

Earlier we named two critical listening behaviors: Giving your total attention to the person who's telling you a story and not interrupting the flow of the story as it's being told to you, even if it's unclear or the details seem out of order. This section gives you a few more listening tips.

Stay away from disrupting the story

"Most conversations are just alternating monologues. The question is, is there any real listening going on?"

— Leo Buscaglia, author and lecturer on human potential

As Leo Buscaglia suggests, most conversations are monologues. You aren't really listening. You're usually caught up in what you're going to say in response. To truly be present in the moment, you need to quiet this internal chatter. You also need to put down your pen or stop clicking away at your keyboard as you listen to the story part of a conversation. Note taking can be a huge distraction to the teller of the story. Let the words wash over you, just like you let water do when you take a shower. Immerse yourself in the total experience.

Listen delightedly

Storytelling coach Doug Lipman calls the type of listening we'd like you to engage in *listening delightedly*. To listen delightedly (when you're in person or even when using Skype or FaceTime), do all the things we've mentioned so far, plus the following:

- ✔ Make eye contact (unless this is culturally unacceptable).

- ✔ Lean in toward the person.

- ✔ Display genuine interest in your body language and facial expressions.

- ✔ Express emotions as appropriate (laughter, sorrow, and so on).

- ✔ Don't fill the pauses with words, unless it's to say, "Go on" or "Tell me more."

- ✔ Use gestures, like hand movements, that encourage the person to continue talking.

What about when you're on the phone? Picture the other person in front of you. Don't you *dare* put yourself on mute so you can multi-task. You'll soon tune out, and the other person will know it.

Respond after you've finished listening

Let's first talk about what you *shouldn't* do right after someone tells you a story:

- ✔ Launch into your own story.

- ✔ Say, "I understand what happened. If I was in your shoes, I would have done it this way …."

- ✔ Offer advice on what to do next.

In each case, you're shifting the conversation back to being about you. And you're subtly undermining the other person and inducing one-upmanship.

Instead, express some form of gratitude. It can be as simple as saying, "Thank you for sharing your story with me." If you feel inclined, you may want to add an empathic statement. Examples include: "I sense it was a difficult one for you to tell" or "What a wonderful memory to have."

Maximize meaning and value

You're not done listening yet. There are several more steps in the process of empowering those you've evoked stories from to feel that they engaged in a great conversation.

Ask reflective questions

Reflective questions (or statements) allow you to make and gain meaning. This is what storytelling is all about — creating meaning. It follows that instead of asking information questions that get you concrete facts, you need to ask questions that get at the meaning of the story for the person telling it. Here are some examples of reflective questions/statements:

- ✔ What do you like about that story (experience)? (Tell me some things you really liked about your story.)
- ✔ What do you like about how you told the story to me? (Share with me what you liked about how you told that story to me.)
- ✔ What does that story (experience) mean to you? (Tell me what meaning that experience holds for you.)
- ✔ What did you learn from that experience? (Tell me what you learned from that experience.)
- ✔ What are your takeaways from that story (experience)? (Tell me what you'll take away from the experience.)

Asking these questions/statements will help you quickly learn more about the person's motivations and view of the world and what the individual values and cares about. You'll be astounded at how fast the relationship deepens.

Give appreciation

Now is your chance to provide the teller with positive feedback about his/her willingness to share and the experience you just heard about. Tell the person

- ✔ Something you liked about the story.
- ✔ What the story means to you.

✔ How the story affected you.

✔ Parts of the story that stand out in your mind.

This sort of positive appreciation continues to make the teller feel good — an important piece of empowerment.

Avoid saying the following:

✔ "Wow, I can really see why you'd be so happy; the same thing happened to me. . . ."

✔ "You might want to think about . . ."

✔ "You know what I would have done . . ."

Sentences like these shift the conversation back to being all about you while subtly undermining the teller.

Keep in mind that launching into appreciations before asking reflective questions interrupts the meaning-making process on the part of the storyteller. When you start signaling what made the story meaningful for *you*, they will validate that instead of telling you what the story means to *them* first.

Ask clarifying and information questions (optional)

If you feel a strong need to do so — and if there's time — ask any clarifying and informational questions you might have. Examples include: What were the names of the people again? When did this happen? Where were you again? This is also where you might paraphrase a portion of what you heard that you want to emphasize or gain more details about.

Thank them again

This is an important step to remember because of all the person has shared with you.

Share a story in return (optional)

If the time and situation are right, go ahead and share a story in return. Do so in a manner that continues the dialogue rather than engaging in a one-sided conversation.

Once the story-sharing experience has ended, it's time to maximize the meaning and understanding you gained from the story. Find a quiet place where you can jot down a few notes about what you'll take away from it:

✔ Note what it was like to listen in this way. How do you feel now about the experience, what happened, and the person who told it?

✔ What insights have you gained? Especially if this experience occurred with a customer/prospect, write down everything you learned about the individual and the situation — demographics, likes and dislikes, challenges, solutions, and the opportunities before you.

✔ What material did you hear that validated what you already know?

✔ What material did you hear that was new to you?

✔ Capture all the visual language you heard, including images that stand out. Note metaphors and analogies that can be leveraged in marketing and communication materials, product/service offerings, and so on.

✔ Record how to apply the knowledge you gleaned from the experience.

Listen to stories deliberately in groups

One-on-one listening helps you establish a solid relationship and understand what makes a person tick. But what if you want to take this further and listen to stories with a group of eight to ten people? Follow these steps:

1. **Set aside two hours.** This gives everyone time to share.

2. **Beforehand, identify what you really want to learn.** For example, are you using this approach to learn about a specific brand, as you would in a focus group? Or do you want members of a new project team to learn about each other and develop a cohesive way of working together? Select at least three story prompts. Send the prompts out to people with a short explanation of the session and request their approval to record it. Why? When you first hear a story live, you'll walk away with certain impressions. When you listen to it again, you'll hear different things that allow your understanding about the person and the story to grow. You don't want to miss out on those extra goodies.

3. **Once everyone arrives, make sure they all understand why they're there.** Let them know you really want to hear their stories. Spend a little time going over what it means to listen delightedly.

4. **Model a story first.** Telling a story to kick things off is the best way to get everyone's minds into story gear.

5. **Ask the first prompt and demonstrate listening delightedly.** Remember to record the stories.

6. **Let others jump right in with their stories.** One person's story will undoubtedly spark a story in another person.

Cruising for stories

A few years ago a major cruise line conducted several story-gathering sessions with their passengers. They anticipated receiving around 40 stories based on previous experience. By the end of the sessions, more than 230 useable items had been identified. These included stories, anecdotes, short quips, and tons of visual language to dig into. What a goldmine!

7. **Demonstrate how to ask reflective questions as you go along.**

8. **Periodically offer specific appreciations for what you are hearing.** This will maintain the energy flow.

9. **When stories about the first prompt wind down, ask another prompt.** You may need to offer a short anecdote of your own to get them started on this new topic.

10. **You'll find the session naturally winds down between one and a half to two hours.** Don't be surprised if people come up to you before departing and share more stories or what they got out of the session. Capture these pieces as well by continuing the recording or taking notes.

11. **Afterward, send a thank-you note to attendees and confirm with them what will happen with their stories.**

12. **Sift and sort through the recording and/or your notes.** Depending on your reason for holding the session in the first place, you may want to identify themes, unique comments, issues, lessons learned, and perhaps follow-up questions to ask or next steps to take. Make sure your notes have everyone's name who attended, the session date and time, and any other relevant information you may need for documentation.

Capturing and Preserving the Raw Story

Rarely has either of us heard the first rendition of a story and said, "Wow. That's well crafted." If you're truly serious about sharing stories from others that compel people to action, then you'll need to spend time capturing them and exploring their various facets. Although this chapter focuses on getting stories from others, use the methods described here for capturing and preserving your own stories as well. This section talks about the types of things you can think about and do to make this happen.

Attend to legal/ethical issues

Before you can use anyone's story, except your own, within your organization or communicate it on a blog, in an article, as part of a presentation, or the like, you need to get permission in writing to obtain and use it. Too often we hear about people who've proclaimed a story (experience) was theirs when it truly is someone else's. Keep in mind that some individuals may not want everyone to know about what they went through, especially if their story will be displayed in social media.

Here are the main elements that need to be a part of an agreement. We encourage you to consult a legal expert for further assistance:

- ✔ **Consent to use:** Is this an exclusive (no one else can use the story) or nonexclusive (the person can give rights to others) permission?

- ✔ **Attribution:** How does the person want to be acknowledged? By name, title, and organization? Or not at all?

- ✔ **Representations and warrantie:** You need to ensure that the story and or information is original and doesn't violate any copyright, personal or proprietary right, or contain any information received in confidence, as a trade secret, or on the understanding that it would not be disclosed or published, nor discloses proprietary information without express authorization of the owner of said proprietary information, nor violate any contract, express or implied. Whew!

- ✔ **Contributor rights:** What rights does the contributor keep? The right to copyright, license others to use the work, create derivative works, and so forth? This also includes how copyright will be noted and obtained.

- ✔ **Duration of the agreement:** How long do you have the right to keep the story and use it?

Create and transcribe an audio recording

One of the easiest ways to capture the raw version of a story and maintain its spoken nature is to record audio of the person telling it. Before you run and record someone else's story, prep them in advance. Make sure you have just the right story (based on your story prompt). Sometimes people think of two or three that would be good, and you need to whittle them down to the one that's most unique.

Also help the individual *frame* the story ahead of time — where it starts and where might it end. Ask the person to share as many details as possible, such as dialogue, visuals, smells, and the like. They can always be removed later. Then turn on that recording device and listen away — in silence, of course.

Once you've finished recording, follow steps 1 through 4 in "Maximize meaning and value." Then have the audio transcribed. You can do it yourself if you have the time; it can help you to hear it again. You can also use software designed for this specific purpose, ask an intern or assistant to help, or hire out the service.

Bullet the flow of the story

Some people feel more comfortable sketching out a story before they begin to craft it. There are two ways to do this: outlining and storyboarding.

Outlining is very likely a skill you learned in grade school. That is to outline the raw version of the story in bullet format with two — no more than three — layers of headings.

The second is to storyboard it. *Storyboarding* is useful if you find it easier to create visually. You'll need a stack of Post-it Notes, 3 × 5 cards, markers, and a large piece of foam core board from an office supply store:

1. **Get an idea.** Select a story to work on — one you've heard through using a story prompt or a hip pocket story from Chapter 4.

2. **Gather all the materials.** Write the following labels individually onto Post-it Notes. Place them on foam core board (maybe several pieces) or along a wall in a line:

   • The hero

   • The enemy

   • The major needs of your character

   • The major issues of the story

   • The kinds of possible resolutions

   • What the major result is

   • Lessons that you might want to incorporate

   • Happy times

   • The problem or conflict

   • Hard times

   • Funny moments

   • The obstacles, challenges, or barriers

   • Victory moment

   • The realization

   • Great parting message

Using blank Post-it Notes, look at each label and quickly draw an image or jot down a keyword it brings to mind. Don't write sentences — only a word if you can't figure out an image. This isn't about art; merely simple drawings to remind you of the images you want to convey. Brainstorm as many images and words as you can. Some categories may only have one or two (hero, for example). Post these images and words underneath the appropriate label.

3. **Mix and match the elements to create a mock-up.** From the images and words you generated while brainstorming, select those you want to convey and stick them onto the 3 × 5 cards — one image/word for each card. Then stack them in the order you think they should go in. This is why we like 3 × 5 cards — you can easily shuffle them to refine the image order. It's fine if you end up with a big deck. You've now created what's known as an *image deck* (or *story line*), even though it also has keywords as part of it.

Write out the raw version

If you like to write, you may want to sit down and let the story flow from your fingertips through your keyboard or pen. Don't edit as you write. Let it be a stream of consciousness that gets captured. Don't worry at this time if you're writing a description of a series of events or you're truly telling the story. Chapter 6 is designed to help you transform it.

Create a video recording

Aren't cellphone cameras, Flip cameras, and laptop visual recording software wonderful inventions? If you're enamored with them, then capture the raw version of a story in this manner. More often than not, you'll still need to transcribe the audio portion so you can polish it based on the tips in Chapter 6. (Unless it's your own story, and you're a pro at being able to look at a recording and tweak it in your mind's eye. We aren't.)

Telling publicly known stories

Name any historical situation — or current world event — and we'll show you myriad versions of what's considered "truth." What does this mean to you? If you want to share well-known stories, we encourage you to capture information from various sources and create an initial rendering that's your own rendition. Or select one perspective and focus on that. In any case, when you eventually share the story, let others know it's your interpretation or portrayal based on your interpretation of the facts.

Part II

Moving People to Action: Creating Compelling Stories

Five Ways to Take a Story from Bland to Grand

- ✔ Determine which structure best fits with a story and use it to ensure the content is in the appropriate order and all critical information is included.

- ✔ Bring the main and secondary characters to life through inner and outer dialogue and detail some of their characteristics and motivations through lots of sensory information.

- ✔ Boost contrast through irony, figures of speech (oxymorons, metaphors, similes, analogies, and aphorisms), contrasting environmental elements, and additional visual scenes.

- ✔ Embellish a story by strengthening emotions and novelty, building tension, adding humor, and incorporating unexpected events or decisions to add drama and surprise.

- ✔ Make the story memorable by strengthening its key message and associated actions and choosing an attention-grabbing title.

Find out how to merge data into a story to prove your point in a free online article at www.dummies.com/extras/businessstorytelling.

In this part . . .

- Take a raw story and transform it into a more formally crafted one that includes a key message and action steps.

- Select a structure for the story and embellish it by bringing characters to life, enhancing sensory imagery and contrast, and using figures of speech, humor, surprise, and drama.

- Take data, even complex data, and craft a story from it that provides meaning, including visuals that may accompany it.

- Identify ways to reduce the length of a story and add in elements to lengthen and strengthen a short story.

Chapter 6

Crafting a Story

. . . .

. . . .

*R*ecall a time when you heard someone tell a story at work and it fell flat. Why? Was it dull and boring? Did the teller wander in several different directions, making it hard to follow? Did the story's main message seem foggy? Were there too many details for you to track?

At the end of Chapter 5, you captured a raw story — your own or one from others — through transcribing an audiotape, bulleting the flow through an outline or storyboard, writing out the raw version, or creating a video recording. It's not unusual for a raw story to be emotionally timid, not well structured, unfocused, too complicated, and weighted down with too many details. If you tell it just like that, listeners may ultimately feel bad for you.

On the flipside, avoid *canned* stories. These are stories that are over-rehearsed, emotionally distant, slick and polished, scripted, told by rote, rigid, perhaps sensationalized and insincere. Canned stories frequently cause listeners to pick apart the teller after hearing the story.

Our goal is to aid you in crafting compelling stories — stories that are well crafted yet flexible and somewhat improvisational, practiced, authentic, and emotionally engaging. You as the teller are present in the moment, your focus is on the audience, and the audience feels connected to you. The next two chapters are all about how to make this happen.

This chapter covers story strategy — figuring out the approach for your story and developing it from a raw story to a more formally structured one.

Story strategy isn't only about the content of the narrative and the milestones within it, it's also about the *turning point* (when the action changes direction, for better or worse) and its *key message*. Story strategy is yours to decide.

In this chapter, we stick with the basics: Stories have a beginning, middle, and end. In business storytelling, you have to pay attention to this simple flow in addition to the who, what, why, how, and when. Here, we take you through a story step-by-step. First, we delve into the point of the story: its themes, key message, and layers of meaning. Then we move on to the heart of the story: its conflict, plot, and arc. From there, we tackle how to start the story and how to end it. Although we've introduced some of these topics in Chapter 3, we're taking a deeper dive into them here. Chapter 7 completes the picture by addressing various story structures and embellishments.

Driving Home the Story's Key Message

In Chapter 3, we stated that the key message is the *most* important point embodied in a story that you want to convey to your audience. It's the one layer of meaning that resonates on a universal level. The key message clarifies the story's value and purpose for telling it. Because of the multiple layers of meaning a story can have, it can be very tough to immediately identify the key message.

To make this identification easier, do this: Figure out the story's themes first, then select its key message, and finally tease apart the layers of meaning and decide which to keep with the story.

Pick a raw story to play with as you go through this chapter. It can be your personal founding story or one of your success stories. It can also be a story you've captured from someone else that you have permission to tell. Or maybe you have a story that attacks a specific need, such as conveying the importance of an aspect of teamwork to your staff. Any of these are fine.

Determine the themes

Sometimes the key message easily pops out of the story. Most times it doesn't. When it doesn't, start by identifying all the themes that the raw story covers. *Themes* are the subjects or topics covered by the story. Go back to Bob McIlree's story in the appendix and re-read it. What are the themes in his story? Here are a few we've identified:

- ✔ Creativity and innovation
- ✔ Revenge
- ✔ Courage
- ✔ Leadership
- ✔ Assertiveness
- ✔ Teamwork and collaboration
- ✔ Perseverance
- ✔ Helpfulness

Bob originally wrote out the raw version of his story. The three themes of the story that resonated with him were assertiveness, perseverance, and creativity.

Now do the same for the raw story you selected (review Chapter 5 if you need to first). Read it out loud, whether you recorded and transcribed it or wrote it down. Go over the bullet points or storyboard and talk out the details if you used either approach. Watch the video if you captured it that way. This is important. Don't shortchange yourself by only thinking about the series of events. Ask, "What themes are embodied in this story?" Write them down. Then, whittle down the list to those critical few that best fit the story. Now you've got a place to start figuring out the story's key message.

To aid you in identifying themes, this is the time to get a handle on the potential audiences for the story — the individuals and groups you may share it with — and their needs and desires. If there are several potential audiences, pick one for now. Picture this individual or group in your mind. Take some notes while asking yourself the following:

- ✔ Who are they (demographics — age range, education, professions, and so on)?
- ✔ What are they wrestling with?
- ✔ What are they feeling and experiencing?
- ✔ What answers are they searching for?
- ✔ Given these responses, what themes have emerged in your raw story and how aligned are they with the audience needs you've identified?

Keep these notes handy. The more closely you're acquainted with your audience's pains, fears, needs, and aspirations, the better equipped you'll be in pinpointing the story's key message. This information will also aid you in crafting the story so that it really resonates with them.

For Bob's story, the primary audience is project managers (PMs) and business analysts (BAs) who attend a workshop that Lori presents on persuasion and influence. They wrestle with how to motivate others to get things done when they, as PMs and BAs, aren't in charge (have no direct-reporting authority). Spurring motivation can be very frustrating without authority. The themes that most closely align with them are teamwork, perseverance, and assertiveness. Perseverance and assertiveness align with what Bob identified.

Figure out the key message

You've whittled your story's themes down to the vital few, but they're likely still too general. Now it's time to figure out your story's key message — what you want to leave people with that will move them to action and inspire them to do something different.

To do so, ask yourself the following questions and add your responses to the information you've already documented. If you're working with someone else's story, you may have collected their views on these when you asked reflective questions after listening to it. Compile their responses with yours:

- ✔ What's your goal in telling the story?
- ✔ What do you like about the story? What draws you into it?
- ✔ What does this story mean to you?
- ✔ What did you learn or gain from this experience?
- ✔ What understanding or meaning do you want others to have grasped?
- ✔ What do you want the audience to believe after you share the story?
- ✔ What do you want the audience to do after you share the story?

Afterward, read through all the information you've documented and the story one more time and identify patterns — information that's mentioned over and over again. From these patterns, you'll be able to choose the key message that captures a specific action you want people to immediately take after hearing the story. For Bob's story, the patterns of *finding ways to have voice* and *needing to be heard* arose several times. Based on this, we selected *assert yourself* as the key message of Bob's story.

The key message is the backbone of the story. Ultimately, you want people listening to the story to repeat both the story *and* its key message. So what are the qualities of a key message?

- ✔ It's a full sentence, not a bullet point.
- ✔ It's a statement, not a question.
- ✔ It's concise and memorable.
- ✔ It's confined to one significant point.
- ✔ It's affirmative, not negative.
- ✔ It conveys a universal message: Everyone who comes in contact with the story is able to connect deeply with it.

Because the key message needs to create a solid, memorable takeaway, use techniques that advertisers employ to get you to quickly recall tag lines for companies (for example, Nike's *Just Do It*) and TV commercials that move you to buy an item. Here are the key messages for stories found in this book:

- ✔ Make a meaningful connection (Cristi's story in Chapter 3).
- ✔ Take the time (Pam's story in Chapter 7).
- ✔ You too can make it happen (Grantmakers' story in Chapter 9).
- ✔ Stretch beyond your comfort zone (Jan's story in the appendix).
- ✔ Give me time (Frank's story in the appendix).

 If this sounds easy, in practice it isn't. It can take a while to arrive at the perfect key message for a story. Sometimes you know the key message in a flash. Other times it gets altered and improved as you try it out. For now, decide on a key message so you can continue to work through the process of crafting a compelling story.

 Plan to revisit the key message as you craft the more formally structured version of the story. It's possible that the key message you thought was the right one needs to morph. Don't worry if it does. Pay attention to how the key message changes and gets better over time.

 What's the use of a key message in story construction? Every part of the story you tell should reinforce it. This is how you avoid adding in too many details or getting sidetracked into other mini-connected side stories.

Tease apart the layers of meaning

As you've just experienced, a single story can have multiple themes and potential key messages. We call those *layers of meaning*. Where do these emanate from? As Chapter 3 says:

✔ Characters can embody different meanings because of how they act and transform.

✔ The conflict (problem/struggle/trouble) can convey different meanings depending on how many obstacles are included and how they're overcome.

✔ What a personal story means to you can shift and change over time.

You may be thinking, "So what? Why do I need to know that a single story can have multiple layers of meaning?" It's important for two reasons.

First, when you start work on identifying the key message, it's possible that what you thought was important to convey turns out to not be, and something else emerges in its place. That's because crafting a compelling story is an iterative process. As you share your story with others, the key message may change based on their feedback and reactions. We talk more about this dynamic and how to handle it in Chapter 10.

Second, when you move from the raw story to crafting the first draft, you have to decide which meanings to keep with the formally structured version of the story. There may be one or more that aren't critical to how the main character is perceived or that minimize the key message.

If you were to ask Bob McIlree what he consciously elected to leave out from his story, he'd tell you something like, "I had other activities and initiatives going on at the time, so the delay in getting access to the database and its data didn't mean that I had nothing to do until it was 'fixed.' I just didn't include them in the story." If he had included these other activities and initiatives, they may have added additional meanings to Bob as a character (for example, he's a workaholic) and to the problem (maybe the situation isn't really all that urgent because Bob is working on other things).

How do you begin to identify these layers of meaning? You need to answer all the questions we put forth in figuring out the key message. And you'll want to test the narrative with others and obtain their feedback while you're crafting the story.

Starting a Story

There are two important aspects to starting a story: Your opening line(s) and what we call *painting the picture* — providing information about the context, setting, and characters. We find it easier to start with painting the picture, so we'll do that first and then go back to crafting the first few sentences.

There's always an opening scene where you're introducing the characters. Remember what we said in Chapter 3? Tell us who the people are in the story, including their names. Because people relate best to an individual and not groups, make sure there's at least one identifiable, named character.

Chapter 7 talks more about bringing characters to life. For now, you need to know some details about the main character of the story (and potentially about other characters) if this information is critical to the key message and how the story plays out. If not, allow people to create their own version of these characters based on personal experiences.

As we say in Chapter 3, use the language of the senses in setting your opening scene. Listeners need to see, hear, feel, taste, and smell where characters are and what they're doing. Paint a picture of the environment and what's going on. Give your listeners images to feast on so their imaginations kick right in.

Go back to the story you're working on and ask the following questions:

- ✔ What's the setting of the story?
- ✔ What kind of day was it?
- ✔ Who's the main character (also known as the *protagonist*)? It could be you.
- ✔ What's the protagonist doing and feeling?
- ✔ What other characters are present?
- ✔ What are these other characters doing? Who is interacting together?

It's likely that the content we're asking you for here is strewn throughout the raw version of the story. Or it may be missing. That means you may need to reorganize your narrative and add those missing details. Rarely have we encountered a raw story in which all the information needed to paint the picture is in place or in the right order.

Here's a problem we see all the time. We call it the *preamble* start to a story, and it goes something like this:

> "I've been with XYZ corporation for ten years, first as a manager in C division, and then moving over to head up sales, before coming to my current job as VP of Operations. My background is in business management and finance, and I have very much enjoyed my career here. I've met many fine people and customers. One day I was called into . . . ."

This narrative isn't the beginning of the story. The true beginning of the story is "One day I was called into . . . ."

How can you avoid a preamble? Dip into the experience and share it. Right away, give the audience an image to feast on so they can place themselves in the situation. Make these images about the setting. Place the main character (again, this may be you) in the experience. *I was out on my walk when . . .* or *Jim was sitting at his desk gazing out the window when. . . .*

With this in mind, let's re-craft the opening to Bob's story (see the appendix) and strengthen it. To paint a picture, he could start his story with any one of these options:

- ✔ "I was sitting at my desk in my office at work when I received a call from Amy, one of the support staff. 'Bob, we can't get the application you developed to function. This is really serious. We need your help.'"

- ✔ "It was getting to be lunchtime and I was starved. I'd missed breakfast because of an e-mail I needed to tackle at home. The phone rang in my office just as I was about to take a bite out of my turkey sandwich with all the trimmings. 'Hi, this is Bob . . . .'"

- ✔ "I was finishing up a report on a critical project when the phone rang, totally disrupting my thoughts. I thought, 'Arghhh, I can't get anything done around here today.' 'Hi, this is Bob . . . .'"

When starting a story in more formal settings, never say, "I want to tell you a story about . . ." or, "This is a story about . . ." Why not? Some people have an unconscious bias against storytelling. If you say, "I'm going to a tell you a story," some say to themselves, "Oh, whatever's coming next is fabricated" or, "I don't want a story, I just want the facts" or, "I don't have time for a story. I'd wish he'd just get on with it." You don't need that low-grade resistance. Just launch into it before they know what's happening.

There's another, more powerful reason to avoid starting a story with, "I'm going to tell you a story about such and such. . . ." When you do that, you're telegraphing the end of the story. You don't want a book to start off by telling you what happens at the end. We doubt you watch a movie for the first time knowing exactly how it ends. Spoiler alert! So don't start your stories this way. If you do, people may disengage — and they'll do so unconsciously. Why should they pay attention if you already told the ending? You just killed their desire and curiosity to know more.

Clarifying the Core Conflict

The middle of the story is where a problem emerges or a crisis happens — some sort of tension is building. The complications don't have to be life-and-death or earth-shattering. They can be small — like losing your car keys.

Once a character realizes she wants something and moves to get it, the story is set into motion. That leads to figuring out the core problem or conflict, the plot, and its story arc. All are closely intertwined:

- ✔ The *plot* reveals what the problem is and narrates the course of events.

- ✔ The *conflict* is the problem/struggle/trouble and what is at risk.

- ✔ The main *character* (protagonist) is the one who's trying to solve the problem.

- ✔ The *story arc* is the shift in awareness that occurs.

- ✔ The *key message* makes the story meaningful by the end.

To be compelling, a story needs to be meaningful. Meaning happens through knowing what the conflict is and seeing how the main character responds to it, how the story unfolds (plot), and how the story creates a shift for the main character from the beginning through to the end (story arc).

Describe the conflict or problem

When incorporating a conflict into your story, describe the problem or issue along with what was frustrating for the main character (which may be you) in the story. Also include the behaviors of the other characters, if appropriate — what they were doing that led them down the wrong path.

There's always someone or something opposing the main character and what they're trying to achieve. The role of the *antagonist* (usually a person but can also be another company, a regulation, the weather, and so on) is to provide this opposition. The villain thwarts the main character. Interestingly enough, a conflict and an antagonist make us care about the characters.

Consider the following progression from ho-hum into a problem, adapted from Dara Marks's *Inside Story: The Power of the Transformational Ark* (Three Mountain Press, 2007):

- ✔ Mary goes to the store (we don't care)

- ✔ to buy some milk (we still don't care)

- ✔ for her baby (we care a little)

- ✔ who is sick (we care a little more)

- ✔ and hasn't eaten in days because she can't get in to see the doctor (we care a lot).

Now consider this progression from ho-hum into a conflict with an antagonist (the neighborhood bully):

- ✔ Mary goes to the store (we don't care)
- ✔ to buy some milk (we still don't care)
- ✔ for her baby (we care a little)
- ✔ who is sick (we care a little more)
- ✔ and hasn't eaten in days because a neighborhood bully stole most of her money on the way home from work (we care a lot).

In both examples, we have the kernel of a story. Before the problem or conflict was introduced, though, all we had were uninteresting events.

Every conflict involves a person or situation that's out of balance. That keeps us on our toes because there's always the danger of loss, harm, or failure if it's not resolved. Something is in *jeopardy*. Once jeopardy is established, the story is propelled toward the end and its resolution. Along the way there's struggle, trouble, and peril, all of which generate dramatic tension. This conflict keeps listeners on the edge of their seats. Listeners remain engaged because they care about the people in the story and want to learn what happens to them.

In Bob's story, the conflict begins when he's denied access to a software application he designed that has stopped functioning. Conflict escalates when the database administrator refuses to budge. It escalates further when Bob approaches Jim's boss and she doesn't immediately resolve the issue. Do you see how the conflict keeps moving the story along while keeping us engaged?

Go back to the story you're working on. To determine the main conflict of your story, ask yourself these questions:

- ✔ What is the core struggle, trouble, or problem in the story?
- ✔ What does the main character want?
- ✔ What are the complications?
- ✔ What are the barriers that stand in the main character's path?
- ✔ Who's the bad guy in the story? Is it some big company, an irritating regulation, maybe the status quo, or a combination?

The simplest stories have one clear conflict. More complex stories (think 20-minute stories or a book) can contain several conflicts. For example, let's say in Bob's story that he also had a side conflict with Jim's boss. Weaving that into the story would have made the piece more complex and longer. However, to keep the story focused on its key message, it wasn't important to go into it. So for our purposes here, keep it simple. Make a decision about what the main conflict is and make sure your story stays focused on that.

Unfold the plot

Okay, you've got the key message and the core conflict. Next, let's tackle the plot. A *plot* is the sum of the events that occur and what happens to the characters — what they do and where they go. Plot is all about how the story unfolds over the length of the telling. It's the unique chain of events that leads to the end of the story.

Here's the plot of Bob's story:

1. He gets a call while at the client site.
2. He is locked out of the databases.
3. He calls Jim, the database administrator.
4. He calls Jim's boss.
5. He files a Freedom of Information Act.
6. He meets with Jim's boss.
7. He withdraws the request.

Yes, this is a simple progression of events. It's the plot skeleton. Eventually it'll get filled in with more details. As you look at the story you're working on, consider the following:

1. How do the events flow in the story?
2. What happens first, second, third, and so on?
3. What steps are taken to bring us to the end?

As we state in Chapter 5, it's important to get the flow down. Otherwise it's easy to drift off into unrelated tangents or side stories. For example, in Bob's story, Jim's story about Bob isn't present. That's because Bob knew, in telling his story, that Jim's side story wouldn't move the plot along.

But both the plot and the key message in and of themselves don't create a meaningful story. They need to be woven together so they follow the story arc, and you have to add to them lots of details and LOTS (language of the senses), characters, motivations, emotions, and context.

Lay out the story arc

A *story arc* is more than just a simple beginning, middle, and end. Think of the story arc as a bell curve. It's the sequence of events that keeps the listener or reader moving along.

The story arc follows a path. It starts with the setting and then presents the core conflict — along with a sense of urgency around resolving it. There's tension from barriers that emerge to block the main character from resolving the conflict, which brings about the rise and fall of hope. Then there's a turning point, an *a-ha* moment, that moves the character to resolve the conflict. The story arc ends with a new reality and finally delivers its key message — the main point that you're focused on making.

It's up to you as the storyteller to carefully select and arrange the material so that the emotional significance of the story and its larger meanings can emerge. You're in charge of how the characters of the story develop and grow into a new understanding or awareness — that new understanding is one of the major differences between a compelling and a ho-hum story.

The setting for Bob's story is the client's site and involves a software application that he designed which uses several internal databases. Things get interesting when the customized application stops functioning. Lots of money is lost if the system is shut down for any length of time, which creates urgency. Tension gets added when a barrier pops up: Jim, the database administrator, refuses to grant Bob access to do his work. Bob is blocked from resolving the initial problem.

Enter *rising and falling hope*: We initially hope the problem will be resolved with Bob's first request for access. But our hopes are dashed. So Bob goes to Jim's immediate boss. Once again, our hopes are lifted. Will he succeed this time? Nope, dashed again. When Bob thinks out of the box, again our hope rises. This time he is victorious! Yeah! That's his defining moment.

Then, a shift occurs when Jim's boss confronts Bob about his tactics. Bob could have made a big stink, but by thinking out of the box, he realizes he's not powerless. He's not out for revenge. He withdraws his request, and his point is made. The key message follows.

Here are a few additional details about the middle, the turning point, and the end of the arc:

- ✔ **The middle:** The middle of the story is when the main character is wrestling with the conflict and its barriers. There's resistance here. Maybe the person is floundering in the unknown, trying to figure things out — or is exhausted. The main character may shift from fear, trepidation, or constraint over to confidence, acceptance, or new understanding.

- ✔ **The turning point:** The turning point between the middle and the end of the arc is the moment of enlightenment — the *a-ha* moment. Ultimately, you want to see what the main character has achieved at the end of the story that they weren't capable of achieving at the beginning.

> ✔ **The end:** With the end of the story comes an experience of release. The journey has ended, we're back in the land of the known, and we feel refreshed or renewed in some way. That's exactly what happened to Bob.

As the story winds down to the end, make sure it's nice and tight. As you craft the setting, the conflict, the *a-ha* moment, and key message, ask yourself, "What moments from this story connect most powerfully to the key message?" As we said earlier, every part of the story should be driving the story to that most important point.

When thinking about the story arc for the story you're crafting, ask:

✔ What are the barriers and resistance in the story?

✔ How are the main character and others in the story feeling?

✔ When is the defining moment in the story?

✔ How is the conflict resolved and what kind of release does the main character experience?

✔ What is the new awareness the main character has that you can share?

Ending the Story: This Isn't Disney

Endings often confound those who craft stories because they haven't figured out the story's key message. Because you've already spent time on that, crafting your story's ending should be relatively easy.

The *ending* is all about how the problem or conflict is resolved. This resolution rights the world in some way — it brings the characters back to wholeness. You can resolve a problem by changing the situation, changing the world, or changing the main character.

Disney is all about happy resolutions. However, in business, "happily ever after" is only one of many ways a story might end. We don't want you to avoid telling stories of failures. Recovering from failures or mistakes can be inspiring and positive. We've all overcome disappointments and can learn different ways to cope from each other.

Many people think the *climax* is the end of the story, but it's not. Once you reach the story's peak, the action slows and the story winds down. In the winding down is where all unanswered questions are answered and the conflict gets resolved. After that, you get to sum up the story and bring it full circle.

With all that in mind, there are four main parts to ending a story:

- ✔ **The resolution** of the conflict.
- ✔ **The key message** of the story.
- ✔ **The transition** to an action statement.
- ✔ **An action statement:** For the listener, the story should answer the question, "What must I do?" In other words, "How can I take action to get the results I want?" The universal key message travels with the story, but the action statement could change with every audience. To see an example of different action statements for a single story, check out the Grantmakers' story in Chapter 9.

Are you interested in knowing what this looks like for a story? Here's the key message, transition to action, and the action statement for Bob's story:

When you can't get what you need to do your job or solve a problem, *assert yourself*. Be vocal. Be creative. Follow up with people who can make things happen. Persist until you're satisfied that you have exactly what you need. Assert yourself even if it means seeking forgiveness rather than asking for permission. If I can do it, so can you.

The key to moving people to action is moving them through various emotions as the story progresses. This is especially important at the end of the story.

Your intention, your story, your key message, and your action statement all need to match up. That's called *congruence*. As you put together the end of your story, the answers to these questions need to align:

1. How is the conflict resolved?

2. How are characters changed?

3. What must listeners do next? What action can they take to get the results they want?

4. How does the ending connect to the beginning and middle of the story?

5. In what ways does the ending allow you to segue into the key message?

6. Does your ending educate, resonate, inspire, and built trust and respect?

Creating a Detailed Story Outline

You entered this chapter with one or more of the following:

- ✔ The transcript of a recorded raw story
- ✔ A bulleted flow of a raw story
- ✔ An image deck from your initial stab at storyboarding a raw story
- ✔ A written raw story
- ✔ A video of the telling of a raw story

In each section of this chapter, we've asked you a series of questions. If you've been answering them and capturing your responses, you have all the pieces necessary to complete the following steps. When you document the results of each step, you'll have created a detailed outline (or a storyboard) of the next version of your story.

We've written these steps so you can use them for any story you might choose to capture and craft in a compelling manner. If you've already done all the work we asked you to do in Chapters 5 and 6, you can skip to step 3.

Step 1: Get an idea

Select a story to work on. It can be one of your own or one you've identified from someone else using story prompts (see Chapter 5). It can also be one of the hip pocket stories discussed in Chapter 4.

Step 2: Gather your notes

Capture the raw story in some form. We give you five ways of doing that in Chapter 5, summarized in the bulleted list that begins this section.

Step 3: Create a mock-up

In its simplest form, the journey your story takes follows this flow. Fill in this outline using your raw story and any other notes you may have about it (answers to reflective questions, archived materials, and so on):

✔ The opening scene

✔ Then something happens (the conflict emerges)

✔ Barriers or obstacles appear

✔ Barriers or obstacles are overcome

✔ Resolution occurs

✔ New insight is gained

✔ The end and parting message is offered

From that outline, transform the story into a first draft of a more formally structured story (or storyboard — see www.dummies.com/extras/businessstorytelling/) for our free extra article on storyboarding. As you're writing or sketching, pay attention to the

✔ First few sentences.

✔ Story's resolution.

✔ Last few sentences, including the key message, transition to action, and action statement.

✔ Possible story title (see www.dummies.com/extras/businessstorytelling/ for an article on this topic).

Step 4: Tighten and toss extraneous details

Review your draft and validate that you've got all the pieces you need in your story and that it's on track to becoming a compelling one. If you've done a storyboard, go through the following suggestions first (if not, skip to the questions that follow):

✔ Walk through your story out loud. Determine all the unnecessary details you can leave out. Remove all images and words that are incidental to the main action of the story and your key message.

✔ The order of the images may change. This is fine.

✔ Don't worry about the pieces you're not going to use right now. Keep them around. You may use them later or when you want to refine or re-craft the story for another purpose.

✔ After this first weeding, review your image deck one more time. Chances are it's probably a lot smaller.

Ask the following questions about your story or storyboard to determine what adjustments need to be made to it. For each one, we ask you to consider what *images* need to be added, because images are how a story is conveyed. Focus on imagery and language of the senses (LOTS) instead of information:

✔ Where should there be outer dialogue in the story? Where should there be inner reflective dialogue?

✔ In addition to what you already have, what LOTS need to be added to the story? What metaphors and images do you need to add?

✔ Where could you add contrast in the story (good/bad, right/wrong, and so on)? What images do you need to add?

✔ What emotions does your audience need to feel? What drama do you need to add to get them to feel this way? What images do you need to add?

✔ How is the reader going to feel when the story is finished? What images do you need to add?

✔ What is your audience going to think, learn, and do differently afterward? What images do you need to add?

✔ Do all the details of your story convey or reinforce your key message? What images do you need to add or delete?

✔ In what ways does your story connect to what your audience values? Does your story convey or reinforce this? What images do you need to add?

If any of these questions spark new thoughts about your story, go back and weave them in. But once again, cut out anything that doesn't directly link back to and reinforce your key message. Don't wander and go off on tangents. Keep the story tight and focused.

Step 5: Try it out

After doing this validation, tossing, and tightening, you're now ready to try out your story.

If you did a storyboard

After the final weeding, restack your image deck, if needed. Now it's time to tell the story as you would with a listener by speaking your story out loud using your deck of 3 × 5 cards. You may want to record this so it can be transcribed if you want a written document.

You now have a choice: 1) Continue writing the story based on your image deck and/or recording, or 2) Leave your story in the form of the image deck without writing it. Yes, you can do that. Many storytellers leave their stories as image decks. Chapter 10 goes into how to practice and tell your story from both a written story and an image deck.

If you did a written story

It's helpful to begin by speaking your story out loud. Often, additional clarity comes through this first walk-through that makes any further writing go more quickly. Tweak the story as needed.

Now share your story with someone to see what's working and what you might want to change. Keep crafting your story until you're happy with it and sense that it'll resonate with the individual or audiences it's for.

In the end, you want to show how a character (you or someone else) succeeds or fails . . . grows and changes . . . through the unfolding conflict . . . from the storyteller's point of view.

Step 6: Save it

Capture all the great work you've done. Save it to your computer. Save it in on Evernote, Dropbox, and so on. Print it. In Chapter 7 you'll have the opportunity to hone and polish your story.

Differences Between Oral and Print

When you're sharing a story orally, you have a bit more time to ease into it and connect with your listeners. But when crafting a written story, either for print or online publication, you have to grab people at the very beginning to keep them reading through to the end. Your opening sentences have to set the scene and present the dilemma or at least an action that gets the story moving right away.

Compare these two examples to get a feel for what we mean:

✓ **Oral:** "For the last six months, I've been working on a cruise ship. Mostly below deck. I used to be a teacher but when I turned 30, I wanted more adventure, so I looked for a temporary job. Working on a cruise ship seemed just the ticket. But after working steadily from January to June, I was ready for a long shore leave. I found myself on Easter Island, which is a port I'd always dreamed of visiting. As I walked down the gangplank, I felt free! I loved hearing the birds. And the green land was beautiful! With only one week to myself, I desperately wanted to see the large stone statues everyone talks about. I also found myself wondering, 'Would I find my destiny here or would I rejoin the ship when it was ready to sail?'"

✓ **Written:** "I was finally getting off a cruise ship after working hard below deck with little sign of light for six solid months. I was free! And I was in a port I'd always dreamed of visiting: Easter Island. I only had a week of shore leave. As I walked down the gangplank, I wondered, 'Would I find my destiny here or rejoin the ship when it was ready to leave?'"

Even if you're writing a story, make the language conversational. That's why two methods we suggested in Chapter 5 were audio and video recording — whether it be someone else's story or your own. Conversational language will help you more quickly connect with your reader and keep them engaged.

Here are a couple of other distinctions between an oral and a written story:

✓ Conversations between two characters:

- **Oral:** Drop the "he said, she said" words and use other techniques, such as vocal intonation changes or where you look in the room, to distinguish between what the characters are saying. Observe everyday conversations where people are informally relaying a story, and you'll pick up on this. More on this in Chapter 10.

- **Written:** Use phrasing such as, "Jim said, 'Blah blah blah.' And Gloria responded, "Yeah, yeah, yeah.'"

✓ Phone conversations (example by Doug Stevenson, May 11, 2013):

- **Oral:** Tell your side of the conversation while inserting what you hear. "Oh, hi, Jim . . . you need what? A horse and a trailer? What for? . . . Huh. Your tractor was totaled? Really? Wow. You hit the guardrail on the side of the road? Geez. How'd that happen?. . ."

- **Written:** Relay both sides of the conversation.

✔ Physicality:

- **Oral:** Demonstrate through body language or facial expressions how a character moves, feels, or reacts.

- **Written:** Describe, using LOTS, how a character moves or feels in reaction to what is happening. "Tim gingerly walked down the street with a painful limp in his right leg." "There was a wry grimace on his face when David heard the news." "Joan's face lit up with joy when Harry said 'yes' to their sales proposal."

Whether written or oral, most stories we review typically make several language mistakes:

1. **They don't use enough LOTS.** The best-crafted stories activate at least two of our five senses: hear, see, smell, taste, and touch. Provide succinct visual images when they're necessary for the listener/reader to have. Otherwise, give them just enough to attach to the visuals they have in their own mind's eye.

2. **There's more describing than telling.** The more you transform a description of events into the telling of a story by adding emotions, inner and outer dialogue, and a variety of sensory details, the more impact you will have.

3. **There's too much industry jargon and acronyms.** This is the opposite of LOTS and is more conceptual than tangible. It's okay to use business jargon in conversation as a linguistic shorthand if and only if the story benefits from it or the audience requires it.

4. **There's too much business speak.** Get rid of it. Business speak sounds like this: "XYZ company offers leading edge services focused on helping leaders and their teams maximize their full potential through organizational cultural transformation. Our statistically validated assessments are benchmarked using enhanced performance technology tools to provide multiple levels of . . . ."

5. **There's lots of repetitious content.** Avoid telling them something and then summarizing what you just told them.

6. **Being outlandish.** There's a limit to what people will believe. Claims like, "$50,000 in revenue will be yours in one month if you buy our product" feels a little too good to be true. Avoid it or your hype will cast seeds of doubt rather than trust and confidence.

7. **Being an advertorial.** This is when an advertisement is dressed up to look like a story or a piece of news. It's misleading. Just keep telling darned good stories. Let them do the work for you.

8. **Inserting data throughout the story.** Read Chapter 8 to learn the best way to refer to data and statistics.

Chapter 7

Polishing a Story: Structure and Embellishments

....

....

We both work with a lot of different organizations and individuals to help them craft and hone their stories. Sometimes this happens in workshops that last a day or two. Other times it's one-on-one in person or over the phone. The feedback we get is almost always the same: "This is hard work! I never knew how much is involved in polishing a story. I keep wanting to make it better and better. There are so many details to think about." We agree. There are a lot of details to think about. Which means there are many ways to embellish a story — to really make it sing. One is to improve its structure. We've purposefully saved this topic until now because you already know it. Yes, we realize this seems counterintuitive. Here's why.

Many times, the first thing Karen's asked is: "What's the structure of a story? Just tell me the story structure, and then I'll know how to tell a great story." Her response is always the same: "This is the simplest structure I can give you. All stories are reduced to this structure. Are you ready? Okay, here it is: problem/resolution. That's it: problem/resolution. Now that you know that, do you think you can tell a story any better?" They often chuckle and say, "No."

In this chapter, we cover a variety of story structures. We also show you how to take a business story from bland to grand by enhancing various story elements.

Choosing a Story Structure

When crafting any kind of story, it boils down to these four pieces:

- ✔ **Plot:** What the problem is and the chronology of events (see Chapter 6).
- ✔ **Story arc:** What caused the action, character intention, and meaning of the story (see Chapter 6).
- ✔ **Elements:** How the story is crafted using emotions, LOTS, drama, contrast, and the like (see Chapter 3).
- ✔ **Structure:** The order in which you put the story together.

We cover story structure before we talk about other embellishments even though we don't suggest you address story structure until you're ready to finalize your story. There are two general types of structure: those from Hollywood and those from the world of business. We discuss both kinds here.

Hollywood-focused story structures

Although these types of structures come from the world of entertainment, they also have a use in business.

Kurt Vonnegut, in a hilarious short video, whips through some very popular story structures (www.youtube.com/watch?v=oP3c1h8v2ZQ). There's the structure of *I'm better off than I was before*, and those that highlight *loss and gain* and *down and out* — much like the movie *The Pursuit of Happyness* starring Will Smith, about the life of Chris Gardner. As you become familiar with the three story structures Vonnegut discusses, reflect on how they fit with your professional and personal experiences. These structures, which are dramatic in nature, make for fabulous business stories when they're tied to a business purpose and include a call to action.

The "I'm better off" structure

The *I'm better off* story goes like this: The main character gets in trouble, then gets out of trouble, and ends up better off for the experience. As Vonnegut says, "People love that story. They never get sick of it!" Many stories that leaders tell follow this pattern. It's the story of struggle and redemption — of losing everything and gaining something better in return. A bankruptcy, being let go from a job, losing a home, and making major mistakes and recovering from them — all follow this structure. All make for riveting business stories.

Wally Amos and his Famous Amos cookies are an example. He lost his company and the ability to use his own name. He re-emerged as "Uncle Noname," which has morphed into the successful Uncle Wally's muffin company. He says the experiences on the roller coaster of life taught him that there really are no tough times, just opportunities to grow.

Larry King's life also fits this structure. In 1971 he was a popular Miami radio show host. At 37 he was charged with grand larceny by a former business partner and arrested. All charges were eventually dropped, but his media career hit the skids. Working in public relations, he kept interviewing athletes and other famous folks. With their help, he rebuilt his career and achieved unparalleled success with his CNN show *Larry King Live*.

The "loss and gain" structure

Creating a story using the *loss and gain* structure goes like this: The main character falls in love with a business or opportunity or is doing work that fulfills their dreams — loses it when something puts those dreams on hold — and then regains it. This also is a very powerful type of story to share.

In Chapter 4, Steve Jobs's *love and loss* tale is both an example of loss and gain and a founding story. Another example is that of entertainer and television icon Dick Clark. Since 1972, Clark enthusiastically hosted ABC's *New Year's Rockin' Eve* celebration and midnight countdown of the Times Square Ball in New York City. In 2004, he suffered a debilitating stroke. His recovery was painful and arduous. In 2006, after teaching himself to walk and talk again, he was back on the show where he remained as host until his death in 2012. "I wouldn't have missed this for the world," he said when he rejoined the show in 2006.

Artist Pablo Picasso's story follows this type of structure too. Early in his career, his friend Carlos Casagemas committed suicide, plunging Picasso into grief, suffering, and despair. For three years these feelings influenced his paintings, causing it to be labeled as his *blue period*. Eventually they passed. With the help of friends and fellow artists, he gained new inspiration and entered into his joyful rose period. His *blue* period and these subsequent art works propelled him into fame and fortune.

You can read more about the stories of Wally Amos, Larry King, Dick Clark, and Pablo Picasso in John A. Sarkett's *Extraordinary Comebacks: 201 Inspiring Stories of Courage, Triumph, and Success* (Sourcebooks, 2007).

The "down and out" Cinderella structure

The *down and out* story structure goes like this: The main character is in a bad spot, a special helper provides gifts, but then the character loses their good standing. Eventually that good standing is restored, and the main character gains incredible bliss. In his video, Vonnegut says, "This is the most popular story in our western civilization. Every time it's retold, someone makes another million dollars." In business, this could be a story of dissatisfying work and living in desperation. Then a mentor comes along and transforms the person's life, but circumstances still hold the person back. These are eventually resolved which leads to the person's dreams being realized.

Remember the real-life, story-turned-movie of Erin Brockovich? As a down-and-out mother struggling to survive, she landed a job doing clerical work in a law firm. Between her own grit and the guidance she receives from others, she perseveres against a utility company and the harm it creates for the town of Hinkley, California. The case takes its toll on both her love live and her health. Her relationship fades and painful injuries from a previous car accident get in the way. While sharing her story with her chiropractor, who knew actor and producer Danny DeVito, Brockovich came to the attention of Hollywood. Winning the case and having her story brought to the movie screen gave her success beyond her wildest dreams.

Business-focused story structures

Sometimes business-focused stories don't quite fit these more dramatic types of structures. And those dramatic structures may not fit with the hip pocket stories provided in Chapter 4. When this happens, try using the components of business-focused story structures we've identified here, which are also powerful and easy to use. Keep in mind that the complexion of the story will change based on the arrangement of the elements that you choose.

With business-focused story structures, the story either starts with a setting or the context — or with a problem. Action is taken to resolve the challenge, the problem, or the hindrance, and the results are shared, revealing how it was all resolved. There comes a point in the story when you get to share the insights you gained (evaluation or lesson) and offer suggestions to the audience about actions or steps they may want to take that are linked to your message.

Following these business story structures is a good idea when you only have a short time to tell a story and want to ensure you hit all the critical points (for example, in job interviews and short presentations). They also work well when you're writing a very short story and want to keep it tightly focused. Because of these needs, a good way to use the elements of any given business story structure is as a check to ensure the first draft of a story includes them.

SHARES

SHARES stands for Setting, Hindrance, Action, Results, Evaluation, and Suggested actions. This structure begins with a *setting* ("I was sitting at my desk . . ."), followed by the *hindrance* or obstacle that's creating a problem. The *action* that was taken by the main character is given next, along with the *result*. The teller then provides a statement *evaluating* the experience ("this made me think about . . ."), ending with *suggested actions* for your audience.

Here's a quick example to show you what we mean: Both Cristi and Bob's stories from Chapter 3 follow the SHARES structure. They start by presenting the *setting* (Cristi puts the finishing touches on a brochure in her office, Bob gets a call at his desk from support staff), then showing the *hindrance* or obstacle that was present (not winning government contracts, being shut out of a critical database). They reveal the *actions* that were taken (Cristi attends the seminar and gives the speaker a brochure and ChapStick, Bob tries official channels and then files a Freedom of Information Act request). Finally they gain *results* (she wins the contract, he gets database access), *evaluate* the experience (thoughts about being prepared, being creative), and *suggest actions* (make a meaningful connection, assert yourself).

PARLAS

PARLAS stands for Problem, Action, Result, Learning, Application, and Suggested actions. With the PARLAS structure, you start by presenting the *problem*. Then you work your way through the *action* taken by the main character to solve the problem, what the *result* was, what was *learned* in the process ("what I learned from this was . . ."), how that learning *applies* to today, ending with *suggested* actions for your audience.

CHARQES

CHARQES stands for Context, Hindrance, Action, Results Quantified, Evaluation, and Suggested actions. The CHARQES structure starts with laying out the *context* — what was happening and why. Then the *challenge* is presented, what *action* was taken by the main character comes next, followed by the *result* in *quantifiable* numbers. After this, the teller gives an *evaluation* of the experience and finally provides *suggested* actions for the audience to take.

CCARLS

CCARLS stands for Context ("It was the bottom of the 9th inning"), Challenge, Action, Result, Lesson, and Suggested actions. This structure starts with the *context* of the issue (similar to CHARQES). Then the *challenge* is presented, the *action* that was taken is brought in, and the *result* is provided — along with the *lesson*. *Suggested* actions for the audience are given at the end.

If you've worked through the previous chapters, you have the first draft of a story. Now you'll want to determine which Hollywood or business structure fits best with it — and if it's missing any of these structural components.

Apply structure to a story

Let's look at a more detailed example. The following is the first draft of a story from Pam Stampen, a corporate executive and former flight attendant. In the text, you'll see bold words referring to various structural elements. You decide which structure it follows. Afterward, decide which structure elements fit with each paragraph (or two or three) in your story and tag them like this:

> As a flight attendant for Northwest Airlines back in 1986, I was working a red eye flight from San Francisco to Minneapolis in the middle of the summer. It was very hot outside for San Francisco. We needed to get to the plane about 8 o'clock at night.
>
> When we got on, it was very hot. Normally an auxiliary power unit keeps the plane cool while it's on the ground when the engines aren't running. But either they didn't have one or it was broken.
>
> We got everything checked out and then folks started to get on the plane. It was packed with people, packed with suitcases — all types of baggage everywhere. People were agitated because it was late. They knew they were going to be flying through the night. Every seat was full. **(context)**
>
> In the very last row there was a single man sitting by himself toward the wall. In the middle seat was a young girl about two years old who was acting out and the mother. The child was very agitated. The mom was very nervous because she didn't know how the child was going to behave on this very long flight in the middle of the night. They were in a row of seats that didn't recline. They had gotten stares from people all around them as they made their way to the back of the plane. **(challenge)**
>
> In the way that I usually do, I went back to go talk to the mom and the child. What usually happens with kids is that if a stranger talks to them they get quiet and attach to their parent. **(action)** You're not trying to scare them; you're being very nice to them. This helps them calm down. You talk loudly enough so the people around them understand that the child might be scared or she might be hot. Flying is hard for kids.
>
> I said, "If she starts to cry during the flight it's probably because her little ears hurt and she doesn't know what's going on. We all need to be patient with that and I know we will." **(action)**
>
> I was trying to set the tone for the people sitting around the mother. I did see some eyes rolling. I saw some newspaper crunching. I saw people in business suits trying to relax, thinking, "This is going to be a very long night." **(context)**

We take off and the little girl is still very agitated. She doesn't want to sit. She doesn't want to color. The mom is trying to do everything she can. **(challenge)** I come by again and I said to her, "I'm really busy right now but when I'm finished with my work can I come back and we can talk and I've got something to show you." The little girl nodded to say, "Yes that that would be okay," and the mom smiled.

I went and did my work. Once we got everything tucked away for the night and everyone was situated, I came back. The little girl was still uncomfortable. I could see that the mother was very, very tired. I remember bringing the little girl a pin shaped like a set of wings. She liked that. I asked her if she was thirsty and she said, "Yes." So I asked her mom if it was okay that she have something to drink. She said, "Yes."

Then I asked her mom if it would be okay if she went on a walk with me. The mom said, "That would be just fine." I think she was running out of energy. So the little girl and I walked up to the front of the plane. We got some juice. And we made a toy out of plastic cups and stir sticks. We put them inside of two plastic cups and bound them together with bandaids — all things that were in the flight attendant kit. We made a rattle — kind of a noisy toy — which she thought was fun. Then I walked her back to her mom. She finally settled in for the night and fell asleep. **(action)**

I was sitting in the back doing a little reading. The mom came back and asked if she could talk with me. I said, "Certainly." So we went in the galley, close enough where she could see her daughter but far enough away where we could have a conversation.

She thanked me for being so kind to them. She realized it wasn't an easy situation and she really appreciated the extra care. She explained to me that her daughter had been taken from her and that she'd been without her daughter for some period of time and had been searching for her. She was just getting her back and was scared. She really, really appreciated that I'd tried to understand and help. It made a difference to her. **(result)**

While I've always felt I was a customer-focused person and understood the value of a client, I gained a new perspective on that day. You never know what people have been through before they get to you and you never know where they're going after they leave you. The only thing you do control is how well they're taken care of while they're in your care. You always need to take the time. This has never left me. **(lesson)** *Used with permission. Copyright © 2003 by Pam Stampen. As told by Pam Stampen and crafted by Lori L. Silverman. All rights reserved.*

In this story, you can see that the structural elements are out of order. Even so, it appears to follow the CCARLS structure, which would mean the suggested actions for listeners is missing. As a result, the ending isn't as powerful as it could be. We'll fix all of this as we go through the chapter.

Getting a Story to Pop

Structure will only take you so far when crafting a compelling story. You also need to embellish it. Each of the following sections poses questions. Not all may apply to the story you're working on — as we'll see with Pam's story. Feel free to follow the sections in this order or skip around.

Bring characters to life

You know from previous chapters how important characters are when you want to engage listeners. To add more zing to a story, detail some of the characteristics and motivations of your characters using lots of sensory information (LOTS). Before you do so, determine where it's important for you to provide these details to listeners. The following questions can help:

- ✔ **What are the distinguishing features and distinctive gestures of your characters?** These could be talents and abilities. Find ways to add these details in where needed.

- ✔ **How can you bring additional dialogue into the story to increase connection and empathy for the characters?** Go through each paragraph and ask whether it would add value to turn sentences into dialogue. For more information, see Chapter 3.

- ✔ **What speaking style do your characters use?** Are they talkative, taciturn, soft-spoken, loud, formal, casual, fast, slow, or have accents? Determine how you can bring out these speaking styles if the story is in print or electronic form (or act this out if you're telling the story).

- ✔ **What is the main character's short-term goals and long-term needs?** Consider whether you need to add in these pieces for some or all of the supporting characters.

- ✔ **What fears do your characters have?** Tell us about them and the growth they achieve by the end of the story.

If your story is about a group, let listeners know which group member is the main character; some are secondary characters — they help the main character to move the story along. The rest will be minor characters who may not even have a role. Give the main character and the secondary characters a name and differing characteristics. Minor characters don't need to be named.

Early on in Pam's story, to convey a better picture of the little girl in the mind's eye, what if this detail:

> The little girl was wearing a short sleeve white shirt with flowers on it and a pair of hot pink shorts. Her sandy blond hair was in pigtails. As she wailed, a river of tears streamed from her puffy green eyes.

Why would you add this level of detail to the little girl versus any other character? Because she has so little dialogue in the story, we did this so you will more strongly identify with her.

Let's go on to dialogue. Where would additional external and/or internal dialogue benefit the story? Consider this paragraph toward the end:

> She explained to me that her daughter had been taken from her and that she'd been without her daughter for some period of time and had been searching for her. She was just getting her back and was scared. She really, really appreciated that I'd tried to understand and help. It made a difference to her.

You could re-craft this text into character dialogue to strengthen the ending:

> "You see . . . I haven't seen my daughter in quite some time. She was taken from me and I'm just getting her back. I've been looking for her for a long time. I was so scared that I'd never see her again. I really, really appreciate your understanding and your help. It's made a big difference."

This dialogue may come from the story transcript or from clarifying questions asked to the originator of the story. If dialogue is needed, and the originator doesn't recall it specifically, ask them to recall the nature of the conversation. Dialogue only needs to reflect the exact words that were said when they are of critical importance to the story or the originator of the story. Now go back to your story. How can you bring your characters to life?

Enhance sensory imagery and contrast

One benefit of adding in LOTS is that you also boost contrast. As we've mentioned, contrast helps create meaning because the mind learns to know the value of one thing when it's compared to another.

Review your story. Strengthen these elements by answering these questions:

- ✔ **What additional visual scenes can you paint for listeners?** What else do you want them to see, hear, smell, taste, or feel tactilely?

- ✔ **Where could you add *stark* contrasts that highlight differences?** Identify those contrasting elements. Examples include: peaceful/angry despair/bliss, and expressive/silent.

- ✔ **Where could you add contrast between environmental elements?** Examples include hot/cold, summer/winter, soft/hard, and smooth/rough.

- ✔ **What irony could you add to further embellish your story?** Phrases such as *"It's raining, and such a pleasant day"* or *"Coffee and donuts, a perfectly balanced meal"* are another form of contrast.

> ✔ **Where could you add figures of speech to boost contrast and enhance visual language?** These include oxymorons, metaphors and similes, analogies, and aphorisms (we talk about all of them in a moment).

Although Pam's story has quite a bit of LOTS and contrast, there are still ways to make it more memorable. For example, you could replace the phrase about the little girl, *She was very agitated*, with one containing more detail and action to clarify what you mean by *agitated*: *The little girl couldn't sit still. She kept trying to stand up. And she kept kicking and punching the seat in front of her. When her mom tried to hold her, she pushed away.*

Use figures of speech

When crafting a story for business use, it's common to be literal in your word choices, which can produce some uninteresting results. Inserting oxymorons, metaphors and similes, analogies, and aphorisms (see upcoming examples) can make your stories more lively, interesting, and entertaining. Figures of speech can help communicate a great deal with just a few words or a phrase.

Here are five questions to ask about your story for each figure of speech:

> ✔ **Could one oxymoron/metaphor/analogy/aphorism be leveraged for your entire story?** One way for this to happen is to link it to the theme of the story (see Chapter 3 for more on themes).

> ✔ **Are there places where an oxymoron/metaphor/analogy/aphorism would enhance languaging and story recall?** Look through each paragraph and see if there are opportunities to use them.

> ✔ **Do you want the oxymoron/metaphor/analogy/aphorism to add humor to the story?** In what ways can you word it or position it in the story for humor to occur?

> ✔ **Do you want the oxymoron/metaphor/analogy/aphorism to enhance or add additional contrast?** In what ways can you do this?

> ✔ **Do you want the oxymoron/metaphor/analogy/aphorism to add human-like qualities to inanimate or non-human entities (personification)?** Personification is a way to give real-life or human-like qualities to objects: *The waterspout danced across the ocean.* Or: *The tiger glided along like a graceful ice skater.* In what ways might you be able to do this in your story?

Oxymorons

Oxymorons link two seemingly contradictory words together into the same phrase. One of the most common examples is the phrase *pretty ugly*. Others include phrases like *true lies, military intelligence, deafening silence*, and *a new classic*. These are all forms of contrast.

Sometimes it's hard to come up with oxymorons. Try this site to stimulate ideas: www.oxymoronlist.com.

Here's a way of inserting an oxymoron into Pam's story. Instead of simply saying, "When we got on, it was very hot. Normally an auxiliary power keeps the plane cool while it's on the ground when the engines aren't running. But either they didn't have one or it was broken" add "It was a fine mess" to the end of the paragraph after shortening the wording. *Fine mess* is an oxymoron and sums up the situation nicely while tickling our funny bone.

Notice that this oxymoron represents an emotion that people in the situation are feeling without having to explain a lot. When you're crafting really short stories, you'll find that all the figures of speech can help in this manner. Take another look at your story. In what ways could you use an oxymoron?

Metaphors and similes

Jumping for joy. The apple of my eye. Leaping with laughter. His stomach is a bottomless pit. All are examples of commonly used metaphors. For more, see www.buzzle.com/articles/metaphor-list.html.

Metaphors are when one thing is represented as, named as, or symbolically linked to something else. Our brains are stimulated by the juxtaposition as we play with linking them together to create a new picture and new meaning. Try this on for size. Reflect for a moment on what comes to mind when you hear the phrase *you're the light of my life*.

Avoid these common mistakes when using metaphors:

- ✔ **Steer clear of common, trendy, and overused metaphors like *fiscal cliff*.** They won't have the level of impact you may need for your story.

- ✔ **Avoid metaphors your audience won't understand.** If they don't know what *purgatory* is, then saying, "The team was headed into perpetual purgatory" will be meaningless.

- ✔ **Don't mix metaphors in the same sentence.** Replace "Our team was digging for treasure when our ship came in" with "Our team was digging for treasure when we struck gold."

Metaphors are very similar to but not quite the same as similes. A metaphor says that something is something else without using the words *like* or *as*. For example, "Your report *is* a bowl of bland oatmeal" is a metaphor. The *simile* would be, "Your report is *like* a bowl of bland oatmeal."

Use this comprehensive listing of similes to stimulate your imagination and develop your own: www.bartleby.com/161/.

Some metaphors and similes connect an abstract thought to something concrete and experiential. They help us construct meaning and structure thought. Consider these metaphors: time (abstract) is money (concrete) and his ideas (abstract) bore fruit (concrete); and these similes: as gentle (abstract) as a lamb (concrete) and as smart (abstract) as a fox (concrete).

Where might a metaphor work in Pam's story? Look at the new dialogue we added. Replacing the last sentence with a metaphor strengthens it even more:

> "You see . . . I haven't seen my daughter in quite some time. She was taken from me and I'm just getting her back. I've been looking for her for a long time. I was so scared that I'd never see her again. I really, really appreciate your understanding and your help. *You're a bright light in the dark of the night.*"

Now, one could argue that this metaphor can't be used because the woman may not have said this phrase. Keep in mind the essence of the comment has been kept intact. What we've done is strengthen the message through a device that also aids visualization and ultimately recall. We talked about this earlier in the chapter when we discussed dialogue.

What simile could we add to Pam's story? Consider: "The mom was very nervous because she didn't know how the child was going to behave on this very long flight in the middle of the night." Let's replace the first part of that with a simile so the sentence now becomes as follows:

> *The mom looked as anxious as a first-time flyer.* It was clear she didn't know how her child was going to behave on this long flight in the middle of the night.

What about your story? Where might you use metaphors and similes?

Analogies

Analogies make comparisons in slightly different ways by using contrasting elements. An analogy is a similarity between like features of two things, so a memorable comparison may be made. Here are a few examples:

- ✔ An annoying voice is akin to nails on a chalkboard.
- ✔ What a general is to an army, a CEO is to a company.
- ✔ Pen is to paper as a keyboard is to a computer.

Here's a listing of analogies to draw from: `http://fos.iloveindia.com/analogy-examples.html`. Here's another resource showing many types of analogies you can create (`http://www.spellingcity.com/analogies.html`).

Sometimes analogies come easy, sometimes they don't. We found one place where we could use an analogy in Pam's story to embellish it in a meaningful way. Here are the original sentences:

> I was trying to set the tone for the people sitting around the mother. I did see some eyes rolling. I saw some newspaper crunching. I saw people in business suits trying to relax, thinking, "This is going to be a very long night."

Here they are again, in final form, with an analogy:

> When I looked up, I saw some eyes roll and I heard the crunching of newspapers. *For some, children on planes are akin to dentists doing root canals.* No doubt those in business suits were thinking, "This is going to be a *very* long night."

Review your story again. Where might an analogy boost a section of it?

Aphorisms

Aphorisms are pithy observations that contain a general truth, much like a proverb. *A penny saved is a penny earned* and *A man is known by the company he keeps* are aphorisms. Here's a site that has captured a number of them: `www. faculty.rsu.edu/users/f/felwell/www/HomePage/aphorisms.htm`.

Pam has used her story at work in large group settings to illustrate two points:

- ✔ **Being open:** We don't always get to pick the "moments of truth" in our lives. Sometimes life picks them for us. But we do get to pick how we respond to them. We need to be open to seeing them when they come. And we need to be open to being "more" because of them.

- ✔ **Service:** We don't know where people have come from before they get to us and we don't always know where they are going when they leave us. All we know and have the power to influence is what they experience while they are in our care.

We've elected to focus on the second purpose and to edit the story with this theme in mind. This means we're only looking for aphorisms (sometimes called proverbs) about *service*. Some examples that came to mind include

- ✔ No act of kindness is too small.
- ✔ A good word costs no more than a bad one.
- ✔ Extending a hand into the darkness can pull another into the light.
- ✔ Pay it forward.

We elected to use *no act of kindness is too small.* In the next section, we give you one way to incorporate it into an action statement for the story.

Take another look at your story. Is there an aphorism that lends itself to the theme you've chosen?

Grab people's attention

Because stories inherently need to have a plot and conflict, heightened drama and tension are key. This means early on you'll want to reveal feelings around the troublesome situation. These might include fear, despondency, frustration, anxiety, or anger. Because we live in a world where we're bombarded with so much stimuli that we frequently tune out, our brains also hunt for — and delight in — novelty and surprises. They amplify engagement. Which means we need to find ways to incorporate all of these elements into a story.

Consider these questions when you want to embellish a story with more emotion, novelty, drama, and surprise:

- ✔ **What can you do to strengthen the emotions already resident in the story and where can you add them to keep people engaged?** For example, instead of describing a character as angry, find ways to demonstrate the anger through dialogue and actions. Also consider using emotional swings such as from happy to sad back to happy again — or from humored to shocked to contented. You don't want to leave your audience in a pit of despair. Nor do you want to spark really uncomfortable emotions in them without resolution. Adding more emotions into the story means you also need to keep them balanced.

- ✔ **What tension can you build into a story by waiting to reveal key pieces of information until the end?** People don't always need to know immediately _why_ something is happening in your story. If revealing this later on adds an element of surprise, delay mentioning it — as long as your intent isn't to manipulate others.

- ✔ **Does the nature of your story allow for humor?** Think about what kind of humor will work (dry, understated, overstated, witty, slapstick) and which is appropriate for the audience (considering such things as cultural background and physical location). Can you slip humor in as an aside, from you as the narrator? In a business setting, it's best to avoid biting sarcasm, put downs, sexual innuendos, ethnic/racial, religious, and political humor — in essence, anything someone might find offensive.

- ✔ **What unexpected event or decisions could you embellish or add into the story to add drama and surprise?** Maybe someone jumps out of a closet and shocks a person. Or maybe there are wrong choices your characters made that could be emphasized. Sometimes a word or phrase has multiple meanings that take listeners in one direction, when in fact, something else has happened. This can add an element of surprise, and even humor. For example, Lori tells a story of a CEO being interviewed on the phone for an article. He interrupts the call several times. The final time he says, "Can you hold for a sec? I've got a big fish here on the line and I'd like to reel him in." Listeners immediately assume he means a big deal when in fact he's in a boat in the middle of the lake, fishing.

✔ **What truly surprising obstacles are standing in the way of the main character?** You may be able to find ways to make the obstacles in the story more dramatic or difficult.

Let's address two things in more detail with Pam's story: the emotions one feels at the end of the story and how drama and surprise enter in. In Pam's story, it's easy for the ending to be somber. When Lori's told it in presentations, it's not unusual for a few folks to get teary-eyed. This is one story where it's important that the transition from the key message (*Take the time*) to the action statement (*Find a way to take the time to care about a colleague. Find a way to take the time to care about a friend. Even when you're sleeping, find a way to take the time to show somebody, anybody, that you care!*) has to include a focus on the resulting joy or hope. Here's one way this transition could happen — note the inclusion of the aphorism (italicized):

> While I've always felt I was a customer-focused person, I gained a new perspective that day on what it means to "take the time." You never know what people have been through before they get to you and you never know where they're going after they leave. The only thing you control is how well they're taken care of while they're with you.

> Imagine for a moment the joy that mom must have felt upon having been reunited with her daughter. And the immense gratitude she felt because someone took the time to care. This is exactly the sort of gratitude you have the power to create when you take the time to help others. *No act of kindness is too small.*

Now let's talk about surprise. Pam's story already has a surprise twist in it. If you've traveled by air, there were likely a few infants or young kids on the flight, and at least one probably cried at some point. That's not unusual. However, what isn't expected is why the child in Pam's story was crying — she'd just been reunited with her mom and was scared. To heighten this twist, keep the disclosure of this reason distanced from the context, challenge, and action. Make these three elements sound as typical and normal as possible. The surprise helps broaden the contrast between the challenge and the result.

In a story, one way to add drama and mystery is to use a *but* contradiction. The audience's imagination automatically starts filling in the blanks and trying to resolve the added tension. Here are some generic examples:

✔ It was sunny, *but* I was emotionally dark.

✔ I was happy as a lark *but* also blind as a bat about Tom.

✔ I went to my job interview *but* was totally clueless.

What can you do in your story to add emotion, novelty, drama, and surprise?

Use humor to lighten the mood

We're not fans of techniques like *Start your speech off with a joke* or *End on a funny note to keep them laughing.* If your humor is real and authentic, then go ahead and use it. But there's no reason to try to be funny or entertaining just because you believe that's what people want to hear. Make sure the humor fits with the setting, is respectful, and actually enhances your story.

Sometimes in the darkest of moments, humor can jump in and relieve the intensity of a situation. In Pam's story, one opportunity might be when she takes the little girl up to the front of the plane and makes a rattle. You could easily improvise in this section, depending on the audience. For example, you could step out of telling the story and make a comment directly to listeners — something like, "I'll bet some of you here would like a flight attendant kit to use at work" and then pause for the laugh before turning back into the story.

Doug Stevenson, author of *Doug Stevenson's Story Theatre Method* (Cornelia Press, 2008) says there are three dimensions to humor in storytelling:

- ✔ **Conceptual:** Conceptual comedy is cerebral. Sit down with a pen and paper and make lists of funny words and phrases and silly ideas and concepts that relate to your story — and start mixing the ingredients, like a chemist.

- ✔ **Physical:** How do you use your body, gestures, and facial expressions to invoke humor? Watch comedy shows and study the actors. For fun, watch a second time with the sound off. Note how they get laughs with or without words.

- ✔ **Vocal:** Pay close attention to rhythm, tempo, volume, inflection, and timing. How you deliver your lines is key to success. You can have great lines and deliver them horribly and lose the vitality of that moment.

Jeanne Robertson is a professional speaker who is fantastic at using humor dimensions within her storytelling. You can view several stories here: www.jeannerobertson.com/MeetingPlannerVideo.htm.

Here are techniques Doug Stevenson suggests in his *Story Theatre Newsletters* (November 2000, September 2005) to help add humor to a story:

- ✔ **The triple.** *Triples* get a laugh because of structure. When you provide one to illustrate a point, use three examples. The first two set a pattern; the third breaks it with a humorous twist. Here's one Doug uses about himself and his son: "My son Bennett and I couldn't be more different. I'm an extrovert, he's an introvert. I'm creative, he's linear. I'm verbal, he's an engineer." Why does this get a laugh? He starts with what's obvious and easy to grasp. Introvert and extrovert sets up a pattern of opposites. The words *creative* and *linear* continue this pattern — creative people are known to be non-linear thinkers. Now, the opposite of verbal is non-verbal. When he substitutes *engineer* for *non-verbal*, it's a surprise. The audience's expectations have been upended. The pattern is broken and gets a laugh.

✓ **Poke fun in a light-hearted way at common foibles and frictions in business and then provide a solution.** Stevenson uses the example of a sales meeting. They're often mandatory, boring, predictable, and too long. Try the techniques of a *setup line* (one or two short sentences) and the *payoff* (the laugh line). Here's an opportunity for sarcastic irony. You could say, "I always look forward to sales meetings (**setup**). They're so exciting (**payoff**). My favorites are the ones that last for four hours (**payoff**). And make me late for lunch . . . with a sales prospect (**payoff**)." Vocal delivery is key here — you'd need to pause after each payoff line, and then look like you discovered another reason before giving the next line. The solution is embodied in the talk that follows.

Once again, it's your turn. What can you do in your story to add humor?

Exaggerate to make your point

Exaggeration is a great embellishment device and comedic tool. Here are four ways to amplify characters, events, or obstacles to strengthen a point:

✓ **Exaggerate the characters and their personal characteristics such as physical body qualities and appearance.** For example, you could exaggerate a character by identifying an administrative assistant as "Miss Gatekeeper." Or, if describing someone making a cup of coffee, go into extreme, minute detail that is way over the top. Both methods can make people laugh because many of them have experienced something similar. Be mindful of your audience if you elect to use this approach.

✓ **Exaggerate an element of the story.** Examples of elements include time (*after six weeks, seven government holidays, and another 150 days of haggling*), the size or dimensions of an item (*it wasn't just a large box, it was the size of Fort Knox*), and something about geography or the location (*New York City isn't just five boroughs, it's the center of the universe*). It's okay to exaggerate beyond belief, too. Instead of saying, *The meeting didn't go well*, you could say, *World War III began in that meeting on Friday. There were hand grenades being lobbed over and under the table.*

✓ **Use repetition for emphasis and more punch.** We're not talking about being redundant and putting people to sleep by saying something like, *The value of having values is the value they bring to your organization's value proposition.* You don't want repetition to become your enemy. Here are some good examples:

- **Add the same word in a repetitive phrase.** For example: . . .*that we shall pay any price, bear any burden, meet any hardship, support any friend, oppose any foe to assure the survival and the success of liberty.* Here, John F. Kennedy uses the word *any* five times to emphasize the point being made in his 1961 inaugural address. An advertising jingle also demonstrates this type of repetition, which you can use in a story: "I'm a Pepper, he's a Pepper, she's a Pepper, we're a Pepper — wouldn't you like to be a Pepper, too? Be a Pepper, drink Dr. Pepper."

- **Repeat a word or phrase at the beginning of a sentence.** Select a word or phrase that would benefit your story through repetition at the beginning of each sentence in a section. Winston Churchill did this when he delivered a speech to the United Kingdom's House of Commons on June 4, 1940: *"We shall fight on the beaches, we shall fight on the landing grounds, we shall fight in the fields and in the streets, we shall fight in the hills."*

- **Repeat a word or phrase at the end of a sentence.** This section of Abraham Lincoln's Gettysburg Address is an example: *". . . and that government of the people, by the people, for the people shall not perish from the earth."*

✔ **Leverage the physical.** Use body movements, facial expressions, and varied vocal tone and volume when delivering different parts of the story to reinforce it. In Pam's story, when she talks to the little girl, she could exaggerate her tone as she would if she were talking to a little girl. She could also simulate kicking when talking about the little girl's behavior.

Before reading further, which technique might you use with your story?

Making the Story Memorable

We've spent time talking about how to increase a story's memorability in other chapters. This section explores various ways to deliver a key message and its associated actions and how to use tag lines and tangible story triggers within a story. We also address how to add action steps to Pam's story to strengthen how it ends and boost its overall impact.

Fix the key message and action

To embellish a story's key message, there are several options you can use to share it and move from the transition to the action statement (see bolded text):

✔ **Do you as narrator want to deliver the key message or do you want your character to deliver it?** The ending to the story shown in the "Heighten emotion, novelty, drama, and surprise" section is told from the perspective of Pam. If you were to tell it from the narrator's perspective, a few words would change slightly:

*While **Pam's** always **been** a customer-focused person, **she** gained a new perspective that day on what it means to "take the time." **As she says,** "You never know what people have been through before they get to you and you never know where they're going after they leave. The only thing you control is how well they're taken care of while they're with you."*

Imagine for a moment the joy that mom must have felt upon having been reunited with her daughter. And the immense gratitude she felt because Pam took the time to care. This is exactly the sort of outcome you have the power to create when you take the time to help others. No act of kindness is too small.

✔ **Is there a question you can pose to your audience that will add power to your key message?** Let's take the last paragraph from the preceding bullet and add a question to the end of it:

*Imagine for a moment the joy that mom must have felt upon having been reunited with her daughter. And the immense gratitude she felt because Pam took the time to care. This is exactly the sort of gratitude you have the power to create when you take the time to help others. No act of kindness is too small. **Each and every day, no matter how chaotic things might be, what can you do to take the time to show others that you truly care?***

✔ **Is there a quotation you can use to lead into the key message, giving it greater weight?** Here's how the key message of Pam's story sounds if we put a quotation before it:

***Ralph Waldo Emerson has said: "You cannot do a kindness too soon, for you never know how soon it will be too late."** While Pam's always been a customer-focused person, she gained this perspective on that day. She learned what it means to "take the time." As she says, "You never know what people have been through before they get to you and you never know where they're going after they leave. The only thing you control is how well they're taken care of while they're with you."*

✔ **Is there a personal reflection you can make that hammers home the key message's point?** Let's stay in narration mode and add this personal reflection into the transition to the action statement portion of the story:

*Imagine for a moment the joy that mom must have felt upon having been reunited with her daughter. And the immense gratitude she felt because Pam took the time to care. **Like Pam, I've experienced this sort of gratitude when I took the time to listen to a coworker when my schedule didn't allow it.** No act of kindness is too small.*

✔ **Do you want to repeat the key message several times or is there a short phrase you can repeat to make the takeaway more memorable?** Here's one way to do this with Pam's story — and add in a bit of humor:

Imagine for a moment the joy that mom must have felt upon having been reunited with her daughter. And the immense gratitude she felt because Pam took the time to care. This is exactly the sort of gratitude you have the power to create when you take the time to help others. No act of kindness is too small. **Find a way at work to take the time to care about a colleague. Find a way at home to take the time to care about a friend. Even when you're sleeping, find a way to take the time to show somebody that you care!**

Back again to your story. Which of these approaches best fits with it?

Identify tag lines

A *tag line* is a phrase that's a memorable way to refer to your story. It could be an analogy, aphorism, or metaphor. It might be one theme from the story. It could also be the story's key message. Steer clear of using the tag line to title the story, though, if it's also the key message. Why? It'll give away the outcome and could cause people not to read or listen to it. This is what news reports do. To arrive at a tag line, think of the crux of the story or the key message. Note as many answers to these questions as you can. Select the one you like best:

✔ Can you create a tag line without giving away the essence of the story?

✔ What tone is important? Funny? Serious? How can a tag line help differentiate you, a product/service, or your organization?

✔ What tag line might connect to what someone wants or needs to answer?

✔ Can one of your story's aphorisms or analogies be turned into a tag line?

✔ How can you include LOTS, a metaphor, or contrast in the tag line?

For Bob's story, which is in the appendix, the tag line is "Make Things Happen." Here are a few ideas we generated for Pam's story:

✔ A Bright Light in the Dark of the Night

✔ The Truth Reveals Itself

✔ Cranky in the Cabin

✔ Seeing the Light at 30,000 Feet

We elected to use a tag line to title the story because it doesn't allude to the key message. The one we chose is "A Bright Light in the Dark of the Night." Now it's your turn. What tag line fits best with your story?

Putting All This Together for Pam's Story

Let's put all of these layers together into Pam's final story (our rendition of it) so we can see how it all hangs together. You do the same with yours!

A Bright Light in the Dark of the Night

I was one of five flight attendants working a red eye flight on a weekday evening from San Francisco to Minneapolis. When we got on, the plane was stifling hot. It was hot outside and the auxiliary power unit that keeps the plane cool wasn't working. What a fine mess.

We'd just completed all our checks when the passengers started to board. People couldn't help but stare at a mother and her two-year old daughter as they made their way down the aisle. The little girl was wearing a short sleeve white shirt with flowers on it and a pair of hot pink shorts. Her sandy blond hair was in pigtails. As she wailed, a river of tears streamed from her puffy green eyes.

The mom looked as anxious as a first-time flyer. It was clear she didn't know how her child was going to behave on this long flight in the middle of the night. (**context**)

They had two seats in the very last row, next to a man seated by the window. The little girl couldn't sit still. She kept trying to stand up. And she kept kicking and punching the seat in front of her. When her mom tried to hold her, she pushed away. To make matters worse, the plane was packed. There were no empty seats or luggage bins on this Boeing 757. (**challenge**)

I decided to speak with the mother and her daughter. If a stranger talks to kids, they get quiet and attach to their parent. This actually helps calm them down. I said, "If she starts to cry during the flight it's probably because her little ears hurt and she doesn't know what's going on. We all need to be patient with this and I know we will." I spoke loud enough so people could understand that the child might be scared or distressed. Flying is hard on kids.

As I looked up I saw some eyes roll and I heard the crunching of newspapers. For some, children on planes are akin to dentists doing root canals. No doubt those in business suits were thinking, "This is going to be a _very_ long night."

The plane took off and the little girl continued to squirm and fuss. The mom tried to do everything she could to calm her. I came by again and asked the girl, "I'm really busy right now but when I'm finished with my work can I come back and talk with you? The little girl responded, "Yes." (**action**)

I said, "I've got something to show you." I gave her a pin shaped like a set of wings. She rewarded me with a smile.

After I was done giving out snacks and beverages and the lights had been turned down, I returned to the rear of the plane. The little girl was still uncomfortable. "Are you thirsty?," I asked. "Yes," she whispered. I asked the mom, "Would it be okay if I took your daughter on a walk to get something to drink?" She just nodded. I could see that she was very, very tired. I took the little girl's hand and we went up to the front of the plane and got some juice. Then we made a toy by putting stir sticks inside of two plastic cups that I bound together with Band-Aids. You have no idea how creative we can be with all the items in a flight attendant kit. I even got a giggle out of her. Then I walked her back to her mom. She finally settled in for the night and fell asleep. (**action**)

I was sitting in the rear of the plane doing a little reading when the mother came back and asked if we could talk. We went in the galley — close enough where she could see her daughter but far enough away where we could have a conversation. She said, "Thank you for being so kind. I know this has not been an easy situation for you. I really appreciate the extra care." I replied, "You're welcome. I'm glad I could be of help."

In a halting voice, she continued to speak, "You see . . . I haven't seen my daughter in quite some time. She was taken from me and I'm just getting her back. I've been looking for her for a long time. I was so scared that I'd never see her again. I really, really appreciate your understanding and your help. You're a bright light in the dark of the night." (**result**)

I paused before saying, "What an incredible story. You're an amazing person to put in the effort to get your daughter back. She'll always be worth it. It's probably going to take a while for things to get back to normal. I know this is very personal to you and I appreciate you taking the time to tell me. It means a lot."

While I've always felt I was a customer-focused person, I gained a new perspective that day on what it means to "take the time." You never know what people have been through before they get to you and you never know where they're going after they leave. The only thing you control is how well they're taken care of while they're with you. (**lesson**)

Imagine for a moment the joy that mom must have felt upon having been reunited with her daughter. And the immense gratitude she felt because someone took the time to care. This is exactly the sort of gratitude you have the power to create when you take the time to help others. No act of kindness is too small. Find a way to take the time to care about a colleague. Find a way to take the time to care about a friend. Even when you're sleeping, find a way to take the time to show somebody, anybody, that you care! (**suggested action**) *Used with permission. Copyright © 2003 by Pam Stampen. Told by Pam Stampen and polished by Lori L. Silverman and Karen Dietz. All rights reserved.*

Chapter 8

What to Do About Data

*W*hether it's business communication or performance management, Karen's MBA students have to produce a presentation/report in story form — which must include at least two pieces of academic research, with data, to back up their arguments — to influence corporate executives to support and take action on a proposed project. They do pretty well until they get to the research articles. Then they fumble. They have tremendous difficulty blending research and data into stories.

What do they do instead? They throw some dense quotes on a slide or a page and wash their hands of it. Or they leave citations at the end of a PowerPoint presentation or a report and never weave them into the document. Sometimes they provide a convoluted chart. Every time, the transitions between the rest of the presentation and the research and the data are rocky.

You likely have this same issue in your work — times when you need to share research or data in your stories. Consider these situations:

✔ Raising awareness about your research findings

✔ Seeking support and using data to add credibility

✔ Producing a new strategy and validating it with data

✔ Clarifying a controversial issue using data or research

✔ Providing data for policy or executive decision-making

✔ Redirecting program or project priorities using the latest research

This chapter explores the unintended effect data has on audiences and how to successfully integrate data into stories while maintaining their power.

Specific techniques for how to share research and data are included, along with how to incorporate complex information, how to make data visual, and when and where to bring data into stories and presentations.

Engaging the Brain

We both like to do the following in workshops: We start by sharing a well-crafted, compelling story. Then somewhere along the way we read part of a research article or a data-rich piece. We ask listeners to raise their hand when they want us to stop. It doesn't take long — 90 seconds at best, somewhere in the second paragraph — before arms start shooting up in the air.

We ask them to describe what happened. They always say these things:

✔ I couldn't think anymore. I got tired.

✔ I couldn't remember what you were saying.

✔ I became totally overwhelmed. My brain hurt.

✔ My mind switched off and I was bored.

✔ I started to daydream and not pay attention.

When asked to repeat back to us what we said, they say, "No." Ever wonder why this happens? If so, read on!

The limbic system is the emotional part of the brain. This part likes stories. It releases oxytocin, dopamine, and serotonin, which stimulate feelings of reward and connection. Compelling visuals and storied infographics can spark the same reaction.

Stories connect directly to the limbic system, but data and information don't. That's why you get the reactions you do when you read research and data-laden articles to others. We don't deny that plenty of minds like information and data. In fact, we're both people who love playing around with numbers to see trends and patterns. Only, we've learned over the years to present story first, data second. And we know how to take data and lay it out as a story.

Think of data in its raw form as a tool. A tool can reveal and help tell stories, but the tool itself isn't a story. Without a translation into meaning, a bunch of data is just that — a bunch of data. Here's a secret: Data isn't worth much unless it's related to something that people are doing. Once you know what your data is trying to say, then you have to figure out how to relay this message to another human being. The human experience is the main experience; the data needs to enhance it. Your job is to make the data story relevant — to spark an emotional or even spiritual — reaction in someone and then move them to action.

Think about it this way. What you have is "not just a bucket of numbers," says Nathan Yau, author of *Visualize This: The Flowing Data Guide to Design, Visualization, and Statistics* (Wiley, 2011). "There are stories in that bucket. There's meaning, truth, and beauty." He goes on to say, "Sometimes you're not looking for analytical insight. Rather . . . you can tell the story from an emotional point of view that encourages [listeners] to reflect on the data."

Distinguishing Data and Information

For clarity, let's distinguish between data and information. By *data* we mean hard data: charts, graphs, facts, numbers, and statistical information. Data is cold and objective. Story, which is warm and subjective, is the vehicle for conveying data. Zachary Meisel and Jason Karlawish, both physicians from the Perelman School of Medicine at the University of Pennsylvania, argue why this is the case in the field of medicine (http://scienceprogress. org/2011/11/the-importance-of-narrative-in-communicating- evidence-based-science/). They say:

> Facts and figures are essential, but insufficient, to translate the data and promote the acceptance of evidence-based practices and policies. Narratives — in the forms of storytelling, testimonials, and entertainment — have been shown to improve individual health behaviors in multiple settings. Moreover, evidence from social psychology research suggests that narratives, when compared with reporting statistical evidence alone, can have uniquely persuasive effects in overcoming preconceived beliefs and cognitive biases.

We believe that's true in other data-intensive industries and fields as well. Take a look at the next example in technology sales.

Dave Brock, CEO of Partners In EXCELLENCE, talks about a challenge when he was the COO of a startup company. As he tells it:

> We provided high end data analytic solutions. Our technology was overwhelming. We were able to solve problems people had never been able to address . . . and provide insights that were previously unthinkable. The problems we solved were BIG problems. With one customer, in just one part of the business, we enabled them to save a $100M annual contract with a customer. Other problems [we solved] produced business value on a grand scale. But we had problems in closing deals. Our prospects could see the analysis, the output of our analysis, and data presented in a compelling manner — yet we struggled with closing [these] deals.

> Suddenly, one of our sales people discovered the secret — it was stories. With stories, all of a sudden the data had a context, it had meaning, [and] people could create mental pictures of what we were presenting. They [became] emotionally engaged with what had previously been very abstract (http://partnersinexcellenceblog.com/sales-marketing-big-data-and-stories/).

Now let's talk about information. By *information*, we mean a description of the data, often presented in conceptual language. *Conceptual language* is composed of words for non-physical objects and abstract ideas. Unlike perceptions — specific images of individual objects — concepts can't be easily visualized. You may wonder how you can storify information if it's conceptual. See the next example.

Here's a random example of conceptual language from the results of an actual study, "The Spiral of Silence and Fear of Isolation," by Kurt Neuwirth, Edward Frederick, and Charles Mayo:

> This study provides general support for propositions about fear of isolation derived from the SOS literature and, overall, provides at least partial support for the bulk of the hypotheses set forth in the study. In particular, the results (a) demonstrate the construct validity of fear of isolation measures and the apparent utility of employing scales derived from the communication apprehension (CA) literature . . .

Let's say you wanted to substitute more conversational language yet still sound professional. You might say the following:

> This study supports general ideas about fear and isolation from previous research. The results show that the measures used to determine silence and the fear of isolation are still valid.

Now let's sketch out the beginning of a raw story about this research:

> Three separate researchers from around the country got together just before the U.S. Congressional elections in the fall of 2002. They asked themselves, "How are fear and isolation expressed in people's opinions? Are historical research methods still valid?" One of them said, "Let's focus on the opinions people express around the debate of whether the United States should invade Iraq." They did. Here's what they found . . .

Information is great, but it's a description, not a story, so it's really not helpful. You need to figure out how to draw meaning and conclusions from it.

When melding story with data or information, your task is to find ways to link the data and information to lived experience so you get the best of both worlds. You need to shift from viewing data as an accounting of something to incorporating personal evaluation and learning experiences. Remember, you need to transform data and information into the ability to take action.

Making Sense versus Making Meaning

Data and information — and the reporting of complex research — are about *sense-making*. Here are reactions you'll get when you use sense-making:

- ✔ Oh.
- ✔ I understand.
- ✔ That makes sense.

On the other hand, story is all about *meaning-making*. Here are some reactions you'll get when you use meaning-making:

- ✔ A-ha! Now I know what to do.
- ✔ I get it and I'm motivated to make something happen as a result.
- ✔ This is how it connects to me.

You need to stretch into meaning-making when melding data and storytelling together. It's not enough to wrap graphics around the numbers and deliver them in a slick package. Nor is it the responsibility of the audience to figure out what you're trying to say or show them, or to extrapolate meaning from the numbers. It's you — the person sharing the data — who has to craft and tell the story. The reaction you want to strive for is, "A-ha! I get it. This is how this data relates to me. I now know what action to take."

Here's a before-and-after example so you can get a handle on the difference between sense-making and meaning-making. It's based on some really cool research conducted by Deborah Small, George Loewenstein, and Paul Slovic (`http://opim.wharton.upenn.edu/risk/library/J2007OBHDP_DAS_sympathy.pdf`). Here's what they concluded. As you read, note your reactions:

> Apparently, statistical information dampens inclination to give to an identifiable victim. This result is consistent with the tendency to give less to an identifiable victim after learning about the discrepancy in giving. When jointly evaluating statistics and an individual victim, the cause evidently becomes less compelling. This could occur in part because statistics diminish the reliance on one's affective reaction to the identifiable victim when making a decision.

The first time we read this, we said, "Huh? What do they mean?" So we went back and read it again. Did you? With no interpretation of what this research means, you're left to your own devices to figure it out — if you have time to do so. In work situations, when results like this are presented along with numbers, some people are naturally inclined to debate the statistics with you. That doesn't help further the conversation relative to meaning-making.

Now, here's the same research as it might typically be delivered in a presentation. As you read this version, note your reaction:

> Deborah Small, a researcher at the University of Pennsylvania, teamed up with two colleagues in other parts of the country to conduct some interesting research. They divided subjects into three groups. The first group received information about a nonprofit and data about its relief programs. The second group received a story about the plight of a young girl and the difference the organization's services made in her life. The third group received both the story with the data. Everyone was given five one-dollar bills and was asked to make a contribution. The first group gave a small amount. The second group, who received the story, gave the largest amount. The third group, who received both the story and the data, gave the same small amount as the first group.

Did you react with "Huh, this is interesting" or "Wow, this is fascinating — I need to tell someone . . . or change my behavior"? Chances are you had the former reaction — a sense-making response — because the information is a description. We still don't have a storified version of this research.

Let's take another stab at transforming this research into a story — one that involves asking listeners a few questions. By the way, this is our rendition of what we think happened based on what's in the research study. It's the version we share in webinars, where we have no ability to get visual cues about whether people are absorbing the content. (We'd tell it a bit differently if we were sharing it in person.) Note your reactions to this version:

> Have you ever wanted to know the *real secret* to getting people to reach into their back pocket, grab their wallet, open it up, and give you money? Deborah Small, a researcher at the University of Pennsylvania, teamed up with two colleagues in other parts of the country to conduct several rounds of experiments to answer that question.

> Participants were divided into three groups. The first group received lots of information about a nonprofit — all the kinds of things you would typically hear: how many years they'd been in existence, the size of their annual budget, how much they spent on various programs, demographic information about their constituents, the size of their staff, a list of their funding sources, and the like.

> The second group received a story about a young girl who lacked food, clothing, housing, and education and how difficult it was for her to live on a daily basis. The nonprofit had provided her with a variety of services which had made a significant difference in her life.

> The third group was given both the story about the young girl and all of the information about the nonprofit that was shared with the first group.

Everybody was given five one-dollar bills and asked the exact same thing: "Please donate." They all made donations. The first group, who received only the information, gave, but only a small amount. The second group, who received the story, gave more than twice as much as the first group.

Now, how much money do you think the group that heard both the story and the information donated? Did you guess that this group gave even more money than the one that received only the story? If so, guess again. Now, this may surprise you. The group that heard the story and the data and information together gave the exact same *tiny* amount as that group that only heard the information. Oh, my heavens. How can this be? It's so counterintuitive!

What do you think happened to generate these results?

Here's what Deborah and her colleagues learned: Data and information didn't create empathy toward the nonprofit or the constituents it serves. As a result, only a small amount of money was donated.

On the other hand, when a story — and only a story — was shared, significant empathy was produced toward the young girl in the story, and people willingly gave more. They could identify with both the girl and her challenges and the difference the nonprofit made in her life.

For the group who heard the story along with the data and information, the researchers hypothesized that the accompanying data and information completely undermined any empathy that the story had created, leaving people with the same lack of emotional connection that the first group experienced. And that's why they gave the exact same tiny amount as the first group.

What's your reaction to this storified version of the research? Did you say, "Wow. That's really interesting. I need to change the way I'm communicating at work." If so, meaning-making has occurred. Which is exactly what you want to do with all that research, data, and information you share at work.

What we also love about this research on sympathy and callousness is that it demonstrates how sharing a story involving one character whom everyone can identify with creates connection and empathy, whereas straight data — or even data combined with a story — leaves us feeling disconnected and cold.

 Numbers affect the left brain. They don't connect emotionally with people. When we remain emotionally neutral, it's easy to fall into debate. Which means you'll likely not get the buy-in you need. Instead, craft a story to tell about the numbers. It'll generate both learning *and* the motivation for action.

 As an aside, when sharing a story based on research, it's perfectly fine to provide the title of the study or offer the article. If you're sharing it in a report, add the citation so others can go back and read it if they'd like.

Including Data Is a Must: What to Do

What do you do when you absolutely must include data with your story? Recognize that both need context. *Context* is more than background information. It also answers the question, "What does this mean?" The purpose of data is to inform people. *You* have the job of interpreting it and telling your audience about the data's impact — creating *meaning* from it.

How do you do this? Sit quietly with the data. Continually ask, "What's this data trying to tell me/us?" Here are other ways of asking this question:

- ✔ **What do people really need to get out of this data?** Think of yourself as a tour guide. Share the who, what, where, when, and why surrounding the data and its collection. How can you make it simple to understand?

- ✔ **Why is it so important that I show this data to others?** Show what's unique about the data. What can they not do if they don't hear this? Or what do they need to stop doing?

- ✔ **What's the topic of the data really about?** This isn't always easy to determine. It's not always about the surface information that the data relay. You need to dig deeper.

- ✔ **What one piece of data will make someone's eyes pop open?** Did something unexpectedly surprise you? Did the data change over time?

- ✔ **What comparisons, trends, patterns, and relationships define the data?** Think about how you can best display and communicate these. Bring connections to life for people.

- ✔ **What do I think the reader should get out of this?** List all the messages the data communicates that are important to relay.

- ✔ **What's the number one reason you are showing this data?** Go through the messages you've already noted and figure out which is most critical to relay to get people to take a specific action.

Now that you have a better sense of what to communicate, here are some pointers to follow to take a deeper dive into creating a story from these data:

- ✔ **Find the face behind the data.** That human face is the main character of your story. It humanizes everything. Tell that person's story and then relate the data to it. Find and weave together little data points of human behavior into a compelling narrative.

- ✔ **Find the dilemma that you want your data to illustrate or inform.** What's the problem or conflict your data raises about the human face behind the data?

✔ **There's no need to include all the data.** That's why we asked you a bunch of questions about what the data means. Determine what's most important to achieving the outcome you're going after.

✔ **Decide on a story structure that helps organize the data and relay the story it tells.** At the very least, make sure your data is presented with a beginning, a middle, and an end. Use the structures from Chapter 7 or consider these other concrete ways to tell a story with data:

- **The Deductive Argument Wrapped in a Story Approach:** Set the context first. Tell your audience the dilemma (problem or conflict) and then run deductively through the steps. *Deductively* means: To do X, you have to take steps A, then B, then C, then D, and then E to reach the conclusion, F. If you take those steps, you'll work through the challenges and resolve the situation. This will lead to your key message.

- **The Butler Did It Approach:** The book *Freakonomics* by Steven D. Levitt and Stephen J. Dubner (William Morrow, 2009) uses this technique. When discussing the drop in the U.S. crime rate since the 1970s, the authors set up the beginning of the story with the context, characters, and problem. Then they go through the data. Instead of giving a chart explaining the number one reason for the drop in crime rates, they pose seven other possible reasons. Could it be this one? Could it be the next one? Maybe it's this reason. They present the final accurate reason as the last option, deliver their interpretation, and then provide the key message.

- **Set Your Story as a Map Approach.** Think of the data as presenting a journey in visual format across space and time. Mapping is as old as the hills. Think about mapping land masses, the human body, time, and the stars. All have a story to share. You can craft a map to tell a story about a journey a character takes. Decide on your key message and action steps and then work through your data or research to display it as a map that helps you deliver the story.

In addition to the key message — the action you want your audience to take after hearing the story — make sure readers or the audience also receive a takeaway about the data or research. Craft it as an *a-ha* moment (a new piece of knowledge) in the story.

Create frames for the data

Language always comes with what's called framing. *Framing* helps people communicate about reality. Framing focuses people's attention, helps them make sense of the world, and provides a quick and easy way to process information so that it's personally meaningful.

Recall the compassion and sympathy research from earlier in the chapter. There are two possible frames that could be used, depending on the audience:

- ✔ **Raising money:** This frame could be used for any audience where donations need to be obtained internally (a business leader seeking funding for an initiative) or externally (funding from financial institutions).

- ✔ **Closing sales:** This frame could be used when speaking to sales staff or account managers — or business leaders concerned about sales.

There's also a third frame that we use with both audiences: *This is a secret.* Why? Scarcity is a tool of influence, and secrets are a form of scarcity: "I know something you don't know and I trust you with it." The compassion and sympathy research truly is a very special piece of research — not a boring project or a common tip. This third frame captures people's attention and connects to an age-old mythological quest for the secrets of a successful life.

Now go back to your story. What frame works best for the audience who will hear or read it? Is there an additional frame you want to use to make the data stand out as unique in some fashion? Add them in.

There are two additional ways to frame data: Leveraging metaphors and using simple contrast.

Leverage metaphors

The best type of framing to use when sharing data is to find a metaphor. How do you find that metaphor? Go back and take a look at Chapter 7. The metaphor you select needs to reflect how you want your audience to think about the data or the facts you're presenting to them.

At the beginning of strategic planning, Lori has her clients conduct an environmental scan, looking out at least five years at the economy, technology, future consumers, and the like. She immerses them in the future. Then she has them compare that future to what exists today. One firm gave her reams of historical financial data. She had a statistician plot it onto control charts to assess variability over time. Something startling appeared: The firm appeared to be going out of business and didn't even know it. When she shared the charts with the firm's partners, instead of talking about each chart, she told a story using the metaphor of a slow-moving cancer to describe the situation. Lori talked about a person who didn't feel well, and then got better and forgot about it. A few weeks later he felt worse, got concerned, but still didn't do anything once the symptoms went away. After a long while, the symptoms didn't fully disappear. He learned he had a slow-moving type of cancer that was progressively getting worse — it was now Stage 4. If he continued to ignore it, death was on the horizon. The time had passed for researching it further. Action needed to be taken immediately.

Go back and take another look at your data. What metaphor can you use within your story to help frame the material and generate meaning?

Use simple contrast

Using *contrast* — comparing things to highlight differences — is another great way to frame data. In her book *Resonate: Present Visual Stories that Transform Audiences* (Wiley, 2010), Nancy Duarte shares a very effective technique for using contrast when presenting information. She suggests going back and forth between painting a picture of the present-day problem and envisioning a desirable future. This not only builds urgency, but also the desire to take action. We talk more about this approach in Chapter 16.

The same technique can help you when presenting your data. Contrast the desirable against the undesirable scenarios or expose the difference between present-day data and future opportunities that the information might be indicating. You can also use before-and-after pictures. Make sure your visuals show a contrasting shift from one situation to another.

Return to your data. What contrasts can you highlight? And what's the best way for you to do so within your story?

Massaging Complex Data

Imagine a group of physicians and medical staff from the U.S. Department of Veterans Affairs who were tasked with traveling around the country to train other VA physicians and staff in new ways of delivering patient care. This multi-day training was one continuous PowerPoint presentation. The slides were dense, and the amount of information was vast. No slide was allowed to be changed. Of course, the biggest challenge was how to transfer all this knowledge in ways that made it meaningful and memorable.

What did they do to overcome this issue? Each person took a slide and circled one piece of knowledge on it that listeners needed to walk away with. That became the key message. Then each person found a personal story that delivered that key message. When the slide came on the screen, the person shared that personal story and delivered the key message. Following this, using the story and key message, the individual referenced the remainder of the complex information on that slide. It worked like a charm. Instead of getting glassy-eyed stares, it was obvious the audience was learning.

If you have complex data to communicate in a slide show, you can use this technique to tell a series of stories about the data. Or storyboard the data to see how it flows together, reveal what pieces might need to be added, and allow the story to emerge from this process. That will help you figure out what data to show and in what form it needs to be displayed in.

It's easy to fall into the *so what?* syndrome with highly complex data. Here's how it happens: Because we dig into the data ourselves, we become entranced with the process of crunching numbers and making charts. We can't wait to show the fruits of our labors. We excitedly present it to a group. But they look at us like we're crazy. Inside, they're saying, "So what? Who cares?" If you can't answer these questions, no amount of tinkering with data will work.

Break data into bite-size chunks

When it comes to data, small is beautiful. Big is not. Break large amounts of complex data into easily digestible pieces. Instead of feeding each person an entire, super-rich ice cream bar in 20 minutes, give them bite-size miniatures they can savor. Share your data in small bits and bytes so the audience can digest what you're saying, comprehend it, and create meaning from it. The left brain needs time to process the information and "get it."

Especially today. More than ever, people are exposed to increasingly chaotic situations. And that's not going away, given our dependency on technology. How does this impact communications? It means you need to lower the complexity associated with them. For example, if you're dealing with a rapidly changing marketplace with new competitors, you need to make the story and the action steps associated with it as simple as you can. The last thing you want to do is present a complex plan. People's brains will go into overload and explode or get paralyzed. In any case, action won't happen.

Display complex data so it tells a story

Several times we've mentioned moving through your data as though you're taking others on a journey. An easy way to do this is to take a story structure from Chapter 7 and share your data using it. Here's an example:

Let's say you're looking at a chart about the consumption of animal proteins from 1910 to 2008 (http://13pt.com/projects/nyt110315/) and want to share it in a presentation. The chart shows the consumption of lamb, veal, turkey, fish and shellfish, chicken, eggs, pork, and beef. The data for each are displayed across a timeline that includes World War I, the Great Depression, World War II, the Korean War, and the Vietnam War. The chart also shows the year the first and the 1,000th McDonald's restaurant opened. Talk about a lot of data!

How do you take someone on a story journey to understand this chart? First, figure out the key message. For us, it's *Make a conscious choice*. With this key message in mind, here's how we might share this data as a story using the PARLAS structure. As we did, we'd point to the data on the chart:

Since my husband's heart problem a few years ago, we've been more concerned about how much beef we eat. **(problem)** I don't recall eating a lot of beef growing up, so I wondered, "How has consuming proteins like chicken, fish, beef, and pork changed over time in the U.S.?"

One day while taking a break, I decided to poke around the Internet and do some research. **(action)** I was curious about a few things. Was pork gaining in popularity over time? Are people eating more or less chicken today? If our oceans are being overfished, does that mean we're eating more fish? And has beef consumption really risen all that much? Inquiring minds want to know!

It didn't take me long before I came across this particular chart. As I stared at it, several things popped out right away. First, I was really amazed at how popular chicken had become. I'd assumed that people were eating pretty much the same amount of chicken over time. I guess that's because we were always eating chicken at my grandparent's farm.

And, despite all of the news about the oceans being overfished, instead of finding a big spike like I was expecting, I found only a tiny increase.

That made me curious about how much lamb and veal people were eating today. They've actually been on a slight decline. That didn't surprise me. I'd never eaten lamb or veal until I was a young adult.

I was also startled to find pork had remain pretty stable, despite how popular bacon has become. It seemed to me that we were always eating baked ham, bacon, and ham balls when I was a kid.

But here's the kicker: The link between the dramatic rise in beef intake and the popularity of McDonald's was stunning. **(results)** Now I'm sure it's not the only reason people love beef, but it's a big influence.

In the end, here's what I gained from this chart: Fast food has radically changed our diets. **(learning)** Personally, I choose to opt out of its advertising influence because I know I have to *make a conscious choice* over the foods I eat. **(suggested action)** Now, what does this chart say to you? Do you need to make a conscious choice over what you eat?

Crafting a Great Story with Data

What a challenge you have when crafting a story, especially if all you have is data. First, you have to aggregate the *data* together and then you have to assemble it into meaningful *information*. After that, you have to figure out what *knowledge* — concepts — it communicates and how to bring about enhanced *understanding*. Finally, you need to move to *wisdom*: increasing the effectiveness of people's actions. This continuum is commonly called the DIKW Model, or Wisdom Hierarchy (http://en.wikipedia.org/wiki/DIKW).

Let's look at a simplified version of this continuum as a visual metaphor for baking a cake (www.scoop.it/t/just-story-it/p/322960589/data-cake-a-brilliant-visual-metaphor-for-data). It goes like this:

- ✔ **Picture 1:** A bowl of flour and a separate bowl with four eggs. This is your *data*.

- ✔ **Picture 2:** A freshly baked two-layer cake cooling on a rack. Your data has now turned into meaningful *information*.

- ✔ **Picture 3:** Each layer of the cake now has white frosting on it. Your information has now been decorated for *presentation*.

- ✔ **Picture 4:** An empty plate with a few remaining cake crumbs. Your cake has now been ingested; the result is *knowledge*.

If you were to extrapolate to *wisdom*, you'd have to ask yourself what could you now do differently and more effectively having eaten the cake?

The next section takes a look at how to use visuals in your story to depict data, information, knowledge, and understanding — and how best to organize this material so it moves people to wisdom.

Create compelling visuals

Earlier we explained the difference between sense-making and meaning-making. Here's a beginning list of commonly used sense-making tools that folks tend to use when illustrating their data and information — often these are enhanced with various colors, sizes, and layouts:

- ✔ Proportions
- ✔ Axes
- ✔ Shapes
- ✔ Flow
- ✔ Matrixes

- Comparisons
- Distributions
- Correlations
- Densities
- Mapping
- Charts, graphs, and graphic lines
- Dimensions
- Patterns
- Bar values
- Stacking
- Connectors

Data visualization isn't about displaying numbers. Data visuals help explain complicated material in a simple way. Because data arrives in a messy, raw state, your job is to find a way to organize it visually. It needs to come together in a way that shares a story and potentially makes a point. Some data visuals don't need to make a point. They might promote a cause or point of view. Some data can be displayed such that we *get it* by simply *viewing it* — so beginnings, middles, and ends don't apply. Much like a subway map, which is designed to provide information. It doesn't need to tell a story.

But if you want to use data and data visualization to move people to action, then melding story and data together is essential. Here are some guidelines:

1. **Show, don't tell.** Leverage the power of images and imagery. When creating your visuals with words, at some point turn off or remove all of the text to see if your piece still tells a story. Words can be a crutch.

2. **Decide what you really want to happen when presenting the visual.** Go back to the DIKW model. Do you want to relay knowledge or understanding? Promote interaction and sharing between people? Cause a strong emotional reaction?

3. **Never assume that your graphics in and of themselves are going to tell anyone anything.** Graphics are often treated as mere eye candy. People like eye candy. Just don't sacrifice your story for eye candy.

4. **If the data tells a great story, pictures and graphics don't need to be slick.** If they're too flashy, they can be distracting and undermine the story you're trying to tell. It's easy to get caught in the trap of thinking that the data is what needs emphasis, when the real key to success is the story about the data. This is no different than where you place emphasis when you say the word syllable (sy-LLAB-le or SYL-la-ble).

Information graphics, or *infographics*, are a popular way to present complex and significant amounts of data, information, or knowledge graphically. They can be educational, humorous, controversial, or newsworthy. (Here's a website that has numerous infographics for you to explore: `http://visual.ly/`.)

Many infographics present a problem but no resolution. Without a resolution, the data doesn't stick. Sometimes, viewers are left to their own devices to finish interpreting the data and make it meaningful and applicable to their own lives. The infographic that took lots of time and labor to create is quickly forgotten or ignored. Don't let this happen to you! Add these story elements from Chapters 6 and 7 to enhance meaning-making and overall value:

- ✔ **Relatable characters:** Connect insights to individual characters.
- ✔ **Problem-resolution displays:** Either show a solution or offer ways to shift/change/act on an issue so it's resolved.
- ✔ **Story triggers:** Use words or graphics that spark a story within the mind of the viewer.
- ✔ **Metaphors:** Compare data to something that's symbolic of something else.
- ✔ **Novelty or cleverness:** Say something surprising about your data/information.
- ✔ **Contrast:** Use vivid examples to emphasize differences.
- ✔ **Emotions:** Make your audience feel something about the data.
- ✔ **Movement through time:** Show how change happens.
- ✔ **Story arc:** Show the shift in awareness that occurs.
- ✔ **Key message and action statement:** Make the story meaningful by the end and give listeners concrete steps to take.

Find the key message: Data into meaning

You still have to find a way to inspire people to action (wisdom) when you craft a story that's all data. When you're presenting lots and lots of data — which implies complexity — keep the chaos associated with it very low. Get rid of anything that smacks of confusion, disorder, or messiness.

Let's look at some possible key messages for an infographic. Here's one infographic that is a story: www.fastcocreate.com/1680831/charity-aspire-gets-funding-through-targeted-emails-bearing-mini-graphic-novels. It's from a U.K.-based charity called Aspire, which obtains specialized lightweight wheelchairs for individuals who have spinal cord injuries. How would you state its key message? We came up with these two ideas:

- ✔ **Make people more mobile.**
- ✔ **Change a life with a chair.** (Our choice.)

Move to action when data's involved

Let's take the key message for this infographic and follow it with a transition and an action statement specific to it. The audience is brand managers whose companies in the sports, automotive, and male grooming industries were targeted to provide sponsorships. Here's one option for wording:

> Did you know that every eight hours someone in the U.K. is told they'll never walk again due to a spinal cord injury? Imagine how devastating this injury must be to someone. How can you help? You can *change a life with a chair.* We all deserve to be happy. To enjoy life. To have the ability to easily move around.

Here's the action statement that follows from this content and the ending of the infographic:

> Take the time to talk with Chris at Aspire. He's the person who'll make it possible for you to change a life with a chair. In the next three days, he'll be calling you to discuss how you and your firm can partner to bring joy and happiness into the life of someone with a spinal cord injury. Please click the phone when he does.

Now, let's go back to your data-rich story. Ultimately, you want to have one or more of the following outcomes happen as a result of it:

- ✔ Did the audience understand the context of the data and its interpretation?
- ✔ Did the data and the story build credibility and trust?
- ✔ Did it evoke an emotional response? Did the audience learn faster or better?
- ✔ Did it spark any personal insights, new questions, or *a-ha* moments?
- ✔ Did the audience share or talk about the visualization or data story? Were they able to confidently retell the story to others?
- ✔ Did they feel they could make an informed decision? Was it persuasive? Did it lead to their knowing what action to take?

Structuring a Data-Rich Presentation

Bring data into a presentation like a drip irrigation system. Start the story and then drip in data. Continue the story and drip in a bit more. To help your audience catch up to the information or data you're sharing, deliberately build pauses into your talk so you don't lose them. Do this until you reach the end.

When you do this orally, use a theatre technique. Find a place in your story to step out of it, share the data, and then step back in and continue the story. You've seen this done on stage when a character steps out of the script, makes a side comment to the audience, and then steps back into acting out the script with the other actors. Do the same when sharing data in your story.

You can use this technique in written materials. As you share the story, find an appropriate break for the data — as a sidebar, text box, indented italicized paragraph, or chart in the margins — without interrupting the story's flow. This can be useful in annual reports, for example. How much better it would be if stories and data about the company and its progress for the year were interwoven together?

If you have a significant amount of data, organize it as a series of small stories. Intersperse each story with bits of data and insights that all lead to addressing the issue you're raising, your key message, and action steps.

You probably don't really need the data

Go back to the earlier story about the research from Deborah Small and her colleagues. Read it again. Do you see any data in it? There's none. On purpose. There's one key thing we've learned through years and tears of helping organizations and individuals storify data: You don't need it (unless it's legally required). Seriously. You don't. If you're really clear on the story's key message (or the key messages associated with the mini-stories for those with highly complex data), you can tell the story without referencing the data that was the impetus for its creation.

We know that's a huge stretch for some. You probably work with individuals who *love* data. But is it really the data that's moving these individuals to action? Or is it something else? Chances are, it's a story that someone someplace is sharing with them. Try it sometime and see what happens.

Chapter 9

Expanding and Contracting Your Story

*L*ori once compacted a 72-page, double-spaced transcript onto two sides of a single page to be used to solicit sponsorships for a community awards ceremony. Karen took a 40-page story transcript down to a few paragraphs for a client to use in its marketing and promotions effort.

Condensing a story down to its core essence, without losing its power, beauty, and significance, is a huge challenge. We cover how to effectively do so in this chapter. We also cover how to take a really short story and expand it without adding nonessential details.

How long your story should be depends on why you're telling it, its business application, the context in which it's told, the medium used to relay it, and the action you want to evoke. For example, web-based storytelling is quite different from face-to-face. If you share a story in an e-mail, it had better be short, sweet, and to the point. If you tell one in a formal talk, it can be longer. When sharing stories in person, a well-constructed story lasting 5 minutes, 10 minutes — even 20 minutes — can be more effective than shorter versions.

Stories are wonderfully elastic. Not only can they take on varied lengths, they can be adapted to various media that we cover in Chapter 11. Your task is to ensure that all versions are truly stories — and that you don't fall into reducing a story to a description, anecdote, or example for the sake of time.

Shortening a Story

You don't always need to shorten a story. Sometimes you can move from the raw story (transcript, bullets, storyboard images, written or a video story) to the first draft and on to the final version, as described in Chapters 5–7. Other times, you'll know before you write the first draft that the story needs to be shorter. It's this latter case that we focus on in this chapter, although you can also use this process on a finished story to shorten it for various media uses.

The story showcased here as an example is from San Diego Grantmakers (SDG) (www.sdgrantmakers.org). This membership association is comprised of philanthropic entities such as corporate giving programs, foundations, grantmaking public charities, giving circles, and so on. These organizations grant dollars to address community needs. In 2009, SDG convened a coalition of philanthropists, local elected officials, and nonprofit service organizations to tackle the severe problem of homelessness in the region. Later, to highlight the coalition's successes, SDG wanted to post a story on its website. That meant the final version of the story had to be very short.

The raw story was initially captured in a 60-minute oral interview with the lead SDG consultant for the project, Barbara Mandel. The other consultant on the project was Mary Herron. A rough and rambling five-page written story was generated after initial editing of the transcript, which we'll call Version 1. (For your own story, this is when you might want to use the framework in Chapter 6, in the section "Step 3: Create a mockup." Or you can use storyboarding — create an image deck as outlined in Chapter 5 and the online article on www.dummies.com/extras/ about this subject.)

Analyze and rewrite

The original story was designed to highlight SDG's work with its members and other stakeholders. We've been given permission to alter the final story and its purpose to fit our teaching needs here. Rest assured, it remains accurate and valid.

Let's walk through how to tame this beast into a short, compelling story. Grab a highlighter and a pen or pencil. Take your copy of "It's Not About Shelters: Version 1" from the appendix. That version is the raw story, so it will have imperfections to it. Follow these directions to replicate our work:

✔ **Read through the entire story and analyze it.**

- Underline the dialogue and the visual language that you really like.

- Use a highlighter to mark passages you think are important and whatever strikes you as new or different about the situation.

- Note in the margins who you think the main character is.

- Circle any messages that strike you as significant.

- Pinpoint problems or conflicts and note how they're resolved.

- Identify key facts, data, and information that need to be kept and mark them, too.

- Identify images that need to be incorporated into the story.

✔ **Rewrite the story.** Leave out all the text that wasn't circled, highlighted, underlined, or marked up in some way. Try cutting it down by one page.

When these two steps are done for the SDG story, our version goes from five pages down to four. It's Version 2 in the appendix. There are still several imperfections in this version.

Build in empathy

Let's talk about the main character. In previous chapters, we promote giving names and faces to individuals in order to reap empathy from whomever the story touches. In this case, the main character is an organization — the Homelessness Working Group (HWG). The supporting cast is SDG. Here, individuals didn't want to call attention to themselves; they wanted the focus to be on the group's work. You too may find this with your organization's stories. That's why storytelling is an art form. Creativity is needed to craft the best possible story given situational constraints you may face.

So how does empathy get built into a story when an organization is the main character? We can think of a couple ways in this story: include more dialogue, add lots of sensory information, and talk about families and their housing struggles so people can closely identify with their experiences. Look for these elements in the next several iterations of it.

Edit to emphasize themes

Before crafting Version 3, address the themes that the story brings forth, the focus (direction) it needs to take, and its key message. Follow these steps:

1. **What themes are in the story?** Chapter 5 covers how to identify the themes associated with a story. Several themes immediately come to mind for the SDG situation: *working collaboratively, strength in numbers, power of philanthropy, leveraging resources, new possibilities, forging partnerships*, and *stronger communications*.

2. **What key message follows from these themes?** We looked at all the themes and noticed a common thread having to do with *making something happen*. We turned that into the key message: *Make it happen*.

3. **What's the focus the story needs to take?** Sometimes a story could go in several different directions, depending on the primary audience for it and the purpose for sharing it. When this happens, you need to decide which direction to take. Is the SDG story about homelessness or is it about a group of people who made a big dent in a very problematic social issue? We chose to focus on the group. This story also needs to promote SDG, so it's important to incorporate how the organization wants to be perceived. To do this, three words — *learning, demonstrating*, and *advocating* — need to be conceptually woven throughout the story.

4. **Whittle the story down one more time.** Take another pass, incorporating the focus, key message, and themes you want as layers of meaning in the story (layers of meaning are covered in Chapter 6).

Look at the results so far

After following the steps in the preceding section, here's Version 3. It's still somewhat raw. Keep in mind that we still haven't re-arranged the pieces to follow any sort of story structure:

> We're familiar with those panhandling on the street, sleeping in a corner downtown, and standing in the bread lines. People who're often feared — the chronic homeless who're mentally ill and whose resources run out 25 days into the month and who aren't able to manage their care themselves.
>
> But the picture of homelessness is changing today. As people lose their jobs and homes, entire families are homeless. Six thousand two hundred children in San Diego schools are identified as homeless or at risk. Many, many more families are coming into the schools for services, who're doubled up, living in their friend's garage, in their parent's living room, in their car, or in somebody's attic.
>
> The San Diego Grantmakers (SDG) Homelessness Working Group asked, "How can we turn our attention to a rapidly growing group of folks? What can we do to get private and public organizations together to tackle this wave of homeless families? Can we tackle prevention?"

Two events came together: a national conference on family homelessness here in San Diego and the opportunity for federal stimulus money. The Homelessness Working Group decided to hold a summit with nationally recognized speakers to present the picture of family homelessness around the country. There was standing room only, including elected leaders or their representatives. We painted the picture of the new face of homelessness, and looked at immediate funding and immediate solutions to create long-term sustainability. The city had been focused for so long on shelter, shelter, shelter. But talking about where to put another shelter was so politicized for most folks that they just shied away from talking about homelessness. When one of the speakers at the summit said, "It's not about shelters — it's about keeping people in their homes," a light bulb went on everywhere. Attendees said, "Oh, well if that's the case, then *yeah* we can get behind that!"

The picture isn't of some grungy guy on the street anymore. It's a picture of a family with children who're struggling in this economy, about kids who're struggling in school because of losing their homes, and what we're doing to really support our families — because if you don't have a home, you cannot find a job. If you don't have a home, your children won't do well at school. If you don't have a home, looking for a job is crazy because you're spending all your time worrying about where you're going to sleep. So you've got to keep people in their homes. Preventing homelessness is really all about housing.

After the summit, SDG convened its first meeting of jurisdictions who were applying for competitive funding from the stimulus package. There were about ten people around the table. They were happy and surprised to be invited to the meeting. One of them said, "You know, we've never really sat together; we've never had a discussion together, we've never talked about this together. We'd be working in our little silos thinking how we were going to spend this money in the same way we've always been spending it." So we talked about what we could do that was different and how we could address things in a new way.

At our second collaboration meeting, we had 25 people in the room and we thought, "Wow, this is really great! This is the place to be. People are really feeling like they want to be a part of this and that's why they're showing up!" Some agencies, when they heard what was going on, showed up, saying, "I want to be a part of this." It really blossomed into a discussion of how, as a region, we make sure that folks get what they need to prevent them from becoming homeless.

Around the table we collaboratively developed a model for doing this work — where health and human services/food stamps folks are sitting down and talking with housing and community development folks in the region; where folks from Oceanside are talking with the folks from Chula Vista about how to use existing resources. It was that strength of, "Okay, if we in the city don't have the capacity to immediately write the rent check, if someone receives a three-day eviction notice, who does?"

Our efforts were really starting to pay off at the state level, too. This teamwork was evident in the strength of each funding application generated to receive federal stimulus dollars. Sacramento officials overseeing state stimulus distribution were also impressed with our efforts, saying we were really ahead of the game through our collaboration and efforts to develop a comprehensive strategy. The group of applicants that the SDG Homelessness Working Group convened became sort of a guide for the state to provide to others on how to connect resources together, how to create a competitive funding application, and identify solutions that work better than others.

And the bottom line? The collaboration garnered and leveraged $13 million in government funds coming into the region. People are excited, saying, "Hey, you know it hasn't taken much but look at how far we're getting." We've built relationships with each other locally and regionally, along with state and federal agencies.

We've also achieved consensus on a model of outreach, point of entry, and data collection. We continue to meet to discuss how to connect the dots between all the resources for families. We're developing regional materials together so all the agencies will know who the players are and will be able to provide a higher level of care and service in their community. We intend to continue meeting every quarter as a collaboration to assure connection and coordination among all the resources.

We hope we can get other funders to say, "Gee, that's a really compelling story! We'd really like to join those efforts, because we see that leveraging that money will create something sustainable and long lasting."

For San Diego Grantmakers, our role will continue to be to convene the meetings, be the working collaborative member's technical assistant and advisor, and to bring information to the table. A few of the cities have said that they wouldn't have applied for this money if they hadn't had our support and assistance. "We wouldn't have bothered," they've said, "Because we wouldn't have known about how to do it."

In the end, a group of funders stepped into this new arena where funders, government, and agencies hadn't been before. They didn't try to solve problems as individual organizations, but collaboratively. They said, "Let's make it happen" and they did! It speaks to the power of philanthropy and grantmaking, in breaking out of the box, being innovative, and taking risks that government agencies can't do alone. *Used with permission. "It's Not About Shelters" version 3 copyright © 2009 by San Diego Grantmakers. All rights reserved.*

Ask questions and edit for structure

Version 3 is almost three pages long — still too lengthy for the website use originally stated or for a short presentation beyond this. Chapter 6 gives questions to answer when building a compelling story. They're also relevant when collapsing a story. They help you think strategically, keep you and the story on target, and cut editing time. Here's a summary of them for the SDG story. How would you answer these questions?

1. **What's the primary purpose for telling the story?** Is it to share a new idea to combat homelessness, to enroll people in participating in the coalition, to highlight Grantmakers' role, or to promote the results of the Working Group? For SDG, it was the latter — promote the group's results. This aligns with the answer to the question about the story's focus.

2. **Whose point of view needs to be taken when telling the story?** For the SDG story, is this the consultants? Grantmakers? The Homelessness Working Group? An agency? Given the reason the story is being captured, SDG elected to tell it through its own lens.

3. **Of the available problems and challenges, which is the primary one for this story?** Based on the focus and purpose of the SDG story ("a group of people who made a big dent in a very problematic social issue"), is the primary problem about homelessness, the economy, lack of coordination among parties, or a small pool of cash? There can be several problems and challenges in a story — the main one helps you construct the plot. For SDG, the main problem was the lack of coordination among various parties.

4. **What elements of surprise can be highlighted in the story?** For SDG, these could be who attended and why, or the amount of money gained.

5. **What additional sensory information, figures of speech (metaphors, analogies, and so on), and emotions can be added to keep the story interesting and spark empathy?** You'll see what was chosen in Version 4, which follows this section.

6. **How does the story need to begin?** For SDG, is this at a meeting? A conference? A Grantmakers' office meeting? At the state legislature? In a HUD (Housing and Urban Development) office? SDG chose the summit on homelessness as the starting point.

7. **Based on the main problem or challenge, what resolution should there be**? For SDG, this needs to be based on the lack of coordination. What other resolutions also need to be included to handle related problems or challenges in the story? See what was chosen when you read Version 4.

This is also the time to evaluate the structure of the story using what we discuss in Chapter 7. Why now and not earlier? You want to ensure all the pieces of a specific structure have been included. This way, you'll know you've hit all the critical points along the way without forcing the story into a structure too soon. The structure you choose will depend on which structure was provided when you captured the story and whether you can alter that, which ones you like best for it, and the context in which you're sharing it.

This story follows the CHARQES structure from Chapter 7's section "Business-focused story structures" (Challenge, Hindrance, Action, Results

Quantified, Evaluation, and Suggested actions). When you overlay that structure onto Version 3, you'll see that the suggested actions at the end are missing. As an aside, we could've used the PARLAS structure and it would've been just as good. Remember, there is no one right structure to use when sharing business or personal stories.

Now make additional cuts and changes to Version 3 based on your answers to those eight questions and organize the content so it follows the CHARQES structure. If you're using an image deck, rearrange the cards so all the pieces flow together. Next, find a great opening for the story. We decided to showcase the situation about homelessness, because it has a slightly different take than how people normally think about the issue. Doing all of this decreases the length of the story to one page.

Look at the results again

Here's Version 4:

> "It's not about shelters — it's about keeping people in their homes!," said a speaker at a 2009 summit on homelessness sponsored by San Diego Grantmakers (SDG) and the San Diego Association of Governments (SANDAG). Without a home, you can't look for a job. Without a home and a place to study, kids struggle to pass tests. Without a home, more families than ever before are doubled up, living in a friend's garage or in their cars. In San Diego County, a whopping 6,200 children are identified through the schools as homeless or at risk. The average cost to have someone move in and out of a shelter is about $48,000 a year. The cost of providing even a $1,000 a month, or $12,000 a year, to keep them in their homes is a quarter of that.

> The Homelessness Working Group, a project within SDG, asked, "How can private and public organizations come together to prevent family homelessness?" With American Recovery and Reinvestment Act (ARRA) money on the table, for the first time ever the county, cities, and public agencies were invited by the Homelessness Working Group to develop a common strategy to tackle this problem and apply for ARRA funds together. A small group of ten curious people came to the first meeting. As one of them said, "You know, we've never really sat together; we've never had a discussion together, we've never even talked about this together. We'd be working in our little silos instead, thinking how we were going to spend this money in the same way we always have." Discussions blossomed about how, as a region, we can make sure folks get what they need to prevent them from becoming homeless.

> More agencies and cities showed up at the next meeting to work together to attract this new funding into our region. Around the table, the group collaboratively developed a regional model to prevent homelessness — Health and Human Services folks from up north in Oceanside were sitting

down with folks from Chula Vista in the south to get things done. Typical conversations were, "Okay, if we in the city don't have the capacity to immediately write the rent check if someone receives a three-day eviction notice, who does?"

Sacramento officials overseeing homelessness dollars were so impressed with this collaboration, they said the San Diego county strategy was way ahead of the game. Thirteen million dollars came into the region as a result of this cooperative effort to keep children and families in their homes.

The San Diego Grantmakers' Homelessness Working Group stepped into a new arena by facilitating and supporting this public-private coalition, venturing where grantmakers, government, and nonprofit agencies had never gone before. They said, "Let's make it happen" and they did! As a result, more people will have a roof over their heads. It is an exciting beginning as the Homelessness Working Group continues to join with its partners in the fight to end family homelessness in our community.

You, too, can make it happen … *Used with permission. "It's Not About Shelters" version 4, copyright © 2009 by San Diego Grantmakers. All rights reserved.*

Weave in the action steps

Based on the key message *make something happen*, what is the transition from it to an action statement and what specific actions need to follow from this? Like many stories, action steps depend on audience. SDG could tell this story to other government agencies, municipalities, and organizations to become part of the project. They could tell it to other philanthropists to build membership, or to legislators when advocating for the power of philanthropy. For each audience, here's how to weave together the actions steps and the key message:

- ✔ **Government agencies and other organizations:** "You, too, can make it happen. Come join us. And don't hesitate to download the toolbox on our website. It's full of information for agencies about what we learned that works. If your organization has a resource we don't know about, please share that with us. To attend our next meeting, give us your card and we'll invite you. And talk to Barbara in the back of the room if you have more questions. We look forward to working with you!"

- ✔ **Philanthropists:** "You, too, can make it happen. Come join us. We invite you to become part of San Diego Grantmakers and our philanthropic community. To attend the next Homelessness Working Group meeting or participate in an upcoming Grantmakers' event, give us your card and we'll call you. Talk to Barbara in the back of the room if you have more questions about the coalition's work. And don't hesitate to contact us if you want to talk with any of our members about our organization. We look forward to working with you!"

✔ **Legislators:** "You, too, can make it happen. Come join us. Don't hesitate to download the toolbox on our website. It's full of information about what we learned that works. Your actions on legislation now and in the future will shape public/private partnerships and the ability of philanthropy to help people for years to come. When legislation is being considered on public/private partnerships, remember what happened here in San Diego. Support collaborative ventures that benefit families and communities and deliver services more effectively while protecting state budgets. If you have questions or want to share ideas, please talk with us before you leave. We look forward to these conversations!"

You may have noticed that cost data was added into Version 4 of the story. It was included to emphasize the benefit of moving people into homes — that building more shelters isn't the long-term solution to homelessness.

Our work with this story isn't done yet. It needs to be condensed to a few short paragraphs. Now's the time to start slashing anything that seems extraneous. How do you pick and choose? By asking yourself two questions:

✔ What's absolutely essential that must survive?

✔ What's the emotional core of the story that must be kept at all costs?

Do you have to make some sacrifices when doing this? Absolutely. Can a story be cut too much? Yep. If you find yourself in that position, add a few pieces back in so it remains compelling.

Appraise the final story

Here's the final product, Version 5. In the first paragraph you'll see two new items: a phrase in the form of a *triple* (the phrase "without a home" is repeated as a memory aid) and how 6,200 homeless kids compares to the number of children in the community. Notice how we continue to polish the wording of the story and what happens to the cost data added in Version 4:

"It's not about shelters — it's about keeping people in their homes!" said a speaker at a 2009 summit on homelessness sponsored by San Diego Grantmakers (SDG) and the San Diego Association of Governments (SANDAG). Without a home, you can't look for a job. Without a home and a place to study, kids struggle to pass tests. Without a home, more families than ever are doubled up, living in a friend's garage or in their cars. In San Diego County, 1 out of every 12 kids, a whopping 6,200 children, are homeless or at risk. Keeping people in their homes is cheap: only a quarter of the cost of moving someone in and out of a shelter.

Formed by SDG, the Homelessness Working Group asked, "How can private and public organizations come together to prevent family homelessness?" With American Recovery and Reinvestment Act (ARRA) money on the table, for the first time ever, the county, cities, and public agencies had a chance to develop a common strategy to tackle this problem and apply for ARRA funds together. Invited by the Homelessness Working Group, a small group of ten curious people came to the first meeting. As one of them said "You know, we've never really sat together; we've never had a discussion together, we've never even talked about this together. We'd be working in our little silos instead, thinking how we were going to spend this money in the same way we always have been spending it."

Sacramento officials overseeing homelessness dollars were impressed with this collaboration. They said the San Diego County strategy was way ahead of the game. Thirteen million dollars came into the region as a result of this cooperative effort to keep children and families in their homes. We've gone where no grantmakers, government, and nonprofit agencies have gone before. San Diego Grantmakers' Homelessness Working Group continues to join with its partners in the fight to end family homelessness in our community. They said, "Let's make it happen" and they did!

You, too, can make it happen . . . (add one ending based on the audience). *Used with permission. "It's Not About Shelters" version 5 copyright © 2009 by San Diego Grantmakers. All rights reserved.*

Time the story out loud

Once you've shortened a story, the next step is to tell it out loud. As you do, you'll discover what's easy to read but hard to say and ways to drop some acronyms and abbreviate sentences. There may also be minor shifts in the order of sentences. This may also happen with your image deck. Time yourself. If it's still too long for the intended use, you'll have to do more editing. We got Version 5 of the story down to two minutes.

Rebuild the story

If you want to rebuild the story, simply add back in details that flesh out the story and enhance its impact. Go back to Chapter 6 for lots of ideas about what to include. Just remember to keep the story focused and on point.

Lengthening a Story

What if you want to pump up a story so it's longer and has more oomph? How do you do that? The best rule of thumb: Add in select details along with lots of sensory information and make sure they help drive your key message. To practice lengthening a story, here's a composite story about a bicycle and pedestrian transportation initiative that we put together. It isn't a great story, nor is it a compelling description. It clocks in at about one minute when told out loud. Whether it stays this length or is elongated, it needs some help:

> For a while, the county had been working with coalition of community groups and city staff to implement a 50-mile bike path through the city and the back country. The project would increase parkland along the corridor, commuting to work by bike, and the safety of the roadways. Everyone agreed on the value of the project. But the coalition got stuck on trying to figure out how to protect the signage from graffiti, road damage, and weather. The project was delayed for months with no end in sight. As an afterthought, one of the coalition members sent a quick inquiry to a manufacturer wondering if they could help. Within days the manufacturer proposed several low-cost solutions to prevent the graffiti and wear and tear from the weather. This led a city engineer to come up with an idea to minimize road damage. These breakthroughs allowed the coalition to complete their work and the bike path was launched.

Map the story's structure

The first step to use with a brief story like this is to identify its structure based on the "Business-focused story structures" section in Chapter 7. Once you've diagrammed the story structure, then you can figure out which pieces are missing that need to be added to it. This story appears to follow the CHARQES pattern: Context, Hindrance, Action, Results Quantified, Evaluation, and Suggested actions. When this structure is applied, the only *result* that's mentioned is that the bike path was launched. More can be added here, along with *quantified evaluation*, which will make the story more powerful. Also, *suggested actions* are missing. As a consequence, the ending is very weak.

As we did here, you might need to locate more information to flesh out the missing structural elements. When we add them here's how the story reads:

> For a while, the county had been working with a coalition of community groups and city staff to implement a 50-mile bike path through the city and the back country. The project would increase parkland along the corridor and enhance commuting to work by bike and the safety of the roadways. Everyone agreed on the value of the project. (**context**)

> But the coalition got stuck on trying to figure out how to protect the signage from graffiti, road damage, and weather. The project was delayed for months with no end in sight. (**hindrance**) As an afterthought, one of the coalition members sent a quick inquiry to a manufacturer wondering if it could help. Within days the manufacturer proposed several low-cost solutions to prevent the graffiti and wear and tear from the weather. This led a city engineer to come up with an idea to minimize road damage. (**action**)

This breakthrough allowed the coalition to complete its work, and the bike path was launched. Within two years, 250,000 people annually used the bike path for recreation and commuting to work, saving the county hundreds of thousands of dollars in transportation costs. **(results quantified)** It just goes to show how one person reaching out can create a breakthrough **(evaluation)**, and that you never know what's possible until you ask. Which is a good thing to remember next time you're stuck! **(suggested actions)**

Structure alone can't fully fix this story if you need it to last five to eight minutes. It needs more work.

Identify the key message

With any brief story like this, you want to identify the key message before adding details. That way, everything you add can reinforce that message.

Sometimes, the wording for the key message is already a part of the story. Look for it. In the last paragraph, you see the phrase *you never know what's possible until you ask*. *Ask* is the type of action you want others to take. This generates a variety of possible key messages:

- ✔ Seek input when you're stuck
- ✔ Ask and you shall receive
- ✔ Reach out and ask someone

We chose the phrase *seek input when you're stuck* as the key message. It's catchy and alliterative, which makes it memorable. At the end of this chapter, we craft several ways to end the story using this phrase. The reason we don't cover this now is that one option for this ending includes knowing the story's main character, whom we haven't identified yet.

Add details to support the key message

Look at the CHARQES structure version of the story again. You'll see it's missing named characters, inner and outer dialogue, a variety of sensory information, contrast, and the expression of emotions. The next rewrite of the story (or image deck, if you're storyboarding the situation) needs to include those missing basic elements to have any hope of turning what amounts to a description into a story.

To increase memorability, especially with a longer story, you should include embellishments such as humor, drama and surprise, exaggeration, repetition, and figures of speech such as metaphors, analogies, and aphorisms. Including embellishments is challenging. The following sections offer suggestions.

Humor

To add a little humor at the beginning, you could say something like, "It's been said that to get something done, a committee should consist of no more than three people, two of whom are absent. But that wasn't the case here …."

Here are several other ways you could get a few grins and giggles:

- ✔ "Members were getting so frustrated it looked like their heads were going to explode!"
- ✔ "You could see that this committee was on the road to perpetual purgatory."
- ✔ "You would think that such a bright group of people juggling suspicious communities, self-interested developers, and countless bureaucrats wouldn't get so stumped over a few signs."

We've opted only to include the first example. We skipped over the second one; not all people know what's meant by *purgatory*. The last comment is also not advisable; it could be perceived as a back-handed slam to the group.

Drama and surprise

Drama and surprise help heighten the contrast between the problem and the resolution while building more tension at the same time. Here's how to add these elements into various sections of the story. You'll see we've started to identify a few characters, some by name (Jeff is the main character):

- ✔ "No one had the right technical expertise. Web searches were turning up dry. Sometimes too many options were presented, and they couldn't evaluate them well enough to make a decision. They were at their wits' end. Everyone got cranky trying to figure out how to balance all these concerns and the budget."
- ✔ "The mayor kept asking for updates. The press kept reporting that progress had stalled. And there they were, thoroughly dejected."
- ✔ "On a whim Jeff sent a quick inquiry to a sign manufacturer wondering if the company could help. He doubted the manufacturer could or would be interested. Mary, the manufacturer's rep said, 'I may be able to come up with some weather solutions, but I don't think I can help with the graffiti problem.'"
- ✔ "Out of the blue, a couple weeks later Mary contacted Jeff again. 'Hey Jeff,' she said. 'One of our engineers just finished field testing a new product that keeps our signs free of graffiti. I had no idea he was working on this! Can I come talk to your committee about our findings?'"

Exaggeration and repetition

Another way to lengthen the story is to use exaggeration and repetition to drive home the challenge: how stuck the team was. You can do that in two ways: by using a repetitive word and by amplifying the characters:

> They were at their wits' end. Everyone got cranky trying to figure out how to balance all these concerns and the budget. Round and round the discussions went with no end in sight. The obstacles felt insurmountable. Discouragement and ongoing frustration colored their meetings. The mayor kept asking for updates. The press kept reporting that progress had stalled. Members were getting so frustrated it looked like their heads were going to explode! In the end, they were thoroughly dejected. "Aaaaaarrrrggggghhhhhh!" Jim thought to himself. "I'm about ready to give up!!" In an act of desperation, he sent a quick inquiry to a sign manufacturer wondering if the company could help.

Figures of speech

What metaphors, analogies, and aphorisms can be added? Go to the final version of the story at the end of this chapter and see if you can spot the four metaphors we added. (Hint: They have to do with river, logs, sea, and fire.) We couldn't find analogies and aphorisms that comfortably fit this story. Sometimes that happens.

Drive home the key message

With this CHARQES story structure you need to add the key message and a transition prior to the suggested actions. You have several options for doing so. As we say in Chapter 7, the main character can make an evaluative comment, or you can pose a question, use a quotation, or add a personal reflection or a repeatable phrase. Let's try these out:

✔ **Question:** "Doesn't it just go to show how powerful it can be when just one person reaches out for help? You'll never know what's possible unless you seek input when you're stuck. So remember this the next time you're stuck — seek input by picking up the phone or sending an e-mail. Stay open to possibilities and be willing to be amazed. I trust your next project will be as successful as this one."

✔ **Quotation:** "As President Barack Obama says: 'The best way to not feel hopeless is to get up and do something. Don't wait for good things to happen to you. If you go out and make some good things happen, you will fill the world with hope, you will fill yourself with hope.' That's what Jeff did. He took a little initiative, and the whole world opened up for the coalition. It just goes to show that you never know what's possible unless you seek input when you're stuck. So remember this the next time you're stuck — seek input by picking up the phone or sending an e-mail. Stay open to possibilities and be willing to be amazed. I trust your next project will be as successful as this one."

✔ **Personal reflection:** "Here's what this story reminds me of: that even the simplest and smallest initiative that I can take might yield huge results, even when I doubt it's going to work. I keep remembering Jeff and how a simple act — seeking input when he got stuck — changed everything for the committee. Next time I get stuck, I'm going to seek input by picking up the phone or sending an e-mail. I'm going to stay open to possibilities and be willing to be amazed. When you do too, I trust that your next project will be as successful as this one."

✔ **Character delivering the key message:** "After the project was over, Jeff was interviewed about his experience. As he says, 'What I learned is that the best way to not feel hopeless is to seek input when you're stuck. Don't wait for anyone else. Just by picking up the phone and making a call as a last resort, a breakthrough occurred. Next time you get stuck, seek input by reaching out or sending an e-mail. Be open to possibilities. You'll be amazed at the success you may achieve.'"

✔ **Repeatable phrase:** "The best way to not feel hopeless is to seek input when you're stuck. Don't wait for good things to happen to you. If you go seek input and take action and remain open to possibilities, you'll feel more hope, those around you will feel more hope, and the world will feel more hope."

The final story

Let's put all these elements together with an ending (we chose the quotation):

It's been said that to get something done, a committee should consist of no more than three people, two of whom are absent. But that wasn't the case here. The county had been working with a coalition of community groups and city staff to implement a 50-mile bike path that stretched through the bustling downtown to the rolling hills and pine forests of the back country, like a serene green river of peace. Not only would the project create scenic parkland along the corridor, many more workers could commute to work by bicycle, while bikers, hikers, and drivers could remain safe. Mike from city planning, Carol from city transportation, and Dave, the city engineer, worked with Sue and Jeff from the regional bike enthusiasts association. In the evenings, they regularly met in the community room of a local branch library with folks from various communities along the proposed bike path.

In between these events, over coffee and doughnuts — a perfect balanced meal — they would swap friendly updates, share the latest family news, and diligently work to keep the project moving along. Everyone was enthusiastic and passionate about the project. But Mike, Carol, Dave, Sue, Jeff, and the others they spoke to got stuck on the signage.

Carol kept asking in frustration, "But if we put these signs up along the roadway, what happens if taggers cover them with graffiti?" Sue and Jeff wondered, "Won't drivers accidentally knock the signs down because they're too small?" Mike pointed out in his grumpy way, "How durable are these signs going to be? Won't they need to be frequently replaced because of all the weather damage?"

No one had the right technical expertise. Web searches were turning up dry. Sometimes too many options were presented, and they couldn't evaluate them well enough to make a decision. They were at their wits' end and got cranky trying to figure out how to balance all these concerns and the budget. Round and round the discussions went with no end in sight. They were log-jammed. The obstacles were feeling insurmountable. The mayor kept asking for updates. The press kept reporting that progress had stalled. Members were getting so frustrated it looked like their heads were going to explode! In the end, they were thoroughly discouraged and dejected.

"Aaaaaarrrrgggggghhhhhh!" Jeff thought to himself. "I'm about ready to give up!!" In an act of desperation, he sent a quick inquiry to a sign manufacturer wondering if the company could help. Mary, the manufacturer's rep, said thoughtfully on the phone, "I may be able to come up with some weather solutions, but I don't think I can help you with the graffiti problem." As promised, within days Mary proposed several low-cost solutions to prevent wear and tear from the elements on the signs.

A few weeks later out of the blue, Mary contacted Jeff again. "Hey Jeff," she said. "One of our engineers just finished field testing a new product that keeps our signs virtually free of graffiti. I had no idea he was working on this! Can I come talk to your committee about our findings?" Sure enough, Mary came to the next meeting, and the talk turned to excitement once again. She helped them sift through various options including graffiti-resistant materials, different coatings that allow graffiti to be washed off, metal baffles, and textured sign surfaces.

Dave, the city engineer, felt his mind open to the sea of possibilities. He was so energized, he came up with an idea to minimize road damage from salts and sands used by road crews during large snowfalls. Other ideas were sparked within the group.

With these breakthroughs, the coalition was completely reignited by the fires of creativity. They quickly finished their work and launched the bike path. The coalition had its own celebration with lots of handshaking and pats on the back as members congratulated each other on their contributions and success. Even the mayor showed up and gave everyone certificates, acknowledging them for their hard work. Within two years 250,000 neighbors, families, and community members annually walk, hike, bike for miles, and easily commute to work, saving the county hundreds of thousands of dollars in transportation costs.

As President Barack Obama says: "The best way to not feel hopeless is to get up and do something. Don't wait for good things to happen to you. If you go out and make some good things happen, you will fill the world with hope, you will fill yourself with hope." That's what Jeff did. He took a little initiative, and the whole world opened up for the coalition. It just goes to show that you never know what's possible unless you *seek input when you're stuck*. So remember this the next time you're stuck — seek input by picking up the phone or sending an e-mail. Stay open to possibilities and be willing to be amazed. I trust your next project will be as successful as this one.

We now have a story that's about five-minutes long when told out loud. Pretty cool, huh?

Here's our one big caveat when you lengthen a story: How a story is written is often different from how it's told orally. As you craft stories for telling, remember that how you say it may change and so can the order of some of the sentences.

Changing It Up: Stories Are Flexible

The funny thing about stories is that your sense of the story won't be static. What it means, how you open and close it, and what details you add or leave out can evolve over time. Compelling stories are always in flux. Even *perfectly* crafted stories and *perfectly* crafted key messages can change.

Why? The more you share a story, the more feedback you'll receive about it. Especially if you tell it orally. Whether to one person or a thousand, body language, laughter, sighs, and gasps from listeners will cause you to change things up a bit. You'll find better ways to word what you say. On top of that, you as the storyteller are always growing and changing, which means the story you're sharing will impact you differently over time.

If you alter the key message of a story, you need to go back and make some modifications to the story to support this message. If you don't, you'll lose the impact of this message, and listeners may get mixed signals from you about what's truly important in the story.

Crafting stories is an iterative process. You have flexibility to change a story as the context and audience changes in order for it to be relevant to them while still authentic to you. What ultimately matters is what the story means to you at any given point in time.

Part III
Sharing Stories for Maximum Value

Five Ways to Start Embedding Story into Your Organization's DNA

- Provide training as part of a continuum of activities that also includes ongoing coaching, teleseminars, webinars, practice time, and follow-up evaluation.

- Connect story efforts to standard operating procedures (work processes), from how input from customers is collected to how the work is performed each day.

- Link story into project work through business cases, knowledge sharing, the ways updates, problems, and risks are communicated, and promoting successes.

- Propose a small story initiative where leaders and staff learn and try out the skills that move them toward a goal, or where they contribute stories to a story bank that everyone can access in their work.

- Attach story to an identified organizational strategy linked to growth, innovation, strengthening a merger or acquisition, or a desired cultural transformation.

Check out how to use stories with virtual teams in an online article at www. dummies.com/extras/businessstorytelling.

In this part . . .

✔ Enhance your storytelling skills and get the most out of practicing your story before telling it.

✔ Identify the pluses and minuses of using story in oral, digital, audio, written, graphic, and iconic mediums and determine which media are best for specific uses.

✔ Incorporate story into your daily work and into projects, standard operating procedures, and the organization's strategies for success.

Chapter 10

Getting Comfortable Telling Stories

*H*ow comfortable are you telling stories at work? What makes you not share your own? If you say, "I don't have any stories to tell," check out Chapter 4 to spark some ideas and memories.

We recognize you may not be ready to tell one of your own or one of your organization's hip pocket stories publicly. That's okay. We address sharing tougher stories at the end of this chapter. Does your stomach gets queasy when telling stories in a group? We talk about that, too.

If you're employed by an enterprise, minimally you need to be able to share personal and organizational stories during staff meetings, when giving presentations, or when training others. These needs also exist if you're job hunting. If you own a business or are an entrepreneur, growing your firm depends on being able to share your personal stories, in addition to business stories, with prospects and clients. Perhaps you feel squeamish because you don't want to be seen as arrogant, egotistical, or as someone who's always bragging. We get this. And we offer ideas on how to overcome these feelings.

There's another reason you need to be able to tell personal stories. As Gail Larsen says in *Transformational Speaking: If You Want to Change the World, Tell a Better Story* (Celestial Arts, 2009), when she became a public speaker, it "stripped me of my façade of invincibility, replacing it with a vulnerability that allowed me to connect more deeply with others." You also need this depth of relationship in any work role you have. When you share yourself with others, you get even more in return. In *Inside Story: The Power of the Transformational Arc* (Three Mountain Press, 2007), Dara Marks says this best: "Open your gift and release into the world of infinite possibilities the sacred truths that reside there — waiting only for you — inside story." We cover how to make that happen for you as well. Read on!

Playing Out the Telling-Listening Cycle

We've said it before and we'll say it again: The true value and magic in business storytelling is in the dynamics between telling and listening. Once you grasp this interaction, your storytelling skills will improve. This interaction includes honoring your gifts and talents, having fun, and tapping your creativity.

Act as the center of exposure

If you're afraid that sharing your stories will make you appear arrogant, boastful, or egotistical, stop right there. That kind of thinking is all about seeing yourself as the center of attention. On one level that makes sense because when you share a story, people are focused solely on you in that moment.

Here's another way to think about it, though. It all boils down to intention. If your *intent* is to be the center of attention, then your stories will come across as boastful. But if your intent is to be the *center of exposure*, then you'll have a very different experience. To embrace being the center of exposure, you need to pull back the veil and authentically share a personal experience and what it means to you. In this way you humbly express your humanity by being in service to others through the stories you tell. When you share from this place, you'll not be perceived as arrogant or boastful.

How does this work? Since 2000, Brené Brown, a research professor at the University of Houston Graduate School of Social Work, has studied vulnerability, courage, shame, and authenticity. She shares her own story at the start of her TED talk, "The Power of Vulnerability" (www.ted.com/talks/brene_brown_on_vulnerability.html).

She learned the value of authenticity and speaking from your whole heart about your business and work, how you lead, and the people you serve. Doing so means you're

- ✔ **Courageous:** You're willing to share authentically.
- ✔ **Compassionate:** You have compassion for others and yourself.
- ✔ **Connecting:** You're willing to be open — and share your stories *and* listen to stories that others share with you — as a means of connection.

Embracing vulnerability is the birthplace of joy, creativity, belonging, and love — the underpinnings of great storytelling. We must believe that our stories are enough at the same time we express them with our whole hearts and allow ourselves to be seen. In doing so, we become kinder and gentler with ourselves and others. This is how you switch from being the center of attention to being the center of exposure.

Acknowledge the gifts you bring as a teller

We're all unique. And the universe is vast. No one person can know all there is to know about the great mystery of life. Through experience, we gain little nuggets of wisdom about this mystery. As we share our stories, we pass these nuggets on to others who find ways to take our learning to heart. In turn, we listen to their stories and the nuggets they've gained and incorporate their wisdom into our lives. Because personal stories often carry universal truths, this sharing allows the sum of our existence to become greater than the parts.

Since your personal stories reflect unique experiences and the lessons you've learned, sharing them provides a gift to others. If you don't bring these gifts forward, they'll be lost forever. That would be a tragedy! As you work with your own stories, you also gift yourself — you learn more about what moves you and what others gain when hearing them. When you share your stories in this manner, they stop being about you and start being about how others can take what they hear and apply it to their own lives. In the end, your stories are more than entertainment. They're your authentic voice.

Presentation techniques about where to stand, how to make eye contact, and how to move your body are valuable — but they're not the primary focus when telling a story. Our goal is to get you to work from the inside out — to enhance how you naturally move and authentically express yourself when delivering a story. This process is less about what needs to be fixed and more about what needs to be found. Practicing your story lets you discover this.

Tell: Transformational or transactional?

You engage in transactional storytelling when you network, introduce someone by sharing an anecdote, and offer storied sound bites in interviews. When you move from transactional storytelling (*I tell a story that results in a sale*) to transformational storytelling (*I tell a story and we both change and benefit from it*), you awaken others to new possibilities and plant seeds for change.

If you want your stories to help people overcome obstacles, foster growth, strengthen a connection, acknowledge contributions, and address uncertainty, then it's time for transformational storytelling. If done well, the story takes on a life of its own and becomes part of the experience of those listening to it. In the moment they hear it, they may get a flash of inspiration. Or they may reflect on that story for months and years and continually gain new insights. You have no control over this.

What you do control is telling the story really well — and allowing it to live on and affect people. Later, that story may return when someone tells you how meaningful it was and what happened in their lives as a result. Greet this blessing with joy, gratitude, and wonder. It'll fuel you to tell more stories.

Enhancing Your Telling Skills

Enhancing your storytelling skills involves more than listening, valuing your stories, being vulnerable, and knowing the difference between transactional and transformational storytelling. It's also about reading your audience and delivering the stories well.

Recognize what's happening to listeners

Quantum physics teaches us that we live in a connected universe where everything is linked. Let's apply this notion to storytelling: We see a person tell a story, the audience hears it, and both audience and storyteller co-create the experience — which melds it all together. Once the event is over and everyone leaves, that exact experience will never happen again. The next time the person tells that same story to another group, it's a completely new and unique event that is co-created in different ways. It's essential in storytelling to connect with an audience in this manner.

How does this co-creation happen? In storytelling, as in live theater, there's a fourth wall. In theater there's the back wall, the two side walls (stage left and stage right), and a fourth, invisible wall between the actors and the audience. Actors deliver the play, but rarely interact with the audience unless the script calls for this. In storytelling, the fourth wall doesn't exist. Every time you share a story — whether it be the boardroom, a meeting room, or the cafeteria — it's a co-created experience. You as teller are always connected to your audience. Consciously or unconsciously, you shift the story in real time to fit that particular moment.

Because of this connectivity and co-creation, selecting the best story to use in formal venues or planned presentations requires forethought. Not every story is right for every circumstance. How do you do that? Pay attention to and keep track of those stories that pop into your mind when an opportunity to share a story arises. Use the following six criteria to finalize your selection. The first five are about context; the last one is about content:

1. **Who will hear the story?** Finding out all you can about your audience beforehand is critical to matching a story to who they are. Remember the "What's In It For Them" (WIIFT) principle:

   - Why has the audience gathered together to listen to me?

   - Is the audience voluntarily joining me or are they required to attend? What's their level of interest in the subject?

   - How large will the audience be?

   - What are their demographics — age, gender, ethnicity, religion, membership in other groups, and socioeconomic background?

   - What's important to this audience? What do they value?

   - What's their world like? What challenges and issues do they face?

   - What answers are they looking for? What do they want to know? What do they need to learn?

   - How do they think? What are they skeptical about?

2. **What objective am I trying to achieve?** Learn the goals for the overall event or meeting and the presentation itself. This doesn't mean the story needs to strictly "fit" the topic; a metaphorical or symbolic story can be just as powerful:

   - What is the ideal outcome for this situation?

   - What do the organizers or those in charge of the event hope my story will add to the outcome of the occasion?

   - What am I responsible for conveying?

3. **Where will I physically be telling the story?** If the story is meant only for a certain audience, learn about the location where you'll be delivering it. Not all building walls are soundproof. Stories like to travel! Know the answers to these questions before showing up to share it:

   - Is the setting formal or informal? What will the general mood be?

   - Is my presentation during a meal?

   - Is the audience going to be seated or standing? Am I going to be seated or standing?

   - What audio visual equipment do I need?

   - Will I be mic'd or need to project only using my voice?

4. **When will I be sharing the story?** To aid you in making some decisions about story placement, get the answers to these questions:

   • What is the timing of my presentation on the agenda?

   • How much time do I have? Have I scheduled practicing the story (and my presentation) so I know it fits the allotted time?

   • How will I get the audience ready to listen? If you know they'll be tired or distracted, open with a story to capture their attention.

   • How can I weave a story into other information that I need to share? Some rules of thumb: If you suspect they may resist what you have to say, relay a story beforehand that helps them understand its importance. If you're unsure they'll comprehend data you have to communicate, follow the approaches we suggest in Chapter 8. If you're skeptical that they'll do what's been asked of them, end with a story that speaks to the need to take action.

5. **How will I be perceived given the story I share?** As discussed earlier in this chapter, this question centers around intent. Decide to be the center of exposure, not the center of attention. Also consider:

   • What does my audience already know about me? What do they need to know about me in advance?

   • What preconceived notions might they have about me?

   • What's my role? Am I the only speaker or one of many?

6. **What's the content of the story?** If the story is about your company or its employees, offerings, or customers, integrate some portion of your own story into it. People need a personal connection to help them meld the lessons into their lives and create their own personal meaning. On the flip side, if the story is a personal one, make sure it has an element that links it to your organization. That gives it the larger sense of belonging that we all desire. Stay away from painful or embarrassing stories or those that speak to life-and-death challenges until you've established rapport and credibility. Before telling a story, you'll want to know:

   • What current events are impacting listeners' lives today?

   • What do they know about my cause, or organization?

   • For my topic, what's familiar to them and what may be foreign?

   • What can or can't I say? The last thing you want is to inadvertently offend someone because of cultural or ethnic nuances — or peculiarities inside a company. For example, some organizations take offense to any type of profanity. Lori shares a story where one character says, "We use that code to identify our PITAs. You know, those 'pain in the ass' customers." Learn in advance whether you can share such content. Not all places are receptive to it.

Know when to speed up and slow down

Rhythm in storytelling occurs through pacing and pausing (for example, fast–pause–slow–pause–fast) and repetition ("around and around they went . . ."). *Pacing* — slowing down and speeding up as you tell different sections of a story — is a way to build variety into your delivery. It can also wake people up and keep them involved and engaged in your story.

Hail to the power of the pause! Often we're so excited to tell a story that we forget to breathe. Pausing is powerful: It's a way to wake people up and build their anticipation for what's coming next. It builds drama and tension.

Pausing during select moments while telling a story also allows people to keep up with you and process what you're saying. As you speak, they're feasting on your images — digesting them and making them their own. Sometimes there's a lag between an image you deliver and the mind of the listener who's internalizing it. Make time for this.

Let's try these skills. Without any pausing, pacing, or repetition, speak the next paragraph out loud. It's from the story we lengthened in Chapter 9:

> For a while, the county had been working with a coalition of community groups and city staff to implement a 50-mile bike path through the city and the back country. The project would increase parkland along the corridor, commuting to work by bike, and the safety of the roadways. Everyone agreed on the value of the project.

Now, add in pauses, pacing, and repetition and hear the difference:

> For a while, **(pause)** the county had been working with a coalition of community groups and city staff **(pause)** to implement a 50-mile bike path through the city and the back country. **(pick up the pace)** The project would increase parkland along the corridor commuting to work by bike, and the safety of the roadways. **(slow down now)** Everyone, everyone **(repetition)** agreed on the value of the project.

Build pauses, pacing, and repetition into your story judiciously. You'll know you have a good balance of rhythm and repetition when a story *captivates* listeners — you'll feel people physically move with you as you share the story, and they'll describe the story as being in sync with their experience.

Identify characters: Gestures and voice

Here's a chance to have fun when telling a story: Add different voices and mannerisms to characters. Doing so brings characters to life and helps listeners distinguish among them and engage more easily with the story.

We're frequently asked about how physical and expressive a teller should be while sharing a story. We've been entranced by a storyteller who traversed the entire width of the front of a room when sharing their stories — and by one who sat still on a piano bench. Both carried great power. In general, it's less about being theatrical or reserved and more about what comes natural. If you've crafted your story well, your sharing and body movements will flow naturally and be authentic because you're *in the zone*.

Whether a story is compelling is driven primarily by how well it's structured. However, assuming you're telling your own story, there's nothing wrong with enhancing your delivery of you. Maybe you need to tone down flailing your arms and pacing across the stage. Or maybe you need to add some hand or arm movements or exaggeration for a humorous effect. Your delivery should be neither distracting nor mousy. Find the sweet spot between driving home your key message and moving people to action, without being disingenuous. This may mean stretching beyond what's comfortable.

When it comes to how you project the other characters in your stories, there are lots of ways to make each character unique. An easy way is to mirror their behaviors — act like them. Talk the way they talk. If they have a British accent, work on making your voice sound that way. If they laugh in a unique way, reproduce it. Stand the way they stand. If they tend to pace back and forth when they speak, do that. Gesture the way they gesture. Use the same facial expressions. We're not talking about mocking anyone, only imitating them. We just want you to bring these characters to life.

When depicting various characters, you may want to stand (or sit, if the story calls for it) in different places in the room. This is especially important when you're delivering dialogue between two characters. There are also techniques you can use to roll back and forth between them while relaying a conversation without saying, "I said . . . and then she said back to me . . ." One of these is called "The Two Character Two Step," where you position your body 45 degrees to the left of center for one character and then shift 45 degrees to the right of center for another, while also switching how you gesture. For further information, check out *Doug Stevenson's Story Theater Method: Strategic Storytelling in Business* (Cornelia Press, 2008).

"Where do I look with my eyes?" is one question we often get about how to share internal dialogue: Look anywhere except at the people with whom you're sharing the story. You might look down or off into the horizon, or off to one side, as you would if you were talking to yourself.

Practicing Your Story

Storytelling is a creative act. How you craft and embellish a story is all about conveying your experience in imaginative ways. When you practice your stories, set up an environment where this behavior can flourish.

Before we talk about how to practice a story, you may be thinking, "Practice? You mean practice telling my stories out loud? Why would I need to practice? I already know it cold." Really? The purpose for practicing a story out loud in a group setting is to get in tune with saying it in front of an audience and experiencing co-creation, as well as learning what works best in the delivery of the story. That may be different from how it's written or how in your mind you think you're going to tell it.

There's absolutely no substitute for practicing out loud. After you've crafted the final version of the story in written form or as a storyboard, begin by working alone. Practice speaking the story out loud. The first time, you'll likely find that the written version needs to be tweaked. That's normal. If you're using a storyboard, you may find that the order of the images needs to be altered. That's normal too. Doing this initial walk-through will help you get a feel for how the story sounds and identify what needs to shift.

Story Lab: Practice with others

After you've practiced alone a few times, now you can set up what Karen calls a Story Lab. This is a process she learned from storytelling coach Doug Lipman, founder of Story Dynamics (www.storydynamics.com). In a *Story Lab*, you bring in others to provide feedback. Chapter 5 also gives you a process for listening to stories. Guess what? The skills mentioned in that chapter apply here too.

Because storytelling is a co-created experience between you and the listener, the best way to practice your stories is with a trusted listener (or group of listeners). This will get you real-time feedback about what works and what doesn't. Their reactions can help you determine how to polish the story. You'll also understand at a deeper level what the story is all about.

The job of the listener in a Story Lab is to "listen the best story out of you." That means the person needs to be in total service to you and the story. She sets aside her own agenda so she can be of the most help to you. When choosing a listening partner, make sure it's somebody who you feel can really take on the role. You want that partner to be able to listen delightedly to you in a selfless way. Have the listener steer clear of sarcasm and negativity in their comments while they do this.

There are two ground rules for the Story Lab to share with your partner:

1. **The teller is in charge.** You, the teller, own the story and the listening process. The listener needs to request permission to ask reflective questions and also provides appreciation so that you stay at the forefront.

2. **Everything that's said is confidential.**

Here are the steps for tellers and listeners to follow:

1. **Listeners listen delightedly.** See Chapter 5 for how to do this.

2. **Listeners ask reflective questions of the teller after gaining permission** (see Chapter 5 for questions). By answering these questions, you as the teller can determine whether you have the appropriate key message, transition, and action statement. You'll also dive deeper into the story, which will inform what you need to bring to the next telling. Keep in mind that it's not yet time to make alterations to the story. That's in step 5.

3. **Listeners give appreciation.** The listener provides positive feedback about all the things that went right in the story related to the following:

   • Plot, conflict, structure, and characters

   • The meaning of the story to him or her

   • The effect the story had on him or her

   • How the story was told

   • Personal style or presence, including gestures and facial expressions

   • Vocal variety, including pitch, pacing, and tone

   • Images, sounds, smells, tastes, and physical feelings (for example, the roughness of a piece of wood) that were evoked

   • Emotions that were conveyed and drawn out

   • Memories conjured up as a result of hearing the story

This positive feedback works because your critical mind kicks in as you're telling the story. You'll say to yourself, "Oh, I want to fix this piece next time," or, "What I just said didn't work. I want to redo that section when I tell it again." Because you already know what needs to be fixed, by sharing appreciations the listener is training you on what really worked, so when you tell the story again, you can repeat those elements.

The teller (you) only needs to say thank you to the appreciations. Engaging in appreciation can be hard for both teller and listener. You may want to discount the praise. Instead of saying, "Thank you," you'll say something like, "You liked it, but I think if I really said it this way, it'd be better." Or the listener may say, "I really liked what you said there, but I bet if you said it this way, it might be better." Neither response is helpful. Why? They can cause creativity to crash. Alterations to the story aren't being identified here yet. At this point, it's more powerful to know all the things that are working well for you and the story. Encourage the listener to be as specific as possible.

4. **Together, come up with as many positive suggestions for improvements as you can.** This step is about generating ideas, not giving advice. The listener's job is to give you, the teller, a choice of a couple different ways to handle a troubling spot so you can decide which works best for you. In this way, you'll continue to share the story from a place of authenticity instead of thinking you need to tell it in a certain way because someone told you to. On the other hand, you need to be open to trying out different solutions.

5. **Before closing the Story Lab, listeners ask what other input the teller would like about the story and its delivery.** There may be one last item that hasn't been mentioned that you think would help you. Ask the listener to share his or her observations on it. Or not. Maybe you aren't ready in this round to hear additional feedback because you have enough material to work with. Keep this last step optional.

Get the most from your rehearsals

Follow your practices with your Story Lab listening partner (or group of listeners) by telling your story repeatedly in informal settings. Here are some ways to do that:

- ✔ **Try the story out on others.** If you'll be telling the story to a varied audience, find people who are similar to those who'll hear it. This is the optimal way to take your story to the next level.

- ✔ **Take your talk on a walk.** Take a leisurely stroll while speaking the story out loud. Let your hand gestures and facial expressions occur naturally. You'll undoubtedly find things you want to change, so carry your written story or storyboard and a pen with you. You're also building a kinesthetic storytelling experience into your body. The story becomes more of a physical experience rather than a mental exercise — which mirrors what will happen in front of an audience.

- ✔ **Practice the story out loud while getting ready for bed, in the shower, when doing housework, and the like.** These are great ways to embed the story in your mind the way you want to tell it so you don't have to rely on your notes. Doing this helps you focus on telling the story in the presence of distractions.

- ✔ **Imagine yourself sitting or standing comfortably with an interviewer or your audience in the room with you.** Practice the first minute or two of the of the story. Then practice delivering the ending. Also focus on the wording of the transitions between momentary events.

Don't go overboard. Too much rehearsing may create an inflexible story. If you get used to telling it a certain way, you'll forget to pay attention to the audience so you can shift and change the story in the moment to manifest a co-created experience. It will become *too* rehearsed, practiced, and stiff with story arthritis. In the long run, you'll become less sensitive to listeners.

Don't rely on mirrors and video

You'll hear people advise you to practice your story (and presentation) in front of a mirror. Or to video yourself as you tell your story so you can make corrections. Ignore both. We want your Story Lab partner and other listeners to be your mirror and video feedback. Looking at yourself in front of a mirror or on camera isn't going to help; it'll only make you self-conscious. We can always tell who's been practicing in this manner and who's been practicing with others. The mirror/video practicers usually sound rehearsed, stilted, and less *alive*. The listener practicers sound more authentic and conversational.

There's one more switch in your thinking to make. Consider video recording one of your audience presentations as an end product, a way to share your stories, rather than as a tool to help you practice.

Ready, Get Set . . .

You've crafted a compelling story. You've practiced with a listening partner and others. And you've used other moments to run through your story. Now what do you do on the day you'll be sharing the story?

Run through it one last time out loud. It can be in the shower or an hour before you'll be telling it. Get comfortable saying the first couple lines of the story. We've found that if you get nervous, after launching into your story you'll more easily overcome your anxiousness when you take this last step.

We both have a few rituals we use right before we speak. We take a few minutes, when the situation allows, to calm and center ourselves and become conscious of our breathing so we can slow it down. We place our notes in a location that's easily accessible, in case we need them. We gently hum to prepare our voices. Sometimes we even say a prayer! Lori walks the perimeter of the room before delivering a keynote with several stories in it to embody it as sacred space. Karen stretches and dances to warm up her body and ground the space. You can do these rituals too, or make up your own. They're easy to do, can be done anywhere, and help get you read to tell.

Begin your story

Here are a couple ways to launch into your story. We assume here that the story is personal or about an experience you've had inside an organization:

✔ **Someone introduces you to the audience.** It's perfectly fine to start with the first sentence of your story as an attention grabber. But, please, please, please . . . pause first. Look one or two people in the eye. Take a deep breath and let it out. Gather your energy. Don't immediately jump into telling your story. When we've had workshop attendees try this, after they've done just the opposite, they'll say things such as, "Wow, what a difference! I not only feel more calm, centered, and grounded, I feel more strongly connected to the audience and more confident." Is there any difference in their story? Yep. It's way better. Try this when sharing a story with your friends. You'll experience the difference, too.

✔ **The presentation or agenda is turned over to you with no formal introduction.** You could launch into your story, but then there'd be no transition between the agenda item before yours and your story or presentation. The audience would be lost trying to make the connection. Here's the perfect place for a *setup phrase.* As Mary Wacker and Lori share in their book *Stories Trainers Tell: 55 Ready-to-Use Stories to Make Training Stick* (Jossey-Bass, 2003), a setup phrase helps create the context so listeners understand why you're sharing the story. Examples:

  • Joe's comments remind me about the time when . . .

  • You all heard Joe's experience. Something similar happened to me once . . .

  • As I was listening to Joe, his situation made me think about what happened when . . .

As with anything in life, there are a few subtleties associated with opening a story. Here are two more tips:

✔ **The story is one you've created from one or more books or news sources about a historical event in your company, another organization, or the world at large.** It's okay to say, "This situation/example/ scenario is my take (or rendition) on what happened prior to when Joe Jackson called to cancel his firm's contract with us."

✔ **You have permission to tell someone else's story.** Take a look at the first line in Cristi's story in Chapter 3. It attributes the story to her and provides her job title and the name of the firm she works for. When Lori introduces Bob McIlree's story in the appendix, she starts out by saying, "My close friend, Bob McIlree, received a call from. . . ." When the story isn't your own, you need to know how the person who gave you the story (assuming they're the main character) wants to be acknowledged. This is part of the permission form found in Chapter 5.

In both cases, notice we didn't say, "I got this story from Bob McIlree that tells about a time he worked on a contract back in 2003," or, "I read this story from author Dave Jones in *XYZ* book published in 2004." Both are terribly boring and don't position you or the story well.

In all situations, consciously signal to your audience that it's time to listen. Claim your space. Don't rush into the story. Collect your presence. Look at people in the room. Take a breath. Then begin!

Stay away from these words

As we say in Chapter 6, never give away the key message of a story when launching into it. Never tell people what the story is about before they hear it. Never give the ending at the beginning. Don't bother giving a really long explanation about the story after you're done telling it. Avoid the maxim "Tell them what you're going to tell them, tell them, and then tell them what you told them." This is storytelling, not a lecture. Last, but not least, never open with the words, "Let me tell you a story." Why? Because this will trigger people's unconscious biases about stories as we discuss at the end of Chapter 1.

Telling Stories: More Considerations

What about those tough stories — the ones you may think you should avoid? Find out here why you should tell them anyways. Do you want to tell stories that aren't your own? You need to know a few things before you do so. Ever consider deliberately not telling an entire story? In this section, we also talk about how doing so can be advantageous.

Make the most of your personal stories

You have many personal stories — some small, some big, some entertaining, some of great importance. Not all will shake the foundations of the universe. But every story can impart meaning. A treasure trove awaits, even if you don't think you have many to share. As you begin to tell your stories (and those of others), you'll discover that more and more stories come to you.

It's easy to take your personal stories for granted. You live with them, you share them privately, and that's about it. But you have another opportunity. As you hone, craft, and share stories — as you articulate their key messages and discover their deeper meanings — you enter a land of ongoing learning. It may surprise you. Like this:

✔ **The key message is no longer the key message.** A story Karen tells about starting her first business has morphed over time. The original key message was *If I can do it, you can do it too.* But she kept telling that story and asking herself, "What do I need to say about the story this time? What do these people need to hear from the story today?" Before long, that story's key message evolved to *When you're really scared, keep moving forward.* No doubt you'll have this experience, too.

✔ **Stories have a life of their own.** If you pay attention, your stories will tell you when they want to be told. You'll be chatting with someone and all of a sudden a story pops in, demanding, "Tell me! Tell me!" Or you'll be going to a meeting where you need to share a story and ask yourself, "What story should I tell?" All of a sudden — zing! You suddenly know exactly the story you need to share without pondering the situation.

✔ **Reframe the story if you're tired of it or if it's lacking juice.** Maybe you have additional options for how to tell the story because of a new audience or a new business context or position you're in. Perhaps one of the layers of meaning now carries more significance. Or a new meaning has shown up that holds more value and should now become the key message. For example, Bob's story in the appendix could be re-crafted to focus on the inefficiencies of bureaucracies — how not to let "rules" inadvertently cause an organization to lose hundreds of thousands of dollars. Which means the key message would shift from *Assert yourself* to *Where there's a will, there's a way around red tape.*

✔ **Retire your stories.** You've told them over and over and over again. They're not attractive to you any longer. It's good to retire stories periodically. They need a rest and so do you. After a while, you may return to tell them in a different way — after you gain a new insight into the situation. It's okay. It's a normal part of the storytelling process.

Communicate really tough stories

Stories come in all shapes and sizes. Some are easy to tell. Some are tougher. Sharing stories about a health challenge, a layoff, losing a business, tragic events, accidents or death, crimes and punishments, and victims and perpetrators are all tough to tell and part of the business landscape. Your work is to understand the meaning of these events as best you can and learn how to share the experiences in ways that help all of us discover and grow.

Loren Niemi and Elizabeth Ellis, both professional storytellers and deep thinkers about the power and responsibility of stories and storytellers, wrote *Invite the Wolf In: Thinking About Difficult Stories* (August House Publishers, 2001). The entire book is devoted to working with tough stories. According to them, here's why it's important to tell tough stories: "We must tell difficult stories to be truly human. . . . How do we learn the impact and consequence of these kinds of events on people's real lives if we do not tell the difficult story? . . . To tell tough stories requires courage, thoughtfulness, and compassion. . . . If we strip stories, whether personal or traditional, of their meaning because we are afraid, we not only do a disservice to the stories, but ultimately to the listener and to ourselves. As much as we need to tell the difficult story, there are those who need to hear it."

Storytelling isn't about doing personal therapy with your listeners. Before you tell it, your tough story and relationship to the experience should already be worked out, and the story should be well crafted, with a meaning that fits the audience. Don't use your audience as a sounding board or to figure out in real time what the experience means for you (unless they're part of a Story Lab). You never want to make an audience uncomfortable or pity you (or flee). Your story is supposed to be a gift — it must truly benefit them.

Karen tells a really tough story about her mom and alcoholism before she died. It's full of humor and tragedy. But she can only tell that story when all the conditions are right: the right setting, the right people, and the right place. She's tried telling it when the timing isn't right and either can't get through it or it bombs. She knows it's an important story to tell — but only when the heavens align.

Sometimes our personal stories, or the stories we tell of others, touch us so deeply when we share them that we re-experience emotions: sadness, despair, anger, or fear. That's the nature of powerful storytelling. Not every telling of a tough story prompts this response, but be prepared for it to happen. All too often, when this occurs, most tellers stop and push their emotions aside. That may work short term. But in the long-term, sadly, they stop telling the story because it's too painful, thus losing the gifts it provides for them and others.

So what are your options? In the book *Sacred Stories: A Celebration of the Power of Stories to Transform and Heal* (Harper, 1993), storyteller and Jungian psychoanalyst Clarissa Pinkola Estes is cited as saying that stories flow where needed — yes, even the stories you share in business. They act "like an anti-biotic that finds the source of the infection and concentrates there. The story helps make that part of the psyche clear and strong again." The marvelous thing about stories, especially the emotional ones that get caught in your throat, is that the more you tell them, the more balm they create. They help heal the hurt and bind the wound.

If the story you share brings up a lot of sadness, allow this to be okay. Carry on by remembering you're there for your audience. Turn your attention back to them and the key message you're delivering. It's okay to pause and explain why you feel the way you do before continuing the story. Know that each time you tell it that the sadness will be lesser, until you finally can share it in a powerful way without feeling the need to cry.

When stories make others cry, it's okay to pause to silently acknowledge what's going on. Sometimes people get "stuck" for a moment because what you're sharing touches them deeply or makes them sad. That's perfectly fine. Keep sharing your story, moving toward resolution and your key message, knowing it will provide hope, meaning, and context for them to resolve their emotions.

Share stories that aren't your own

When we tell personal stories, we *relive* the experiences. When we share the stories of others, we must find ways to *imagine* and *embrace* their experiences. That's not easy. It requires you to be in their shoes and reflect the story from their point of view. That means you must do your homework. How do they talk? How do they normally behave? What goes through their mind? This is where audiotaping the raw story can really help. You capture the sound of their voice and their vocal intonations as well as colloquialisms they use as they talk. If the person is no longer alive, such as a historical figure or a company founder, read about them. If possible, talk to people who knew or worked with them. If none of that's possible, do the best you can.

Your responsibility when using someone else's story is to tell it authentically. In other words, remain true to the story. If you want to tell the story a certain way, or emphasize a different key message, ask the person whose story you're using for permission to alter it. You can also keep the original key message and then share the meaning the story has for you, which is *your* key message.

When you're telling someone else's story, actually share it. Don't fall into the trap of telling *about* them. Share the story as it was told to you. To refresh, first person uses *I* language, second person uses *you* language, and third person uses *he/she* and *they/them* language. Always seek approval to tell it in first person voice.

When using other people's stories, get permission from them and properly attribute it. We talk about how to do that in Chapter 5. Also acknowledge how you learned about the story and how you came to tell it.

Know when not to tell the whole story

Because everything we've said up till now speaks to telling a complete story, this may sound like an odd section for this book. We want to let you know there are at least three situations where *not* sharing the entire story is advantageous:

✔ **Using stories in training:** Let's say you're teaching a workshop on customer service. Or using a staff meeting to talk about your company's core value around customer service. Consider taking a real-life situation and only giving people the story through the conflict portion. Then have listeners create the ending. Some may be told to craft the best possible ending. Others may develop a worst-case scenario. And a few may be asked to come up with the most likely ending. Afterward, talk about all three and draw meaning from them. In this way, you help others develop critical thinking skills about the subject matter. You can also use *Harvard Business Review* case studies (some of which are stories) in this manner.

✔ **Unfolding stories** involve a single story with individual pieces revealed over a period of time in order to create and heighten drama and interest. The old Taster's Choice commercials are an example of this. You can view the 1987–1992 U.K. Nescafe version of these commercials, all strung together, at www.youtube.com/watch?v=meJDrMW6mns.

✔ **Big experiences or adventures:** These are stories that take an hour or two — or more — to tell. Karen's story of her 30 days in India in 1979 is like this. Those 30 days were filled with so many different experiences that there's no way she could pare them down to 10 or 20 minutes. This is what's called a *story cycle* — mini-stories about a specific event that are best treated as a series of stories. At any given time, Karen can dip into that treasure trove, pick one or two that are relevant to the audience in that context, and share them.

Another way to treat a group of mini-stories within a larger story is to serialize them. Serializing can be particularly effective for articles, blog posts, and web content. You can either tell the stories as they happened over time, arrange them by theme and tell them, or choose a specific mini-story to fit an immediate need.

Chapter 11

Moving Stories into Multiple Media

. . . .

. . . .

A large organization asked a colleague of ours to bid on a digital storytelling project. It was obvious that the client had focused on the technology — not on the story itself. They didn't have a clue about what story needed to be told and why, its key message and purpose, the audience for it, or how to craft it before deciding which medium to use. Our colleague covered these missing items in the proposal. A few weeks later she got a call saying she'd won the contract. She was the only one of six bidders who talked about the strategy for the story and its crafting. The rest had focused solely on the technology.

Sadly, this situation isn't unusual. Overall, we find a significant lack of understanding about what's gained or lost when moving stories into different medium. Assuming you've crafted a wonderfully compelling story based on the previous chapters, there's a continuum of media (also called *communication channels*) you can use to share it. Each medium is suited to different purposes. This six-channel continuum, ranked by *distance to the storyteller*, assumes that the closer you are to the teller, the more powerful the experience. For example, because the graphic capture of stories is visual, many elements of oral, digital, and written stories are missing from them. We explain more as we go along in this chapter. Here's the continuum:

- ✔ **Oral:** One-on-one or group setting in person (most effective).

- ✔ **Digital:** Video, film, slides or SlideShare, and so on. Although we realize almost anything can be digitized, *digital storytelling* specifically refers to the media listed here. Remember this as you read the chapter.

- ✔ **Audio:** Radio or recordings delivered online, via MP3, or on CD.

- ✔ **Written:** Blogs, newsletters, e-mails, websites, and so on.

✔ **Graphic:** Photo novellas and comics as well as posters, infographics, photomontages, and collages.

✔ **Icons:** Tangible objects (least effective in certain situations).

The medium (or media) you choose has an impact on connection, audience experience, repeatability, and other critical factors — all covered here.

Criteria for Deciding on Media

We use eight criteria for deciding which media to use for sharing a story. You can use them on your organization's stories and your own. We comment on each one as we take you through the six communication channels:

1. **Audience experience:** How engaged or passive will the audience be when consuming the story?

2. **Availability of connection:** The kind of link the story will have — will it be to you, the company, a piece of technology? We also look at the quality of this link and how long it takes the bond to occur — is it immediate or delayed?

3. **Richness of channel:** How much and how dense does the sensory data, language of the senses (LOTS), and body language need to be?

4. **Flexibility of the medium:** How malleable is the media for changing and adapting the story over time?

5. **Audience recall:** How will the media affect someone's ability to remember and share the story?

6. **Scale of delivery:** How many people need to be reached?

7. **The ability to stimulate change:** How well is the media suited to promoting the change and how fast does that change need to happen?

8. **Impact opportunity:** What's the overall effect the story may have on Trust, Engagement, Relationship, and Authenticity (TERA), and the best media to achieve these results? We explore each of these concepts earlier in this book. They're being brought together here because collectively they influence the degree of impact on an audience.

Oral: Storytelling in Person

In-person telling can happen one-on-one or in groups small or large. It can be broadcast simultaneously on a screen if the telling is part of a formal event. There are many ways for in-person telling to occur, including standing in front of people without props, employing PowerPoint as a visual aid, using puppetry, and performing a short skit with others:

1. **Audience experience:** Consumption by the listeners is first-hand. Oral storytelling is an active co-created experience. As the telling occurs, direct feedback is available for both the teller and the listeners.

2. **Availability of connection**: There is a direct and immediate human connection between the listener and the teller. With a well-told story, listeners are engaged, and the storyteller can openly interact with them.

3. **Richness of channel**: Oral storytelling is the richest communication channel. There are many options for using LOTS and for adding physicality and vocal shifts through body movements, gestures, facial expressions, characterizations, and the like. These and the ability for live audience interaction create deep experiences for people.

4. **Flexibility of the medium:** Flexibility is at its maximum with in-person telling. It requires no special equipment and can happen anywhere. In the moment, a story can be changed to meet the audience's immediate needs.

5. **Audience recall**: The ability to recall and repeat an oral story is exceedingly high, particularly if there's a strong story arc embedded with lots of LOTS, a key message, and action steps — and when a teller uses physical movements, facial expressions, gestures, and the like.

6. **Scale of delivery**: Surprisingly, oral storytelling can be experienced by thousands of people at once. On the flip side, it can be scaled to intimate settings. There are still some limitations to widely disseminating a live oral story across time zones and countries, but it can be done through multiple, simultaneous tellings by different tellers.

7. **The ability to stimulate change**: Because there's a live audience to gauge reactions and adapt the story, and the connection is immediate, the ability to stimulate change is high, assuming a well-constructed story is being delivered.

8. **Impact opportunity**: The degree of impact is greatest because all the elements of TERA are maximized.

Time and again our experience has demonstrated that telling stories orally in a face-to-face setting is the medium of choice above all else. The chance to impact many people on multiple levels is higher. The audience is engaged and so are their imaginations, which means recall of the entire story is at its strongest. Sensory data is at its richest point, and there's maximum flexibility to change and adapt the story in real time. It's a whole brain/whole body experience. Everything is optimal for getting action to happen afterward.

If one reason for sharing the story is to build TERA, then oral storytelling is key. This doesn't mean TERA can't be built through other media. However, you have to take trade-offs into account.

Digital: Visual Storytelling

Digital storytelling involves creating and sharing a story via video or a tool like SlideShare. Here's a terrific website by Alan Levine that takes a simple personal story and moves it into 50 different digital storytelling tools: http://50ways.wikispaces.com. On this site you can gain an understanding of the software that's available and how to translate a story using each kind. You can use digital stories in many ways. They can be posted on a website and used in presentations and in-house meetings or training:

1. **Audience experience:** Because consumption is second-hand (the telling isn't "live"), digital stories are a more passive experience than in-person storytelling. People get to choose whether to click the play button or do something else. Direct feedback is lost (beyond Likes, Shares, tweets, or comments). If someone does comment, you may or may not learn what's working in the story and if it resonates with them. But in some respects, you've lost control.

2. **Availability of connection:** Viewers of a digital story are one step removed from direct human experience — the connection is between them and the screen. Co-creation and the ability to immediately tailor a story to bond more deeply with viewers are lost. If resources are available, there are technologies that can connect in real time with viewers.

3. **Richness of channel:** When the video of a teller is shown, this channel can contain very rich and dense sensory information and body language. Adding photos, film, and music enhances the sensory experience, which is a good thing. Sometimes when stories are rendered digitally, photos that fade one into the other are shown in progression, with the story told in voiceover. Moving from one image to another while sharing a story can be effective. However, what's missed are gestures, body language, and facial expressions that convey so much meaning.

4. **Flexibility of the medium:** Digital storytelling is somewhat static. You can't immediately alter the story. That would require editing, re-recording, and the time and financial resources to do it well. And video, despite technology advances, can be expensive. You need to create a script and figure out which tools to use (editing software, cameras, microphones, tripods, backdrops, or digital tools like Prezi and VideoScribe). You might need to do a storyboard, find music, make the voiceover, and capture however many "takes" it requires — sometimes with a professional videographer — to get it to where everyone is happy.

5. **Audience recall:** The ability to recall and repeat the digital story is fairly high if there's a strong story arc embedded with lots of LOTS, a key message, and action steps and a teller who uses physical movements, facial expressions, gestures, vocal shifts, and the like.

6. **Scale of delivery:** With the proliferation of the Internet and the wide variety of sharing sites, there's a huge opportunity for reaching countless people. This assumes the target audience has easy and convenient access to technology and the Internet.

7. **The ability to stimulate change**: Because there's no live audience to gauge reactions, although you may hope that the digital story stimulates change, the results can be variable. On the other hand, if a digital story is disseminated widely, stimulating change could very well happen.

8. **Impact opportunity**: The degrees of TERA, although close to oral in-person storytelling, are compromised a little because of the limitations in directly connecting with others. As of the publication date of this book, the best videos of speakers are those in front of live audiences. Yet, even here, something is lost because viewers of the video are one step removed from a direct experience.

Audio: The Sound of Storytelling

Have you heard Garrison Keillor of *The Prairie Home Companion* radio show (http://prairiehome.publicradio.org) share a story? Have you ever seen him on stage telling his stories? His physical movements are sparse. Yet he weaves magical stories together through the power of imagery, imagination, and voice. You can learn from him. Here we discuss moving stories into various audio formats such as audio recordings, webinars, teleseminars, and the like:

1. **Audience experience:** Consumption is second-hand. Audio stories are a more passive type of experience because listeners aren't in the teller's presence. Listeners might be multi-tasking: doing chores, playing computer games, checking e-mail, or driving. They get to choose whether to push play or not. Direct feedback is lost (beyond Likes, Shares, tweets, or comments — but if listeners are multi-tasking, they might not even be able to do that).

2. **Availability of connection:** A degree of connection is lost because the relationship is between listeners and the audio device, not the teller. Without a direct storytelling experience, co-creation is also lost. Once again, if you have the resources to target specific listeners, craft relevant stories, and deliver them in a specific context, it's possible to increase connectivity.

3. **Richness of channel:** With an audio recording, you can't see the teller, which means sensory material is less rich because of the lack of facial expressions and body language. With diminished visual cues (which help to embed a story in the listeners' imaginations), the ability to recall and retell the story is compromised, even when given the slide pack for a webinar. To make up for what's lost, more attention needs to be paid to adding vocal variety, pausing, and repetition while avoiding rushing or speaking too fast.

4. **Flexibility of the medium:** The strength of audio recordings is their ease of duplication, dissemination, and portability. Even webinars are easy to record. The end result can be easier to edit and change than video. The

expense is relatively low, although time to make the recording is still required, along with a high-quality microphone, editing software, and the like. Access to a recording studio and professionals can help. The stories remain somewhat static because change happens via editing, or through rewrites and an updated recording.

5. **Audience recall:** The ability to recall and repeat the audio story is somewhat high if there's a strong story arc embedded with lots of LOTS, a key message, action steps, and a teller who uses a significant amount of vocal variety to maintain interest. If possible, providing visuals along with the audio may help.

6. **Scale of delivery:** With the proliferation of the Internet and many types of sharing sites, there's a huge opportunity for reaching countless people, if you can get them to notice what's being offered and then listen.

7. **The ability to stimulate change:** Similar to digital storytelling, you may hope that an audio story stimulates change, but the results may be variable if it's not recorded with a live audience that's given the chance to comment in real time. If it's disseminated widely, stimulating change could happen.

8. **Impact opportunity:** The degrees of TERA may be somewhat compromised because of the limitations in connecting with others and the other confines already mentioned.

You can use audio recordings as complementary material to other media (such as a blog post or e-books), when mass distribution is desired, or when building relationships with people isn't as critical simply because it's more important to just get the story out into the world.

Written: Old School Stories

When incorporating written stories into blogs, e-books, e-mails, newsletters, marketing materials, and websites, we often assume they need to be short, sweet, and to the point. However, there's value in long-form storytelling on the Internet. The *New York Times* article "Snowfall: The Avalanche at Tunnel Creek" is a great example: `www.nytimes.com/projects/2012/snow-fall/#/?part=tunnel-creek`.

You also have the opportunity in e-mails and newsletters — and sometimes with blogs — to take a longer story, break it up into smaller chunks, and release it over a period of days or weeks:

1. **Audience experience:** Consumption is second-hand. Written stories are a more passive type of experience since readers aren't in the presence of the author. Again, consumers control whether to read the story or not. Direct feedback is lost beyond a Like, Share, tweet — or a book review on a site such as Amazon or a blog devoted to the book.

2. **Availability of connection:** A degree of connection is lost because the relationship is between the reader and the text/paper/device, not the author. There's less opportunity for a direct human connection. Co-creation is lost because it's difficult to engage with readers directly unless an item's original content is co-created in real time on a website or blog. In the digital world, targeting written stories to specific customer groups and delivering stories with specific contexts is easier and less expensive.

3. **Richness of channel:** Because text is the medium, written stories are somewhat compromised unless storywriting skills are excellent and the reader's imagination is well stimulated.

4. **Flexibility of the medium:** The flexibility of this medium is variable. Changing written stories on websites and blogs is easy and cheap to do. They aren't as static as digital or audio stories. Changing e-book stories gets more complicated. Altering printed books or materials is far more complicated and expensive in terms of time, money, and resources.

5. **Audience recall:** The ability to recall and repeat the written story (or its essence if it's really lengthy) is somewhat high if there's a strong story arc embedded with lots of LOTS, a key message, and action steps.

6. **Scale of delivery:** The proliferation of the Internet and the wide variety of sharing sites means a huge opportunity to reach countless people, if you can get them to notice and read the story. Independent of length, written stories are easy to disseminate, and audience size doesn't matter.

7. **The ability to stimulate change:** As with digital and audio storytelling, the results can be variable because a live audience isn't available to gauge reactions so it can be adapted. On the other hand, if you can get the written story disseminated widely enough, broad change can happen.

8. **Impact opportunity:** The written word has launched revolutions and changed history. The degrees of TERA could be great if the story is exceptionally well crafted. Alternatively, its impact could be somewhat compromised because of the limitations discussed earlier.

Graphic: Sharing via Graphic Works

There are several kinds of graphic works: photo novellas and graphic novellas (a type of comic book) and posters, infographics, photomontages, and collages. We discuss them separately because photo/graphic novellas are more like books, whereas the other graphic pieces are usually displayed as one frame or one canvas.

Photo novellas and graphic novellas

Photo novellas and graphic novellas (a type of comic book) have been used with great success in public health campaigns in various countries to effect change. Photo novellas are mini-books that tell a story through photos, along with character conversation and thought bubbles. Check out this example: www.camh.ca/en/education/about/camh_publications/Pages/photonovellas.aspx. Graphic novellas are similar but use drawn images instead of photos. Here's one: www.cdc.gov/phpr/zombies_novella.htm. Both media can be very powerful for sharing stories, particularly among select age groups and in specific cultures where photo and graphic novellas are popular:

1. **Audience experience:** Consumption is second-hand. These stories, often communicated via print, are passive — they aren't being read in the presence of the teller. If consumed on the Internet, direct feedback from readers is lost beyond Likes, Shares, tweets, or a website comments. If technology isn't available to capture feedback, direct contact with the reader population or word-of-mouth research can provide insights.

2. **Availability of connection:** When a story is moved into a photo novella or a graphic novella, the distance between the reader and teller increases. The connection is to the visual representation of the story/art piece, or medium in which it's shared, not to the teller. In many ways, co-creation is lost, and there's less opportunity for a direct human connection. Readers control whether to access and read the story.

3. **Richness of channel:** Because photo novellas and comic books are visual stories, this medium can be a rich communication channel. There is the opportunity to use lots of LOTS, facial expressions, body language and movement, along with colorful images and creative designs.

4. **Flexibility of the medium:** The media is fairly static. If something in the story needs to change, most likely the entire artwork needs to be redone unless it's a simple alteration to a panel or two. That requires time and the resources to republish it. Digital formats are easier to change than print versions, where expense can increase dramatically, so the flexibility of this medium is variable.

5. **Audience recall:** Because of its visual elements, the ability to recall and repeat these types of stories is somewhat high if there's a strong story arc embedded with lots of LOTS, a key message, and action steps.

6. **Scale of delivery:** With the proliferation of the Internet and the many types of sharing sites, there's a huge opportunity for reaching countless people, if they're receptive to this type of story. For print versions, the resources available for distribution impact the scope of dissemination.

7. **The ability to stimulate change:** Delivered to the right audience, in the right context, with clear messages, photo novellas and graphic novellas can be potent tools for educating readers and changing their behaviors. It's not quite as high as in-person telling because of the unavailability of

a live audience to gauge reactions and adapt the story. If these stories are disseminated widely enough, broad change could happen.

8. **Impact opportunity:** The degree of impact could be large if the story is exceptionally well crafted. Because of the lack of direct interaction with the creator, TERA will always be somewhat compromised. In addition, limited resources, not connecting with target markets, lack of audience participation, and the media not being flexible enough to meet the immediate need can also affect these outcomes.

Posters, infographics, photomontages, and collages

As we showed in Chapter 8, infographics designed as a story or that use many story elements can be quite helpful. So are stories created from a series of photos or images — much like what's on SlideShare (www.slideshare.net) or in a photo collage. These media let your imagination and creativity soar.

Technology such as Stipple (https://stipple.com) allows you to take a photo and add text to it to transform it into a story. As you hover over a portion of a photo, the text is displayed. This can be lots of fun and fairly cheap to do. You can shorten the story down to the size of a Twitter post —140 characters — or break your narrative down into several pop-ups per image. You can also take several images to which you've added text and link them together for a more complete story to post on your website or blog. This isn't an easy task to do and still keep a story arc and all the elements that make a story a story. To see a Twitter-length story that Karen crafted, check out Chapter 14.

Vuvox (www.vuvox.com) lets you put photos together in a photo collage and add text. On Glogster (www.glogster.com), you can put together a poster that tells a story, like this example: www.glogster.com/kdietz/the-shoes/g-6m8fqf4lqbtpa48add0kqa0.

When you put a story into a poster or photo collage, it may become a representation of it instead of an effective way to tell it. In essence, you've turned the story into a type of story trigger, discussed in Chapters 5 and 15. This happens when the skeleton of a story is presented through a series of images and short texts. In this case, people may need to know some parts of the story first before they can gain meaning from a poster or a photo collage:

1. **Audience experience:** Consumption is second-hand, resulting in a passive experience. Direct feedback is lost beyond social media responses when the item is provided electronically. When housed in printed material, people may pass it along and comment on websites, if they have access. When seen as an original piece of work, they may take a photo of it and share it through social media.

2. **Availability of connection:** The distance between viewers and the teller increases because the connection is to the visual representation of the story or the medium in which it's shared, not the creator. In many ways, co-creation is lost, and there's less opportunity for a direct human connection. Viewers decide whether to consume the story.

3. **Richness of channel:** Because posters, infographics, photomontages, and collages are visual stories, this medium can be a rich communication channel when combined with text. There's the opportunity to use lots of LOTS, along with colorful images and creative designs.

4. **Flexibility of the medium:** Digital formats are easier to change than printed ones, so the flexibility of this media is variable. If any part of the piece is hand-crafted, then it becomes more static because changes may require pieces to be reworked. If there's a need to move the piece into a printed product, expenses in reproduction and dissemination increase dramatically.

5. **Audience recall:** Posters, infographics, photomontages, and collages can be great mediums for a story but can be tricky. Audience recall could be comprised if the context of an item isn't deliberately woven into the piece to bring it meaning or if viewers don't have insider knowledge about the story being referenced. If the desire is for people to both share the piece and re-tell the story, they need to be packaged together.

6. **Scale of delivery:** The Internet could be a powerful vehicle for sharing stories of this kind. There's a huge opportunity for reaching countless people, if you can get them to consume the piece. If using the Internet isn't a good option, then the resources available for printing the work will determine the scope of dissemination.

7. **The ability to stimulate change:** Welcome to unchartered territory. Delivered to the right audience, in the right context, with a clear message, stories told in this way could be powerful. Although there are plenty of opportunities to be creative and experiment, it's unclear if these media will stimulate change. Posters have been successfully used in resistance movements (http://en.wikipedia.org/wiki/Protest_art), though they're used more as triggers to activate a story inside the viewers' minds. In addition to sharing or sparking a really good story, for change to really happen, public participation needs to be added to the equation. Having people participate in the actual creation of the piece — or contribute their own creations — activates individuals and/or communities to become "catalysts for change." Participation becomes an act of self-expression, empowering people to share voices and stories with one another about an issue in which they have a personal stake.

8. **Impact opportunity:** The degree of impact could be large if the story is exceptionally well crafted. TERA will always be compromised if there's lack of direct interaction with the creator of the piece. In addition, limited resources, not connecting with target markets, lack of viewer participation, and the variable flexibility of the medium to address the immediate need can also affect outcomes.

Icons: Sharing Iconic Stories

By *icon*, we mean that a single image or object serves to trigger the story in the minds of those who come upon it. Stories portrayed in this manner are the furthest removed from the teller. Here's one example: Imagine an employee who is well regarded in his company. He once saved the day with a customer, and that experience has become folklore around the firm. People love the story. It's a great reminder of the desirable action steps this employee performed for the customer, based on the company's values. His last name is Bear. Even after Bear retires, when employees talk, all they have to do is say the word *bear* and everyone laughs. They connect to the story being referenced and how it fits into the current conversation. What if they put up a bear icon or piece of artwork on a wall in the company to remind people of the story? That bear is the icon for the story about Bear, the former employee.

You may want to use an icon as a reminder of one of your hip pocket stories or as an educational prop to reference a story during training workshops. You can also use an icon during presentations as a take-away (in Chapter 7, if you were Pam Stampen, you could give people a model airplane to take home):

1. **Audience experience:** Consumption may be first- or second-hand. For this medium to work, people have to know first-hand, or be taught, the story. Insider knowledge is required. If insider knowledge and the story are known, audience experience is more direct. If not, audience experience is about the icon; the experience of the story is minimal at best.

2. **Availability of connection:** When a story is moved into an icon, the connection is to the visual/physical representation of the story or the medium it's shared in, not the creator or storyteller. Thus, the distance between the audience and the storyteller becomes greater. Unless the icon triggers conversation, co-creation is lost, resulting in less opportunity for direct human connection.

3. **Richness of channel:** Although the icon can be a potent visual image in and of itself, the richness of this channel is somewhat compromised because of the lack of text, language, physical movement, and the like.

4. **Flexibility of the medium:** Because digital formats can be easier to change than hand-crafted artistic media, the flexibility here is variable. If the icon is digital, it can be very flexible. If any part of the piece is hand-crafted, it becomes more static because changes may require the entire piece to be reworked. Expenses and resources increase dramatically.

5. **Audience recall:** Audience recall could be comprised. For the icon to be meaningful, the viewer has to know the story, its context, and have insider knowledge. There's more opportunity for an icon to be remembered and the story retold if people have access to the story. This can be a great medium for triggering a story, but it can be very tricky.

6. **Scale of delivery:** Technology provides many opportunities for disseminating and sharing a story represented as an icon. But it only works if people viewing the icon have access to the story, its context, and some insider information. Otherwise the icon won't be meaningful and reach is compromised.

7. **The ability to stimulate change**: This is unchartered territory. Similar to protest art, icons can powerfully promote a change, as evidenced in the United States by the Spring 2013 DOMA (Defense of Marriage Act) decision and how an icon for it went viral (www.adweek.com/news/advertising-branding/doma-nation-148206). Surely, characters like Mickey Mouse or Superman trigger stories in the minds of audiences. But linking specific stories to icons meant to stimulate large-scale change doesn't guarantee success. Delivered to the right audience, in the right context, with clear messages, stories told through icons can work, as shown here. Like posters, infographics, photomontages, and collages, public participation might need to be employed to stimulate change (see preceding section).

8. **Impact opportunity**: The degree of impact could be great if the story and its icon are exceptionally well crafted and strongly linked together. TERA will always be somewhat compromised because of lack of direct interaction with the story's main character and creator. Unless people know the story and the information surrounding it, impact will be compromised. In addition, limited resources, not connecting with target markets, lack of audience participation, and the medium not being flexible enough for the immediate need could also affect outcomes.

Deciding Which Medium Fits Your Needs

Both of us have experienced this impulse when working with leaders: They want to polish a story so they can be videotaped telling it, be done with it, and then get back to work. Our reaction is always, "Oh no, that's the last thing you want to do." Why? As a leader, manager, small business owner, nonprofit executive, or government director, people want to experience *you* first-hand. They want to directly experience your authenticity. They want to connect with you, trust you, and have a relationship with you. Face-to-face telling gives you maximum impact in all four areas — whether you're focused on change, raising funds, managing a team, or growing a business.

Now, we know that isn't always possible. And that your department, business, or nonprofit may need to disseminate stories widely. Time, money, and resources all come into play. How static, flexible, and adaptable the medium is also has a role. To figure out which media on the continuum will get you the results you seek, answer the questions we pose in the next two sections.

Find the purpose of sharing

Before you do anything else, outline who the audience is for the story. Be as specific as possible in identifying it. Then determine the desired effect the story needs to have. This is separate from the story's content. (Audience and effect are both discussed in Chapter 10.) The effect is what the story needs to do for you personally or for your business — the communication channel (that is, media on the continuum) that's going to provide the best chance of getting stated results. Issues to consider include:

- ✔ How broadly the message needs to be disseminated.
- ✔ How strong a relationship needs to be built with the audience for the long-term.
- ✔ The degree of authenticity the audience needs to experience.
- ✔ How strong the need is to document and preserve the story for the long-term.
- ✔ The speed needed to get the message to the audience.

Don't skip these items. Your answers will help you filter through your responses to the questions that follow.

Determine what's desirable

There are lots of choices and decisions to make when shifting an oral story into different media. Here are the eight criteria again, with questions you can answer based on your specific needs. After answering the bulleted questions, in each section determine which medium will serve the need best:

1. **Audience experience:**
   - Is the audience going to be engaged in an active, co-created experience or will it be more passive?
   - How much does the audience need to be directly engaged with the teller, or does it matter if their experience is more passive?

2. **Availability of connection:**
   - How important is it to have a direct connection?
   - How much of a direct connection do I or my organization need with the audience given the identified purpose?
   - Will the chosen medium create an immediate connection or will the audience have a choice about listening to the story?

3. Richness of channel:

- How important is it to have the story be densely packed with LOTS and physical movement?

- How rich and dense with LOTS, physical expression, and the like does the medium need to allow for given the identified purpose?

4. Flexibility of the medium:

- How flexible does the medium need to be for changing and adapting the story?

- What are the costs of changing the story at a later date?

5. Scale of delivery:

- How many people need to be reached?

- How can technology be used for delivery purposes?

6. Audience recall:

- How important is it for the audience to recall and retell the story?

- Which medium will allow for the strongest amount of recall so the audience will be able to remember and repeat the story?

7. The ability to stimulate change:

- How could each medium inspire the needed change?

- Which medium would be the fastest at stimulating the change?

8. Impact Opportunity:

- How much TERA is needed (trust, engagement, relationship, authenticity)?

- Which medium will best leverage TERA based on stated needs?

Now that you have the answers to all these questions, identify the medium that fits the best with all of these criteria, that also meets the purposes identified earlier, and matches the targeted audience.

Choose a medium using story length

You can always expand and contract a story to fit different media (see Chapter 9). Here are a few examples:

You can take a 10- or 20-minute story, reduce it to its core essence as a 1- to 3-minute story, and then share it as a digital story, a quick audio file, or SlideShare program. Or you can create a photo story. Maybe it can be turned into an infographic or reduced to two or three paragraphs as a written story. In this way, you get the same story out in a variety of formats, including telling it orally face-to-face. The story structures from Chapter 7 can help you here. Use them to shorten a story without losing its impact.

You can also expand a story by adding maps, videos, infographics, and other supporting materials to create an even richer piece. Likewise, you can use the material in Chapters 6, 7, and 9 to expand your story and really heighten the transformation that occurs.

Creating Stories That Go Viral

The gold standard for leveraging a story is whether it goes viral through word-of-mouth. That's everyone's dream. There's an art and science to creating a story that will go viral. Today it's mostly art, but more science is coming forth. Here's what we know as of the publication of this book.

Chip and Dan Heath are best known for their book *Made to Stick* (Random House, 2007), which focuses on what makes people *remember* information. Jonah Berger, author of *Contagious: How Things Catch On* (Simon & Schuster, 2013), goes a step further and addresses those factors that stimulate us to *share* information with others. According to Berger, certain emotions increase the likelihood that a story will spread. He learned the following:

- **On average, positive pieces are shared more than negative ones and high-arousal emotions, whether positive or negative, increase sharing.** The first part of this statement may seem like common sense. The surprise is the latter piece. Even though some negative emotions like anger or anxiety actually increase sharing because they move us to action, sadness doesn't. When we're angry, we want to throw a temper tantrum, scream and yell, and jump up and down. We do the same when we're excited, but in a positive way. Excitement, humor, and awe are all high-arousal positive emotions.

- **Controversy, or being controversial, doesn't increase sharing.** Berger learned that the more controversial the topic, the less conversation it sparks because the controversy makes us feel uncomfortable. As a result, we don't talk about the subject and we don't share information about it.

Here are some other drivers of sharing that Berger found:

- **Social currency:** A piece gets shared when it makes us look great or knowledgeable. We share content when it's something worth thinking about and because it arouses us, whether it's true or not. The more practical value we perceive it to have, the more we'll share it. We do this because we're trying to help others.

> ✔ **Triggers, public visibility, and stories:** If people see someone doing something, they're more likely to do it themselves. Making something more observable makes it easier to imitate. This is called *public visibility*. This begs a question: How can you use stories to make a behavior more visible? Regarding the sharing of stories, make sure the information you want to convey is wrapped up into the story arc so tightly that people can't share the information without the story.

As Berger asks, ". . . will applying [my findings] make it more likely that 10 people will hear [your message] rather than nine, or that your sales will increase by 20 to 40 percent? Certainly." (`www.gsb.stanford.edu/news/research/why-some-ideas-spread`) We don't know about you, but we think this impact is significant.

Reflect on what you want to accomplish by having a story go viral. Then select the medium that best supports that outcome. If you're a leader sharing a story in your firm that demonstrates a particular value that you prize — such as innovation — you want employees to talk about and share that story. At the same time, if you want to build trust, authenticity, and deep relationships, then oral storytelling is the best medium. If you're telling the story to advance a cause, fund a Kickstarter campaign, increase visibility, or get more website hits, then a digital story that could go viral across the Internet might suit your needs better.

Recognize the art, science, and mystery

The art of storytelling is the crafting. Part of the science of sharing stories is mastering the media continuum — and keeping up with future developments. Even though the guidelines for crafting a compelling story have remained the same for years and years, what's new and different are the multiple media available for sharing a story, which are unprecedented.

Every person, organization, and brand has a story to tell. How we elect to share that story is shaped by the available media. Today, people can access content from TVs, game consoles, computers, tablets, and mobile phones — who knows what else is on the horizon. That means there are more ways than ever to connect with others.

It also means you need to tell your stories across a wide range of platforms using a variety of tools. Find creative ways to share them, personalize them, and have an audience to engage with them in different media. It's easier now to target by audience, demographic profile, behavior, purchase habits, and many other indicators. We're sure there are even more creative tools, platforms, and experiences waiting for us. Let us know what you find!

Chapter 12

Incorporating Story in Your Organization

· ·

In This Chapter

▶ Knowing what causes resistance to storytelling and ways to overcome it

▶ Finding ways to incorporate storytelling into your daily work

▶ Identifying ways for your organization to benefit from storytelling

▶ Being mindful of ethical issues associated with business storytelling

· ·

*Y*ou don't need permission to try business storytelling approaches in your daily work. As we mention in Chapter 2, that means you have the personal power to move others to action. At the other end of the people continuum, we haven't yet found an organization that's incorporated story into *all* aspects of its DNA as a core competence, internally and externally. Yes, it takes time and effort. But as Chapter 2 shows, story use in all business functions can get results.

This chapter is the bridge between using storytelling on your own and getting your organization to embrace it. You can use storytelling in a work process, a project or program, in the way leaders behave with staff, for a specific function such as operations or customer service, or as a strategy. In this chapter, we highlight why some people resist using story, suggest several tools to individually and organizationally assess story use, and discuss many ways to introduce story into your organization. We also talk about setting up a *story bank* (also called a library, database, repository, or repertoire) to draw on, when needed. And we cover ethical considerations for using stories in a business setting.

Overcoming Resistance

There are some business functions and professions where story is more naturally embraced. For example: Those in sales will tell you they have a predisposition to tell stories. The same thing is true with individuals who work in marketing and branding. Journalists and writers, along with lawyers who practice in the courtroom, financial advisors who are focused on people realizing their dreams, professional speakers, training professionals, public relations folks, and the like are also prone to tell stories.

It seems logical then, that there are careers and functions where it's harder for people to wrap their heads around the benefits of story. These are professions where information sharing is what's taught in college and reinforced in the workplace. They include data-intensive, research-oriented, scientific, or highly technical roles where staff relay pure facts.

In the blog article "Tall Tales: The Strength of Storytelling" (`http://rw connect.esomar.org/tall-tales-the-strength-of-story telling/`), at an ESOMAR congress in Athens, Patrick Young of DVL Smith gives a reason as to why this might be. ". . . the craft of storytelling demands that there be a new project stage inserted between data analysis and presentations; that of creating the story. We need to make time to turn our evidence into a story. And unfortunately some organizations may not be prepared to make this adjustment."

Chapter 1 addresses one aspect of the time problem. We said: "People will spend the time to listen to well-constructed compelling stories, which means structuring them well is your issue." However, Smith raises a related time challenge — how to provide people the time they need to structure stories well from the data. What we've learned is it's a chicken-and-egg question: Until leaders hear a compelling story and experience the outcomes of using stories with groups, they're not inclined to give staff the time to craft them. Our advice? Find the time. If you believe it's important, don't wait to be given time. Make time to fit this work into your schedule.

The same blog article offers another reason storytelling efforts get stalled. Alison Esse, co-founder of The Storytellers, a U.K.-based consultancy, says: "The very nature of storytelling tends to be viral, ethereal, and intangible. This makes it difficult to implement in organizations with clear hierarchies and structured processes and systems."

Stephen Denning, author of *The Leader's Guide to Radical Management: Reinventing the Workplace for the 21st Century* (Jossey-Bass, 2010) and several books on storytelling, agrees. In "Leadership Storytelling 3.0: From Arithmetic to Calculus" (`www.storytelling.es/leadership-storytelling-3-0-from-arithmetic-to-calculus-2/`), he says, "We need to change the very processes and systems that drive the organization. If those processes and systems remain focused on the manipulation of things — outputs, demand, human resources — [they] will undermine deliberate attempts to make the organization more people-focused." Denning continues, "In order to create people-centered organizations, organizations need people-centered processes." He says asking for customer and user stories and using value-stream mapping to create "the story of the organization from the customer's point of view" can be valuable.

Before we leave the topic of resistance, we can't overlook how you might sabotage yourself. Here's what we've observed and heard from people over many years — and how this book can help you:

- ✔ **Not getting trained or educated in storytelling:** Kudos to you for reading this book!

- ✔ **Thinking stories have only limited applications in an organization:** Read Chapter 2.

- ✔ **Thinking you personally can't tell great stories:** Read Chapter 10.

- ✔ **Thinking business stories are only fables and fairy tales:** Read Chapter 4.

- ✔ **Telling other people's stories without permission or acknowledgement:** Read Chapter 5.

- ✔ **Thinking that just because you tell stories, you'll be successful. Listening is as important — sometimes even more so:** Read Chapter 5.

- ✔ **Not being humble in your stories and messages:** Read Chapter 10.

- ✔ **Neglecting to practice telling stories:** Read Chapter 10.

- ✔ **Being too scripted and rote when telling stories:** Read Chapters 6 and 7.

- ✔ **Mandating someone else do all the storytelling:** Read the rest of this chapter.

- ✔ **Not linking vision and value to stories and daily work:** Read Chapter 4 and the rest of this chapter.

In addition to the ideas offered in this section, the remainder of this chapter focuses on helping you overcome these barriers. Read on!

Assessing Storytelling Competence

There are several kinds of tools available to diagnose both your organization's competence in story use and your own personal skills and style. Here are a few assessments we've run across in our work:

- ✔ **Story IQ — Narrative Intelligence:** Karen has developed a three-part assessment (www.juststoryit.com). Part A focuses on how confident you are in your personal storytelling skills. Part B looks at how much knowledge you have about the topic and the dynamics of storytelling — how and why it works and how to find, mine, evoke, and work with stories. Part C assesses how aware you are about various applications for using stories within and outside your organization.

✔ **Story competence and application assessment diagnostic:** Developed by Graham Williams, founder of The Halo and the Noose, this tool reveals an organizations' strengths, weaknesses, and opportunities to apply story processes, techniques, and approaches in advancing corporate goals (http://storytellinginbusiness.blogspot. fr/2012/04/get-your-complementary-story-competence. html). Two sets of outcome measures are provided: level of story competence displayed by the organization (capturing, listening, and telling) and the degree to which story is deeply understood and applied throughout the business. Here, *story* means all oral and written versions of narrative, metaphor, and personal anecdote; biographical, histori-cal, mythological, metaphorical, and wisdom stories; past, present, and future stories; and fact and fiction.

✔ **Professional Values & Story Index (PVSI):** Developed by consultant, facil-itator, and coach Cindy Atlee of The Storybranding Group, based on the 12-archetype model created by Dr. Carol Pearson, this instrument (www. storybranding.com/site/take-the-pvsi-survey.php#step_1) measures how much you identify with the attitudes and behaviors of 12 mythical or archetypal characters, called *story types*. The results tell you what's most meaningful and motivating to you in the workplace and how your strengths and values portray a specific story type.

What does the future hold for assessment and diagnostic tools? Those avail-able as of this writing only help you and your organization obtain measure-ments of storytelling readiness and competency. Given the measurement approaches emerging in the field (see Chapter 19), the next level will hope-fully address organizational progress on two fronts:

✔ Measuring and documenting the achievement of key strategies and enhancement of core business processes through storytelling.

✔ Measuring and documenting the quantifiable impact of story beyond anecdotal and action research on knowledge transfer, leadership, and management effectiveness, productivity, customer loyalty, and the like.

In both cases, the challenge will be teasing out the contributions of storytell-ing from other factors that may be causing the change.

Taking Personal Ownership of Story

What does it take to become a *story pioneer* (a term first used in *Wake Me Up When the Data Is Over*, Jossey-Bass, 2006) — a person who uses business storytelling approaches day in and day out? Just do it! There's no reason to announce to the world that you're embracing business storytelling. Each time you use a story or a story-related approach, you're modeling a new way of communicating. Be mindful of this and intentional in your efforts so that others see and experience the positive results of story use in the workplace. In this way, you'll help others to overcome any resistance they may have.

You can do a variety of things:

✔ **Keep track of your personal stories.** Use the list of hip pocket stories in Chapter 4 as a guide. You can keep a journal of story ideas, put notes about individual experiences onto notecards, or create a database of situations to translate later on into stories on your computer.

✔ **Find opportunities to orally share your personal stories and those of your organization.** When might a story be useful in relaying your work to someone? When might a story be a good way to communicate an issue? When might a story help someone you've been asked to train?

✔ **Talk about the difference that storytelling has made in your work or organizational life.** Showcase your experiences and those from others.

✔ **Encourage those around you at work to use storytelling.** When it makes sense to do so, suggest the approach when coaching and mentoring folks.

✔ **Evoke stories from your coworkers, customers, and others that you come in contact with on a regular basis.** Instead of asking questions, look for ways to use story prompts to get a richer picture of what they went through or a problem they experienced.

✔ **Listen, listen, listen.** When you hear a story, use the listening approach outlined in Chapter 5. Listening delightedly to these stories will give you insights into these individuals and their experiences.

✔ **Identify opportunities to relay stories in writing.** How could you include them in a proposal? A business case? A status report?

✔ **Find ways to attach a prop to a story you tell.** Refer to the prop as you tell your story to give your words another "real-life" dimension.

How can you identify these opportunities? Answer these questions:

✔ **What work processes are part of your job responsibilities?** How can you incorporate various story techniques and approaches into how you perform them?

✔ **What projects are you working on?** Relaying lessons learned, risks, and status updates all benefit from sharing stories within a team.

✔ **How could you enhance your communications with your boss through story?** In what ways can you use story to convey best practices, issues, work progress, and results to upper management?

✔ **What meetings do you regularly attend?** How might you use story in staff meetings? Committee meetings? Task force meetings? Status meetings?

What about leaders? Leaders need to think of storytelling not as another tool to use in their work, but as a fundamental way in which their work is carried out. There's no special place for *leadership storytelling* to happen. Stories need to be shared in both formal and informal situations: one-on-one, at social gatherings, in speeches, and everywhere in between.

As Paul Smith in his book *Lead with a Story: A Guide to Crafting Business Narratives That Captivate, Convince, and Inspire* (AMACOM, 2012) points out, David Armstrong, former CEO of Armstrong International, would post stories on bulletin boards around the office, stuff them into paycheck envelopes, record them on CDs for his salespeople, and broadcast them on TVs on the factory floor. "In short," says Smith, "It's hard to think of a place [leaders] shouldn't be telling stories." Smith links sharing stories to 21 tough leadership challenges, including setting policy without rules, building courage, demonstrating problem-solving, helping everyone understand the customer, valuing diversity and inclusion, delegating authority and giving permission, and encouraging innovation.

In his article, "Corporate Storytelling: The Wave or Particle Theory?" Richard House, who's worked as a journalist and as a communications consultant for leading international companies, sees four of these challenges as key for leaders (http://storyfountain.wordpress.com/2011/09/18/corporate-storytelling-the-wave-or-particle-theory/):

- ✔ **Translate formal company information.** Transfer strategic objectives, issues, and market information into simple messages and easy-to-understand stories that are relevant to employees and teams.

- ✔ **Create emotional bonds**. Find ways to use the practice of storytelling to motivate employees and teams — and to increase employee satisfaction and engagement — by making people feel heard and understood.

- ✔ **Transmit values**. "Formal company values . . . can seem dry, lifeless, and forgettable if remote from employees' daily work — however long a task force has spent crafting them." Increase your authenticity by sharing stories that draw on work examples and personal experiences that help employees "make sense" of these ideas. (We would add that you also need to help employees "make meaning" from these stories so they can easily align their behaviors to these core values.)

- ✔ **Stimulate the imagination to conceive other outcomes**. ". . . Focus not so much on the goals at hand, but how things will look once today's goals have been achieved." Work to get staff to say, "We can do it here." Do this by using story to present new perspectives or "alternative versions of the future," so people can imagine bolder possibilities. (We touch on future stories in Chapters 4 and 16.)

If you're a leader, storytelling can help you build "presence" and your signature leadership voice. However, House believes that before you can unlock this step as a leader, you have to work first on building skills and qualities related to effective communication. This involves some attributes that even high-level senior managers may take for granted, especially in hierarchical institutions or workplace cultures where power-distance is traditionally high. These include "showing up with the whole self," "active listening," and "experiencing the other." Who said that taking personal ownership for stories in leadership is easy?

Getting Story into an Enterprise's DNA

 Our goal is to have story permeate all aspects of how an organization functions so that it's elevated to a core competence for all employees and the broader enterprise. But we know this isn't where most organizations start, and that's okay. We'd rather you find small ways to get people to embrace what's in this book than fail at gaining acceptance to a larger organizational initiative. What follows are ideas on how to start small and build large.

Provide training and coaching

One of the easiest ways to introduce a new concept or skill or practice into the workplace is through coaching and training. However, if you treat training as a one-and-done — an event — instead of a series of activities, of which one is training, you won't get the results you seek. Based on what we've seen work and fail, here are our thoughts on a few options:

✔ **Coaching without training:** If you model skills related to story, you'll open up opportunities to coach others. People will notice that you're getting results and want to achieve those themselves. Offer your help when you hear situations where a story skill would be useful to someone.

✔ **A one-hour, in-person presentation:** As you gain personal traction using a variety of story skills, you may be asked to present what you know and have learned to your coworkers or team members. How do you determine what's most important for them to learn? Focus on immediate issues or a specific need that could be addressed through story. And make it simple. If it seems overwhelming or complicated, or too theoretical rather than practical, you won't get others to embrace trying something new. Offer to coach people afterward so you can continue to develop them. If you're a speaker doing a one-hour keynote talk, find ways to ascertain needs and potential applications in advance so your talk can be tailored to the audience. In all cases, find a way to do one or two short activities so people get a chance to practice skills in real time.

✔ **Webinars:** There are a couple ways to use webinars:

• **Use a webinar similar to an in-person presentation.** The challenge with this is there's no real chance for follow-up unless you build it into the process. Nor is there the opportunity for people to practice in real time.

- **Use a webinar as a way to introduce the topic of story prior to a training workshop.** We've found that assigning homework between the webinar and the training doesn't mean it will get done. For this to work, a system of accountability needs to be built into the process.

- **Use webinars as a follow-up to training, once attendees have gotten a chance to practice.** Build it around actual challenges they may be experiencing and feature success stories from those who have gotten results.

✔ **Formal training (half day and longer):** The key question here is "What do attendees need to be able to do differently after training?" Without knowing this, chances are the workshop won't include enough practice time or the right knowledge so attendees have context around what to do with their stories.

We've both conducted training events that have lasted a half day to many days in length. For skills to take hold, it's imperative that this training be part of a continuum of activities. Here's one option: Have people read a very short article, watch a short video, or attend a webinar in advance. After this, assign a small task for them to prep for the training. It could be, "Here are some story prompts. Using one, come prepared to work on a specific story." Lori's gone so far as to ask attendees not only to find a story but to audio record and transcribe it prior to training. It worked because internal staff followed up on this assignment to ensure it was completed.

If you can, present the training over a period of time. Do a piece and then let attendees go practice. Have them bring their knowledge to the next workshop and build on it. Repeat this process several times. After the training is complete, have attendees fill out multi-part Action Plans (one copy stays with them, a second gets sent to them in six weeks, and a third goes to their boss for coaching purposes). If you're coordinating the training, retain a fourth copy for yourself so you can summarize people's commitments and identify themes for follow-up. Use the six-week mark to get feedback on how well attendees have done. Also schedule a follow-up webinar to address successes and skill-enhancement requests.

You can offer training and coaching with the intent of beefing up people's skills. Or you can do it more strategically, like the Association for Public Health Laboratories (APHL). Through APHL's emerging leaders program and its advocacy work, three workshops on story use, ranging from one to three days in length, were offered to members across the country over the course of ten months. Prior to each one, interviews with at least five attendees occurred to collect examples of story use and find a single story to capture and craft to start out each training. As workshops progressed, stories that prior attendees and staff had developed anew were incorporated into the next offering. Simultaneously, Lori offered one-on-one coaching to staff and attendees.

Before the advocacy workshop, Lori taught a webinar and provided attendees with pre-work. Following training, workshop attendees, accompanied by staff, took the stories they developed to Capitol Hill to test them with legislators and their aides. A debrief occurred afterward, and the next versions of the stories were submitted to APHL for feedback and honing. Now the organization is moving toward creating an overall story strategy for APHL as an association as it continues to offer additional training and coaching to promote and communicate the role of laboratory science in the national public health dialogue.

Hitch story efforts to work processes

Every organization has lots of work processes or procedures in place. Most places have standard operating procedures for these. Often, surrounding this work is a continual improvement initiative or International Organization for Standardization (ISO) initiative. What's great about these efforts is that they are the perfect opportunity to introduce story.

No doubt, you're asking, "How so?" Try a couple ideas for your work group. We're positive you'll be able to come up with more:

- ✔ **Create a vision for how the work process needs to flow.** Have people share a future story of how the ideal work flow might occur. You can also act out this story (that is, do a walk-through of what life would be like) to make it more tangible for others.

- ✔ **Collect input from customers and consumers.** Instead of asking questions, use story prompts. The resulting stories will give you more explicit information about requirements and how critical they are. These stories may also uncover needs you hadn't previously considered.

- ✔ **Listen to feedback from those doing the work.** Collect their experiences in the form of stories. Listen delightedly to draw out more opportunities for improvements and innovations.

- ✔ **Make meaning from the data that's being collected.** Chapter 8 gives you a host of ideas on how to craft stories involving data.

There are also certain work processes for which incorporating story techniques makes sense for an entire department. Use staff meetings — or whatever committees are in place to discuss work flows — to generate ways to incorporate story into them and to talk about how story has improved work process performance over time. Some examples include:

- ✔ **Recruiting:** Relay stories about the company when advertising a position and explaining its core values. Use them at job fairs.

- ✔ **Hiring:** Use story prompts to evoke stories from candidates.

✔ **Onboarding new hires:** Provide historical stories about the enterprise. Get leaders to share stories about themselves. Ask new hires to share stories about what brought them to the organization. Tell stories about how products and services have made a difference in people's daily lives.

✔ **Providing on-the-job training:** Provide stories about what can happen if mistakes are made.

✔ **Conducting performance appraisals:** Ask employees to put together stories that highlight their successes and accomplishments.

✔ **Pitching a prospect:** Communicate stories you've heard about the challenges the company is facing and those from other clients who have overcome similar issues.

✔ **Putting together a budget:** Collect stories that exemplify the needs for monies being requested.

✔ **Innovating new products or services:** Collect customer stories about their pain points and use them as fodder to brainstorm new or improved products or services.

✔ **Researching competitors:** Seek out stories about them from customers, new recruits, colleagues, professional association members, and the like.

Here's a specific example of what we mean: Coca-Cola has entirely revamped it marketing processes to be story based. Instead of focusing on a traditional *creative excellence* strategy, the company's approach has evolved into one of *content excellence* — what it calls Content 2020. Coke has released two videos on YouTube to discuss this shift, which includes moving from one-way to dynamic storytelling, where the company and its customers share stories back and forth.

In Part 1 (www.youtube.com/watch?v=LerdMmWjU_E), we learn this approach is based on brand stories creating "liquid and linked ideas that provoke conversations that [Coca-Cola] need[s] to act and react to 365 days a year." It's acknowledged that consumer-generated stories outnumber Coco-Cola stories on a number of its brands and that the company wants consumers to continue to take the lead in storytelling. In the third chapter of this video, the company states five key storytelling areas it will pursue: serial storytelling, multifaceted storytelling, spreadable storytelling, immersion and discovery storytelling, and engagement through storytelling.

Like Coca-Cola has done, how do you make story use a standard way of working within your function or department versus a one-time occurrence? Here are four ideas:

✔ **Alter work processes and procedures — and the documentation associated with them — to reflect the routine use of storytelling.**

✔ **Tie engagement in storytelling activities to job descriptions and performance appraisals.** In this way, their use will be measured.

✔ **At staff meetings, ask for stories and make time for folks to share them.** It could be a story that highlights the topic of a specific agenda item. Or it could be a set agenda item where the open sharing of stories occurs. Include time for reflection on these stories, using the techniques mentioned in Chapter 5.

✔ **If you're a leader, when you hold individual meetings with staff, regularly prompt for interesting or unique stories.** Also, share one if there's a lesson that can be put to immediate use by the employee. This is especially helpful when coaching and mentoring or helping staff deal with a performance issue.

Link story into project work

Proctor & Gamble does it. So does NASA. In fact, NASA publishes lessons learned stories in *ASK* magazine (`http://appel.nasa.gov/ask-magazine-issue-50-spring-2013/`). There are a number of ways to link story to various aspects of the project-management lifecycle. Which of these could you try on a current or future project?

✔ **Gain buy-in and funding for a business case.** In Chapter 14, we outline several types of stories that work well here.

✔ **Get to know team members.** For example, have members share a story about their best and worst project experience to learn what works best for them individually.

✔ **Relay expectations — yours and those from the sponsor.** How do you want people to handle conflict? What is meant by "on-time?" Share a story so all of you have the same mental picture.

✔ **Explain concepts that aren't always easy to grasp.** Some of these include dependencies, duration versus effort, and how quality is being defined.

✔ **Aid in identifying business requirements.** Be careful. Something may be labeled a *user story* but may be nothing more than a descriptive phrase or paragraph about a requirement and its functionality from the perspective of the user or the customer of the system.

✔ **Identify risks.** Have team members share stories of possible failures and their effects to tease out risks and how to mitigate them.

✔ **Manage scope creep.** If you've articulated a future story at the beginning of the project, refer back to it to demonstrate scope creep when a change request is put forth.

✔ **Assess and maintain stakeholder commitment.** Evoke stories from stakeholders when determining what they need and what they can give to the project. Continue to request project-specific stories from stakeholders to engage them throughout the project and showcase those that exemplify their involvement.

✔ **Get status updates at meetings.** Instead of talking through a bulleted list of accomplishments, hand it out and relay stories that stress something of high importance on the project.

✔ **Suggest ways to address issues or problems.** Depicting the issue or problem that needs to be addressed is best done through a story or series of them. How an issue was handled successfully on a prior project could also be brought in through story.

✔ **Promote successes and accomplishments.** Tell the story surrounding the positive outcome that was achieved so other members can benefit from the experience.

✔ **Gather best practices during a project close-out.** Find a way to document and share this type of story with other teams and functions.

If you're a project team member — or an individually contributing change management or communications resource — once again, no need to ask for permission to use storytelling in your project work. If you're a sponsor or project or program manager, strategize how you want to introduce and use storytelling with your team. In other words, lay out what you want to accomplish by using stories within the project or program and the steps that need to be taken to make it all happen.

Here's an example of why you need to strategize. When Karen worked with a national retail bank in the late 1990s, silos between divisions were pretty rigid. As a result, significant parts of the organization's history were being lost. As she collected historical stories in each division, she learned that some groups had some parts of the larger story, and other groups had different pieces. But no one group or division knew the entire story. So she and her team began to share the different parts of the story across silos, particularly the pieces that each group didn't know. Staff would consistently say, "Wow, I never knew that!" Pride in the organization and appreciation for coworkers significantly increased. Were silos broken down? No. Did significant cracks develop? Yes. Did greater acceptance and acknowledgement for other's work increase? Yes. All good things!

In this situation, Karen used story listening to cut through barriers and heirarchies and boldly go where no one had gone before. To have a crack at the successes that she enjoyed, you've got to know how to effectively listen for and evoke stories from individuals and groups — and how to share them in a way that they're well received in a culture that hasn't resonated with the practice in the past.

Propose a small story initiative

Sometimes the route to bringing story into an organization isn't a direct one. Like this example from Karin Hurt, an experienced executive (http://letsgrowleaders.com/2012/09/20/strategic-storytelling/).

Years ago when Karin worked in human resources, she and a colleague worked for almost a year on building a comprehensive frontline leadership development program, from competency models through the development of the curriculum with outside experts. Then, as she puts it, "The whole thing came to a screeching halt. A big merger was announced, and the program was put on hold." She and her coworker had a realization. "The best leaders we saw at the front lines were the ones who had some scar tissue from experience, combined with other leadership competencies. If only we could help to accelerate the learnings of that experience to others. How could we do that? For free? Our answer . . . storytelling. Without announcing our intentions (just a causal whisper to our bosses), we created a series of strategic storytelling workshops designed for various levels of the business."

In summary, Karen and her coworker asked leaders to identify a personal story related to how they viewed and practiced leadership and share it with their team. Together the leader and the team were to identify story themes and use them to create team norms. Leaders were also asked to identify ways to "incorporate strategic storytelling into their communication plans." After meeting with the "friendliest senior leaders" to pitch their idea, Karin and her colleague were invited to give it a go. The technique they used, along with key lessons, can be found in *Storytelling, an ASTD InfoLine* (ASTD Press) (`http://store.astd.org/Default.aspx?tabid=167&ProductId=8028`).

What can we take away from Karin's experience? Identify leaders in your organization whose styles are amenable to storytelling. Maybe they already tell stories or advocate for their use. Leverage these individuals and their groups to spearhead a storytelling initiative. Allow it to grow from there. Let these folks be your advocates.

The book *Wake Me Up When the Data Is Over* (Jossey-Bass, 2006) was specifically designed to collect examples of story initiatives, especially those initiated at the grassroots level. Here are two examples:

- ✔ **Jodie Beverage, RN, Operating Room, Rush-Copley Medical Center:** She introduced story to nurses in the operating room and was able to grow it further from there. She got stories from nurses about their work with patients inserted into a monthly newsletter and in an annual publication called *Extraordinary Care: A Collection of Stories from the Nurses at Rush-Copley Medical Center*. This work contributed to a significant reduction in turnover.

- ✔ **Bruce Neeb, Government Outreach Supervisor, West Central Region, State of Wisconsin Department of Natural Resources:** As part of attending the DNR's year-long Leadership Academy, Bruce undertook an oral history project with John DeLaMater, his mentor and supervisor for 32 years. After identifying ten leadership competencies from organizational documents, and after talking to those who knew John to pinpoint times he exemplified those competencies, Bruce captured 13 stories that were distributed via cassettes and CDs through the Division of Forestry.

To learn about new story initiatives like these and others that are broader in scope that hit the media, sign up to receive the articles that Karen scoops daily at www.scoop.it/t/just-story-it/.

Bank and access stories

You as an individual, and your organization as a collective whole, will benefit from having a variety of hip pocket stories on hand, as described in Chapter 4 and the cheat sheet linked at www.dummies.com/extras/business storytelling. Often, the totality of these stories is called a *story bank* or *library*.

Your own stories

Both Jodie Beverage and Bruce Neeb created a bank of stories through a small story initiative. Just like them, you can create your own personal bank, library, or database of stories. They may include your personal stories. And they can include those you hear from others that relate to your work. Maybe you're a fundraiser and you regularly hear stories from donors that you want to remember for use in newsletters, reports, or proposals.

There are several simple ways to note these stories for future use. Get a pack of notecards or Post-it Notes and document a few sentences about each story, including possible key messages. Or do the same electronically. Lori has a journal where she writes possible stories for development. Karen keeps an Evernote notebook filled and tagged. Organize them any way you want — by subject, key message, possible audience uses, or actions steps. We recommend categorizing them by key message because that focuses on the meaning of each story and gives clues about how best to use it.

Your organization's stories

Your department, division, business unit, or organization may also choose to create a story bank. Families USA describes how it developed one in *Sharing Across the States: Strategies for Story Banking*: http://familiesusa2. org/assets/pdfs/health-reform/Across-the-States-Story-Banking.pdf.

How can you do this? Here are some general steps and questions we like to go through with groups who want to create a project to collect stories:

1. **Purpose:** Why does your organization want to collect stories? What sorts of stories does it want to collect? Why is this? Why is it necessary that these stories be stored in a story bank over the long haul? How will these stories be used?

2. **Infrastructure:** Where will this initiative be housed, first, as a project, and second, as a part of daily work? What staffing will it require? What type of training or skill development will be needed? What about budget for both the project and the ongoing work?

3. **The stories:** Who will these stories come from? How will you solicit for them or evoke them? What sorts of permissions need to be obtained? Will these folks want to share their stories? Will raw stories be collected or will they be polished? If it's the latter, who will do this polishing work? How many versions of a single story will exist and in what media?

4. **Collecting stories:** Will the stories be collected in person? Individually or in story listening sessions? Through a website? Via social media? How will this process be set up? Can its viability be tested before investing huge sums of dollars?

5. **Housing stories:** Will technology be used? If so, what type of program or software is best? What sort of security needs to be put in place? Will the system be static (a compelling story is shared; at most feedback is allowed on them) or dynamic (stories shift and change in the moment by those who interact with them)?

6. **Entering the stories into the story bank:** How will the stories be tagged for retrieval? Who will enter them and make decisions on coding?

7. **Retrieving stories:** Who will have access to the stories? Are passwords needed? How do the permissions that have been gained (or not) impact access? Will those who retrieve them be able to alter them? If so, how will these alterations and any lessons that come with them be captured?

8. **Distributing stories:** In what ways is it appropriate to use them, and has this been built into the permissions that were obtained? Will distribution be regular (blog or newsletter) or when the situation calls for a story (such as a presentation that would benefit from a story in the bank)?

9. **Tracking story use:** How will tracking happen if use is an important metric? How frequently will they be used? What if a story isn't used — does it get pulled out of the bank? What if certain stories get used more than others?

10. **Tending stories:** Periodically review the stories to ask what new insights you're gaining from the stories. Do they need to be further polished? Do their tags need updating? What new opportunities do you have to share them? Don't let them collect dust or get lost in a database black hole.

Don't get wrapped around the axel when you code stories. Here's why. In the 1950s, a seven-volume typed index was created to capture fairy tales and folklore stories across all cultures. This categorization became so detailed (for example, stories about animals that bury bones) that it lost its value. Over time, folklorists stopped categorizing stories because each story's meaning-making component was missing. That's why we suggest organizing stories using their key messages. A useful system needs to go beyond taxonomies.

You may wonder whether you need to go through all the steps outlined in this section. Nope. You don't. However, that could cause you some hiccups later on. You don't want to be the organization we know about that spent significant dollars collecting stories from leaders only to discover the stories served no long-term value.

Build storied work environments

If we're hard-wired for stories, think in stories, and talk in stories, then it makes perfect sense that we build storied work environments. Walt Disney knew that and designed his theme park as storied spaces that people move through. Yet all too often we're confronted with buildings and landscapes with no soul. Such places and spaces don't enliven anyone.

Tony LaPorte, environmental branding director at Kahler Slater, a global architecture and design enterprise, helps businesses tell their unique stories through their physical environments. His company worked with Mesirow Financial, a 1,200-person employee-owned, privately held, global, diversified financial services firm to help tell its stories in its new Chicago headquarters. These stories held special importance since this was the first time many diverse business units had been brought together under one roof (www. forbes.com/sites/barbaraarmstrong/2011/12/08/storytelling-is-overlooked-in-workplace-design/).

As he describes, "Through a series of in-depth, interactive sessions, we helped Mesirow executives uncover the company's most meaningful stories. Then we aligned those stories with an environmental branding program, pinpointing several key locations throughout the new headquarters. For each location, unique branding elements, with a mix of mediums and media, were designed to tell a specific story." Here's one example: "The central hallway features a large history mosaic, created from moveable, multicolored glass tiles, which marks the company's many milestones over more than seven decades. The story: Mesirow Financial celebrates their rich history and accomplishments."

Is there a way you could use your own personal workspace to tell a story? How might your organization, on a much smaller scale, find ways to turn certain spaces into places that tell a story? How can your organization provide comfortable places for storytelling to naturally happen?

Attach story to organizational strategy

We know that having a story initiative be supported by top management is critical to long-term success. Yet because we've also witnessed storytelling initiatives be successfully birthed from grassroots efforts, we left a discussion of attaching story to strategy until now. Here are five ways to do this:

1. **Use story approaches in strategy work.** As outlined in Chapter 4, future stories can be used in scenario planning and when articulating an organization's vision and individual long-range strategies. Shawn Callahan, founder of Anecdote, adds two additional story-based strategy applications that he used with a pharmaceutical company in Vienna (www.anecdote.com.au/archives/2013/04/pulling_the_str.html): On the first day, as he helped leaders create a massive visual history, he says, "We delved into the important events that have shaped them and the lessons they've learned so far. We looked at the challenges they faced and told stories of how these challenges were really impacting their work. . . . On the second day, we focused on the future. I stepped them through a visualization to get them out of their heads and then we shared stories of where the future was already happening in their business. We call these Gibson stories inspired by William Gibson who is reported to have said: 'The future is already here, it's just unevenly distributed.'"

How do you get all employees to live and breathe the elements of strategy in their daily work? William Arthur, a division of Hallmark, used videos of customer stories and testimonials that linked all employees to its brand promise, strategic goals, and vision of the future: www.tlnt.com/2012/10/04/the-power-of-customer-stories-testimonials-to-engage-employees/. One video shows Elaine Baker, owner of Paper Potpourri in Havervill, Massachusetts, recounting the reaction of a customer of hers to the invitations she had ordered from Elaine's business. "'I have had work done for years and never, never, never have I ever had a finished product with the quality of the paper and the colors so true to what I had requested.' Elaine then goes on to say how each contributor at William Arthur plays a vital role in her ability to deliver these kinds of customer-delighting results."

2. **Strategically build story into the organization from its birth.** Here's how it happened for a nonprofit called Kiva that connects entrepreneurs to loans as little as $25 while treating them with dignity and respect (https://gsbapps.stanford.edu/cases/documents/M325.pdf).

In March 2004, Jessica Jackley was working in East Africa with the Village Enterprise Fund. Her job was to assess the impact of the $100 grants this nonprofit gave to entrepreneurs to start or grow small businesses. She says, "I would sit down with a goat herder and listen for an hour or two about whether they received the money, what they used it for, what their business was, and whether their lives had changed because of the funding." She was deeply inspired by these stories. "Yes, there was need, but they were stories of triumph and stories of effort and of people doing extraordinary things with a little bit of money."

Matt Flannery who came to visit her on this trip, experienced these stories first-hand. She says, "After hearing all these stories, we knew they had to be shared." This desire to share authentic stories about the people being served, their funders, and the experiences of their staff inspired them to conceive Kiva. What has resulted from Kiva's storytelling efforts (www.kiva.org/about)? Between 2005 and 2006, its first official year, the organization distributed $500,000 in loans to entrepreneurs. The next year, more than $14 million was distributed. In 2012, the nonprofit made more than $453 million in loans in 70 different countries with a 99.02 percent repayment rate.

3. **Make story a strategy, among others.** Coca-Cola's Content 2020 initiative is an example of story as a conscious strategy. It's now being instilled at the work level into all of the company's marketing processes. Vanessa Chase, a writer, nonprofit collaborator, and philanthropy advocate, talks about how to infuse this type of cultural strategy within a nonprofit (http://pfa-blog.com/home/how-to-create-a-culture-of-storytelling/#ixzz2ZhowtQXT). She says, "Decide at an organizational level what your priorities are for program development and fundraising; then create some strategic messaging around those priorities. Once those have been set, you can clearly communicate to all staff members what kind of stories you are looking for."

4. **Attach story to another strategy.** Here story is the means to an end, not an end in itself. This is what happened at U.S. Geological Survey, a scientific organization with 10,000 staff in 400 offices, as cited in *Wake Me Up When the Data Is Over* (Jossey-Bass, 2006). As Nancy Driver, Leadership Program Manager in the Office of Employee Development explains, "Part of the organization's strategic plan is to develop innovative leaders. Our vision is to create a leadership-centered culture." She goes on to say, "We established our leadership program in 1999 and purposefully integrated story into it. . . . Because story falls under the umbrella of leadership, it works." Leaders are accountable for modeling story both within and outside of the classroom environment.

5. **Make story a core competence, both internally and externally.** Here, story becomes part of the organization's DNA. It's woven into all external-facing processes and strategies with consumers, customers, partners, and others. It's woven into the organization's mission, vision, values, and all internal processes and systems — the daily work of all employees. And it's woven into the employee lifecycle, from recruitment and selection, to job descriptions and performance appraisals, to the time staff depart the organization. As we've shared, this is our dream. We've found organizations that come close, like Erbert & Gerbert's Subs & Clubs. But none that has fully embedded it as we've described here.

Where's the easiest place to start infusing story into strategy? We've found attaching it to the implementation of another strategy and introducing it during strategy work to both be viable opportunities.

Reward the practice of storytelling

Do internal contests or giving people mugs and plaques for telling stories work? Not really. Employees are humble. They don't always like to stand out. Asking people to share stories about coworkers doesn't help either. What works? Try placing a policy into the employee handbook and making it a job expectation. Or do what Gaylord Hospital did. To help with a financial turn-around, Gaylord married new financial metrics for each department to story-telling. As staff found ways to generate savings or income, their stories were shared and heralded. It had a snowball effect, including moving from being in the red to being in the black in one year. The story of how that happened is told in *Wake Me Up When the Data Is Over* (Jossey-Bass, 2006).

How about web contests? We know that asking customers or members to share stories by clicking a link doesn't appear to work all that well. At best, you might get endorsements, testimonials, or anecdotes, but not full-fledged stories. For more on this, check out Chapter 14 which talks about the link between storytelling and marketing. It remains to be seen if Coca-Cola's mar-keting strategy can make inroads.

Avoiding Ethical Problems

Because stories are an essential part of what it means to be human, they have a great deal of power. Storytelling, whether written or oral, is an ethical and moral act because it has the ability to validate or change both the teller and the listener. We offer a few tips to keep you aware, safe, and out of trouble:

✔ **Get permission to tell someone else's story.** Stories have intellectual property rights attached to them, so credit the source of any story that isn't your own. Acknowledge your own interpretation of the story. Be able to tell it in front of the people it came from. (See Chapter 5 for more.)

✔ **Stories need to be told with the context associated with them.** Taking stories out of context often twists their meaning. When divorced from its original intent and meaning given to it by the owner of the story, a story can be used to manipulate.

✔ **No story is innocent.** Stories have effects on the teller, the listener, and on organizational systems. Have awareness and concern for the long-range consequences of telling particular stories.

✔ **Do no harm.** It is unethical to knowingly use stories for the purposes of oppression, or to support hatred, racism, or sexism of any kind. Before telling a story, even in casual conversation, ask yourself, "Is there some positive message here? Is there something that could create a negative impact? If so, how can I mitigate that or turn it around?"

✔ **Let people tell their own stories.** Everyone has the right to tell their own story rather than someone else telling it for them. For example, it's easy for a leader to hear a story about an employee's work and want to share it with others. When possible, invite that individual to share their story instead of telling it yourself.

✔ **Any story that silences the people the story is most likely to effect is narratively unethical.** When you use stories to silence others, you're *over-storying* that person or group. Don't assume you know someone else's story and try to impose your interpretation of their story on them.

✔ **There is danger in the single story.** No one has the full story and no single story can ever capture or do justice to the richness of business or human life. Gather, preserve, and tell as many different stories as possible to bear witness to the collective truth of organizational and human experience.

✔ **Storytelling rights should be given to everyone in the organization.** This includes customers and consumers, vendors, and external partners, not just leaders or human resources, corporate communications, and marketing departments.

Part IV
Tailoring Storytelling to Special Circumstances

Five Ways to Give a Presentation that Gets People Committed and On Board

- Start with a **Now Story** that brings together the pain points, the opportunity, and the obstacles to heighten urgency and stimulate action right now.

- Tell a **Future Story** to paint what life will be like when the program or project is fully implemented.

- Use the **Your Story**, which highlights why *you* are passionate about solving a particular problem or supporting a cause, to disclose the risks of not moving forward and/or the dangers of remaining at status quo.

- Paint the desirable future again through the **Future Story** and engage listeners in co-creating the **Our Story**, which shows what all of you can accomplish by working together.

- Suggest and clearly communicate simple, concrete, and practical action steps.

Find out how to write story titles that grab people's attention in a free article at www.dummies.com/extras/businessstorytelling.

In this part . . .

- Help funders tell their stories, craft storied presentations to get people committed and on board, go after external venture capital, and raise monies from funders.

- Push stories about your organization and its products and services to consumers, get consumers to tell their stories, and integrate storied approaches into marketing and branding materials.

- Incorporate various story approaches before and during prospecting, when calling on a prospect and asking for the sale, and once the sale is complete.

- Use varied story approaches to heighten commitment, strengthen and communicate the vision of the change, and mitigate risks, overcome obstacles, obtain resources, and get things done.

Chapter 13

Storytelling to Fund Your Passion

In This Chapter

▶ Getting to intimately know those you go to for funding and support

▶ Helping funders tell their own stories

▶ Structuring storied presentations to gain support and funding

▶ Applying the unique qualities of funding, support, and advocacy stories when crafting them

Do you have a social cause you want to promote? Are you an entrepreneur seeking investors and startup funds? Are you in an enterprise or government agency that needs to find backing for a project? Are you a program or project manager in need of resources? Do you need to bring more donors into your nonprofit to serve more people? If so, this chapter offers specific storytelling techniques and best practices to help you on your way.

The study of storytelling and raising funds is still in its infancy. New research is emerging all the time. What follows is what we know at this time.

Getting People to Open Their Wallets

We've both experienced it — coaching someone to tell their story to a group of donors to raise big bucks. At one meeting, when a representative of San Diego Grantmakers shared the homelessness working group story (see Chapter 9), an audience member walked up and handed her a $25,000 check. After being coached, a young girl from Just in Time for Foster Youth shared her story at a gala fundraiser and helped raise $75,000.

Need more confirmation of the power of story in fundraising? As part of raising $6.8 million in a single day (October 24, 2012), Columbia University used the story (what we'd call an anecdote) of Morris Kaunda Michaels, a Sudanese refugee who came to study at Columbia with its alumni. Check it out at: www. brandstories.net/2013/08/05/columbia-giving-day-storytelling-helps-raise-6-8-million-dollars-24-hrs/. Imagine how much more could have been raised if stories as we define them in this book had been used.

It doesn't matter if you're a project manager or sponsor pitching a project to obtain internal resources, an entrepreneur needing to raise capital, or a non-profit leader seeking ways to fund your organization's goals. It's important to get clear on the answers to four strategic questions before starting out:

1. **What problem will various stakeholders be able to solve?** Select those few stories that speak to the main problem that'll get solved. Don't get distracted by side stories — those that relate to the beneficial ripple effects beyond the original idea or solution. Even though these can be pretty awesome, keep them in your hip pocket early on.

   Here are some specific audience needs to keep in mind:

   • **Internal staff:** Both pain and urgency are key here. To communicate pain, incorporate into stories how the program or project is going to solve problems that'll make their daily work life better. You'll also create urgency when these stories address what staff stand to lose. There's more on stories to heighten pain and urgency in Chapter 16. To galvanize action and create possibilities for a brighter future, include benefits for the end customer, consumer, or constituent.

   • **Customers, consumers, community members, or constituents:** In the public sector and nonprofit worlds, it's not about your mission, demographics, policies, or programs; it's about how constituents' lives will be different because of the solution you're providing. If you're a startup, project manager, or business leader, it isn't about your new cool idea; it's about why what you're proposing makes a difference. Don't tell stories of program or project features and benefits. Compare and contrast the present day with what'll be new or different in the future. Convey what's unique and hook people emotionally. Don't forget to also speak to pain points.

2. **When did you (first) realize that doing the work you do and solving the problem were important?** People will want to know why you're asking for funds or resources, no matter what you're seeking them for. Tell them why you're personally engaged and committed to the program, project, and/or organization. Through your stories, share what you gained from the original incident that sparked your interest — how it changed you, taught you a lesson, or provided an insight that's led you to speak to them. Skipping this step will compromise your ability to gain emotional and financial support.

3. **How personally invested are you in the resolution of the problem?** One of the biggest problems in gaining support or raising funds is a lack of genuine connection to the project or cause. Do you really believe in it? Why are you choosing to fight for it? Are you truly motivated to solve it? How much time are you willing to devote to the issue, beyond what's merely required? Get clear on why you're inspired to do this work and share that story in addition to inspiring supporters or funders.

For example, if you're an entrepreneur seeking venture capital, potential investors will want to know your personal stories related to the company and the product or service. They want to hear what inspires you to hop out of bed in the morning and devote your time to bringing this solution to the world. This passion also needs to be infused into the materials you send out. Giving boring formulaic material full of abstract mission and vision statements, financial data, and anonymous bland profiles to supporters or funders isn't effective storytelling. Sanitizing (watering down) stories is a surefire way to lose connection to the cause, project, or new product or service you're wanting to move forward.

4. **Whom are you really trying to influence?** Knowing the chain of influence will help you find, craft, and target stories to fit the needs of each audience and the different contexts you find yourself in. For example, an entrepreneur raising capital initially needs to influence an investor. A manager working to gain resources for a project initially needs to influence colleagues and executives. A nonprofit raising funds initially needs to influence grantors, donors, or funders. Who needs to be influenced beyond this first layer? What other partners and stakeholders — and ultimately customers, consumers, or constituents — need to be impacted? Dedicate time to mapping this chain of people and audiences.

Four Things to Keep at the Forefront

There are four unique twists and turns when working with stories to raise funds. And you thought this was going to be easy. Ha! Let's dig into these topics.

Spark desired emotions in others

We've talked a lot about the role of emotion in stories. The words *motivation* and *emotion* come from the same Latin root *movere*, which means "to move."

When we reviewed Pam's story in Chapter 7, we spent a little time talking about why you don't want to end a story on a somber note. For her story, we showed you how to shift this emotion to one of hope. This shift is even more important when seeking funds, resources, or support. Think of how you feel when you see data about children going hungry — usually not so good. You never want to leave people with unresolved negative emotions. For example, if you stoke righteous anger about an injustice, avoid leaving them without hope for solving the problem. In all cases, don't leave them feeling . . .

✔ Pity or despair.

✔ Depressed or anxious.

✔ Stressed or worried.

✔ Guilty or embarrassed or shameful.

✔ Scared or fearful.

✔ Disgusted or angry.

✔ Dismayed or hopeless or filled with loss.

If your project, product, service, need, or social cause makes people feel bad when they hear the problem, your job is to quickly transition those emotions into positive ones. Provoke these emotions instead. Leave them feeling . . .

✔ Respected or dignified.

✔ Hopeful and excited.

✔ Triumphant and satisfied.

✔ Determined and persistent.

✔ Encouraged and heartened.

✔ Redeemed and loved.

✔ Excited and joyous.

How can you make this shift happen? Try these suggestions:

✔ **Make sure your story has a transformational story arc.** A traditional story arc moves from setting/present day to problem/challenge, to turning points, and finally to resolution, followed by a key message and action steps. Rarely is the main character's inner transformation a part of this equation. A transformational story arc follows the same structure — *and* reveals the main character's inner transformation (see Chapter 6). At the start of the story, this character is shown to be blind, naïve, or unaware. Tension builds. Then, there's a turning point — an *a-ha* moment — the challenge is overcome. This results in greater awareness or an awakening that provides the person with insights into their own self. Because of this heightened contrast, the ending to the story is more powerful and inspiring, which leads to more meaningful action steps.

✔ **Give people small, specific action steps they can take immediately to make a difference.** Provide easy tasks to help overcome the obstacle you've presented in order to capitalize on the positive emotions sparked by the main character's personal transformation.

✔ **Open with an opportunity:** As we share in Chapter 7, the most common story structures present the problem, followed by the solution. When you want to win support for a project, raise money, or obtain resources, you may need to change tactics. Why? The problem-solutions structure can make some people feel so miserable and overwhelmed about another problem, need, or issue on top of all the others on their plate that they can't see the positive solution. Here, it's better to open the story with the opportunity before presenting the obstacle.

At www.getstoried.com/inside-the-storytelling-matrix-part-1-problem-and-paradox/, Michael Margolis, CEO and founder of Get Storied, discusses this alternative. He suggests presenting a possibility — a dream, a promise — based on what's known to be true today. Follow this with the obstacle that's preventing this possibility from happening, how others have already helped to (partially) remove the obstacle (if indeed that's the case), and the action steps your audience can take to overcome it.

For an example, see this "story" from Kiva, the nonprofit mentioned in Chapter 12 (http://fellowsblog.kiva.org/2013/07/20/kenneth-kiva-zip-and-klean-energy). Although not a perfect story, it starts with the successes that several entrepreneurs are having in their businesses. It then outlines how they want to do more — grow beyond where they are today. But they need energy — their primary obstacle. The story goes on to talk about the solution. There's no pity party here. Everyone's a winner and quality of life improves.

Think about what you need to communicate. How can you use this approach?

Highlight the challenge

When raising money or asking for resources, highlight the obstacles that stand in the way of the opportunity for a better life. But don't make them insurmountable. Demonstrate they can be overcome with the help of a sponsor, funder, or donor.

Here's another example from Kiva's website (there's no key message or actions): http://fellowsblog.kiva.org/2013/07/10/the-good-nurses-of-busia-county. This story presents opportunities and challenges woven together, one after the other, in a pattern (opportunity-challenge, opportunity-challenge, and so on). This ebb and flow between highly visible possibilities and obstacles does a masterful job of creating positive emotions at the beginning, middle, and end of the piece.

Lead with respect

It's deceptively easy to talk about or present stakeholders, constituents, or customers as helpless or hopeless victims — but for your intervention. Guard against this at all costs. People who are experiencing difficulties or crises, who face inequities, who are at risk in some way, or who are part of a system that produces inequities or inefficiencies — we've been trained by the media to depict them as defenseless, lazy, or powerless. Talking about them in this way may produce a solution for an immediate crisis. But it won't help you find support for or fund sustainable solutions over the long haul.

So, what does work? Craft stories that engender respect and dignity for those you serve. As you've probably noticed, Kiva does a marvelous job of this. So do the stories on the website of No Barriers, an organization that also uses stories to raise funds. Check out `www.globalexplorers.org/blog/entry/8150/get_outta_here/` and `http://www.globalexplorers.org/blog/entry/8148/a_tennessee_transformation/`.

Building Co-created Worlds and Story Fields

Lori's conversations with foundation and development leaders has led her to create a diagram about the types of connections (also called touch points) necessary to garner support and dollars. Figure 13-1 shows the diagram.

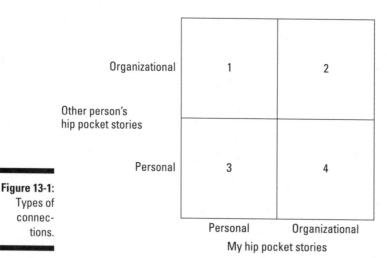

Figure 13-1:
Types of connec-
tions.

Illustration by Wiley, Composition Services Graphics

What's the ultimate goal between you and another person? To forge links between the two of you in all four quadrants. Why? The more links you create, the more intertwined the other person is with you and your organization. The more intertwined they are (assuming these are positive connections), the greater the potential for co-creating stories about the future that involve support, resourcing, and/or funding.

How do you use this diagram? Pick someone whose support you'd like to have or who controls funds you need or desire. Explore all four connections you and your organization have with the individual and his/her enterprise by writing the answers to the questions posed here in the boxes. Then do the two story tasks that follow:

- ✔ **Box 1:** How do your personal experiences connect to the other person's organization? What have you read about the enterprise? What previous interactions have you had with this organization? What were they like? Who do you know who works there and what kind of relationship do you have with him or her? (Note: If you both work for the same place, *organization* could mean department or unit.)

- ✔ **Box 2:** What is the relationship between the two organizations? How well are their goals, values, philosophies, visions, and strategies aligned? Does it makes sense to have a relationship of some kind? If so, how might this work?

- ✔ **Box 3:** What personal experiences do you and the other person have in common? Did you grow up in the same home town? Go to the same schools or universities? Have the same hobbies, interests, or career path?

- ✔ **Box 4:** What connections does the other person have with your organization, now or in the past? Have they been an employee? Member? Board member? Constituent? Customer? Consumer? What were those experiences like? What bonds would they like to have in the future?

Based on your answers, you now have two story tasks. First, draw specific stories out of the other person and listen delightedly to them, as discussed in Chapter 5. Add these stories to the chart. Second, use the stories and the messages you hear to select stories to tell about yourself, your organization, its supporters or funders, and those it impacts — and how lives are different as a result. Then add these stories to the chart. Even if you both work in the same enterprise, you still need to connect in all four areas. Start with Box 3 — building a personal relationship if one hasn't been developed yet.

By sharing stories back and forth within these four touch points, you're creating a *story field* (www.co-intelligence.org/StoryFields.html) that consciously shapes and influences future actions, behaviors, and values. A story field also allows you to co-create the future with others. When you co-create stories with others about the future, you heighten the chance they'll support you, your cause, and what you need financially and otherwise.

Help supporters tell their stories

Too often funders and other supporters experience a "culture of distance" after contributing money or supporting a cause. All they may hear is that the program was felt to be a success. They never learn the true impact of their actions unless an organization tracks outcomes — but outcomes aren't stories. Even if you're working in a public or private enterprise, often those who provide resources to your program or project don't directly experience the results of their decisions and actions. All they may see is high-level data throughout the timeline.

How do you overcome a culture of distance? Get stories from the mouths of sponsors, supporters, or funders of how their contributions made a difference to them and to your organization and include the results that came from their support. This may mean you need to educate them about how their money was used. This huge source of untapped stories can help the organization and its supporters build pride, closer ties, and deeper relationships.

How untapped is this in the nonprofit arena? Most provide a yearly listing of contributor names, sometimes with very short profiles of top-level donors. There's hardly a donor story to be found. If it's true that donors are shifting toward being social problem-solvers rather than philanthropic investors (www.tacticalphilanthropy.com/2011/03/an-investment-approach-to-philanthropy/), they'll want to know the impact of their actions in order to tell these stories to others. "Culture of distance" won't work with them.

This is the case with venture capitalists and many financial lending institutions — there is no "culture of distance." These folks keep a closer eye on how their money is being put to use and the results from that because they expect an economic return. Often they're more intimately involved in the progress of the business. Consequently, they're more prone to share this kind of story within the investment community. That's good news for you if you're the organization they've invested in. These stories have the ability to positively influence other investors and provide future funds to your organization if and when they're needed.

You may be asking, "Why would I want to capture and share these funder stories?" Influence research has shown that others are more likely to take an action if people they admire and respect have already done so. Now imagine if potential donors were to receive a compelling story and a call to action directly from these admired contributors whose money has made a difference.

Here's your challenge: Many people are often reluctant to share that they supported a project/cause or donated money to an organization. So how do you create a space for them to share their own stories of their engagement with you? If supporters for your project know how their behaviors directly led to overcoming a challenge that resulted in fixing a problem, they'll feel excited. If donors know their money bought Susan her schoolbooks, they'll experience pride in the visible and tangible results of their action. It's all about the results and how positively they feel when they hear, see, or experience these outcomes.

How can you assist these funders in building their story? Begin to create a story field by following these steps:

1. Share stories with them about how their actions led to specific results. We specifically did not say, "Share statistics and information with them."

2. Ask them for the story of what led to their support. Listen delightedly.

3. Ask them what that support or funding has meant to them.

4. Ask them if they'd be willing to share their overall story with others so that additional people might also support your program, project, organization, or nonprofit. This story is not about the kind of support they provided or how much money they gave. It's really about how they worked together with you to create an amazing result.

Have you ever seen or heard program or project sponsors in public or private enterprises tell stories like this? Occasionally, we'll hear one anecdotally. Most times the story is told from the team's perspective rather than from the sponsor who is supporting and funding it. This is no different from a donor giving money to a nonprofit for a specific project. What if these leaders were to tell the type of support or funding story we've just outlined here — or co-create it with the team and tell it jointly? These stories could then be used strategically to spark additional investments on the part of other leaders within the enterprise, especially those who are risk adverse.

Structuring Storied Presentations

If you're putting together a very short proposal, you may only have room for a single story. Depending on the audience's tolerance for problems, you'll want to either use a story focused on the main problem or one focused first on opportunity. If you have the chance to provide a multi-page proposal, grant request, or pitch or give more than a five-minute oral presentation, there are four core stories that are important to craft and tell:

- **The Now Story:** This story brings together the pain points, the opportunity, and the obstacles to heighten urgency and stimulate action right now. (This is a special type of story not covered in Chapter 4.)

- **The Future Story:** This is a story that shines a spotlight on what the future holds if specific action steps are taken today. (This type of story is covered in Chapter 4 and Chapter 16.)

- **Your Story:** This story highlights why *you* are passionate about solving a particular problem or supporting a cause. It's one that's often skipped. If people don't know who you are and why you're involved, they won't know why you're asking for resources. Nor will they have a reason to trust you. (This is a special type of story not covered in Chapter 4.)

- **Our Story:** This story of inclusion puts forth what you and the sponsor, supporter, or funder can accomplish together. (This is a type of future story covered in Chapter 4 and Chapter 16.)

Here are some general comments about these four stories:

- **Data:** Use Chapter 8 to add data and information to these stories when it's absolutely critical to do so. That may be necessary when speaking to proof of impact and measurable outcomes.

- **Transformational story arc:** As best you can, make sure you're using it when you craft these four types of stories.

- **Key message:** There are two levels of key message to attend to in a presentation (or proposal): The one for the overall presentation and those for each story. They all need to complement one another. When you get good at this, you'll be able to link together all the individual story key messages into a series of statements that highlight a broader message.

- **Action statement:** Because the action steps are the same for each story. Share them after telling all four rather than after each individual story.

- **The need:** Is your need to get people on board? To excite opportunity and mitigate risk? Or to tug at heart strings? How you use and present these stories and their associated action steps and data will change depending on this need.

Get people committed and on board

Project managers and leaders often need to sell their programs and projects to sponsors, stakeholders, and the project team. The business need has to be defined before initiating the effort. The main question here is: What's the justification for spending time, money, and people resources on this project?

As outlined in Chapter 8, sharing exciting technical details won't get you the support you need, nor the resources. Without committed resources (time, money, people, equipment, and so on), there's no program or project. You have to make sure that the stories used within the business case speak to how critical the effort is to the organization's vision, mission, and overall strategy. This will determine how much support is received in return:

✔ **First level:** "This is a worthwhile endeavor. I can see some solid reasons why you need my support."

✔ **Second level:** "I can see the business case and there's an ROI that I can defend."

✔ **Third level:** "Wow, this is game changer. I can see this significantly altering our position in the marketplace. We really need to do it."

✔ **Fourth level:** "This is a critical project because of safety, regulatory, or compliance requirements, demands from customers, or serious dangers in the marketplace. If we don't do it, the whole organization is at risk."

Here's a suggested structure for a storied presentation that will help strengthen support for your project:

1. **Use the Now Story to set the stage.** Gather stories from end users about their pain points. You'll have to decide whether you start with these or with a story about the compelling business value opportunity. Be careful about how you relay data here.

2. **Tell the Future Story to paint what life will be like when the program or project is fully implemented.** Collect input from potential sponsors and key stakeholders to understand their points of view. Get examples from those who've had successes doing some version of what's being proposed. If these aren't available, include a simulation that makes the outcomes more tangible and possible. Combine these pieces together into a single future story.

3. **Use the Your Story to disclose the risks of not moving forward.** Include end user input about the dangers of remaining at status quo.

4. **Paint the desirable future again through the Future Story and Our Story.** When you get comfortable at evoking stories in the moment, if the culture allows, engage those who are listening to your business case in creating the Our Story.

5. **Suggest simple, concrete, and practical action steps.** Be clear on what you're seeking and ask for it.

Make sure these stories stay front and center throughout the project. Update them as milestones are achieved and new information becomes available. You may need them again to ask for additional resources.

Go after external venture capital

We've listened to venture capitalists and financial institutions tell us what they want in a funding pitch in order to help entrepreneurs and growing businesses secure funding. If you've watched *Shark Tank* or *Dragon's Den* on television, you've seen this in action. The main rule of thumb is understanding what your prospective investors care about. They invest in momentum and want evidence of market demand for your product or service.

Here's our suggested approach for crafting a storied presentation to raise capital. You'll notice there are several places where data factors in:

1. **Begin with a short, simple, memorable introduction.** For example, "Mint.com is a free and easy way to manage your money offline."

2. **Convey the problem and the opportunity through a Now Story.** Link this story to current events. Validate it with outside experts, or sales, or awards, or good beta tests.

3. **Share your solution and the story of you through a Your Story.** Demonstrate transformation — of yourself, of the company's finances, and of your customers. This is the time to show a demo and mention your proprietary technology or intellectual property. Part of the Your Story needs to be about how long you've been working, and in what amount of time you've been able to achieve market results. The shorter the time and the higher the results, the better.

   If you just present the before-and-after picture over a two-year period, it won't look like you're moving very fast. But if you share the alpha phase of your product or service, the beta phase, and then the launch phase, investors will be able to see how fast you're truly moving. You'll also show that you're learning and improving.

4. **Tell your firm's Future Story.** This is your story about traction. Traction is about momentum that's supported by quantifiable evidence which shows you're on a highly profitable trajectory. Numbers that support this are profits, revenues, customers, and clients (especially how you're going to gain new ones), partnerships, and engagement — in that order. Outline how you plan to *make money* — and highlight customer, intellectual property, or partnership revenue sources. Also touch on your competition. Focus on building an upward path in this story. This is one place where numbers are absolutely critical. Cloak them in story to provide context for potential investors. See Chapter 8 for help.

5. **Share the story of your team — the Our Story — and how additional funding will help you catapult forward.** Present the money milestones: fundraising goals, where the money will be spent, and financial overview including breakeven and profitability targets, capital, and valuation.

6. **Deliver action steps.** Make these simple next steps for funders to take.

7. **Close with an inspiring ending.** Refer back to the Future Story. Leave them wanting to know more. Leave them a memento (a story trigger).

Keep the presentation simple with very few bullet points. Better yet, replace bullet points with visual images. Avoid puffery, outlandish statements ("no one ever has made a product like this before"), confusing people with things they might not understand, presenting material that's unclear and requires your audience to think too much, inconsistencies (make sure all your numbers make sense together), typos, errors, and being unprepared. Always remember, your presentation has to answer these questions:

- ✔ What's the problem you're trying to solve?

- ✔ Who's your target market and how big is it?

- ✔ What's unique about your product or service from what already exists today?

- ✔ How do you intend to build more customers?

- ✔ What you need from your investors?

- ✔ Where will the money be spent?

The reasons investors want this information is so they can mitigate risk. That means the stories you share must also address these risk factors:

- ✔ **Are you capable of building your product or delivering your service?** What's the strength of your team?

- ✔ **Will people actually use what you're offering?**

- ✔ **Will people pay for it?**

- ✔ **Is the opportunity significant enough to support ongoing growth?**

- ✔ **What's your weakness?** Every business has weaknesses, so be authentic and own up. Don't dwell on it, but you do need to acknowledge it.

Raise money by tugging on heart strings

Most people associate tugging at heartstrings to be the goal of a nonprofit. If you're pitching a program or project in a public or private organization, you can use the same tactic to incite imagination and vision, deepen understanding and tolerance, and build common purpose among diverse people. It's just easier to see how that's done in the nonprofit arena.

To engage funders emotionally, share stories that convey a moral purpose and touch universal truths about what it means to be human, that surround the people your organization, program, or project serves. Your end goal is to create personal empowerment for the funder.

Through this heightened appreciation for others, funders can also become familiar with the unfamiliar and get connected to a new reality. But be careful here. The key is understanding the underlying reason why an organization is doing what it's doing. Here's an example from the Global Soap Project's story (www.globalsoap.org). It's a big mistake to think the reason this organization collects a portion of the 2.6 million daily bars of partially used soap from U.S. hotels and reprocesses them into new bars to distribute to people who lack soap is to make those people less vulnerable to disease (http://blog.rally.org/the-power-of-storytelling---takeaways-from-social-media-for-nonprofits-in-atlanta/). The real story isn't about making people less vulnerable to disease; it's about the long-term consequence of children not having access to soap — the leading cause of child death globally is hygiene-related diseases. Handwashing with soap decreases this outcome.

This example demonstrates that to effectively tug at heart strings requires moving a story from *how* to *why*. Habitat for Humanity (www.habitat.org/stories_multimedia/volunteer_stories) is good at this. The people who help build houses are a large part of its story. The stories from these volunteers showcase why they are involved. Powerful stuff.

With all this being said, the greatest difficulties you'll face with funders are avoiding compassion fatigue and breaking through inertia. Compassion fatigue comes in two types. The first is funders who resist hearing one more gut-wrenching story and the accompanying plea for money or other kinds of resources. The other type has to do with your telling the same story over and over again until it feels dry — you've disconnected from it.

How do you overcome these challenges? Switch from the problem/resolution story structure to the opportunity/obstacle structure in your Now Story.

The best fundraising presentations follow this structure:

1. **Share the opportunity that led to the creation of a project through a Now Story.** Include a personal story about one of the people facing this challenge and the impact that's also had on others. A terrific example of this type of story comes from this blog posting by nonprofit marketer Nancy Schwartz: http://gettingattention.org/2013/05/non-profit-storytelling-9/. She takes a less-than-compelling story and rewrites it into awesomeness.

2. **Tell the Future Story.** Highlight the solution you provide, explain why it's the best one possible, and paint a picture of how the future would look once the solution is fully realized.

3. **Share the Your Story.** What is it that makes your organization so passionate about this project and the cause associated with it? Share a few quantified results to satisfy the analytical brain and add additional credibility.

4. **Tell the Our Story.** Convey what's made possible by working together that wouldn't be possible otherwise. This is where you get to show the impact dollars from funders can make in someone's life.

5. **Provide a call to action.** Outline a few easy, immediate steps people can take to create this desired future with you.

Here are three questions to answer when collecting and sharing stories about people that your organization, program, or project serves to use in a Now Story or in an Our Story:

1. **Who gets to tell the story?** Is it the organization, program, or project? Or is it the actual person being served? There are two issues here — whose perspective you take in telling the story *and* which voice will be used to tell it. For example, you could have the story crafted from the perspective of the person being served, and you tell it. Or, the same story could be videotaped with the person being served telling it.

2. **Who gets to ask the question that begins the story?** In Chapter 10, we said most stories have a "setup phrase" that needs to be delivered before you start telling the story. In this case, we suggest a question. Here's what you have to decide. Is the organization posing this question from its perspective? Is the interviewer who collected the story posing it through his or her lens? Is the question from one of the people or a group you serve? Or is it a question from the person whose story you're sharing?

3. **What exactly is the question you need to ask?** To develop this question, be clear on the purpose for sharing the story and the key message you're after.

There's a tricky part with collecting stories from those you serve. What happens if some of them aren't ready to share their personal story? What happens if a story is too painful for them to tell? What happens if a funder asks one of these constituents to tell his or her story, but the person doesn't want to? Storyteller Donald Davis shares one model for understanding what's happening in these situations (www.ddavisstoryteller.com):

- ✔ **Front porch stories:** These are public stories that folks easily share with people they don't know but have just met.

- ✔ **Living room stories:** These are more private stories that you share with people once you've gotten to know them better.

- ✔ **Kitchen stories:** These are the intimate stories that you share with people you fully trust and have known a long time.

What often happens is that we request kitchen stories from the people we serve, but they're only willing to tell us front porch stories. We must be sensitive to the kinds of stories we're asking for. This means accommodating their needs, being patient with them, and helping them find acceptable ways to share their stories so they don't feel violated, exploited, or victimized. Here are three questions to aid in that process:

1. What would you like to share about your story?

2. What's important for people to know about you and your story?

3. Where would you like to begin your story that feels the best for you?

Here's how this works. In a coaching session, a young woman shared that she'd come through the foster care system. Part of her story was very emotional. It was very private and not for public consumption. She wanted to make sure that her story exposed common stereotypes about foster care children. Her goal was to inspire people to donate to the organization that had helped her so much but not feel exploited when she did so. After chatting for a while, she found a way to start the story and tell it in an inspiring way that allowed people to experience her foster care life without sharing too many private details. Her goals were accomplished, but it took a lot of work. This outcome would never have been achieved if someone had stuck a microphone or video camera in her face and said, "Tell me about what happened to you."

Change stories as organizations mature

Whether you need support for a program or project, need investments, or desire donations for your cause, there's one important piece of information to keep in mind: As your organization grows and matures, so will its stories.

Think about a program or project as it goes from initiation, to the creation of a project plan, through implementation and monitoring, and finally to close-out. Midway through the effort, when an unexpected problem appears, you wouldn't want to tell the Now Story that you initially used in the business case to gain support to solve it. You'd want to include progress made to date.

The same is true for startups. You'll have new stories to share once your product or service hits the marketplace, your customer base begins to grow, and the organization expands. Shift your stories to communicate these new realities.

In situations where fundraising is a never-ending process, keeping the stories we've talked about here fresh and alive means continuing to connect with your passion for the cause and uncovering new stories to share. As donor money produces results, obstacles are overcome and successes occur. Update your stories to reflect these outcomes. When donors say, "I can see myself in the work you do," then you'll know you've hit pay dirt.

Using Funding Stories in Other Ways

Some of the stories you'll craft will have a short lifespan. Because they're so specialized to the audience and circumstance in which you're seeking support or resources, they may only have a one-time use. For example, the Your Story you create for a unique internal project may only be applicable when you pitch the effort.

On the other end of the continuum, some stories are timeless. They take on a life of their own after their initial use. The Your Story that an entrepreneur creates to pitch an investor has many uses. So do the stories you collect from those you serve and those who benefit from your organization's products and services. How might you use stories that were originally created to fund a specific passion in other ways? Read on.

Put stories into corporate communications

Review the stories you've crafted to garner support and/or funding. How useful would their key message be with other audiences? Who else could benefit from reading or hearing them?

These stories can be inserted into annual reports, promotional materials or e-mails, state, federal, or foundation grants, and online and print versions of newsletters or magazines. They can be translated into videos or webinars and placed on websites or pitched through social media outlets. Incorporating them into onboarding efforts or specific training programs may be valuable.

Don't overlook having them become the backbone of advocacy and ongoing fundraising campaigns. They may also have a role in public relations or marketing campaigns.

Fuse stories into the grant process

You'd think there'd be a tremendous opportunity to share stories in your grant proposals. Unfortunately, many proposals must be completed in very specific ways. Rarely are compelling stories as we've described them requested separately or as part of official proposal forms. At best, you may be able to share anecdotes or vignettes. Those are better than nothing, but they aren't as powerful as a full-fledged story.

What can you do? Think of other ways your stories can become part of the proposal process. For example, do you have the ability to send supplementary materials to augment your grant proposal? Perhaps written stories could be incorporated into these. Is there a place where you could provide links to stories on your organization's website?

Sometimes in the grant process, there's an opportunity for you or the people you serve to be interviewed by representatives of the grantor. Karen had this experience. She helped a local community go after funding from a large national foundation. Part of the process included having each organization provide an in-person presentation to a panel comprised of foundation staff. In this case, it wasn't just the leader of the community who gave the presentation. Six community members were selected to join the leader onstage. Each person had a story to share. These individual stories were woven together like a tapestry into a marvelous, larger community story. The community won the grant hands-down.

Don't get stuck thinking that if the grant proposal has no place for you to share your stories that you've lost an opportunity. Find creative ways to get around this in the grant process.

Meld stories into advocacy campaigns

The final San Diego Grantmakers (SDG) story provided in Chapter 9 was used to advocate for philanthropy. The organization's goal was to craft the story in such a way that it could be placed onto its website and also used in short e-mails that were sent to state legislators. SDG used this story to create awareness about the results of the working group's fundraising efforts — raising $13 million for the project — and is now a model for other groups to emulate around the country.

When you're sharing stories for the purpose of advocacy in order to obtain funding, there's one key thing to keep in mind. Before we share it, read the following piece. It's the first couple of paragraphs from the first version of a story that Robyn Atkinson-Dunn, PhD, Director of the Utah Public Health Laboratory, put together for Lori to review. This real-life situation was slated to introduce the beginning of a short, written proposal for state funding for the Toxicology Section of the laboratory. Based on the story, the request would either be approved for a presentation to Health Department officials or set aside for consideration for the following fiscal year:

Three-year-old Le'A had no idea what was happening to her; all she knew was that she didn't feel good. Her mommy had just given her lunch, but something was different this time. She could see mommy but her cerebral palsy kept her from being able to say, "Mommy, my tummy hurts," and that something was terribly wrong. The only communication her little 41-pound, wheelchair-bound body could muster was the tiniest whimper of pain and agony before her world faded into darkness.

It was impossible for Le'A to comprehend that her mother had allegedly used vodka instead of water to make her lunchtime slurry to feed her via her feeding tube. She could not speak for herself; yet the highly skilled toxicologists at the public health laboratory were able to give her a voice. They were able to tell the world that sweet Le'A was poisoned. She had a blood alcohol level of 0.9! That is the highest level the laboratory has ever detected in any human, dead or alive. The toxicologist reviewing the case thought "Wow! How is this young girl still alive? Even a 6 foot, 200-pound adult might not survive this level of intoxication."

Imagine if your daughter or loved one were drugged in this manner; wouldn't you want someone to speak for them?

The public health laboratory is the only entity of its kind in the State of Utah. We're uniquely involved in the lives of every citizen in the state at some time during their life. . . .

Based on this narrative, is there any reason the toxicology section should receive funding? The group did exactly what it was asked to do. And it provided data that saved a young girl's life.

That's the problem. By writing the Now Story from the perspective of the little girl, all the empathy goes to her. None of it goes to the toxicology section. All your focus is on the child and her health condition. There's nothing that speaks to anything that happened in the laboratory itself. None of the staff are mentioned. Nor the work that any of them did.

Now read this next version of the story (we realize this excerpt doesn't contain the key message and the full call to action). What comes to mind afterward?

"Russ, come see me ASAP – Gambrelli," read the note. Panic, fear, and nervousness set in. "What could be going on?" Russ thinks as he hurries to Gambrelli's office.

"Hi, Gambrelli. What's up?" She says, "The detectives in Weber County are investigating the possibility of a mother intentionally poisoning her 3-year-old little girl named Le'A. We received a blood sample this morning and I need you to include it on your ethanol run today." Russ's mind races back to last evening as he replies, "Yes, I heard about this case on the news. I believe she has cerebral palsy. I'll get to it right away."

Russ rushes back to the lab and works diligently to set up the samples. He thinks, "What sort of dire circumstances would compel a parent to commit such a horrible act? I can't imagine anything like this happening to my four kids." That afternoon, Russ scrutinizes the results. "What's going on here? I can't believe what I'm seeing. This little girl has a blood alcohol level of 0.9!" He manually double-checks and triple-checks the result as he thinks, "Wow! How is this young girl still alive? Even a 6 foot, 200-pound adult might not survive this level of intoxication." What he does know is that this is the highest level the Utah laboratory has ever detected in any human, dead or alive.

It was impossible for Le'A to comprehend that her mother had allegedly used vodka instead of water to make her lunchtime slurry to feed her via her feeding tube. The only communication her little 41-pound, wheelchair-bound body could possibly have mustered was the tiniest whimper of pain and agony before her world faded into darkness. She was unable to speak for herself. Yet Russ was able to give her a voice. He was able to tell the world that sweet Le'A was poisoned.

Imagine if your daughter or loved one were drugged in this manner; wouldn't you want someone to speak for them?

The public health laboratory is the only entity of its kind in the State of Utah. We're uniquely involved in the lives of every citizen in the state at some time during their life. . . . The Utah Public Health Laboratory is requesting $xxx in this FY15 Building Block Request.

You now know more about the Toxicology Section. You have the names of two staff members, and you know what Russ did. As a result of this shift in story focus, Robyn's request went through to the next round. She's already crafted a presentation using the suggestions we offer in this chapter and pitched the need. Guess what? She achieved success. The building block was submitted by the Health Department officials to the Governor's Office as part of the health department's next budget. We have our fingers crossed that she'll clear this final hurdle.

Take a look at the Now Story you're using to advocate for money. Does it highlight the group that needs the funding or the person or people being served?

As you can see, when crafting stories to use for advocacy, you must be very clear about whose point of view the story reflects. That will determine who becomes the hero of the story. When the agency or the organization is the hero, you'll experience better results in your advocacy campaigns.

Chapter 14

Storytelling in Marketing

*E*arly in this book, we talk about how stories pull people in. When used this way in marketing, storytelling is an invitation extended by an organization to the marketplace for an ongoing, interactive engagement with customers, consumers, clients, or partners (we refer to these collectively as *consumers*). Though bottom-line benefits of this new way are significant, organizations typically do the opposite — they push marketing messages to consumers.

A new day has dawned in the marketing, branding, public relations, and advertising worlds. Storytelling — written and visual — is slowly becoming the new cornerstone. Because the shift from push to pull is so profound, companies are still learning how to do it. As we show with Coca-Cola in Chapter 12, a few large companies are doing it pretty well. But results are inconsistent. In this chapter, we share the best examples, ideas, and tips we've found so far for incorporating storytelling into marketing, on both the push and pull sides of the equation. At the end, due to space limitations, we briefly discuss the implications of all of this to branding. We recognize that the subject of story branding is deserving of its own book.

Defining marketing and branding

In the book *M: Marketing* (McGraw-Hill/Irwin, 2009), Dhruv Grewal and Michael Levy define marketing as "the activity, set of institutions, and processes for creating, capturing, communicating, delivering, and exchanging offerings that have value for customers, clients, partners, and society at large."

As distinct from marketing, in the book *Managing Brand Equity* (The Free Press, 1991), David Aaker defines *brand* as "a distinguishing name and/or symbol (such as a logo, trademark, or package design) intended to identify the goods or services of either one seller or a group of sellers, and to differentiate those goods and/or services from those of competitors." The Tronvig Group elaborates by saying branding is "what sticks in your mind associated with the product, service, or organization — whether or not at that particular moment you bought or did not buy" (www.tronviggroup.com/the-difference-between-marketing-and-branding/).

Telling Consumers About the Enterprise

In 2012, Edelman Berland surveyed 1,250 adults in the United States, 18 years of age or older (1,000 in the general population, 250 marketing decision-makers), about the state of online advertising. This market research firm asked them to rate 17 statements that included phrases such as "people buy what celebrities wear or like," "advertising works better on men than women," and "in-store experiences trump online experiences." The top result was crystal clear: Consumers want to be told a story. Seventy-three percent stated that advertisements should tell a unique story, not just try to sell (www.adobe.com/aboutadobe/pressroom/pdfs/Adobe_State_of_Online_Advertising_Study.pdf).

Give consumers sharable stories

What sort of story do consumers want to be told? Good question! Ed Keller and Brad Fay, authors of *The Face-to-Face Book: Why Real Relationships Rule in a Digital Marketplace* (Free Press, 2012), say, "Start a story that consumers will want to talk about." To find the story, answer the question, "What messages about my organization's brand and category are talk worthy?" This question stems from Keller and Fay's research showing 90 percent of word-of-mouth brand conversations take place offline and are primarily face-to-face. Marketing is often charged with developing these messages (hopefully in the form of stories), but remember that internal staff have authentic sharable messages and stories for the outside world, too.

What's one kind of story that consumers find to be "talk worthy?" We all desire products and services that simplify and ease our lives and are less expensive. But above all, we each strive for meaning. One example is TOMS Shoes. The company's multitude of fans support the firm because staff personally distributes free shoes to Argentine children for every pair sold, creating a meaningful experience for both customers and employees.

This means your organization needs to ask: "What do we stand for?" Follow these steps to uncover stories that answer this question:

1. **Gather examples of each type of organizational hip pocket story mentioned in Chapter 4.**

2. **Dig into each of these stories.** Go below the surface. Identify those core beliefs, philosophies, and values that are *routinely demonstrated* by the organization and the fundamental assumptions that underlie them.

3. **Pinpoint stories that best showcase what the organization stands for and how it provides meaning.** These stories embody the organization's fundamental assumptions, beliefs, philosophies, and values.

Giving people stories that spark conversations keeps your enterprise top-of-mind. They also connect your firm to the values, beliefs, and feelings of your audience that build sales, profits, and a long-term relationship with them.

Provide insider stories

Because humans are curious souls, consumers also want insider knowledge. They love to peek behind the curtain to learn the inner workings of your organization. It makes them feel special. We previously mentioned "back stories" in Chapter 4, but here's a new kind to consider: the stories associated with a product or service's entire life-cycle, from beginning to end. This set of "supply chain" stories also reflects your organization's values.

So, expand your thinking beyond "Here's a story about how we make ABC product" or "Here's a story about how we crafted XYZ process" to "Here are the stories along the entire life-cycle of this one product (or service)."

In May 2007, sharing with consumers the environmental impact of every link in the supply chain for five of its products was the original goal of Patagonia's first review (www.fastcompany.com/756443/measuring-footprints). Ten employees traipsed across the world to document these steps. In the spirit of transparency, the company shared all findings, both good and bad. Because of consumer feedback, Patagonia shifted some of its practices. On the Footprint Chronicles website (www.patagonia.com/us/footprint/), you can click on the supplier map and learn about a supplier's environmental behavior. Our wish? If we could just get these folks to tell better stories!

Close the gap between inside and out

An organization will come across as insincere if it jumps on the "we do good in the world" bandwagon and treats finding and telling sharable stories as another project to check off the list.

With more than 185 bakery-café locations around the world, Le Pain Quotidien is renowned for the quality of its boulangerie fare and baked goods, made from organic ingredients when possible. Inspirational speaker and skills trainer Andrew Thorp visited one of these restaurants in London (www.andrewthorp.co.uk/bread-time-stories-pull-marketing-corporate-storytelling/). On each table, he saw a fold-out card with a cartoon strip on it that shared the story of the company's origins. As Thorp tells it, "We were served by a charming young woman and when I mentioned the cartoon story she confessed she wasn't really familiar with it. This surprised me. I assumed this would form a fundamental part of her induction, but perhaps like so many inductions it focused on the practicalities — in this case, how the till works, what's on the menu, and how to clock in and off." He goes on to say, "Your corporate story is only as good as the people living it and delivering it."

Whether you're a micro-entrepreneur or part of a mega enterprise, the inside and the outside stories have got to match if your organization's credibility is to be maintained in the marketplace:

✔ Employees need to know what stories are being conveyed externally *and* have the ability to elaborate on them. Ideally they need to be able to engage people in an exchange about these stories.

✔ As an organization, don't claim to offer happiness, inspiration, or greatness when the internal culture and tone don't match these messages. You'll be found out and talked about on the Web or elsewhere, as Thorp has done on his website.

As consumers, we like to align with enterprises that speak to us authentically, answer our questions, engage us in dialogue, and solve our problems so we can live the life we're inspired to live. The following is an example of how inside stories about core values can spark a unique external marketing effort and generate word-of-mouth stories.

Holstee, known for its greeting cards, posters, t-shirts, and wallets, says it "Exists to encourage mindful living. We hope to change the way people look at life by designing unique products and sharing meaningful experiences" (http://shop.holstee.com/pages/about). Since its inception, because it has continually talked about and valued both *mindfulness* and *using less and doing more* with its employees, in 2012 the company renamed Black Friday (the shopping frenzy that happens the Friday after Thanksgiving in the United States) as Block Friday (www.fastcoexist.com/1680958/a-companys-quest-to-bring-mindfulness-to-black-friday). Block Friday encouraged customers to block off a portion of the day for a personally meaningful activity — whether it be sitting quietly and reading a book or taking a walk with a close friend.

How does this relate to storytelling in marketing? Given the unusual nature of the day — to block off time for meaningful endeavors — we suspect that customers spread stories via word-of-mouth about the company in several ways. First, it's likely they talked about Holstee's invention of Block Friday when they enlisted others to join them in meaningful activities. Second, we assume they mentioned the company again when sharing stories in response to questions about how they spent the holiday weekend.

Providing Stories About What You Offer

It's easy to get caught up in describing product or service features and benefits and thinking that they'll sell what your organization has to offer. Only, these don't cause people to buy anything. What does make them act?

Tell the story behind your offering

Chapter 2 discusses the Significant Objects Project, where attaching a story to a flea market item increased its purchase price by an amazing amount. You may wonder how many companies are actually selling products through storytelling. The following example may pique your interest.

Field Notes produces durable notebooks. Most fit in the pocket of a pair of pants or a men's shirt. Now, how the heck do you market a product most people consider a commodity? Especially if it's being introduced in a bold new color, which might not be well received? First, give it an unusual name: Red Blooded. Second, craft a story, but not just any old story. Nor do you release it on any old date of the year. Nor do you say anything about the company until the very end — and when you do so, you use a humorous twist. Check out this video: `http://fieldnotesbrand.com/redblooded/`. The company didn't stop here. It made another video that showed how critical the notebook is to one of its customers: `http://fieldnotesbrand.com/2012/05/07/aarons-red-blooded/`. For more examples, go here: `http://fieldnotesbrand.com/films/`.

You can do this too. Consider these possibilities as ways to find these stories:

- ✔ Reveal the inspiration or a-ha moment behind creating the product or service. Tell the story about the idea that created it or the story about the need or issue that caused it to be brought into your business to sell.

- ✔ Relay stories about how consumers can use the product or service in their lives.

- ✔ Tell stories about how a product is made or how a service transpires. Share pictures that document these processes. Place them on your firm's website or in a retail store. Knowing the story behind age-old processes used to create the offering makes it desirable on a very different level.

- ✔ Show the workmanship and quality inherent in the product if that's what helps makes it special. If people only see a photo of a scarf or a pile of rugs, it might not be of interest to them or worth the money.

To step this up a notch, check out Story, a unique store in New York City that carries a variety of Big Apple products (http://thisisstory.com/#). Every four to eight weeks, the shop chooses a theme, changes its inventory, and creates a new "story." To select brands and products that fit well with the story, the store owners ask questions like, "Is this product relevant to the story?" Each display is arranged, and products are placed together, in an attempt to tell a narrative. In our humble opinion, what would strengthen this concept even more is if individual items also had great stories attached to them.

Speak to the why

When you're focused on features and benefits, you can easily lose sight of the larger story — the story of *why*. To create both meaning and a meaningful connection, find stories that talk about why consumers need your products or services and why they should care about your organization.

To do this, use the popular problem-solving technique called the 5 Whys, which originated at Toyota (http://en.wikipedia.org/wiki/5_Whys).

1. State a problem that the product or service addresses.

2. The 1st Why is: Why is that important? Because . . .

3. The 2nd Why is: Why is that important? Because . . .

4. The 3rd Why is: Why is that important? Because . . .

5. The 4th Why is: Why is that important? Because . . .

6. The 5th Why is: Why is that important? Because . . .

7. The ultimate Why is:

Here's a way to use it in marketing to get at a product or service story:

1. Our product makes stinky sneakers smell better.

2. Because stinky sneakers turn people off.

3. Because when they're turned off, they won't want to hang around you.

4. Because if they don't hang around you, you can't get to know them.

5. Because if you can't get to know them, you can't date them.

6. Because if you can't date them, you won't get one to marry you.

7. The ultimate Why: If you have smelly sneakers, you'll never find your mate (and never get married).

8. And . . . now you have the framework for a great story!

Okay, it's silly. But you get the point. Try it! You may learn something new.

Sharing Stories About Consumers

There are two ways your organization can develop stories about consumers. The first is to gain a deep understanding of market segments through crafting representative consumer personas. The second is to uncover stories and ways to promote heroes and underdogs within each segment.

Develop personas and archetypes

Your organization has a *persona* embedded in its brand image. There are also consumer personas that embody each market segment. We focus on the latter here because they can also aid in new product or service development.

The strength of a great story depends on its characters and how well they're fleshed out and developed. The same is true in marketing and branding: Digging deep into the personas of consumers to get at their emotional core — gathering as much information as possible about them — is an important step. What do you need to develop these character personas, assuming your organization has already identified its market segments? Try the following:

✔ Dive into who they are and what their lives are like. Identify likes, dislikes, values, favorite hobbies and activities, where they live, what they physically look like, their age range, marital status, ethnicity, city of origin, how they make decisions, and whatever else makes them tick.

✔ Flesh out their needs — beyond the expressed, "I need a new shoe." In his book *Grow: How Ideals Power Growth and Profits at the World's Greatest Companies* (Crown Business, 2011), author Jim Stengel suggests identifying consumers' higher-order needs expressed as ideals:

• Safety and security

• Variety and adventure

• Respect and acknowledgment

• Connection with others

• Enlightenment and growth

• The ability to make a contribution

> Conducting interview research using the story-evoking techniques we discussed in Chapter 5 can help here. So can using methods such as the Zaltman Metaphor Elicitation Technique mentioned in Chapter 5.

> ✔ Dig into consumer stories that your organization has collected over time and identify common characteristics, their emotional nature, and sensory information that resonate with them.

To strengthen these personas, identify the archetypes associated with them. The best resource we've found to aid your marketing efforts is the book *The Hero and the Outlaw: Building Extraordinary Brands Through the Power of Archetypes*, by Margaret Mark and Carol Pearson (McGraw-Hill, 2001). It incorporates Pearson's research, based on Jungian psychology, which defines archetypes as forms or images of a collective nature, which occur both as myths and individual products of the unconscious. The authors believe iconic individuals, brands, and organizations, many of which we've mentioned in this book, captivate us because they carry the mythic power of an archetype.

With this information, craft stories about each persona. Use words and visual images that represent who they are at the core of their being. Several online tools and articles can assist you, such as `www.mltcreative.com/up-close-and-persona/` and `www.toprankblog.com/2011/12/story-telling-persuasion-content-marketing/`. Keep these stories visible and available to staff.

Build stories in which others are the hero

Business storytelling in marketing is far more about consumers as heroes than your company being the hero. These stories need to focus on their journey — how they overcame challenges and saved the day in their own enterprise, family, or community. Your organization is one of the supporting characters who helped them reach their goal. It's a subtle but important shift.

Why don't we want you to tell stories about how your enterprise helped them succeed? As we've mentioned, people identify more closely with individuals, not organizations. The folks they most closely identify with are people just like them — those who have similar issues, problems, calamities, and challenges. When consumers are the heroes, other consumers and prospects see the results these folks have received, how far they've come, and the impact they're having — all because of the hard work, persistence, and help your organization has provided along the way.

How can you make the shift to having consumers save the day in your organization's stories?

1. Uncover the obstacles and challenges that your consumers face.

2. Learn the results they experienced with your product or service.

3. Identify how the product or service made a difference in their life.

Now look at your company's current marketing materials. Then ask yourself:

✔ Does the copy show that we get who our consumers really are? Does it go beyond simple titles and stereotypes? Have we built strong characters and personas that other staff can identify with?

✔ Does the copy really articulate the specific obstacles and challenges that consumers face in their work or personal life?

✔ Does the copy specify what the future could look like if those obstacles and challenges were removed? Is there any mention of how consumers experience hope and inspiration?

✔ Does the copy offer images of how consumers' lives are truly different after using our product or service? Or how they're able to be victorious at work or in their personal life because of our help? Or are we just selling a drill without being interested in the kind of hole it makes?

One more thing before we leave this topic: Never put down your competition. Speaking ill of other enterprises just reflects badly on your organization.

Leverage the underdog

We all love underdogs. We cheer them on. Underdogs are unexpected heroes confronting seemingly insurmountable odds. Think David and Goliath. Think Rocky. These folks need or seek redemption. Many of your consumers also have hard luck and turnaround stories in which they're redeemed in the end.

What do marketing-based underdog stories look like? Check out New York-Presbyterian's *Amazing Things Are Happening Here* website: http://nyp. org/amazingthings/. Each featured patient has at least two versions of his or her story on the site. As you can see, these stories are practiced — they aren't spontaneously told. It appears they were generated by the hospital, not directly by patients. Graeme Newell shares other examples of underdog stories in this video clip: www.talentzoo.com/beneath-the-brand/blog_ news.php?articleID=16649.

What's the overall structure for this type of story?

1. **Describe the significant struggle the person has experienced.** This could be a series of difficulties over many years or one major calamity that has resulted in catastrophe of one kind or another.

2. **Insert a hint of hope.** Somebody shows up to help. A product appears that's in the testing stages. A new article cites a piece of research that suggests a possible solution.

3. **Share the moment of deliverance from the struggle.** In this big moment, the struggle is no more, and hopes and dreams are fulfilled. Embedded here are steps people took, or attitudes they adopted, to realize their deliverance.

4. **Provide the key message.** What do you want others to take away from the story?

5. **Reference back to the implied action steps or attitudes if this can be done appropriately.** You won't need to hit people over the head with these because they've already been brought forth in the story. Sometimes you can just slip in a gentle reminder.

6. **Show how your organization is celebrating the success.**

Return to back stories — from consumers

How awesome would it be to promote consumers by sharing their back stories? And get your organization a brief mention too? Back stories from consumers build their reputation and yours as well. Not only is this sort of story unexpected, your consumers will love you for it.

Renee Whitworth highlights the power of this type of back story in the article "Brand and Social Storytelling: Getting an 'A' for Effort" (http://popsop. com/2011/11/brand-and-social-storytelling-getting-an-"a"- for-effort/). Imagine stories where consumers talk about what it's like to wait in line for the latest Apple product or for Black Friday sales after Thanksgiving, or about the special trip they made to a Levi's store to be specially fitted for new jeans, or the hunt for the perfect furniture piece and their delight once they found your company's product.

Getting Consumers to Tell Their Stories

As marketer Dominic Payling says in "Social Storytelling: How Brands Are Streaming Stories" (http://blog.mslgroup.com/social-story telling-how-brands-are-streaming-stories/), ". . . being able to listen and engage with audiences about their own personal stories is the first step to being a competitive, 21st century company. The most forward thinking organisations go a step further and are building marketing and communications strategies that actively encourage, amplify, and reward customers' stories, rather than assuming that the company is the only entity capable of telling stories about a product. They know how to translate the process of storytelling into a valuable outcome and ensure their own stories are being listened to."

Pull stories from your community

When done right, storytelling creates more than engagement and the opportunity for interactional excellence — it fosters ongoing, back-and-forth exchanges with stakeholders and others interested in your enterprise. How do you make this happen? Here are a few ideas:

✔ **Request customer stories.** Be strategic in collecting them. Asking for stories on Twitter, Facebook, LinkedIn, or on a blog or web page by saying "Submit your stories" rarely works unless you offer an extremely provocative story prompt. Instead, provide a story and ask for one in return. Give people something to react to — a situation or a problem that others regularly face — and follow that with a story prompt. Link to a short video and ask folks to respond with stories that come to mind.

Ever used Penzey's spices? We have. Wow. They're amazingly flavorful. We both get the company's monthly catalogue that includes recipes and consumer stories. How does it get these stories? One way is through a Calling all Cooks! link at www.surveymonkey.com/s/R95TGXY. A second way is through unsolicited e-mails and letters. A third route is triggered when consumers call in to order spices or ask a question. If a representative hears an interesting story, it gets passed on to the catalogue department.

To see sample stories, take a look at the Great Milwaukee catalogue issue (www.penzeys.com/images/GreatMilwaukee.pdf). On page 3, there's a story from Bill Penzey, Jr. that speaks to how this issue was conceived during a chat he had with a woman in Dallas, who once lived in Milwaukee and missed the city. This shows how a single story can spark innovation. The issue itself contains numerous stories from locals.

✔ **Reach out to folks who comment about your organization on social media.** Ask for the story behind what they've shared. Use this when an issue has been mentioned and you don't know what precipitated it. You'll have to decide whether to reach out privately or publicly.

✔ **Create online communities for people to exchange stories.** Facebook fan pages are one place to do this. So are online portals hosted through your organization's website. Membership organizations such as professional associations often do this, but it's becoming more prevalent in other organizations. For example, Marriott offers a site for its reward members to share all sorts of information and stories at www.rewards-insiders.marriott.com/welcome.

✔ **Find existing online communities and seed them with story prompts.** Quora — "your best source for knowledge" (www.quora.com) — is a terrific place to ask for a story and receive lots of insights. Even though the site asks specifically for questions (those on the day we looked included "What's the shrewdest, smartest maneuver you've ever seen in business?" "What were the most ridiculous startup ideas that eventually became successful?"), place a story prompt here and see what you learn.

✔ **Seed a conversation and allow consumers to actively join in and co-create the rest of the story**. It's easy to imagine how this could be done online. Especially with a tangible product. Assign a person in your company to start a story and allow others to chime in and shape it.

Can you do co-created storytelling with something invisible? Intel and Toshiba partnered on a six-week episodic story called *The Beauty Within* (www.youtube.com/watch?v=qyMQIMeSCVY) to promote a new central processing unit (CPU). Alex, the main character, wakes up each day in a new body. To keep track, he keeps a computerized log. One day he falls in love, which makes everything change. Seriously . . . how can a person have a relationship if his outward appearance changes daily? Audience members were invited to play Alex. Anyone could do so since his appearance differed each day. Isn't it interesting that the story isn't about the CPU? It's about how a computer chip allows interactions, connections, and events to happen.

Inspire: A new way of engaging others

Another aspect to this conversation has to do with aspiration versus inspiration. Marketing has traditionally focused on appeals to people's larger aspirations: buying a big house, fancy car, the latest branded clothing, and so on. This approach assumes you can buy your way into a better life.

The following three companies have taken a different approach: They focus less on what they can give (aspiration) and more on what people can achieve (inspiration):

✔ **Levi's:** Go Forth key message campaign as told through a young boy's eyes (www.youtube.com/watch?v=2YyvOGKu6ds).

✔ **Red Bull:** Its Stratos Project depicts a symbiotic relationship between the brand and its Mission to the Edge of Space extreme sports story (www.fastcocreate.com/1681748/red-bull-stratos-shatters-records-and-traditional-notions-of-marketing#1).

✔ **Google Chrome:** Dear Sophie story (www.youtube.com/watch?v=R4vkVHijdQk).

The call to action these three examples put out isn't about your buying a product or service — it's to help you create or achieve a goal or dream. What these companies offer is the motivation for achieving a solution, not the solution itself. Market data shows that connecting through inspiration helps these organizations forge stronger bonds with their market segments and prospects, successfully weather tough times, and foster growth in good times.

Here's the inside scoop on the approach that Honda uses with story to spark inspiration. Matt Kapko shares how this happens in this blog posting "How Honda's Agency Taps Authentic Stories for Social" (`www.clickz.com/clickz/news/2208520/how-hondas-agency-taps-authentic-stories-for-social`):

1. Uncover authentic Honda customer stories through all sorts of media.

2. Connect with those customers and make them feel comfortable sharing their story.

3. Build the customer's confidence that Honda is truly listening to them.

4. Emotionally connect a fan milestone to a Honda brand milestone.

5. Find ways to share these customer stories but *not* as a campaign.

How does this work? Someone at RPA, Honda's agency of record, discovered that a band called Monsters Calling Home had shot a music video inside their Honda vehicle. It eventually found its way to J Barbush, VP and director of creative social media for RPA. Instead, of "Liking" or reposting it, he and the agency saw it as an opportunity to take the story a step further based on the "Honda Loves You Back" theme. See what they did here in this Honda-branded video: `www.youtube.com/watch?v=0Y7AzNj2s28`. This effort is part of ongoing online and offline story sharing with customers. Honda's Facebook fan page is tagged with "Your Story is Our Story" (`www.facebook.com/Honda/app_315041098593551`).

Your organization's consumers, customers, partners, and prospects have *Unique Customer Aspirations*, or UCAs, which you can discover by evoking stories from them about what they find meaningful in their lives. Think of these not as pain points but dreams, hopes, ambitions, and desires. Be prepared to be changed by the interaction.

Storifying Marketing Materials

Like a treasure chest, here's how your organization's core stories can enhance websites, e-mails, social media, and any other print and online marketing and promotional materials you need.

Integrate story into websites

It's true that you can take a conventional website design and populate it with a variety of stories in various media. But this approach is giving way to building websites in more storied formats. To successfully do that requires you have these inputs: the organization's brand, the organization's persona embedded in this brand, along with those personas that represent various market segments, and the narrative to be shared on the site.

With these in hand, here are three ways to integrate story into website design:

✔ **The architecture of the site:** Architecture encompasses all navigation and page flow. Design this flow similarly to how a story logically follows the flow of the plot. Storyboarding can help. Here's an example of what we mean: `http://salleedesign.com/home/`. You can also storyboard what website viewers experience as they move through the site. Because people jump back and forth between pages, go through the discipline of thinking about how the pages flow together as a narrative, even when accessed in random order.

✔ **The storified graphic layout of the site:** Try these approaches:

- Strategically place visual content throughout the site so that it collectively tells a story. Add visuals that enhance individual stories: photos, images, illustrations, slides, videos, graphic scribing, infographics, cartoons, and the like. A 2012 study by ROI Research showed that 44 percent of Facebook users are more likely to engage with brands that post photos (`www.slideshare.net/performics_us/performics-life-on-demand-2012-summary-deck`). As of 2013, each day 300 million photos alone are uploaded to Facebook. Besides conveying emotions and a sense of humanity, visual content can enhance your organization's brand and market position, help educate customers, and launch and sell products and services.

- Use mascots, as external observers or internal characters, to transmit your organization's story. Axure has done this on its website: `www.axure.com`. The Geico gecko is seen frequently on TV commercials (see how he came to be here: `www.geico.com/about/corporate/word-from-sponsor/`). There's also an entire page devoted to his journey across the United States, including a graphic map and a rolling blog with photos: `www.geico.com/about/gecko-journey/`.

- Build interactivity into a story like this website put together by Slavery Footprint: `http://slaveryfootprint.org/#where_do_you_live`.

- Use scrolling. Have a story unfold as the viewer moves down a page. Accessible through Nike's website, this webpage, which promotes an agenda for physical activity, is an excellent example of a scrolling story that also includes data and several action steps: `http://designedtomove.org`.

✔ **The content used to populate the site.** Populate individual stories throughout a website using varied media (written, audio, and visual, to name a few). In this engaging video that uses beavers as mascots, technology company Loggly relays a story on its home page: `http://loggly.com`. As you design each page, ask yourself what type of story would be beneficial to share. Use the hip pocket story types in Chapter 4 and all the various stories we've introduced in this chapter to guide you.

Capitalize on "audio branding" by linking music (after you have permission) into key organizational business stories.

"About" pages

About pages are one of the most underutilized parts of a website. On this page, your enterprise has the opportunity to reveal its personality and offer a real story about who it is and why it does what it does. It's the perfect place to draw people in and start building a relationship with them.

Crafting a storied About Page is hard. Daniel McInerny of The Comic Muse shares his back story of struggling with the development of one for his firm's website here: `http://sevenstorylearning.com/sales/about-me-pag/`.

Here's a great About Page: `www.problogger.net/about-problogger/`. Darren Rowse tells the story of how he started problogger.com and takes the opportunity to market to the reader. Yes! The entire text is a story. He's included a video where he shares more about his personal experiences. In case readers want to dig deeper into who he is, he provides a link to a longer blog post where his full story is available. The end result? Masterful.

What sorts of stories can be placed on or linked from your About Page? Consider these stories referenced in Chapter 4, along with one more:

- ✔ How the organization was conceived — its founding story.

- ✔ A story that demonstrates what your firm stands for.

- ✔ A story that showcases what your enterprise does.

- ✔ Stories about the founder or key leaders — or the entire organization, if it's small. Include photos. Here's how Ishita Gupta describes herself `http://ishitagupta.com/about/`.

Before you design your About Page, ask yourself, "Who's going to visit it?" People who want to work with your enterprise? Absolutely. Prospects? Yep. First-time visitors? Probably. Current clients? Maybe. Then ask, "What do they want to learn that will also get them to take action? "And, What do we as an organization need them to learn so they'll take action?" By *action*, we mean a call, e-mail for more information, or ping your organization via social media. Then share a story or two with these action steps embedded at the end.

Forms

Ever been to a wonderfully designed website and wanted to take action — fill out a contact form, survey, or application of some kind — but that moment of interaction was so cumbersome or ugly that you left the site and did nothing? What's a business to do? Consider narrative web forms. These are forms that literally follow narrative structure. Look at the differences here: `http://blog.kissmetrics.com/narrative-web-forms/`.

The examples shared on that blog post are brilliant. These forms have been shown to increase conversions by 25 to 40 percent. Why? D. Bnonn Tennant, author of "How to Increase Your Conversions with Narrative Web Forms," says they work for three reasons:

- ✔ "Narrative forms create a context your prospect cares about."
- ✔ "Narrative forms closely mimic your prospect's thought sequence."
- ✔ "Narrative forms reduce visual friction. [They look] easier to complete."

Create dynamic e-mail campaigns

How do you get people to open up a marketing e-mail and actually read it?

Having an interesting or provocative subject line is critical. Here's a great resource for creating dynamic headlines from marketing guru Brian Clark, at Copyblogger: www.copyblogger.com/magnetic-headlines/.

What type of stories work well in e-mails? To connect on a personal level to customers, Replacements — the world's largest supplier of old and new china, crystal, silver, and collectibles — has been known to put stories about employees' pets into its electronic correspondence. Here's a link to some of them: www.replacements.com/mfghist/pets01.htm. You can also share raving fan stories, customer-of-the-week stories, or other kinds of marketing stories mentioned earlier in this chapter. Or ask customers to send in photos and stories and run a contest with prizes for the best ones, like Interval International does in its monthly member magazine (www.intervalworld.com/web/my/home).

To maintain reader interest, when sharing stories in e-mail campaigns, on a website, and in blog posts, do the following:

- ✔ Break a single story into shorter paragraphs or add a few bullet points. You aren't changing the story; you're changing its visual display so people can quickly digest it. Try it with images. If the story is short enough, superimpose the text over pictures, drawings, and so on.

- ✔ Block the story into three major sections and send them in separate e-mails over a designated time period. The first section is the setting and the setup. The second is the conflict. In the third section are the resolution and call to action. Each section could be divided further into two to three e-mails, depending on the length of the story. Don't drag the story out too long or people will lose interest. Ensure the transitions between the e-mails lead from one part of the story into the next.

- ✔ Send different but related stories over a span of weeks.

Storytelling and Social Media

Call us purists. Many of the tweets, online comments, and Pinterest pins we've seen aren't stories. At best, they may spark a conversation. Can you craft really short stories? Of course. Here's a 140-character one that Karen created: "From my window in Palm Springs, golfers whack the balls. Who will win as they swagger through the greens? Ahhh, the boss prevails again."

In social media platforms that allow for longer posts, like the discussion groups on LinkedIn, Quora, Google+, and Facebook fan pages, mini-stories can be shared. Only it's mostly marketing staff having conversations with others or soliciting anecdotes. Opportunities for heightened engagement are being missed.

If you really want to leverage business stories in social media, try these ideas:

- ✔ Use a provocative headline and link to a story.

- ✔ Offer short text stories to your fans as a way to trigger theirs. Respond to those they share back with you to continue the dialogue.

- ✔ Use visual storytelling methods like those mentioned in Chapter 11 to transmit or trigger stories.

- ✔ Take advantage of visual platforms like Pinterest, Instagram, Vimeo, Vine, and others. All kinds of graphics and images — including behind-the-scenes photos and snapshots of people interacting with your product or service, even those that are humorous — help project depth into your organization. And stay tuned: Social networks such as Google+, Facebook, and LinkedIn are turning their platforms into visual media.

Building a Storytelling Strategy

You have many opportunities to use stories in marketing. Figuring out what to share and where to share it are tactical feats. But tactics will only take you so far. Better to first think strategically and then build a story strategy that includes these tactics. Base the strategy on these four interconnected I's: immersion, interactivity, integration, and impact:

- ✔ **Immersion:** Through marketing stories, you're creating both experiences and entertainment. When hearing or reading a story, listeners become immersed in the story world being shared. What steps are you taking to invite people into your organization's stories? In return, what are you doing to become immersed in the stories they share?

✔ **Interactivity:** Create situations where people can both immerse themselves in the story and interact with it to affect its outcome. How might this happen? They can write their own ending and share it (or choose a different ending), share a story from a character's perspective, create different plots for how the story should go, or create a parody of the story to share. You can also offer interactivity through additional links, videos, maps, and the like to relay different facets of the story.

✔ **Integration:** Seamlessly connect stories across all marketing platforms. Don't replicate stories in different media; share different parts of the story in different media using a unified original story line. That means you need to decide on the messages, values, and qualities that need to cross all media channels. For example: Tell the main story of a product or service in one media, stories from customers elsewhere, and employee back stories about the process in another channel. Here's another example using the Cinderella fairy tale. Tell the popular tale on one channel. Have the Fairy Godmother tell her side of the story on another channel. On a third channel, Prince Charming delivers his take on the story. Link all stories together online so they feed each other. Are you thinking of your marketing stories in this way? What theme or themes can you use to link them together and create integration?

✔ **Impact:** What kinds of emotional, social, and psychological impacts are your organization's stories having on people? Using quantitative and qualitative measuring tools is important here. Are marketing stories offering action steps for these folks to take based on what they learn by engaging with these stories? Always remember that the degree of impact connects back to the strategies and storytelling techniques being used to accomplish immersion, interactivity, and integration.

Storytelling in Branding

Here's a cautionary tale — one we stumbled upon a few years ago. It seems a fairly large company wanted to get its *meta-story* down pat — the one story that it would be known for. Someone hired a consulting group that went high and low throughout the organization to collect a boatload of stories from staff. Afterward, the consultants returned to their offices, studied all the stories, did a wonderful analysis, and generated the company's meta-story. They came back to share it with company executives. Everyone agreed it was a good one. With much fanfare, together they rolled out this wonderful meta-story to all the staff. The reaction was swift and ugly. Staff turned to each other and said, "That's not the story I told them." Or, "Where did that story come from? Doesn't sound like our story at all."

The problem was that people couldn't see themselves in this rarefied meta-story. That's not the worst of it. Staff felt betrayed by the entire experience. Once they'd been excited to share their stories, believing their voices were being heard. Now they felt invalidated. They'd been given a story that was totally disconnected from what they held to be true and valued. The inside joke became, "Oh yeah. We've been storied!"

How do you recover from a situation like that? It's easy to fall into the trap of believing that your organization can be known by one single story that captures the essence of an entire enterprise. No one story can ever fully reflect all of your business. In fact, a meta-story is made up of a whole host of smaller stories, some of which we outline in Chapter 4. If you work in branding, your role is to first recognize that all these stories coexist side-by-side and then manage the dynamic and informing that happens between the meta-story and these smaller stories.

What's one way to connect story in marketing to branding? A *story brief* is a way to align stories associated with a brand to story-based initiatives in marketing. Because it includes the challenge marketing faces, which must be solved, along with an assessment of the opportunities available, the story brief becomes marketing's back story and can serve as input to marketing tactics. Here's a high-level overview for putting one together:

1. **Articulate how the organization's brand is characterized through its persona and active archetypes.** Include brand values and its belief system — what the brand stands for. Do a reality check to make sure that the organization actually walks its talk in the marketplace and that the brand values match the organizational culture. To aid you, in the article "72 Questions to Help You Dig Deep in Telling Your Brand's Story," David Masters provides questions in addition to those we pose earlier in this chapter (`http://lorirtaylor.com/72-questions-to-help-you-dig-deep-in-telling-your-brands-story/`).

2. **Add in consumer personas that represent the market segments served by the organization.** Include customer, consumer, client, and/or partner needs, problems and challenges, and the conflicts creating obstacles for them. Also list any universal needs and ideals operating in their lives, like the search for meaning, redemption, or belonging — and articulate the beliefs that are shared between you and these stakeholders.

3. **Connect the dots between the results of steps 1 and 2.** Look not only for needs and ideals that can be fulfilled by your organization's offerings, but also at beliefs, attitudes, and worldviews you also share. Dig deeper into the stories captured in steps 1 and 2 to identify these items. You'll miss the target if you take shortcuts here.

4. **Articulate marketing obstacles more fully.** These obstacles fall into four basic categories: Are these stakeholders even aware of your enterprise? Do they comprehend what the enterprise stands for and what it has to offer? Do they have enough confidence in your organization for them to buy? Do they have a close affinity with your enterprise that will lead to ongoing relationship? Find and share stories about these obstacles to better understand the context behind them.

5. **Prioritize and summarize the obstacles and state the actions to be taken.** Here's where all the tips and techniques we've presented in this chapter have a home. Finding methods and resources around these obstacles needs to be embedded in marketing's story-based tactical steps. By conducting a more storied situational analysis, you'll end up with deeper, richer, and more accurate information.

Chapter 15

Selling with Stories

*T*he times they are a-changing. No longer is selling only the responsibility of those in sales or account management. If you have a profile on LinkedIn, you're definitely selling, not only yourself but the places to which you're attached — be it an employer, where you volunteer, or the associations to which you belong. We're all trying to do the same thing — move others by selling, persuading, and influencing them. What a perfect place for story.

If you're in a formal sales capacity, you also know that tweaking compensation plans, requiring folks to do more warm and/or cold calls, or working longer hours only gets you so far in the marketplace. Transactions aren't sufficient; transforming prospects through the sales process is. The same can be said of success stories. Though important by themselves, they aren't sufficient to move others to action.

This chapter looks at the use of story within all facets of the sales cycle, starting with how you prepare to prospect to what you do post-sale. Along the way, you'll get introduced to a few new applications of the practices we've mentioned so far in this book such as using story to overcome objections.

Shifting the Sales Cycle

Back in 2009, when we were writing an article called "Winning Customers Through Story: A New Take" (www.trainingmag.com/article/winning-customers-through-story-new-take), we scoured the sales literature for what people had written on story use in sales. We didn't find much on the subject at that time, but one item that we saw again and again is a time-honored sales process that goes something like this:

✔ What to do prior to prospecting to prepare yourself and your prospects

✔ The act of prospecting

✔ Calling on a prospect (in person, over the phone, or through an electronic connection)

✔ Asking for the sale

✔ What needs to happen post-sale to keep the buyer coming back for more

If you've read Chapter 14, you've learned how the marketplace is changing. And you may have experienced this shift yourself. Reflect on a recent major purchase you've personally made. Maybe it's a car or an appliance, a laptop, or an expensive handbag or piece of luggage. Did you do any research before talking with a salesperson? If so, what kind did you do? Did you do an online search? Did you look at any expert opinions or customer reviews? Watch any videos or listen to any testimonials? Did you talk with friends and family? Were you searching for stories? Did you find any? With the advent of smartphones, checking anything out in advance with just about anyone is as close as your fingertips. We as prospective customers are shifting the very way buying and selling occurs.

Is it any surprise that research by Google and the Corporate Executive Board (www.executiveboard.com/exbd-resources/content/digital-evolution/index.html) found that customers reported being 57 percent through the sales process before engaging a sales rep, regardless of price point? Although this research was done in the business-to-business (B2B) space, it still applies to individual purchase decisions.

In a November 2012 presentation at the SES Conference & Expo (www.clickzintel.com/abstract/optimizing-b2b-content-sales-lee-odden-15767), Lee Odden, CEO of @TopRank Marketing, ups that number. He cites research from SiriusDecisions 2012 that says 70 percent of a B2B buyer's journey is complete before a sales lead. He takes what he calls the customer's journey (awareness-consideration-purchase-retention-advocacy) and maps all different kinds of content to it to demonstrate what he believes potential buyers are researching:

✔ **Awareness:** PR, radio, TV, print, word of mouth

✔ **Consideration:** Online ads, e-mail, pay-per-click, social ads, reviews, blogs, media

✔ **Purchase:** E-commerce, brick-and-mortar store, website

✔ **Retention:** Community forum, frequently asked questions (FAQs), knowledge base

✔ **Advocacy:** Promotions, blog, social networks, newsletter

This social change is one reason why this book has a chapter on story use in marketing and why we're addressing the use of story throughout the sales process: A whole variety of story practices can be integrated into all these mediums and outlets. In addition, if prospects are truly shifting the sales process — which means they may be calling on your organization rather than you calling on them as prospects — you'd better know the stories they've already heard and seen about your organization and your competitors through these outlets. You'd better know stories about their industry or demographic. And you'd better be prepared to evoke these stories from them. They're not going to respond favorably to hearing you spout success stories. They already know them. That's why they're talking to you and your firm in the first place.

Create deep affinity and chemistry

What's the upside here? The good news is that the marketing stories your organization has planted in the media will (hopefully) give you and your organization a unique voice, automatically creating distinctions between you and your competitors. When written well, these marketing stories can engender the four types of connections we mention in Chapter 1: physical, mental, emotional, and the human spirit.

If you're in sales, you know that selling a product or a service's features and benefits doesn't engage people emotionally or at the level of the human spirit. That's why we suggest you ask prospects and customers how they *feel* about your product or service throughout the sales cycle and their experience of it, and why they chose you. Notice we didn't say what they *think* about it — yes, even with products or services considered to be commodities, like fruits and vegetables (if you're a street vendor) or grass cutting (if you have a lawn service company). Not only might you be surprised by what you hear, the information will help you identify the prospect's *Emotional Selling Point* (ESP). Once you have this ESP, you'll be able to wisely choose and share hip pocket stories to solidify this connection.

To be able to ask about how they feel and what they've experienced, more than ever you need to forge a relationship with prospects and buyers that can withstand the test of time. Ironic, isn't it? In a world that's more electronically connected than ever before, developing a trusted, authentic bond is still key.

Before Prospecting

Chapter 14 provides a number of different types of stories that will interest prospects. Read that chapter, especially if you work in a formal sales capacity. You've got some other homework to do, too, when it comes to story use. You need to collect and/or create stories about the industries your prospects are in. Learning more about the demographics associated with potential prospects is also key. From former sales rep and sales manager–turned storyteller Linda Goodman, a story called "The Bag Lady" (http://lindagoodman storyteller.blogspot.com) highlights how assumptions about a prospect almost cost her a huge sale.

Identify awareness level

Given the shift in consumer behavior we've just outlined, it's important to know from a sales perspective how aware prospects are of your organization and its products and services. In his book *Breakthrough Advertising* (Bottom Line Books, 2004), Eugene Schwartz, who wrote brilliant advertising copy for direct marketers, outlined five levels of customer awareness, which today are sometimes called the five levels of market sophistication.

Why do you need to know about these levels? We believe they impact what prospects want to know before they contact you or you reach out to them. These levels, in more current terminology, are as follows:

- ✔ **Unaware:** Prospects aren't aware of their desire or need — or aren't yet ready to admit it (think products that reduce facial wrinkles in men). Or the need is so general, it's hard to describe.

- ✔ **Problem aware:** Prospects have a need — a specific need — but haven't yet made the connection that your product or service can fulfill it.

- ✔ **Solution aware (what Schwartz calls "introducing new products"):** Prospects know they desire a product or service that does what yours does, but they don't know there's a product or service — specifically your product or service — that will do what they need.

- ✔ **Product aware:** These prospects know the product or service, but they don't yet want it. Why? They may not know all it can do, aren't fully convinced of how well it works, or haven't yet been told how much better it is than what competitors can provide.

- ✔ **Most aware:** These prospects have picked your organization. They know your products and services, what they do, and that they want what you offer. They just haven't gotten around to making the purchase. Apple, Rolex, and Harley have many of this kind of prospect.

Subscribing to a relationship-based sales and marketing approach implies connecting with prospects and turning them into loyal customers by building a long-term relationship with them (for ongoing sales). This means having stories for each level:

- ✔ **Unaware** may benefit from stories that draw them into knowing more about the product or service. First you have to make people aware of what you offer, in a way that intrigues them. Then stories on your website can educate them about the product or service.

- ✔ **Problem aware** may want stories from others who had a similar problem that's now been solved by what you've offered them.

- ✔ **Solution aware** are best pitched by an opportunity/problem story. The article, "How Siemens Uses Storytelling to Emotionally Engage Clients and Staff" (`www.marketingmag.com.au/news/how-siemens-uses-storytelling-to-emotionally-engage-clients-and-staff-39705/#.UZLfao5p3Rd`) offers an example of a solution aware story about a dairy farmer in Cobram in Victoria, Australia who wanted a technology solution to help him be more productive on his farm. He approached Siemens about creating a solution to allow him to milk 240 cows in an hour.

- ✔ **Product aware** may benefit from customer stories about how well the product or service works and how it goes above and beyond anything else on the market.

- ✔ **Most aware** may enjoy stories from customers who are currently using the product or service about how their lives are different as a result.

Have stories to address all five awareness levels in your hip pocket at all times. After you assess the awareness level of the prospects you're going after, or get this information from market research staff in your organization, you can then tailor your conversations and offer the appropriate stories.

Now, these stories are primarily customer stories. Which brings with it a special consideration, first mentioned in Chapter 4, when we discussed organizational customer experience stories, and again in Chapter 14. For maximum effectiveness, make the customer the hero of these stories. When the customer is the hero, your prospects will see themselves as the next potential heroes — and as your next customers. That's a good thing.

To get more familiar with this distinction, look at this excerpt from a blog posting by Bob Apollo titled "How to Turn Every Sales Person Into a Top Story-Teller" (`www.inflexion-point.com/Blog/bid/93451/How-to-turn-every-sales-person-into-a-top-story-teller`). It says:

> "One of our customers, [*company name*] a [*type of company*] first came to us because [*brief description of critical issue*]. It was causing [*consequences*] and affecting [*people/departments/functions affected by the issue*].

They had tried dealing with it by [*previous unsuccessful initiative, if one existed*], but had struggled because [*reason why previous attempts had failed*].

Working with their [*key sponsor's role*], we helped them implement [*brief description of our key capabilities*] that allowed them to [*brief description of benefits*]. But that wasn't all — as a further unexpected benefit they found they were also able to [*unexpected benefit*]."

Here's how we'd reword the third paragraph to make the customer the hero:

Working through their [*key sponsor's role*], our client was able to use our [*brief description of our key capabilities*]. As a result [*THEY were able to accomplish...*] that allowed them to [*brief description of benefits*].

Know the market segments you serve

In addition to the stories just mentioned, you need to do some other home-work — or once again get this information from market research. What specific market segments are you serving in your sales capacity? Are you like the account managers that Lori worked with at a large U.S. company that sell cable TV commercial time to markets as diverse as legal, cosmetic dentistry, community banking, credit unions, fast-food, and full-service restaurants, and nontraditional student education? Or do you sell within a single industry?

In either case, you need to flesh out the stories behind the market segments you serve. Get intimate with the biggest pain points and what's changing in the industry, the solutions that potential buyers are seeking, as well as the opportunities that exist within these segments in the future. Notice we did not reference success stories here. Where might these types of stories come from? They could be

✔ Personal stories, based on experiences you've had with products or services offered within the market segment — or those of your family or close friends. Maybe your spouse and four of your friends and relatives have had cosmetic dentistry, and that's the industry you need to learn more about. Get their stories and learn from them.

✔ Stories that you specifically craft after reviewing industry-specific or demographics-specific information on each target market.

✔ Stories from current customers in the markets you want to continue to serve, or even one customer in a new market. Remember to ask for permission to craft and share these stories.

Storytelling While Prospecting

Everywhere you go, and in most places you visit online, you have the opportunity to connect with possible prospects. Even somewhere that has nothing to do with your work, like the dog park! This section discusses some ways you can leverage these situations through story.

Use story when meeting face-to-face

Where do you go to meet new contacts face-to-face in ways that you know will pay off for you? Chamber of Commerce meetings or local networking and charity events? Trade shows? Industry gatherings? When you attend, how do you use story when meeting others? Here are several ways you can do so:

- ✔ **Someone asks you what you do.** Two choices are available. One is to offer a story trigger phrase, which Lori sometimes does by answering this question with, "It depends on the day of the week and what month it is." After laughing, almost everyone responds by saying something to the effect of, "How about Tuesday next week? What are you doing then?" That opens a door for her to share a story. Your second option is to share the first few sentences associated with a story about what you did recently that is really compelling. If the other person shows interest, tell the entire story.

- ✔ **Wear a unique item that has a story attached to it.** Maybe you have a pocket watch that was handed down to you from your father. Maybe you have a colorful piece of jewelry that you saw being made while on vacation in Peru. Perhaps it's a scarf that you made yourself. All of these can function as story triggers. If you're asked about the item, tell the story. If you can, link it to your work. It may encourage a story to be told to you in return.

- ✔ **You're introduced to someone for the first time.** Your job is to get the other person to start telling you about themselves. What story prompts might you use? Consider using one related to the event itself, something the person is wearing, their name, or something you may have heard them say as you were being introduced.

- ✔ **When reconnecting with a person you haven't seen in a while.** Here's another opportunity for a story prompt. Use one that relates to something you already know about the person. For example, "The last time I saw you, you were training for a half marathon. Tell me about a memorable moment during that experience."

If you have the chance to participate in a golf outing or another situation where you'll be spending several hours with a few people, it's the perfect time to get to know more about them. Do your research in advance. Learn about them personally and professionally through LinkedIn or other social media sites. Scope out their organization — review media articles, annual reports, and the website. Use this information to craft several story prompts. Remember, these events are social; it's not exactly the opportune time to press for a sale, but to build a relationship instead.

Capitalize on online opportunities

What about connecting to new prospects online? How can you use story?

✔ **A prospect reaches out to you via e-mail or a contact form.** When responding via e-mail or a phone call, add in a story prompt or two to learn more about their request. One great prompt, if they've not shared it in their first correspondence, is to say, "Tell me about that moment that triggered you to reach out for help/assistance/information."

✔ **You're involved in a listserv, a discussion forum on a site like LinkedIn or Quorum, or want to respond to a blog posting.** Observe the conversation. Add in a story that provides an idea or information that no one else has offered so far.

✔ **You write blog postings, e-newsletter articles, or posts on social networks like Facebook business pages.** What a perfect place for a story. You have all sorts of choices here: one you own, one from a client, one sparked from a news article, or one from the latest research in an area where you're an expert. If the story is lengthy, use the first paragraph or a teaser and provide a link to the full version.

Calling on a Prospect

Getting a prospect to give you their undivided attention isn't an easy task these days. We're all on overload. So when you get the chance to meet with someone in real time via Skype, a phone call, or an in-person meeting, you can't afford to blow it.

Dig deeper through prompts, not questions

Almost every sales book or training course advocates asking probing questions. As we've said before, if all you're seeking is information, go ahead. Ask questions. But if what you desire is to move your prospect to action and create meaning, you need to get them to tell you some stories.

Here's what you need to do. Take the questions you've been asking and transform them into prompts. Here are a few typical questions and the prompts we suggest:

- ✔ What was their defining moment or defining experience that led them to possibly need you and what you have to offer? *Prompt:* Tell me about that moment that sparked you to say, "I need to call XYZ and talk to them about ABC."

- ✔ How did your business get started? *Prompt:* Tell me about the situation that triggered the founding of the business.

- ✔ What motivates your customers to buy from you? *Prompt:* Tell me about an experience one of your customers has shared that demonstrates what inspires many customers to buy from your firm.

- ✔ Is there anything in your industry that alarms you? *Prompt:* Tell me about a recent experience that you or others in your industry have had that alarms you.

- ✔ What does your competition do that you admire? *Prompt:* Tell me about a time when one of your major competitors did something for their customers that you deeply admire.

- ✔ How is business compared to last year? *Prompt:* Tell me about a recent situation that shows a significant change in your business from last year to now.

- ✔ If I had a magic wand and could grant you one wish, what would that be in your business? *Prompt:* I suspect you have a vision in your mind of what you would like to see in your business. If I were to give you a magic wand, tell me about one situation that you'd immediately change to achieve that vision.

Asking the prompt is easy. The hard part is listening. Chapter 5 discusses how to listen delightedly to a story, along with how to respond to the other person afterward.

As a reminder, the steps to listening in this way are:

1. Ask a story prompt.

2. The customer answers with a story.

3. Respond to the story by listening delightedly without interruption.

4. Ask reflective questions.

5. Give appreciation.

6. Ask clarifying and information questions (optional).

7. Share a story, if appropriate, or ask another story prompt.

What will you learn if you do this? Stories you hear can help you identify a person's personality temperament, how they think, their underlying mindset, the core need that's driving them, what motivates them to buy from one organization over another, their long-term goals, and more.

In the blog post "Just Listen! How Sales Reps Can Listen to Customers More Effectively" (http://labs.openviewpartners.com/just-listen-how-sales-reps-can-listen-to-customers-more-effectively/), Dave Kahle shares some listening techniques you can use to affirm what the prospect has said.

Get prospects to open up with triggers

If you decide to share a story in response to one that you hear, know that it may trigger an additional story from the prospect that's related to what you're sharing. If this happens, stop talking. Then start listening in the manner we've just described.

If you're meeting a prospect in person, be observant when you walk into that person's work space or office. Look for story triggers you can use to get the other person to talk. One day, Lori was meeting with a CEO in his office about the possibility of a new contract. She was seated facing him at his desk. When she turned around to leave, above the door she saw many unique swords of all different sizes. After gasping, she turned back to the CEO and said, "Tell me about that moment when you decided to create this collection of swords." After telling her the story, he awarded her the contract.

Relay a variety of stories

Before you can tell stories, you need to deliberately create a library of them. Start with stories of the market segments you serve and the five awareness levels we mentioned early on in this chapter. To enhance this story bank, you'll also want to add these to the mix, specific to each prospect you're calling on:

✔ **Your experiences with the prospect's organization:** Have you ever been a customer of the prospect's organization? If not, has anyone you know been a customer of that business? What did they experience? Were there any challenges or wow moments? What insights can you glean? Be ready to share these stories, good or bad.

✔ **What you know about the prospect's organization:** Learn everything you can about the prospect's organization in the time you have available. What's its founding story? Are there any stories about its core values in action? What folklore is often shared about the enterprise? What stories are currently in the news media?

✔ **What you know about the person(s) you're meeting/chatting with:** What can you learn about the people you'll be speaking to? Their likes and dislikes? Where did they grow up and go to school? Who do they know that you might also know? What hobbies do they have? Find stories that relate to what you learn. Social media sites are a great resource to find this kind of information. Reach out to friends and colleagues who might know this person. These stories could be about the person(s) you're meeting with or a personal story that relates to them (for example, you both went to the same university). Here's an example: Before Lori met a corporate executive who was in town from Finland at a U.S. facility, she learned he loved to fish. When she greeted him for the first time, she shared a personal story about how her entire family often went fishing on Sunday afternoons after prompting and listening to one of his fishing stories. When this gentleman introduced her to his colleague who was traveling with him, he put his arm around her shoulder and said with a smile, "Please meet my new best friend!" The story had built an instant bond.

✔ **Stories that enhance your credibility:** Frank Sherwood, Director of Global Corporate Services for CBRE, Inc. has a story like this that you can read in the appendix. Frank uses this story with prospects to get new business in addition to showcasing the credibility of his team and their skill set. What's neat about his story is that its key message (*Give me time*) also heightens urgency in those prospects who assumed they had the luxury of time to make a decision about hiring him and his team.

✔ **Personal stories:** You could tell one, akin to Lori's fishing story. Or you might share one that functions as an analogy or metaphor for your prospect. The following is a story Lori tells in workshops, about Denise's interactions with a food and beverage manager, which has a personal story from Lori embedded in it.

Story: Soup's On!

As a sales rep for a major food distributor, Barb works diligently every week on finding new prospects. Last fall, her boss expanded her territory to include two additional cities, both of which are an hour from her house. The first week in December, she made her first cold call to the purchasing manager at a casino that gets 100 percent of its food from a competitor. The response? "You come in every week. And I'll see what I might be able to give you."

So she did. The next week she brought in a brochure. And she got the leftovers. The third week she brought in a sample. And the response? She got the leftovers. The fourth week, the leftovers. By the fifth week, she'd worked herself up to about 5 percent of the sales. The sixth week? Voila. She was given an appointment with the food and beverage manager for the following week.

Knowing she needed a home run, she called Denise who works as a food broker. "Denise, they're giving me the opportunity to meet with the food and beverage director next week at a casino. I'd really like you to come with me." Denise responded, "Absolutely, Barb. I'll be there." Her company hadn't been into this casino either.

The following Thursday, Denise drove two and a half hours from her home to meet Barb and head over to the casino for the 11 o'clock appointment. They arrived 15 minutes early and checked in with the head of purchasing, who said, "He's not ready to see you yet. But I've set up some time for you to meet with the woman who's in charge of the gift shop." Which they did. They showed her some snacks — potato chips and candy bars and the like. And she seemed interested.

Around 10 minutes after 11, they were able to meet with the food and beverage director. He'd just come out of a long morning meeting. You could tell he was very flustered. After they introduced themselves and Denise started to chat, she knew by the way he looked at her that something wasn't quite right. She asked, "Sir, do you want us to come back?" He replied, "Yeah, I have to go on the buffet. I have to carve the prime rib and the turkey for lunch." She responded, "When would be a good time for us to come back?" He answered, "1:30." Denise replied, "You sure that's good or do you want us to come back later?" And she heard, "2 o'clock. Make it 2 o'clock." To which Denise replied, "Sir, we'll be back here at 2 o'clock."

On the way out, Denise and Barb stopped to tell the purchasing manager, who said, "Oh, no. What are you going to do for the next few hours?" Denise nonchalantly said, "Don't worry. We'll be here at 2 o'clock. We'll be ready for a presentation at that time."

Denise and Barb left and made another sales call about a half hour away. They came back around 1 o'clock to prepare. Denise had made a list of all the code numbers for the products she planned to show him. Barb put that information into her laptop so she could start getting prices and packaging information.

At 2 o'clock, the purchasing manager took them into the kitchen where the executive chef, the sous chef, the food and beverage director, and the woman from the gift shop were waiting. Denise knew that every night the casino did some sort of buffet — Italian or Mexican or Chinese or seafood. So, she'd organized her presentation in this manner.

First she showed them seafood. She had stuffed crab shells and some breaded calamari. The food and beverage director seemed a little interested. Next she showed them some frozen vegetable blends and the same gentleman muttered, "Huh. That would be different." But he wasn't giving her any eye contact or asking her any questions.

Denise proceeded on to some pork items. Sausage patties and sausage links and bacon and little precooked pork shanks. The director just kept moving the products around on the table. Then they went on to some name brand dressings. His response? "Oh, we make our own. But let me look at this anyway. Even though a product is a name brand, how am I to know if it's good or not?"

Denise immediately stopped and said, "You know, when I was first married, my husband and I were watching our money. Like most newlyweds, we were pinching our pennies every chance we could get, especially at the grocery store. One night I came home with regular nondescript grocery store soup. As I was unpacking the bag, my husband looked at me and said, "Don't you ever, ever bring that kind of soup home again. I only eat Campbell's.

Now I didn't know this about him. Nor did I really understand his need at the time. But I listened. And since then, I've never ever bought anything other than Campbell's soup. And I've learned, *you've got to know it and like it* to eat it. If you pinched your pennies in some areas, you could go for the name brands that you and your customers were brought up on. It's what you like. It's what you're used to."

And he said, "You're absolutely right. You have to go with what you feel comfortable with and what your customers want, whether it's a name brand that they can relate to or some private label item. We get so stuck with the same items over and over again. We need to look beyond them but at the same time keep in mind what everybody might want. That's why we need to have change. I need some new items so I keep people interested and we stand out from other places."

The next thing you knew he was asking to see the desserts and having his executive chef fry up the calamari and the hot wings and the stuffed crab. He then asked for pricing on them along with a couple unique vegetable items and the pork shanks. He changed out items on his Super Bowl and Valentine's Day menus and on several of his buffets, even though the menus had already been written — good thing they hadn't gone to the printer yet.

At the end of the presentation, he turned to Denise and Barb and shook their hands and said, "Thank you very much. You brought a lot of new items that'll help us. You're welcome back any time."

So what did Denise do to get the food and beverage director to let his guard down — and give Barb the chance to capture about 40 percent of this casino's business down the road? She knew what it meant to *stand out **and** be heard*. She didn't give the same old responses when she sensed his disinterest. She told a personal story that he could relate to without ever knowing he was looking for new items to use on his menus.

What about you? How are you going to stand out and be heard in your job or in your sales work?

And that's why we're here — so you can learn how stories can help you stand out from the crowd — and have your voice be heard no matter what your role is in sales. *Used with permission. Copyright © 2009 by Lori L. Silverman. All rights reserved.*

How can you easily and quickly get these five kinds of stories into your own story bank and help create them with a sales team as well? Here's one way, independent of whether you're an entrepreneur or part of a large enterprise. We've adapted an approach that Michael Harris describes in his blog post "Selling Blind — Turn the Lights on with Customer Knowledge Story Coaching" (http://insightdemand.com/business-storytelling/customer-story-sales-coachings/):

1. Keep a running list of the most pressing challenges that your sales team members run up against when prospecting for new business — or trying to extend business with current clients.

2. Ask a sales rep to select an issue that resonates with them that they've been able to successfully tackle. The sales rep is responsible for crafting a three- to five-minute version of the story to tell before the next sales meeting. (**Note:** In the first go-round, it's really hard to craft a well-written two-minute story as Harris asks for, so we suggest it be a little longer.)

3. In each meeting, have a standard agenda item that encompasses listening to and providing feedback on a story. Allot about 20–30 minutes for this item (depending on the size of the sales team).

4. Have the sales rep deliver the story.

5. After the sales rep delivers the story, have the other reps act as story coaches. The team members listen to it as outlined in Chapter 5 if it's only to provide feedback on the story's content, or as outlined in Chapter 10 if it's also to provide feedback on story delivery.

6. Based on the feedback, the sales rep edits the story, writes it up, and distributes it to the team so everyone has another story to use when speaking with prospects.

Overcome objections through story

How many times have you heard these objections or some version of them?

- ✔ "I'm happy with my service provider. I don't want to change."
- ✔ "I'm okay with the way things are right now."
- ✔ "I'm too busy. My group has a lot on its plate right now."
- ✔ "How do I know you really have the necessary experience to do this?"

- ✔ "We've just posted an X billion-dollar loss this past year, head count has been frozen, and people we've let go will not be replaced."

- ✔ "I have a friend who I trust that can help me with what you're offering."

In Bob Croston's blog post "Are Sales Objections Driving You Nut$? Keys to Overcoming the Four Types of Objections" (www.rainsalestraining. com/blog/nuts-keys-to-overcoming-sales-objections/), he says all objections boil down to four common types: lack of need, lack of urgency, lack of trust, and lack of money.

- ✔ We've already discussed the types of stories that get at heightening the *need* — these may come from your market research or how your current customers' problems were solved by what you provided them.

- ✔ Frank's story is one kind that addresses lack of *urgency* as well as lack of *trust*.

- ✔ Lack of *money* can also be addressed through a story. All we have to do is shift Croston's question, "If money were no object, what would be your ideal solution?" into a story prompt that begins to co-create a future story: "Let's pretend for a moment that money is no object. Paint for me the picture of what a perfect day/week/month would be like if you could have the ideal solution." Shifting the conversation like that moves from problem to opportunity, a story structure discussed in Chapter 7.

Asking for the Sale

Maybe you've talked to the prospect once, like Denise, and landed a sale. Good for you! Maybe you've submitted documents several times through a vendor selection process, as Cristi's story mentions in Chapter 3, without any initial positive results.

In complex sales situations, or ones where the customer's initial investment is significant, you may spend a year or more just getting to know the prospect personally before ever being considered as a supplier or vendor. Even then, you may need to go through a request-for-proposals process. If you clear that, you could end up on a short list that requires you to give a presentation. How does story factor into all these situations?

Incorporate story into the proposal

If you're writing a sales proposal that must follow a very structured process, you may benefit from reading the section in Chapter 13 on fusing stories into grant proposals. If you have the flexibility in how the proposal is crafted, here are a variety of ways you can incorporate stories into the document:

✔ **Stories from the prospect:** You need to show the prospect you've heard what's been shared with you. How could you start out the proposal with a story or two that highlight the problem/need? If the prospect has already tried some solutions that haven't worked, and yours differs from those, where could this story fit into the proposal? If the prospect has conducted research that led the organization to you or the type of solution your enterprise provides, how can you fit this in as a story?

✔ **Stories about your organization:** Frankly, the prospect already knows these stories. If you choose to add any into the body of the proposal, do so only if it significantly increases its value or if the story is a very recent experience that prospects don't know about. Otherwise, add an appendix to your proposal that includes stories your prospect has acknowledged are important to have as the proposal is passed through the organization for review and acceptance.

✔ **Stories from your customers:** Notice we didn't say "stories about your customers." Instead of including testimonials, what customer stories would benefit the proposal? Also figure out which customer stories to include based on your prospect's current awareness level.

✔ **Stories about past failures:** There are two types of failure stories: those about prospects that chose not to embrace what your organization has to offer (especially those who elected to do nothing) and those customers who didn't fully utilize, follow, or implement what you provided to them. Why do you want to tell these stories to prospects? The first one speaks to the risks of doing nothing. The second is an opportunity for you to talk about what can happen if customers misuse a product, don't properly implement a service, or ignore your advice. It's also a chance to talk about how you recover customers when things go awry.

Sharing these stories also shows you're willing to be vulnerable and talk about difficult situations so your prospect can learn from them. This humanizes you and your organization. If you aren't yet convinced, read this summary of a study by Vinit Desai, Assistant Professor of Management at the University of Colorado Denver Business School, which demonstrates that failure is a better teacher than success, and that the knowledge from failure is retained longer: www.eurekalert.org/pub_releases/2010-08/uocd-uoc082310.php.

Create a story-based presentation

For over 40 years (yes — a long time) 90 percent of my selling technique was "story telling" and 10 percent was closing the sale. I had already done my "prospecting" to find the client and now it was time for my "presentation" (prior to the close) and while my competition would try to sell the "we are great" concept, I sold "the story." The sad part (for many small businesses), many people today that are reading this don't understand what I just said.

— Jerry X Shea, author/inspirational speaker/small business consultant

Chapter 13 covers many different types of presentation structures that also apply to sales. So does the present-future presentation structure we mention in Chapter 16. In this section, we talk about a few nuances that apply to the use of story in short list or introductory sales presentations.

While you're reviewing the visuals you plan to use, take a look at this blog post called "How to Add Stories to Your Presentations" (http://insight-demand.com/business-storytelling/ppt-buying-simulator/). It'll help you storify your PowerPoint presentations. We summarize Michael Harris's approach here and provide our own commentary:

1. **Begin with no more than four value assumptions based on research you've conducted.** These are pain points or problems that you perceive prospects have. Do so to establish credibility. Tell the stories. We mention how to craft them earlier in this chapter.

2. **Share relevant customer stories that reveal pain points.** Harris says "before and after" drawings can be helpful here. We suggest switching the order to "opportunity/problem" to shift the conversation toward what's possible in the future. Any visual that helps depict this will be helpful. Consider using a whiteboard versus a slide. Why? Keep reading.

3. **Listen to the customer's story.** Frankly, you should already know this. Here we suggest you hone in on co-creating a future story with the prospect (discussed in Chapters 4, 13, and 16), or getting the prospect to enhance the one you've previously discussed.

4. **Provide proof.** Although Harris suggests showing proof, from your perspective, of how your product or service has solved problems, we suggest inverting this. Make customers the hero by showing how they achieved success.

Does using lots of sensory words in a conversation with prospects, when you tell a story in the manner we discuss, mean people will pay more for an item? The answer is yes, according to research cited by Steve W. Martin, who teaches sales strategy at USC Marshall School of Business, in his blog article "Research: How Sensory Information Influences Price Decisions" (http://blogs.hbr.org/cs/2013/07/research_how_sensory_informati.html). When groups were asked to give the price of several items, those given both visual images and descriptions, with dramatic emphasis and inflection about a product/service, priced them the highest. Surprisingly, lengthy product evaluations were found to lower the perception of its value. Martin also spends time discussing why both what you say and how you say it are important. Tone, tempo, and demeanor appear to have more impact than your actual words. You'd better go back to Chapter 10 and practice your stories!

Well, here's a sad statistic: Only 13 percent of salespeople use an interactive writing surface such as a whiteboard to support their customer conversations (www.admarco.net/inbound-marketing-messaging-sales-performance-blog/bid/93032/Visual-Storytelling-Survey-Yields-Startling-Results). Yet, December 2012 research by the Aberdeen Group found "conducting an interactive whiteboard conversation (as opposed to a static presentation) leads to a 50 percent higher lead conversion rate, 29 percent shorter time-to-productivity, and 15 percent average shorter sales cycle." So let us ask the obvious: When and how are you going to include this visual storytelling technique in your presentations?

Using Story Post-Sale

Once a sale is made, follow-up needs to occur if you want repeat business. Now, some of this follow-up may come through your organization's marketing function. Other pieces are the responsibility of the sales function.

So where might story fit in?

✔ **Building referrals:** Descriptions of features and benefits or all the cool processes your company uses aren't the stories that bring referrals. The kinds of stories that do are the personal experiences people have had with you or your organization's product/service. How do you get customers to sing your praises — and do so through story? Check out how Greta Schulz does it for the surgeon who did her Lasik surgery in this blog post: www.bizjournals.com/bizjournals/how-to/growth-strategies/2012/03/how-storytelling-can-help-to-build.html?page=all. First you need to engage in memorable behaviors that go above and beyond. Then you need to help your customer find ways to tell the story on your behalf. They go like this: "I was really in a pickle. Jim came in to work with me and his company solution saved my butt. Let me tell you what happened." Or: "I loved working with Mary. I was really struggling until she came in for a few sessions and showed us exactly how to overcome our obstacles." You can also tell these sorts of stories yourself, but when your customer does it, it has far more impact. Ask to audio or video record these stories for use on electronic devices.

✔ **Engaging through story triggers:** Imagine your last name is Foxx (name changed to protect the salesperson). And your sales numbers have been low. Your sales manager is not too happy with you. One Saturday, you go to a yard sale and miraculously find ten lawn ornaments with a fox on them for a dollar apiece. You buy them all. Every time you make a sale, you take one lawn ornament and stick it in the carpet in front of your sales manager's desk. After doing this four times, it hits you. Why are you giving your boss a reminder of you? Why not do this for your customers? So you go in search of tchotchkes and promotional product items with a fox — holiday ornaments, chocolates in the shape of a fox, t-shirts and hats with a fox symbol on them, and so on — items that regularly remind people of you and all the stories associated with you.

✔ **Following up for feedback:** For those in formal sales roles (outside of a franchised restaurant or perhaps a large brick-and-mortar retail firm), we assume you check in regularly with your customers about how they're doing with what you've provided. Do you prompt for stories in these meetings to assess how well you and your company are performing? If not, get to it! Traditional surveys won't get you the depth of information you need to ensure all is well.

✔ **Collecting and analyzing stories to improve the sales process:** How do you find better ways to support and engage an existing sales force when they're selling a well-established medicine yet still need to increase sales? Pfizer did just that by gathering stories from sales reps in 11 cities spanning six countries within a four-week time span in 2010, using *anecdote circles*. The methodology is outlined in the article "Using Stories to Increase Sales at Pfizer" (`http://cognitive-edge.com/library/more/articles/using-stories-to-increase-sales-at-pfizer/`). After stories were collected, they were analyzed for overall patterns. It showed that the sales rep's attitude about how they viewed the product and their experience selling it trumped product knowledge as a revenue driver. Several areas for improvement were surfaced, including how to overcome objections. The process also identified 18 stories that helped sales reps address those objections. Attitudes shifted, confidence increased, and they were now ready to take to the field to close contracts.

✔ **Incorporating story feedback into ongoing staff meetings:** Through Angela Prestil's role as Director, Sales Culture Development at Credit Union National Association (CUNA), credit union leaders are taught sales, sales leadership, and coaching skills. In training, skill practices based on "worst-case scenarios" give attendees a chance to try different responses so they can see how the interaction might play out differently. They're also encouraged to pre-plan calls with members using the same techniques so they can practice prior to calling the member.

Back at work, in ongoing staff meetings, stories of situations that have gone extremely well, those that are difficult, along with next steps continue to be solicited to encourage reflective learning and additional insights. Supervisors also listen in on conversations to encourage continual improvement of staff skills against identified service standards that are specific to each credit union. One key skill area is to get staff to anticipate the member's next need. For example, if a member comes in for a mortgage, a next need might be the ability to purchase furniture for their new home. Staff are encouraged to use stories here to help understand financial needs at different life stages.

REAL LIFE EXAMPLE

✔ **Celebrating successes:** In one company Lori worked with, a bell was rung in the main corporate building when a large sale was closed. The bell served as a story trigger, signaling that it was time to celebrate and share stories about what had happened to solidify the sale. What a great way to maintain momentum.

Chapter 16

Using Stories to Spark Change

In This Chapter

▶ Heightening commitment by using story sharing during the entire change initiative

▶ Strengthening the vision through dream stories and future stories

▶ Using stories to mitigate risks, obtain resources, overcome obstacles, and get things done

Change initiatives have a dismal track record. From 1995–2011, numerous studies have shown the failure rate is approximately 70 percent (www.onirik.com.au/media/Whitepapers/Cracking%20the%20Change%20Code%20White%20Paper.pdf). Reasons include lack of leadership support and follow-through to using models of change that just aren't very helpful.

We believe storytelling practices can positively move this needle. At its core, *change* is all about changing stories — whether the change is personal, organizational, or societal. When faced with change, we might not know the right choice to make or the right way to act. To address this need, we often recall a true or fictional story that provides both a lesson and meaning about the situation to guide our behavior. You need to work to consciously uncover and transmit stories that provide this guidance. Not only will people seek these stories, to align their efforts they need to hear them.

Together we have more than 50 years of experience working on change initiatives, but this chapter isn't a primer on the subject. It's about the interface between change and various storytelling practices — why they're needed and how you can make it happen.

Story Sharing versus Storytelling

In their blog post "Changing the Conversation in Your Company" (http://blogs.hbr.org/cs/2012/05/in_our_experience_its_rare.html?awid=5438240191344385513-3271), Boris Groysberg and Michael Slind write about what they learned after surveying around three dozen extremely diverse senior leaders who attended a Harvard Business School program. Ninety-two percent agreed that "the practice of internal communication 'has undergone a lot of change' at their companies 'in recent years.'" This research confirms what the researchers found in other studies and in cases they cite in their book, *Talk, Inc.: How Trusted Leaders Use Conversation to Power Their Organizations* (Harvard Business School Press, 2012) — "old 'corporate communication' is giving way to a model that Groysberg and Slind call 'organizational conversation.'" This shift alters the very nature of leadership. They highlight four steps an organization can take to engage in this new way:

- ✔ **"Close the gap between you and your employees."** What would it take in your organization for leaders to be more direct, open, and honest in their communications to employees? Instead of top-down communications, how could exchanges become more personal?

- ✔ **"Promote two-way dialogue within your company."** What channels are available in your place of business to allow ideas to move in multiple directions? How could you create ongoing dialogue where staff shares with leaders what life is like in their world? What would it take for leaders to evoke stories from them and listen in return? See Chapter 5. This isn't about messaging; it's about give-and-take conversation.

- ✔ **"Engage employees in the work of telling the company story."** Hallelujah! This is what we've been saying all through this book. What would it take to encourage, invest in, and promote employee's ability to share their personal version of the company's core stories we outline in Chapter 4 and in Chapter 14?

- ✔ **"Pursue a clear agenda."** What are the overall strategy and the objectives that ground the conversation? How can leaders replace corporate speak with engaging stories that have clear key messages and action statements? See Chapters 6–9 on how to craft and tell them.

The book *Homo Imitans: The Art of Social Infection: Viral Change in Action* (Meeting Minds Publishing, 2011) by Dr. Herrero Leandro supports this research. He says, "Communication is not change." What does that mean? Hierarchical, top-down communications that push change messages to employees aren't effective. This is no different than what we advocate in Chapter 14 about communicating with consumers: a pull approach to communications that invites employees into a process is far more engaging than pushing messages to people, which often results in resistance.

Although change is easier if the top brass are behind it and involved, for change to be accepted and take hold, story sharing, not storytelling, is more critical. Give up thinking that employees will get on board and change their behavior if executive messages via glitzy campaigns and giveaways from corporate communications tell them enough times what the change is and what to do. Adages like, "Tell them, tell them what you told them, and tell them again" and "People have to hear the same message between 8 and 12 times before they get it" don't really work here. In addition to what Groysberg and

Slind suggest, what else do you need to pay attention to relative to story? Try these ideas:

- ✔ **Embrace story sharing as a practice in your change effort.** Embed it up front when you're facing a change or conducting a change impact assessment. Evoke and listen to stories on all facets of the change effort.

- ✔ **Figure out how to share the right stories at the right time to keep momentum going.** Throughout this chapter we make suggestions about the types of stories to flesh out and when to relay them to others.

- ✔ **Find and promote the right behaviors and then make them visible.** As social animals, we watch what other people do. The tendency to copy others is called *social proof*. Whom do we copy in a change? For sure it's not official "change agents." That's like copying the teacher's pet in elementary school. We copy those we feel an affinity with and those we respect, trust, and admire — like the cool kids in the schoolyard. You're more likely to find them in informal peer networks. Identify these folks. Engage them in story sharing about the change and forward steps.

- ✔ **Showcase stories that go beyond demonstrating the need for change.** Make visible stories showing progress, collaboration, persistence, ingenuity, how milestones were met, and the like. Broadcast these throughout the enterprise. Show your staff as the heroes they are.

It's not our intent to throw the baby out with the bathwater. For change to occur, we recognize the need to leverage people structures, communication channels, intrinsic motivators, external rewards, and all else we've said here.

Creating the Need for the Change

A compelling story is critical for any change effort. But a great story from the C-suite isn't enough. One big mistake leaders make is thinking that what motivates them is what motivates their staff. That's far from the truth. Before crafting a compelling story, change efforts start with listening for, evoking, and gathering stories from all levels of the organization. Why? For the story to connect and stimulate action, you have to know your audience.

Get to know stakeholders through story

Up front, engage with audiences who are most likely to be affected by and able to implement the proposed change. You don't do that through e-mails, voicemails, or PowerPoint presentations. You do it by showing up in person.

We're not talking about a roadshow here. Nor is it only about the business case for the change and what lies ahead. Think conversation — give and take. This is where ideas and desire come to life. Try the following:

- ✔ Identify key stakeholders and schedule one-on-one meetings with them.
- ✔ Craft story prompts in advance that get at what you want to learn.
- ✔ Evoke stories to learn stakeholders' needs and points of view.
- ✔ Share stories of similar experiences, as appropriate. To build trust and rapport, include your own personal stories.
- ✔ Provide a story that touches on the opportunities that present themselves when the change is ultimately achieved.
- ✔ Respond to questions stakeholders may have.

Ground all the stories you tell in the three factors Dan Pink, author of *Drive: The Surprising Truth About What Motivates Us* (Riverhead Books, 2009), has identified through a review of extensive research on personal motivation: autonomy (self-directed work), mastery (ongoing learning and improvement), and purpose (being in service to some greater objective).

Why do this, you ask? Here's an example that behavioral psychologists Emily Lawson and Colin Price mention in their article "The Psychology of Change Management" (*McKinsey Quarterly*, June 2003): www.mckinsey.com/insights/organization/the_psychology_of_change_management. A financial services company launched a cost-reduction program with a change story that spoke to typical conventions: The change was needed to increase their competitive position and ensure their future, yadda yadda yadda. Three months into the program, employees were still very resistant to the effort. So the change story was re-crafted to include

- ✔ **Purpose:** To deliver affordable housing.
- ✔ **Mastery:** For customers: fewer errors for customers and more competitive prices. For the company: revenues need to grow faster than expenses. For employees: more attractive jobs.
- ✔ **Autonomy:** Working in teams results in less duplication and more delegation.

The result? A 61 percent increase in motivation in one month. Wow!

Find stories of pain and urgency

There are two kinds of communications that enterprises often use to launch change. The first says, "Historically we've had an advantage over our competitors. This has eroded. Now our customers' needs are changing. We can regain our leadership position and be prominent once more if we change."

The second one says, "We're performing below our competition. To survive, we must dramatically change. We can become a top performer by leveraging our current competencies and focusing on growth." Both sound like lofty pronouncements from on high. Don't use them. Go deeper with stories.

People embrace change primarily because of pain and urgency. Collecting stories that portray these at various levels creates the contexts for change that are relevant to the different audiences. For example, if the change is to enhance customer service, the pain and urgency related to this in IT probably differs from the pain and urgency associated with it in the marketing group.

Gather real stories of the struggles and challenges that people face because of broken systems, inefficient processes, marketplace threats, consequences for customers, and so on. Connect these struggles to the organization's potential fate. These stories reinforce the fact that maintaining the status quo isn't workable. Distress about the way things currently work provides motivation, more so than the vision of what's possible. When gathering these stories, invite people to articulate their understanding of this need for change and bring their passion to it. This will help align them around the purpose of the change. Without Purpose, Mastery, and Autonomy, along with urgency and meaning, you pay people for tasks but don't touch their hearts.

This is the only time to actively evoke "Ain't it awful" stories in one-on-one conversations. Be careful here. A steady diet of this kind of story can be debilitating for everyone. How can you get around this conundrum?

1. When you hear an "Ain't it awful" story, never, ever just say, "Thank you" when the person is done telling their tale of woe.

2. Instead, right after the story is told, ask the person what they'd like to see happen to change it into a better one. Ask for specific steps that would help get them and others there. You'll leave the conversation on a high note for both of you and have gained valuable knowledge about the kind of future they want to see and possible paths forward.

3. Move into providing hope by sharing the future story of what's possible. More on this later in this chapter.

There's another place to get fodder for stories related to urgency and pain. Go into the future. Do an environmental scan looking out five to ten years. Identify trends, threats, and *wildcards* — highly unlikely events that would have huge impact if they were to happen. Craft stories for your change based on this information. As before, tailor stories to the various groups within the organization and to what will propel them forward. This approach can be useful in all settings, but it's especially valuable in enterprises that are highly successful but have significant potential upsets looming ahead. Often leaders and staff don't see any need to change because the organization is doing well. It's also beneficial in places where complacency and mediocrity have set in so deeply that employees see such behavior as acceptable. In that situation, having environmental scan data and information to look at can prevent finger-pointing from taking place and undermining the change effort.

In all cases, avoid the following scenario. In your personal life, let's say you're faced with an urgent and painful need. You share it with friends and family. You find helpful resources and begin to figure out what to do. Though these folks want to hear about your progress, you keep sharing the same story about the urgent and painful need. They respond with, "Yeah, yeah, yeah. We got that. But what's your progress been?"

The exact same pattern is true for organizations and social causes. Over and over, leaders share an urgent and painful "need for change" story. After staff starts taking action, those same leaders come back and tell the identical change story! Forward progress stalls. Why? These leaders haven't crafted the next part of the story to engage staff, thus showing they're completely out of sync with what's been happening.

Demonstrate that change is possible

Once change is imminent — you're assured the organization is embarking on this journey — collect stories in which people survived a personal or organizational change that's significant to them. Surfacing these stories highlights qualities that got these people through these difficult situations, which pinpoints for other leaders and employees what they'll need to bring forth for the change effort to succeed. It also helps folks who hear them overcome feeling lost and anxious as they move into the unknown. This type of story is a great way to build a bridge to walk away from the past and present into the future.

Evoke this kind of "change is possible" story by asking the following questions:

- ✔ "Tell me about a time when you were faced with an unexpected change in your life and what you did to get you through it successfully."

- ✔ "Tell me about a time in your life when you greatly resisted a change, and when you embraced it, many opportunities presented themselves."

- ✔ "Tell me about a time when a group you were part of (in the organization or elsewhere) went through a big change that no one thought could be accomplished — yet it was successful — and what made that possible."

Jan Pulvermacher-Ryan, former National President of the American Legion Auxiliary, worked with Lori to craft a "change is possible" story. You can find it in the appendix. She shared it with a diverse cross-section of more than 300 members, leaders, and staff across the country, ranging in age from 20 to 85. They were attending a strategic planning event over a weekend, which culminated in the National Executive Committee successfully ratifying a new five-year strategic plan.

Following Jan's story, the key message of *Stretch beyond your comfort zone* was reinforced through a facilitated small group meaning-making activity focused on translating the organization's proposed mission statement into everyday work activities. Participants were asked to write what they'd done personally to serve 1) veterans, 2) their families, and 3) their communities, and to share those responses with others at their table group. The debrief of the activity showed everyone that they were already actualizing this proposed mission in their work while building confidence that they could indeed stretch beyond their comfort zone into the proposed new strategic plan. Later in this chapter, in the section "Embody the future story," we describe the story-based activities that came after this to introduce the organization's proposed vision and strategies for the five-year plan.

A "change is possible" story also conveys the unwavering commitment needed to realize the ultimate outcomes of the change. This is exactly what a *burning platform* is intended to communicate. Daryl Connor introduced this term through a story about one of 63 survivors of a massive oil rig explosion who risked jumping off of a 15-story platform to save his own life (`www.conner-partners.com/frameworks-and-processes/the-real-story-of-the-burning-platform`). This story is about the significant implications of not changing that derive from problems and opportunities — current or anticipated. These implications imply a non-negotiable commitment to the change, no matter how difficult, and evoke what Connors calls a "shift from peril to resolve" that engages the hearts and minds of those who hear it.

Apply story structures to launch a change

Chapter 7 introduces different types of story structures. Here's how they work when crafting stories that include pain and urgency or those that demonstrate that change is possible:

- ✔ **I'm better off:** Here's what happened to us. Here's how we can meet the challenge. Here's how we'll be better off.

- ✔ **Highlight both loss and gain:** Here's what we had that was so wonderful. Here's what we've lost. This is what we need to do to rebuild and create something wonderful again.

- ✔ **The Cinderella down-and-out story structure:** We were in a bad spot. Then a partner stepped in to help us. Despite that, we ended up in a dark and dreary place. But now because of XYZ, our future is bright. We can get back on top by specifically doing ABC.

- ✔ **SHARES (Setting, Hindrance, Action, Results, Evaluation, and Suggested actions):** This was where we used to be. Now an obstacle or hindrance blocks our path and threatens our existence. But these are the results we desire. We've evaluated (or can evaluate) our strengths and weaknesses. These are the specific actions to take which will secure for us a new day.

✔ **PARLAS (Problem, Action, Result, Learning, Application, and Suggested actions):** Here's the problem we face. These are the results we desire. This is what we've learned from our recent experiences. This is how we're going to apply these lessons going forward. These are the actions we need to take to bring us into our desired future.

✔ **CHARQES (Context, Hindrance, Action, Results Quantified, Evaluation, and Suggested actions):** This is today's situation. Here's the challenge we face. If we take action, we can realize these results which we'll quantify and report on — so we can consider how we need to adapt in real time. To bring us into our desired future, here are the specific actions we need to take.

✔ **CCARLS: (Context, Challenge, Action, Result, Lesson, and Suggested actions):** This is where we are today. This is the challenge we face. This is the action we need to take to achieve these results. This is the lesson we've learned. Here's what we need to do to bring us into our desired future.

Communicating the Vision of the Change

No one can fight with a personal dream you share about the future of a project, a business, a product or service, or an enterprise. It's yours. You own it. However, they can always fight a future story that's created by a group of people because they weren't involved in creating it or it doesn't jibe with what they think it should be.

How might you deal with this dilemma, especially because both dream and future stories help relay the vision of the change? Here's what we've learned so far through our experiences with all types and sizes of organizations:

✔ In organizations that employ small numbers of people, the founder may choose to share their dream for a change or have everyone collectively create the future story for the change. We suggest both!

✔ In organizations where there are multiple partners (law firms, accounting and physician practices, and the like), it's critically important that the principals discuss their individual dreams for a change. If they aren't aligned, it may mean a partner needs to reconsider involvement with the firm. This is one type of organization where a collective dream story works best to show unity. If the firm is small, a single future story of the change generated by employees is also useful. If there are multiple units, each unit will want to create its own future story based on this dream.

✔ In organizations that have one site (or a large presence through a couple sites in a community or region) and a large staff, the most senior executive, in addition to all senior staff, need their own dream stories in an enterprise-wide change. It's not important that these stories be identical. However, before deploying them, ensure dream story alignment, conceptually and philosophically. Future stories need to be specific to each area of the organization. For example, in a hospital, the CEO's dream may be about patient-centered delivery of care. Each group then creates a future story of what actualizing this dream would look like to it. Marketing's future story would be specific to marketing. The operating room's story is specific to it. Critical care has its own future story too. Aligning these departmental future stories is key to alleviating potential conflicts and synergizing initiatives across groups.

✔ In an organization-wide change within an enterprise with multiple sites scattered across a large geography, decide how localized the dream story needs to be to incite change. Strengthen the dream story shared by corporate executives at these local sites by tailoring the message to the audience and having it shared at the same time that the local leader shares his dream story. Future stories need to be localized.

✔ There are multiple considerations in membership organizations such as professional and trade associations, where there's a paid staff and volunteer leadership changes every year or two. Staff and volunteer leadership need to be aligned in their dreams. A single, collaboratively developed dream story is key for the dream to last beyond anyone's tenure, especially if the change is multi-year. Individual chapters and special interest groups will want their own future stories. Remember that active volunteers are attracted to organizations where a dream's been articulated and members and staff are bringing it into reality.

✔ In government organizations, there are multiple constituents and stakeholders whose dreams and future stories need to be accessed. The leader's dream for the change needs to be shaped by input from these various individuals and groups. Once that's happened, different units can develop their individual future stories and rally behind the shared dream.

Here are three nuances that play into each of these situations:

✔ **Have employees write their own dream or future story of the change.** Much of the energy invested in communicating is better spent listening, not telling, say Lawson and Price. They found when employees choose for themselves (autonomy), they're more committed to the outcome by a factor of almost five to one. Traditional approaches to enterprise and project-oriented change overlook this fact. Many leaders naively say, "Why not just tell them and be done with it?" This raises a critical question: If employees have no personal story to share about the change, how can they take ownership of it? This example that Lawson and Price share has something to teach us. Prior to 2003, oil and gas company BP wanted to develop a training program for frontline leaders. A decision was made early on to involve every key constituent in the design of the program, allowing them to write their own ticket. It took 18 months to complete the process, but the results have been immense. Now in implementation, 250 senior managers from across the organization willingly teach in it, and the program is the highest rated of its kind at BP. Attendees are consistently ranked higher in performance by their bosses and direct reports. As a side note, we don't know if the Gulf oil spill that happened a few years later has impacted the program.

✓ **Have all staff participate in crafting the overall dream or future story.** Here we can learn from the field of appreciative inquiry. Consider holding a series of gatherings where groups create their own dreams or future stories. These roll up from the grassroots and are aligned throughout the organization. Eventually, the collaboratively developed dream or story makes it way back down through the enterprise to all.

✓ **What to do when multiple visions need to be crafted.** Sometimes a large change, such as implementing a new strategic plan, has multiple types of visions. There's the vision of the change related to the plan's overall impact on the organization. Then there are visions associated with each strategy (or goal or objective, depending on your organization's nomenclature) that also need to be fleshed out. In these situations, we encourage the overall vision to be driven by a dream and for each strategy to be guided by its own future story.

Structure a dream story based on the past

If you're the leader who's spearheading a major change, your job is to offer people a dream and allow them to articulate their version of it. Sometimes these dreams emerge from seeing what's possible in the future. Sometimes the dream comes from the past — a video of a talk from a leader who has since died, an unrealized project, archived materials, or the organization's founding.

Warren Bebbington, Vice Chancellor and President of the University of Adelaide, who arrived in mid-2012, went backward in time to find a story to compel staff to embrace a new strategic plan (www.lhmartininstitute. edu.au/insights-blog/2013/02/115-finding-the-narrative-a-key-to-leading-a-university). At that time, the primary focus was on making the institution a great research university. But in the battle against larger and better-equipped universities, it had become like other worn-down, research-intensive campuses. Staff morale had plummeted.

Bebbington was shocked to find out that the university in its early years had been on the cutting edge of higher education. It had been 40 years ahead of other similar English-speaking institutions in admitting women to degree programs and produced two Nobel Prize winners in its first four decades. During that period, its first Vice Chancellor, Dr. Augustus Short, was the visionary hero. It struck Bebbington that the 140-year old institution had forgotten its origin.

When launching the new strategic plan, Bebbington took staff back to the original vision and the heroic story of the university's early history. He traced the energy and qualities of those early years to the present-day plan. To return to its individual discovery and small-group learning roots, Bebbington used metaphors such as the "light of learning shining against the dark southern skies," which showed the uniqueness of the university. It captured wide attention. Staff is energized and excited to complete the plan in 2014.

This kind of thing can happen for your organization, too. When sharing a dream, explain to people why they're the only ones who can do it. Signal that there isn't anybody else who's going to show up and save the day. Add the notion that you're all in it together — you're all in the same boat at sea. When you put it all together, it's really hard to say no.

Follow King's "I Have a Dream" approach

Dr. Martin Luther King articulated what he saw as possible in the future in his 1963, "I Have a Dream" speech. In just 17 minutes, his speech had a massive impact on changing American life that is still felt today. By understanding how he delivered this message, you can create dream stories that do the same.

View the text and listen to the audio of the speech here: http://www.americanrhetoric.com/speeches/mlkihaveadream.htm. Analyze it along with us. Based on Nancy Duarte's book *Resonate: Present Visual Stories that Transform Audiences* (Wiley, 2010) and several articles on rhetorical analysis, Karen's examination shows that King outlined a picture of hope utilizing a back-and-forth current state/future state structure. For the first three and a half minutes he paints a picture of the current state. Then he offers a brief glimpse into the future. For the next minute, King talks again about the current state and then for another minute about the future state. Twenty-four times he moves back and forth between what is and what could be. To inspire people to action, he focused the last four minutes on the hopeful future.

Here's how Dr. King encapsulated many of the story elements we discuss in this book. Consider these when crafting an "I Have a Dream" story:

1. **Know the audience and what they need to do.** Dr. King was very clear about wanting to reach average blacks, whites, and people of any color who viewed the civil rights movement negatively — in this case, anyone who viewed the movement as violent. He made sure the tone of his speech promoted movement but not anger, hatred, or violence.

   • Who are the different audiences for the change in your enterprise?

   • What behaviors need to be promoted? What one or two behaviors do people need to move away from?

2. **Create emotional connection.** King directed people's attention to hating racism — through describing the everyday lives of blacks and the daily struggles they faced — instead of hating each other, while at the same time delivering his wish for a new and better world without racism.

   - What's the deep enemy in your organization? It typically isn't your competitors. It may be constraints like time, cumbersome customer-facing processes, legacy technologies, and the like.

3. **Appeal to people's moral ethics to do right.** King cites the U.S. Constitution and Declaration of Independence as promises to be kept. Ethically, most people believe it's necessary to keep a promise. He also refers to the Emancipation Proclamation that President Abraham Lincoln signed 100 years earlier. He uses this evidence to show that those who've passed before us desired to move away from racism and into a more hopeful future. In this way, he used credibility and social proof, both forces of influence, to make his points.

   - What social proof, from other sources, can you draw on that speaks to moral imperatives and sparks the desire to do right?

4. **Provide context.** King builds parallels between the struggles that black individuals faced to biblical references and William Shakespeare's play *Richard III*. Both remind people of important parts of the past. These references also allow King to build images in the audience's mind of cooperation and collaboration together, being brothers and sisters united against the evils of racism.

   - What key themes need to be reinforced in your change's dream story? Which historical events related to the organization, its industry, or the general marketplace can be provided as context for them?

5. **Include figures of speech.** Throughout his speech, King uses metaphors and similes to bring forth vivid images and numerous kinds of repetition to enhance memory, such as "We will be able to work together, to pray together, to struggle together, to go to jail together, to stand up for freedom together. . . ." He says, "We will not be satisfied" multiple times. The constant repetition between the phrases "I have a dream," and "Let freedom ring," creates rhythm, connects ideas, and builds hope.

   - Chapter 7 outlines several types of story embellishments. Which can be used in the dream story you're creating?

6. **Use contrast.** When King says, "The Negro lives on a lonely island of poverty in the midst of a vast ocean of material prosperity," he effectively uses contrast. He employs it again to move us to the end of the speech when he states, "1963 is not an end, but a beginning."

   - How can you employ the contrast provided by "what is" and "what could be" to enhance the distinction between the current world and what's possible in the future?

7. **Move people to action.** To do this, King again uses repetition. When he says, "Go back to Mississippi, go back to Alabama, go back to South Carolina, go back to Georgia, go back to Louisiana," in addition to telling people not to give up and to continue their cause, he tells them to continue to take action so that freedom can ring from everywhere.

- What exactly do people in your organization need to do differently? What actions can they immediately take?

Process for developing a future story

To move people to action, a future story (also called a vision story) needs to be based in imagery, not business speak and highfalutin' concepts. This imagery must create a picture in the mind that connects both emotionally and to the human spirit. There are several ways to generate a future story. In *The Story of the Future, Told in a Day: Building the Energy to Achieve the Future* (www.pelerei.com/immediate-resources/articles.php), executive management consultant Madelyn Blair, PhD, shares a group process that links the past to the present and then the future. Lori's process for developing a future story is different (http://partners-forprogress.com/FreeArticles.htm). It creates a story grounded in the future that looks back at current reality, what technology futurist Daniel Burrus calls FutureView (www.linkedin.com/today/post/article/20130826190831-48342529-why-martin-luther-king-jr-did-not-say-i-have-a-plan?trk=mp-reader-card). Both approaches are valid. Your organizational culture will influence which one you elect to use.

Future story: Try present-future structure

How do you construct a powerful future story that moves an enterprise or a group from current to future state? Go back and forth several times between painting the picture of the present and that of the future, as author Nancy Duarte explains in her article "Structure Your Presentation Like a Story" (http://blogs.hbr.org/cs/2012/10/structure_your_presentation_like.html). Doing so creates clear contrasts between the undesirable present and the more desirable future — a classic storytelling technique.

This story structure makes use of the opportunity-problem approach introduced in Chapter 7. The difference is that it does so repetitively:

1. Start out by painting the picture of the current reality.

2. Introduce the first turning point — the urgent call to do things differently.

3. State what could be.

4. Outline what is (based on another part of step 1).

5. State another example of what could be.

6. Outline what is (based on another part of step 1).

7. State another example of what could be.

8. Outline what is (based on another part of step 1).

9. Introduce the second turning point — the call to action — and articulate the finish line and problem resolution. These are action steps that'll resolve shortcomings in the current reality and bring about the future.

10. End on a higher plane. Have proof of a happy ending to share so folks know their hard work, dedication, commitment, and perseverance will pay off. They'll have a greater commitment to taking action knowing it won't be easy, but worth it.

Can any of the other business story structures we cover in the "Apply Story structures to launch a change" section be used to craft a future story? Yes, with some adaptation. Place much greater emphasis on the future piece of each of these structures.

Embody the future story

There are many ways to symbolize a future story. Here are a few to explore:

✓ **Graphical illustration of a co-created vision story:** To help employees embrace a new high-end growth strategy at Endevco, a Meggitt Group company, the enterprise translated its strategy timeline into an illustrated story map that moved from the past (shown as an old castle of grandeur) to a future based on technology yet to be invented (depicted as a space-age metropolis). Representative employee input was captured in ten discovery sessions through responses to "What do we share and care about the most?," "What's the vital spark that's sustained us?," and "What do we see as the best of Endevco?" Past and present stories, as well as layoff-rumor concerns, were captured on each session's story map. Later, at a company-wide town hall meeting, several poignant stories were told. Leaders also addressed employee anxieties. The various story maps were displayed in the central employee break area, along with a roadmap that reinforced the company's strengths, mission, and guiding principles. Through story sharing, the company became more unified and committed to change while remaining proud of its heritage (*Wake Me Up When the Data Is Over*, Jossey-Bass, 2006).

✓ **Collaborative painting to co-create a vision story:** After four years of growth, the Ginger Group Cooperative brought painting techniques into its executive retreat when meeting to envision their future. After some prep work, each of its 15 members began painting, in silence, in response to "How do I see my world?" and "Where am I at?" Discussion followed. Then came a second round of painting. Each person responded for one minute to "If Ginger were a garden of paradise, what would it look like?" After this, they moved from their original painting to the one on their left. With the same question in mind, they painted on the other person's canvas for another minute, repeating the process until each painting was its own unique collective vision. The debrief that followed focused on the metaphors embodied in the paintings. As Kate McLaren states in the book *Wake Me Up When the Data Is Over* (Jossey-Bass, 2006), "Painting got us out of our cognitive, explanatory, analytical headspace. We didn't start with narrative but a story emerged from the process." Marilyn Hamilton adds, "Building on that story, we've learned to work together. We broke through a lot of blocks. Now we know each other's strengths and capacities."

✔ **Portraying the dream or future story as a skit or play:** Let's return to the American Legion Auxiliary (ALA) strategic planning event. After Jan's story and the activity that followed it, three leaders who were potential successors to the position of president created a joint "I Have a Dream" story. Audio was recorded, with their voices blending mid-sentence from one to the other. The dream was showcased onstage: The setting was a bedroom where each leader was shown journaling in their own unique way as the audio was played. This was followed by a three-act play. Each act was an eight-minute portrayal of a future story related to a specific strategy. The actors were the team members who had fleshed out the first year's project plan for that specific strategy. All four were videoed for future use. The next point explains what followed this.

✔ **Visual meaning-making of a dream or future story:** Continuing with the ALA example, following the dream and the three future stories, each attendee table group was asked to create a poster-sized collage that told a story about what they'd heard. These collages (of which there were more than 30) were placed on easels around the meeting room for viewing that evening. The activity helped attendees actively process all the vision-related information they had heard and gain a clearer picture of where the organization was headed over the next five years. This prepared them to articulate next steps the following morning for their state's department and their own local unit.

Initiating the Change

Depending on your organization's culture and history, you may want to give your organization's outmoded stories a Viking funeral. In Marla Gottschalk's article "Set Your Counter-Productive Strategies Out to Sea with Story" `http://marlagottschalk.wordpress.com/2013/02/01/set-your-counter-productive-strategies-out-to-sea/`, she shares a story from her husband about an organizational change process he observed at a European client. When the client group launched its change project, it honored the past by sending old strategies out to sea, reflecting through story on what had passed, while at the same time anticipating what was to come.

Lori's done a similar observance with a client. A grave was dug on company property, and a makeshift coffin built. As each employee passed the coffin, they placed a letter inside that included stories of the past, along with policies and procedures they knew would change. Then the coffin was set on fire, and a bonfire was held with a lunch to celebrate the possibilities of what was to come — complete with hot dogs, hamburgers, s'mores, and a great deal of conversation about the past, present, and future.

Identify what needs to get done

As change moves from planning to initiating, ask people what needs to be done to solve problems. We aren't suggesting a pity party, nor should this spiral into an "Ain't it awful" session. What you want to do, in this order, is

1. Evoke stories about the challenges people face around a specific issue.

2. Learn how they currently get around or overcome those challenges.

3. Gather their best ideas to solve the problem.

Pinpoint and mitigate risks

Part of this discovery process will lead you to identify risks and ways to mitigate them. Stories to evoke to get at these topics include the following:

- ✔ "Tell me about some of the risks you've experienced that we might need to address if we change XYZ."
- ✔ "Tell me a story about a risk you're thinking could possibly happen during our change effort."
- ✔ "Tell me about a time during another change effort at the company when you stumbled upon an unforeseen risk and what happened as a result."

In each instance, find out what was or could be learned and how it might be applied to the change that's underway.

Implementing the Change

Once you've launched the change, a different set of stories kick in. Having leaders role model desired behaviors up and down the organization is now more critical because you want to give people stories that depict how those at the top are embodying the change. Once again, these are stories you evoke from others and share. Here's how viral the behavior can become when you do so: www.youtube.com/watch?v=fW8amMCVAJQ - at=31.

Obtain the resources you need

One forgotten type of story in the change process is about resources — those you need and the ones you've provided. If you're lacking resources, use the tips in Chapters 12 and 13 to find and tell stories about the need, opportunity, and solution. Likewise, to ensure everyone wins, share stories about the resources provided to another person, department, or program involved in the change. These aren't boastful stories; they're stories of camaraderie, collaboration, community, and support for the betterment of all.

Evoke these stories by asking the following story prompts:

- ✔ "Tell us about an experience you're now facing with this change that requires resources which weren't budgeted up front."

- ✔ "Now that you have the resources you need, tell us about how they made a significant difference in moving this change forward."

- ✔ "Tell us about a situation where you shared resources outside your group to create a win-win for everyone."

Leaders need to find and broadcast both kinds of stories. Relaying stories about needed resources can help galvanize people to open up and share. Once the request is fulfilled, don't forget to tell the follow-up story of how this catapulted progress. On the flip side, stories about giving acknowledge those who provided resources for others so the change could continue. This recognition continues to actualize the shared vision and showcases tangible, visible results beyond talking about the data.

Overcome all kinds of obstacles

Obstacles, small and large, are the daily experience of any change effort. The steps people take, and their creativity and ingenuity in overcoming them, deserve our highest applause. Searching for, finding, and sharing these stories across the organization is about acknowledging the people who are doing the heavy lifting as heroes. Whether that person is a janitor, repair person, mid-level accountant, or senior executive, momentum will continue to build when extraordinary persistence and resilience is championed. Find these people:

- ✔ Successful outliers — folks who've already figured out a solution to a problem, except others are unaware of it.

- ✔ People who toe the line, yet make a big difference.

- ✔ People who move the project forward because they found a way around an obstacle.

Set up systems so leaders can locate these individuals and obtain stories from them (with permission) to share in e-mails, newsletters, status updates, and so forth. Begin meetings by having staff share stories of the obstacles they've overcome or the solutions they've created to keep things moving. Use this time to honor their contributions.

Build skills

Lawson and Price talk about a bank that discovered its sales-per-banker were falling behind those of its competition. It appeared the bankers were spending much more time on paperwork than interacting with customers. To turn this around, the organization launched a change effort. The loan origination process was reengineered to cut down on paperwork so the bankers could spend more face-to-face time with customers. Only, it didn't work.

Digging further, management learned the bankers preferred doing paperwork. They found customer interactions uncomfortable because of their introverted personalities and poor interpersonal skills. Plus, they felt inferior to their customers who, for the most part, had more money and education than they did. Lastly, the bankers hated viewing themselves as salespeople. The picture in their minds was of a used car salesman in a bank branch.

Armed with these insights, the bank offered training to build the bankers' skills and reframe the notion of sales. Within six months, the program was back on track, and the bankers were exceeding their original targets. Of course, this also required giving them time to experiment, implement the new skills, and teach others what they'd learned. This practice time and knowledge transfer ensured they didn't revert back to their old ways of doing things and that resources were well spent.

This story is a great one to tell about change and for the bank to harken back to during other change programs. It shows the organization was paying attention, spent the time to uncover the real issues, and then dedicated resources to help build skills so people could be successful. It also gave staff stories to share about leaders and managers modeling important behaviors.

How can you highlight stories like this during a change in your organization? If there aren't any, what is that telling you?

Adapt as we go

"Adapt as we go" stories are about course corrections that happen once the organization gets deep into the change. Course corrections are a common experience and should be acknowledged as such. What's important isn't that a course correction happened. It's what caused the correction to be made, what was learned in the process, and how people responded to these lessons.

This knowledge is important to populate across the organization. Others may receive inspiration about adaptions they need to make, take comfort in realizing they're facing similar issues, or gain new insights from these experiences. Find ways to capture and share these stories to foster continual learning and demonstrate that adaptation is a normal part of change.

Closing Out the Change

As the change winds down and heads for the finish line, it's time to pay attention to capturing best-practice stories and celebrating successes.

Capture best practices

Although we've left the subject of capturing knowledge and best practices to the end, we encourage you to collect them all along the journey. You can do that in many settings: with the executive or project team responsible for the change, within groups that had responsibility for implementation, and with various groups of leaders throughout the organization. Here are several prompts to systematically capture these best practices:

- ✔ "Tell us a story about something that happened in [xx] phase of the change that really made an impact on you (or your team or department)."

- ✔ "Tell us about the most important (or significant or moving) story you've heard about this change project."

- ✔ "Tell us about a situation in which you gained a personal insight about this change that will continue to influence how you approach your work long-term."

- ✔ "Tell us a story about a specific action that you (or your team or department) took that really helped to solidify the change."

- ✔ "Tell us about something that happened in this change that you would suggest we not repeat in a future change initiative."

After hearing each story, allow the teller to evaluate what's important about it and its meaning. Capture each story and this additional information. Then share this information with the group that's spearheading the change and/or the entity responsible for the organization's change efforts. Read the stories out loud. Use them to spark in-depth discussions about the value of these reported changes and the process by which they occurred. Have the group identify the most significant stories and articulate why they were chosen. Share the stories and what was learned from these discussions with staff. Also capture knowledge about what worked and what didn't for future use.

Celebrate results

It's motivating to celebrate successes all along the change journey. Whenever the change is fully implemented, it's also important for the organization to collectively acknowledge all the work that's been done, express gratitude for everyone's efforts, and celebrate achievements. Respect and appreciation bring people together and help bring closure to an initiative. Just as movies, plays, and TV shows have credits at the end, so your change story has a list of credits too. Honoring the accomplishment of a dream is a group effort.

What types of stories do you want to evoke throughout the organization? Consider these prompts:

- ✔ "Tell us about the most important thing you (or we) have accomplished."
- ✔ "Tell us about your biggest high during the change."
- ✔ "Tell us the story about how we made it happen."
- ✔ "Tell us about a major obstacle we overcame."
- ✔ "Tell us a story about someone who really made the change happen."

Capture these stories for use in a variety of media. As you share them, keep in mind that the end of a change effort is really a new beginning. This celebration signifies the closing of one chapter and the opening of another.

Part V
The Part of Tens

For an extra Part of Tens chapter on the ten (or so) things you should always do when working with stories, head on over to www.dummies.com/extras/business storytelling.

In this part . . .

- ✔ Avoid potential problems and pitfalls when crafting and telling stories.

- ✔ Expand your story repertoire, design storied keynotes and short presentations, and enhance your storytelling ability.

- ✔ Identify how to qualitatively and quantitatively measure the results of a story project in your organization.

- ✔ Read compelling stories and use a story-crafting template to ensure you have all the pieces of a story in place before communicating it.

Chapter 17

Ten Things You Should Never, Ever Do

In This Chapter

▶ Steering clear of problem situations

▶ Knowing the potential unintended negative consequences of your actions

*W*e grew up in the 1960s, the era of the science fiction TV series *Lost in Space*. Accompanied by a robot and an air force pilot, the Robinsons leave Earth on the spaceship Jupiter 2 to colonize a planet circling Alpha Centauri. Only, they crash on an alien world. One family member is a young boy named Will. During an episode called "The Deadliest of the Species," the robot warns Will and his family members of impending danger, giving rise to the catchphrase "Danger, Will Robinson!"

That's what this chapter is all about — danger. We've witnessed many unfortunate situations related to crafting, telling, and using stories in business. We don't want them to happen to you. You've heard us say them once. We believe they're worth repeating.

Focusing Exclusively on Telling Stories

We both belong to a number of groups on LinkedIn related to storytelling, human resources, and organization development. It's not unusual for us to see postings like these:

- ✔ "Five coaching skills that every manager needs to have."

- ✔ "I'm looking for a creative way to cascade my company's conduct document among a staff of approximately 275 people."

- ✔ "What are the best ways that HR can improve creativity and innovation?"

What's perplexing is that responders only talk about story*telling*. They don't mention evoking stories from others or listening to them. They don't acknowledge that staff have stories on these subjects. They only talk about pushing stories out to others, as if that were the secret sauce.

The secret sauce is missing an entre. The entre is recognizing that the emphasis should be on *listening* — that the majority of your time should be on developing and using story prompts to learn about the experiences of others. And that often the best telling involves remembering and then recalling the stories that people have shared with you.

Everyone has a voice that must be honored. As you go forward, we estimate that 80 percent of story use is about listening, no matter what role you're in. Only 20 percent has to do with telling. Take time to use all the listening approaches we offer in this book.

Assuming There's a Formula for Crafting

Before Lori began a client workshop, two members of another organization were invited by a senior leader to talk about their story initiative. Lori and her client contact weren't aware that they'd be speaking. Imagine their surprise when these guests said, "Oh, crafting stories is easy. In fact we've hired an intern to do it. We gave her a template with a bunch of questions on it, and she's churning out several stories each week."

The biggest mistake people make is starting with a structure — a single structure. They then ask questions to select and mold the story to fit the template — add one or two essential story elements afterward — and call it a perfect story. We don't recommend this mechanistic or formulaic method. Why? The chance of generating a story, much less a compelling one, is slim. At best, this paint-by-numbers approach generates anecdotes, examples, or case studies that look and sound the same. Rarely is there a key message, let alone a call to action.

We prefer a story-crafting process approach that is dynamic, organic, and iterative in nature. It builds on how the brain codifies experiences and captures the totality of what the person went through in story form. One of the reasons we cover different story structures in Chapter 7 is to demonstrate the importance of having the flexibility to select the optimal structure for your story after you've captured the raw version and turned it into a first draft. This means you're using structure — and the elements of story that accompany it — to evaluate and polish the story, while continuing to honor its overall intent.

Storytelling is an art form full of wonder, discovery, and magic. Treat it as such.

Neglecting the Beginning and the End

When we review stories that our clients have taken time to craft, one characteristic stands out: They ramble at the beginning and at the end. The middle piece of the story arc is usually pretty clear. But the beginning is filled with a bunch of descriptive information that's intended to set up the story. The ending is similar — a bunch of rambling sentences that don't provide the full resolution of the story or an effective key message, transition, and action statement. We find the same to be true when we randomly go online and look at websites that purport to have stories on them (if indeed they are stories).

When you neglect the beginnings of your stories, your listeners or readers lose interest before you ever get into the meat of the situation. And when you neglect the endings, they leave wondering why you told them the story, beyond its entertainment value.

What can you do? Follow the approaches we've outlined in this book to turn your raw story into a first draft and then hone it and add embellishments that really make it sing. Always remember the beginning and end need to be crisp and clear. Spend the most time on developing these sections.

Telling On-the-Fly in High-Risk Situations

Relaying a story one-on-one with a close friend is a low-risk situation. You already have a trusting relationship, and chances are you feel great about sharing what happened to you. You aren't trying to get your friend to change. You can tell that story on-the-fly — we wouldn't expect you to craft it in advance.

That's not true with stories used in business. In high-risk situations, you can't afford to wing it. You *must* take the time to craft it well. High-risk situations — where there's a risk if action doesn't happen — include these:

- ✔ You're introducing a transformational project requiring deep change.
- ✔ You only have one shot to talk to people about taking action.
- ✔ You're launching an initiative in front of a very large group and can't afford to botch the communications.
- ✔ You need to communicate a topic that requires an immediate decision and follow-up action to a business leader.

Getting Lost in Digressions

Have you ever told a story and had it trigger a random thought that causes you to digress for a few minutes? If it hasn't happened to you, have you been present when it's happened to someone else? What's it like?

When storytellers digress in the moment, they cause listeners to work harder to follow the train of thought. The audience assumed the story was going in one direction, but now it's going in another. No matter how closely related the digression is to the story, as soon as you say, "Oh, that reminds me of something else" or, "Allow me to digress for a moment," you potentially lose them unless you've mastered the digressive storytelling style. Once you break the chain of the story, you open yourself to interruptions — they may start asking questions, fidgeting, or stop paying attention altogether.

Because stories are co-created when told orally, and people change over time, they're always a bit in flux. But that doesn't grant you blanket permission to randomly switch it up by going down rabbit holes that add little if anything to the core of the story. In fact, the digression may take away from the power of your key message. Stay focused on what you had planned to say. And say it.

Skipping the Meaning-Making

Often when people tell a story, they neglect to share the meaning-making section at the end. This includes the story's key message, a transition to action, and what action(s) you want listeners to take. Why is that? If it's your own story, this material may not be embedded in your memory as deeply as the story or you may not have given much thought to its meaning. If it's someone else's story, you'll probably spend more time ensuring you recall the story than on practicing these pieces. In both cases, you may also run out of time to tell them. Here's why you *must* share this information:

✔ **For you:** The key message and transition to action pieces provide what the story means to you and why you think it's important. Sharing this information helps you stay humble with your audiences. The action step gives you an important reason to tell the story other than merely flaunting your experience.

✔ **For others:** If you want them to remember and retell the story and take action after hearing it, you can't afford to leave off this information. It's the point of the story and the reason you're sharing it with them.

When you do your Story Lab, spend time ensuring that you practice this ending piece so it becomes a natural part of telling the story. Time your story with this in it so you're clear how much you need.

Playing with Emotions

We spend a lot of time in Chapter 10 talking about how important it is for you to tell tough stories. How do you know you're ready to do so?

- ✔ The time is right for the story to be told (for example, you have the right audience).
- ✔ You've worked through your emotions and have come to a place where you're able to be a passionate dispassionate teller.
- ✔ The other people referenced in the story are okay with your telling it.

It's possible that you'll have an extremely sad story, like one that Karen heard from her hairdresser, where there's no way to resolve it *and* bring in a positive emotion or an a-ha! at the end. Here's a synopsis of what Karen heard: *A baby was born very ill. The doctor told the parents the baby would shortly die. The mom and dad were so upset they couldn't hold their newborn. The hairdresser was their friend. She took the baby into another room, sat in a rocking chair, and held the baby until it passed away.* If you share a story like this, even with a meaningful ending, just know there's a low probability that it'll be repeated. The only real impact that story has is with those in the room at the moment it's told. Be very judicious about sharing a story like this so you don't mess with people's emotions.

Alternatively, you don't want to pull a Paula Dean. Her June 2013 television interview with Matt Lauer on NBC's *Today Show* about racially insensitive comments will live on forever. Was she really being sincere in the emotions she displayed? Experts in the field doubt it. Watch the video to decide for yourself (www.youtube.com/watch?v=zW9PRStPtps). Make sure you don't insincerely express emotions while telling a story just for effect. Your audience will catch you at that game.

Using stories is contextual. Whether it be the context surrounding the story's content, who created the original version of the story, or the context around people's lives in general, you need to do your homework in advance of using any of the story practices we've covered in this book.

Using a Story Without Knowing Its Origin

In Chapter 16, we introduce the phrase *burning platform*, coined by Darryl Connor (www.connerpartners.com/frameworks-and-processes/the-real-story-of-the-burning-platform). We discuss how the story that sparked it has been misunderstood and, as a result, has probably been misused and misinterpreted. The same thing happens with research, as with the compassion and sympathy piece cited in Chapter 8. We read several composites of the research, some of which only gave a small piece of the story and another that wasn't accurate.

Go back to the source. Get your story straight.

Telling Someone Else's Story as Yours

In *Stories Trainers Tell: 55 Ready-to-Use Stories to Make Training Stick* by Mary B. Wacker and Lori L. Silverman (Jossey-Bass, 2006), professional speaker Chris Clarke Epstein recounts receiving a seminar brochure from a highly respected firm. She attended the workshop. It was everything she'd hoped for. The trainer told a humorous story about his mother attending one of his sessions. It was all so magical. Three weeks later, she was speaking at a conference where this firm was also presenting. Because she had been so impressed, she attended the session. Guess what? A different trainer talking on a different topic told the exact same story as though it had personally happened to him. How would you feel if you'd been Chris?

Imagine hearing a story of your own being shared by someone else with no permission or attribution! Don't risk your credibility by doing this.

Assuming You're Doing No Harm

When you ask others to share their stories, they become vulnerable when they disclose personal information. There needs to be a high degree of trust present for this to work. If you ask for a story, don't do any of the following:

- ✔ Use a story prompt in a group that you've not tested one-on-one. It may provoke stories you and others aren't equipped to handle in that moment.
- ✔ Make a joke out of what's shared with you, no matter how funny it is.
- ✔ Use someone else's story purely for entertainment purposes.
- ✔ Discredit the story by intimating it couldn't have happened that way.
- ✔ Tell people to ignore a personal story because it appears to negatively impact them. It's one thing to reframe the ending or the interpretation of a story. It's disrespectful to wholeheartedly discard it.

In Chapter 10, we ask you not to use your own stories as therapy in front of a group. On the flipside, you can't practice therapy on other people using their stories. That crosses an ethical line. Every time you use a story prompt or request a story, be consciously aware of what you're seeking. Honor all stories that are told to you.

Chapter 18

Ten Storytelling Tips for Speakers

*T*raining workshops. Talks at company or industry events. Presentations to prospective and current customers or clients. Keynotes at conferences. All these situations call for the use of compelling stories. They are the secret sauce between good and great — and truly awesome speakers.

We both know this first-hand. Lori didn't start crafting and telling stories in the manner we describe in this book until 2002. As she reflects on the evaluations she's received from workshop attendees and keynote audiences, she notes a marked difference in the scores before and after she solidly incorporated well-crafted and purposefully chosen stories into these talks.

Karen's experience is similar. Coming from academia — where data, facts, and information are king — she had to learn how to make her points come alive with stories. Now, instead of dreading those boring presentations, she finds them more fun and meaningful, and they pack more punch.

Whether you're a professional speaker using stories in your talks, a member of Toastmasters who wants to hone your telling of stories, a business leader who's called upon to give presentations, or a staff member wanting to do more speaking, the tips in this chapter will help you. You'll learn other ways to expand your story repertoire, ways to design presentations with stories, and a couple ways to enhance your storytelling.

Identifying Your Signature Stories

Any personal hip pocket story can become a *signature* story. Signature stories are those handful of stories that, like your John Hancock, uniquely identify you. They may be defining moments in your life or situations of extreme significance. They're stories that are so compelling they deserve to be told time and time again. They are *your* stories — no one else owns them or should tell them.

For example, only Aron Ralson can talk about what it was like to make the decision to cut off his own arm after being trapped for 127 hours in Utah's Blue John Canyon (www.youtube.com/watch?v=3ud5i1_-nf0). Only Jackie Nink Pflug can talk about what it was like to be a hostage on the hijacked EgyptAir Flight 648 and survive being shot in the head over Thanksgiving weekend in 1985 (www.jackiepflug.com/story.htm).

We realize your personal signature stories may not be this extreme. That's fine. Lori tells the story of becoming a competitive swimmer at age 10 after overcoming a fear of water than was so consuming that her mom couldn't wash her hair. Karen tells the story of her 30 days in India and the 10 years it took to recover from the experience. What's most important are the key message and the actions you want to engender in others after telling it.

The following questions and answers will help you uncover and use your signature stories:

✔ **How do I know which of my stories are really signature stories?** There are a couple of ways you can figure this out. One is to do a timeline of your life and reflect on those events and experiences that truly define who you are today. You can also refer to the list of hip pocket stories we share in Chapter 4. Another way is to ask colleagues, family, and friends to share with you which stories of yours they find to be unique. You may be surprised at what you hear.

✔ **Do I craft signature stories any differently than my other personal stories?** Nope. All the tips we've provided in this book apply. Your challenge will be to figure out how to tell it in a way that balances all the details with the key message and actions you want to convey.

✔ **How often do you tell a signature story?** Some speakers, like Aron and Jackie, will share their stories forever or until they retire them — or until audiences stop finding them compelling. Some stories have a limited lifespan. Be careful that you don't overuse the story to the point where it loses its effectiveness and luster.

✔ **Is it okay for your personal signature story to be a well-known public story?** Some speakers may take on the persona of a historical figure such as Abraham Lincoln. In this case, the stories they would tell would be about the most memorable moments in Lincoln's life.

✔ **What if I hear someone else telling my signature story?** Well, now that's a problem, especially if they don't acknowledge you. We encourage you to contact the individual, express your concern, and request that they stop using it immediately. If this level of intervention doesn't curtail the behavior, we encourage you to seek legal advice on the options available to you.

Refashioning a Tale

Up until now, we've discouraged you from using *tales* — fairy tales and folklore — in your business storytelling. Why? Every workplace has *story skeptics* — those who don't believe in the power of story. If you share a fable in an internal work setting, other employees and even leaders may respond in a dismissive manner toward you. They won't listen to your message, no matter how important it may be. Now, if you're a professional speaker in a public setting, you might get a little different response if you're using a tale to both entertain and transmit a message. Then again, people came to hear you — your ideas, your messages. There's truly more power in personal stories in a business setting.

That's why we encourage you to reserve telling tales until you've spent a couple years sharing your own personal stories and developing trust within an organization.

Especially if you're a leader. Employees don't want platitudes. They want you to show up authentically and demonstrate your vulnerability.

We haven't yet found a traditional fable that has a built-in key message, along with a transition to suggested action(s), that is suitable for business use. This means you need to craft an appropriate key message for any tale you may use at work — which might also mean tweaking its content to reinforce the ending elements.

There's another thing that happens with fables. Let's take the example of one that's well-known: "Sharpening the Saw." Here's a website with a nice (not perfect) version of the story: www.capstonemedia.com/sharpen-the-saw/. Stephen Covey popularized this story in his book *The 7 Habits of Highly Effective People* (Free Press, 2004). This story has been told over and over and over again. Before using it, you'd need to assess how much value you're going to get out of it in a group setting. That means assessing what percentage of your audience might already know it.

In the end, if you're going to use a fable, make sure the key message has a business purpose and that you can fashion suggested actions from it that fit your audience. The book *Stories Trainers Tell: 55 Ready-to-Use Stories to Make Training Stick* (Jossey-Bass, 2006) has a few business-ready fables in it. Aesop's Fables are also easily recognizable. Here's a website that has a lot of folklore and mythological stories for you to browse and determine whether they might have a business use: www.pitt.edu/~dash/folktexts.html.

Opening with a Story

Why would you want to open a presentation with a story? First, it's one of the most effective ways to capture people's attention — especially considering their addiction to all the technology they've probably brought with them. Second, the key message of the story is a perfect way to set the stage for the content to follow. It can form an umbrella for the rest of your talk. If all you use is an opening story, remember to circle back, at a minimum, at the end of your presentation to the key message and suggested action(s).

Using a Story in a Short Presentation

Other than opening a presentation with a compelling story, where else could you use a story within a presentation that may be no more than 10–30 minutes in length? Here are a few thoughts:

- ✔ To introduce a new idea or unfamiliar concept.
- ✔ To present data as we discuss in Chapter 8.
- ✔ To transition from one part of your presentation to another.
- ✔ At the end of a talk to bring together everything that's been discussed and move people to action.

Crafting a Keynote Solely Based on Story

Let's say you have 45–60 minutes for your keynote talk. Frankly, that's not a lot of time to transmit more than a few ideas to your audience. If you figure that the average length of a well-constructed story is somewhere between 5–8 minutes in length, and you want to share additional content after each story, or have the audience do a short activity, then you're talking about one story approximately every 15–20 minutes.

There are two considerations when using stories in this manner:

- ✔ **How to find and select the stories:** We encourage you to interview a select number of audience members in advance about your topic. Our rule of thumb is no less than five interviews. In the interviews, listen for a story that you could craft for the opening of your presentation that relates specifically to the subject. Lori often finds stories from her audience members to share in her talks — and so can you. The interview might also trigger you to recall one of your own stories that would be perfect to include.

Also listen for audience needs and expectations. Once you summarize the comments gained in the interviews, identify themes and choose stories based on them that will provide the most benefit to the audience. For example, Lori gives a talk that ranges from one to two hours on the topic of resilience. She has a database of about 30 personal stories to choose from on this subject — mostly her own, mixed with a few from others. Every time she gives this presentation, it changes based on what she learns from the pre-presentation interviews.

✔ **How to organize the stories for maximum impact:** Once you know the stories you want to tell, look at the key message and layers of meaning attached to each one. From that, determine how they would best flow together — and how they create an overarching story arc that depicts transformation (real or possible) for the entire talk. Then take the key messages from these stories in the order in which they were presented and string them together into a logical flow. Repeat them at the end of the talk. That reinforces what people need to take away from the experience.

You Sure You Want to Use PowerPoint?

How often have you seen or experienced the following? A set of PowerPoint slides is prepared for a talk. Every word and picture has been carefully selected. Then something happens. Maybe there's no projector. Or the laptop goes on the fritz. Or there's no screen and none of the walls can be used. Or the file doesn't properly open.

Here's how we suggest you prepare for the unexpected. Carefully craft your stories — and the other parts of your presentation — so audience members are given enough sensory information to be able to create pictures in their mind's eye. We really do believe that a well-crafted, compelling story should be able to be told without any slides. You owe this to your audience, especially if you're being paid to speak.

Then, when you do use PowerPoint, you can use it to enhance your stories and your talk. Here's a great infographic that mentions several story elements to help guide you: `http://smallbiztrends.com/2013/06/` `presentations-make-your-message-stick.html`. Keep this cheat sheet handy for when you need to make a presentation or use PowerPoint. Or get Andrew Abela's book *Advanced Presentations by Design: Creating Communication That Drives Action* (Pfeiffer, 2013). Here are a few more points relevant to PowerPoint and story use:

✔ Use a powerful visual to back up your point.

✔ Have one succinct message per slide.

✔ If you feel you have to use bullet points, limit yourself to no more than three per slide, preferably only one.

✔ Remember to end your stories — and your talk — with suggested action steps. Never leave your audience guessing what they should do next.

✔ Practice, practice, practice — so giving presentation is more fun. That's another reason to build stories into your slide deck or design your entire PowerPoint deck as a story — it's more enjoyable and easier to deliver.

Using Memory Devices

One of the best measures of whether a story is truly compelling is whether listeners repeat it, along with the key message, to others. Here are some small things you can do — in addition to all the embellishments we've spoken about — that will get people to repeat your stories:

✔ **Sprinkle the words from the key message individually throughout your story.** Go back to Pam's story in Chapter 7. Note that the words *take* and *time* are woven throughout the text. By the time listeners hear them together at the end, they've heard them several times.

✔ **Use words in the key message that start with consonants.** Consider this key message as an example. Which sounds more powerful: "Promote the positive" or "express appreciation"?

✔ **Incorporate and exaggerate the emotional swings in a story.** We mention this briefly in Chapter 7. It's not always easy to do. Once you've identified a structure for your story — and reorganized content around it — find ways to bring opposing emotions into the story. For example, if a story follows the SHARES structure, can you enhance differing emotions in the Hindrance and the Action sections? Or the Hindrance and the Result pieces?

✔ **Find ways to provide a tangible object or image as a story trigger.** For example, when telling Cristi's story from Chapter 3, you could provide everyone who hears it with a tube of ChapStick to take away. You could even print the key message of the story onto the tube. If the story you're telling is about personal transformation, and you're speaking to a group of women, you could provide them with the image of a butterfly on a note card that they take away — or they could record what they learned on the card and place it in a self-addressed, stamped envelope that's sent back to them six weeks following the talk.

Co-creating a Story with the Audience

Go back to the story we crafted about the compassion research in Chapter 8. We provided you with the version we use in webinars. If you were to tell this story in a group setting, you could easily ask the audience questions and have them interact with you and the story in real time.

To go a step further, you can actually have an audience co-create a story with you through the use of questions. If you're setting the context at the beginning of your story using the CCARLS structure we spoke about in Chapter 7, and the temperature in your story is hot, you could say something like, "What's the hottest climate you've ever been in?" and then weave the responses into your story.

This is especially helpful in these situations:

✔ **You've told the story so many times that it's lost its luster for you as the teller.** Switch it up a bit by getting the audience involved in the telling. Spend some time in advance thinking about how you could do this.

✔ **The audience is one that likes to talk during a presentation.** This can be cultural or an organizational nuance. Play off of this audience strength.

✔ **If you're not getting the reaction that you normally get with the story, consider improvising in the moment.** As a speaker, you should know the stories you tell really well and how audiences typically respond to them. If you normally get a laugh in a particular spot, but don't get one — or if the audience seems disengaged (perhaps something happened ahead of the meeting to distract them) — go off script and find ways to get them to participate in the story.

What to Do If You Screw Up the Story

Oh, the mistakes we've made in telling stories. They happen! Even when you practice your story out loud dozens of times or have even told it for years.

One time Lori said the opposite of what she intended to say when setting up a story. She stopped, turned in a complete circle, and said, "Take two" before starting over at the beginning. The audience laughed and continued on with her. Once when this happened to Karen, she waved her arms and said, "Wait. Wait. Wait! Stop. Stop. Stop! I said it wrong. Let's do it again." The audience laughed and everyone continued. These sorts of faux pas make you human. They are also opportunities to poke fun at yourself and generate humor.

When you make a mistake, the audience only gets as upset about it as you do. If you seem visibly flustered or thrown by the error, the audience will get upset, too. But if you seem relaxed and comfortable, and have fun with the mistake, then it becomes entertaining and the audience empathizes with you — and they love you even more for handling the situation gracefully.

If you notice that you've made a grammatical mistake — said words out of order or mispronounced a word — we encourage you to stop and correct yourself immediately. This automatically builds credibility. This is why we encourage you to pay close attention to your audience's reactions as you speak. Many times when we misspeak, our own brains never tip us off because we're thinking about what we have to say next instead of what we just said. If you say something backward or mix up your words, you'll usually see it reflected on the faces of your audience — sometimes a chuckle, a puzzled look, or a quick shake of the head from one person. In most cases you can quickly replay your mental tape and realize what you said wrong.

Preparing for After the Presentation

Here's what we know with 100 percent certainty: If you incorporate compelling stories into your presentations, people will approach you afterward to share their own story or comment on yours. So be ready for this.

This means you have to do two things:

- ✔ **Be very conscious of the stories you select to share.** If you tell a story about a very difficult personal experience, audience members may feel compelled to share their own difficulties with you. The more revealing your story is, the more their stories will be too. Stories are like viruses; sharing a story sparks one in return. Always.

- ✔ **Be prepared to quickly shift from telling to listening mode.** Center and ground yourself and pay attention to what people say. At the very least, express appreciation for the stories you hear, as we talk about in Chapter 5. If you need to leave the room because others are using it after you, ask people to join you elsewhere to continue the conversation.

Purposefully build in time after your presentation for these interactions to happen. Be willing to put aside your own person needs for a bit to accommodate your audience's needs (for example, you may want to process the content of what you just said on your own).

Chapter 19

Ten (or so) Ways to Measure the Results of a Story Project

In This Chapter

▶ Identifying various qualitative and quantitative measures to assess your project

▶ Figuring out the return on investment on business storytelling in your organization

The first step in measuring the results of a story project is to lay out your objective and what you seek to accomplish. Do you want more loyal customers, more engaged employees, increased sales, improved leadership, better performing teams, and the like? The methods you use to collect or validate evidence also define your measures. This chapter has tips on story research methods and reviews the kinds of returns on investment (ROI) that your story project can produce.

Collecting Evidence

Narrative analysis contains a set of methods for working with stories and measuring their return. If you're serious about validating material and gaining deeper analysis of results, working with a PhD narrative researcher can help. Start by learning quantitative and qualitative methods related to storytelling.

Quantitative methods analytically treat stories as units of measure. The simplest quantitative approaches include counting the number of collected stories, creating a list of the collected story types or doing a pattern analysis of them, and generating statistics on these findings. Other quantitative tools include determining whether your story project generated results through website stats, social media analytics, numerical split test results, and so on.

Those trained in statistics can generalize a sample of stories into conclusions about an entire population. For example, researchers could collect a body of stories from a statistical sample representing the U.S. population, evaluate those stories, and determine that the Hero's Journey is the most popular story in the country. It sounds simple, but it's hard work to isolate story from other variables to generate meaningful results.

Qualitative methods, rather than treat stories as units to statistically analyze, look for the construction of group identity or community. Here are five qualitative methods your organization can use to collect this evidence:

1. Collect anecdotal evidence.

2. Conduct thematic analyses of the collected stories.

3. Run a structural analysis of how collected stories are put together.

4. Analyze performance dynamics of stories being told and listened to.

5. Direct an analysis of how stories are conveyed visually.

Gaining Return on Investment (ROI)

This section outlines seven types of ROI from a storytelling project.

Validate that the message was heard

The most basic and common kind of validation for a story is knowing whether your message has been heard. It may sound silly that you need to seek this validation. But frankly, if you haven't been heard, you have no chance of finding any other ROI because it doesn't exist.

Capture changes in behavior

In their book *Influencer: The Power to Change Anything* (McGraw Hill, 2008), Kerry Patterson and his co-authors point out that stories are one of the most powerful tools for changing behavior. Stories create vicarious experiences — the next best thing to direct experiences. Researchers Arvind Singhal and Everett M. Rogers have proved that when subjects are exposed to believable experiences where behaviors are modeled via stories, their thoughts, emotions, and behaviors change. It's up to you to determine which specific behaviors need to shift and how to measure this change over time.

Track engagement

Engagement is the degree to which you and your employees or customers, members, clients, or patients are talking together, sharing stories, acting on those stories, and receiving mutual benefit from the interaction.

Engagement can be measured through web-based analytics: retweets, blog comments, Pinterest re-pins, and the like. Qualitatively, you can measure it through the quality of the stories shared (such as when customers share stories with you in return) and the resulting interactions. Even better is when customers become brand evangelists and create ads for your firm — think 2013 Super Bowl and Doritos (www.youtube.com/watch?v=4d8ZDSyFS2g) — or come to work for your enterprise. Engagement is also evidenced when employees share stories to demonstrate a positive view of their work, entice colleagues to apply for jobs, and transfer knowledge to coworkers.

Document financial results

This category includes traditional ROI measures:

- ✔ Measuring financial results stemming from an increase in sales.
- ✔ Tracking the number of prospect appointments and closed sales, and the time it takes to turn a prospect into a customer.
- ✔ Using measures in place through your firm's performance management system to document gains in productivity.
- ✔ Documenting product creation and licensing opportunities.

You can also document the statistical number of collected items available for use in marketing and branding purposes, as illustrated in Chapter 5's sidebar "Cruising for stories."

Measure emotions

Return on emotion is about you and your customers feeling emotionally connected to each other. *Evangelists* (raving fans) are people who are so emotionally attached or invested in your company and its products and services that they praise you everywhere they go. Measure return on emotion via social media stats, stories from sales representatives, interviewing longstanding customers, number of referrals received, and the like.

Loyalty is another term for this ROI. Return on emotion could also be called *return on meaning*, because meaning is the end result of an emotional connection. People feel connected because they find something meaningful in the interaction. In some way you've emotionally connected with or satisfied a deep emotional need. A return on meaning and emotion can be applied not only to external customers and clients, but internally to coworkers, staff, leaders, and anyone you want to influence.

Here's an example: Jonathan Harris takes comments people make on the web and creates emotional clouds about how they're feeling (`www.ted.com/ talks/jonathan_harris_tells_the_web_s_secret_stories.html`). You can take the same approach to analyzing how emotionally connected people are to your organization's brand, products, and services.

Track relationships

Here are three ways to think about *return on relationships* as an ROI:

✔ In virtual workspaces where work teams are flung far and wide, you can measure storytelling's impact on forming and cementing relationships and sustaining those relationships over time and distance.

✔ In high-performing teams, you can track how stories are used to help transfer knowledge amongst team members and the speed at which they cycle through failures while achieving successes.

✔ You can measure the life-cycle of your clients. The return on relationship is the difference between short-term transactions and longer-term relationships. Because it costs more to acquire new customers than to maintain current ones, you can document shifts in the quality and quantity of relationships and their length via a story initiative.

Innovate and be creative

Often stories help people expand their thinking, consider different options, and so on. An example is Gaylord Hospital, cited in *Wake Me Up When the Data Is Over* by Lori Silverman (Jossey-Bass, 2006). The hospital's conscious use of stories about innovative solutions and cost-cutting measures that staff came up with spurred other staff to think of innovations and created an organizational culture that pulled off a quick financial turnaround.

Applying Story Tools to Daily Work

Track how effective storytelling is in getting you work results. Are you accomplishing your work more quickly? Are you forging better relationships? Are you resolving conflicts more easily? You can also track the impact of storytelling using existing team measures. These include productivity, cost, quality, and satisfaction metrics. The challenge here was mentioned earlier: Teasing out the contribution of storytelling from other influences.

Appendix

Real-Life Stories and a Template

. . . .

These stories are referenced throughout this book. They're here for ease of access. The story template is a synopsis of key points covered elsewhere.

The Price We Pay to Get Results

Told by Robert McIlree, crafted by Lori L. Silverman

I received a call from the support staff in the information systems area. A customized software application that I'd developed as a consultant to a federal government agency had stopped functioning. This particular application makes extensive use of internal databases and is very useful and popular with agency staff charged with controlling budget dollars. Lots of money is lost if this application is shut down for long periods of time.

Now, I'm properly and officially credentialed with this agency. I have a badge to enter their facilities, complete access to the computer systems that I support, and a small office where I'm required to work onsite due to federal computer security restrictions. When I began to work the problem, I kept getting error messages that said I didn't have permission to view the databases. Somehow my security level had been altered. The only way this could've happened was if the database administrator had removed my clearance. This didn't surprise me. He was known to have an insatiable thirst for power and control over his domain.

I immediately placed a call to him. "Jim, I'm having trouble looking at a couple of databases. I keep getting error messages that tell me I don't have access." He replied, "Oh. We've just implemented our new 'cyber security' scheme. It's a requirement of Homeland Security." I barked, "Well, I have a problem — a real live support issue that needs to be addressed right now." He quickly countered with, "You'll have to get me some sort of documentation for the permission. Then it'll have to go through the proper channels and be approved by a committee. You know, I really don't have the time to deal with this right now." I said, "Thanks." And hung up. Right then and there I knew I'd have to go around him. All he'd given me were excuses. As far as I was concerned, he'd arbitrarily and without notice removed permission for me to access the databases.

It didn't take me more than five seconds to call the government manager in charge of my activity. She also happened to be Jim's boss. I told her what had just taken place. All she said was, "Thank you. I'll take care of it." She didn't need to say any more. Her words were as good as gold. Within minutes she called me back to say she'd directed Jim to restore my access even though he'd claimed to her as well that he and his staff were "too busy" to immediately respond. She was under the impression I'd get my access within 24 hours.

I waited out the day. No access. One day turned into two days. Still no access. Then it became three. After 72 hours, I still couldn't access the databases. My manager was now out on vacation. And Jim was ignoring my ongoing request for a completion date. I'd been stonewalled. What was I to say to the support staff? They were furious. I couldn't fix their pressing production problem.

Not one to give up, I started mulling over strategies to work around, through, or over the problem. I quickly hit upon an idea. While risky and long-winded in process, it would send a clear message that something was seriously amiss. I had decided to file a claim to access the data under the Freedom of Information Act — what we folks in government affectionately call FOIA. This meant working through the "front door" of the agency — the one the general public must use to get information. By law, the agency must allow or deny the request within a limited period of time. I figured none of the data I needed was sensitive or secret. And even if it were, the FOIA request would be routed to the proper department and eventually to my manager for decision and disposition.

From the agency's internal website I printed out what needed to be included in such a request. I wrote up a couple of pages including my name, who I was, and what I specifically needed. Then I took it downstairs to the public affairs people. They accepted it and I got a receipt from the office. Word of what I'd done leaked out faster than a broken water main. People either laughed hysterically or shook their heads wondering why it took a stunt like this to point out a glaring deficiency in the organization.

The next week my request landed like an F-16 fighter jet on my manager's desk. Which prompted her, of course, to come and see me in my cubicle. "I got this FOIA request. What's going on?" I replied, "Jim's group never responded. I still don't have access. They basically blew me off and they blew you off too." Without saying a word, she picked up my phone. "I asked you a couple weeks ago to give Bob access to these databases and he never got it. What's the deal?" I could hear Jim stuttering on the other end of the line. When she hung up she looked straight at me and politely asked, "Why did you do this?" I replied, "Because I wasn't getting any results. I came to you and you also tried getting results. They don't seem to care. They want to be masters of the universe and control everything. I did it kind of as a gag and to bring attention to the fact that things needed to change around here. I can't do my job and neither can others."

With a twinkle in her eye, she replied, "I understand your point completely. But, please don't do this again." I asked, "How do you want to bring this to closure? Do you want to deny my request and fire it back at me or do you want me to go down and close it?" She answered, "I want you to close it." The next day I went downstairs and withdrew the request. She quickly corrected the problem and I was able to proceed with my work.

When you can't get what you need to do your job or solve a problem, *assert yourself*. Be vocal. Be creative. Follow-up with people who can make things happen. Persist until you're satisfied you have exactly what you need. Assert yourself even if it means seeking forgiveness rather than asking for permission. If I can do it, so can you. *Used with permission. Copyright © 2003 by Lori L. Silverman and Robert McIlree. All rights reserved.*

It's Not About Shelters: Raw Version 1

By Barbara Mandel of San Diego Grantmakers

The Homelessness Working Group (HWG) has been, since the first couple of years, really trying to focus on what we can do to reduce the most visible problems in our community regarding homelessness. What's always been the picture most people have about homeless people is those on the street panhandling, sleeping in a corner downtown, standing in the breadlines downtown — those that many people kind of fear — the chronic homeless. In San Diego, many of those people are chronically mentally ill individuals who are on the street because their resources run out on day 25 of the month and they are not able to manage their care for themselves. Over the last few years there has been a group that the San Diego Grantmakers (SDG) Homelessness Working Group (HWG) has been very instrumental in — and that is the plan to end chronic homelessness.

It's been one of the goals of the HWG to support the plan and to create some long-term sustainability. They did so by supporting the plan and by putting a number of people on working committees — and now on the board of the plan — to end chronic homelessness. The idea behind the whole plan is that if you have a small group of people using 70 percent of the resources in San Diego County, and you give them the appropriate resources, you will have more resources to spend on those folks who don't fit into that typical homeless population.

With the economic crisis we are starting to see a whole new group of people who are homeless — and we never really saw them before. But what's starting to happen is, with more people losing their jobs and homes, we are starting to see a lot of people in families, we are starting to see whole families who are homeless. And it's really apparent in the schools. The school homeless liaisons are the ones who have been instrumental in raising the red flag in a very quiet way. It's not until you ask them what's going on that they say,

"Gee, we are seeing a lot more families coming for services who are doubled up, or living in their car, or living in somebody's attic." And it's allowed the Homelessness Working Group to really start to focus in a different direction. "Okay, now that we've done what we can to launch the plan to end chronic homelessness, and we are supporting the Corporation for Supportive Housing to provide the appropriate resources for this group, how can we turn our attention to a rapidly growing group of folks?"

So we've been building a relationship with the National Alliance to End Homelessness in Washington, D.C., as well as with the folks from Funders Together and another charitable trust. And we learned that the National Alliance was going to have their national conference on family homelessness here in San Diego last February 2009. So we thought it would be a great opportunity for us to create greater public awareness — particularly among elected leaders — that there's a whole new group of people out here that we are not paying attention to. The perception is that there is a disconnect between county and city and whose responsibility aspects of homelessness are. And as a community, cities focus on housing plans, while the county focuses on services. We decided to hold a summit and ask some nationally recognized speakers to present what the picture of family homelessness is around the country. We ended up with standing room only at the NTC Promenade at Liberty Station; those attending were either elected leaders or their representatives. We were there to not only paint the picture about what the current situation is, but also to call to attention to some federal stimulus money coming down the pike, and this was a great opportunity to look at some short-term funding and solutions and build them into some sustainable long-term kinds of results.

We did learn that in San Diego Country HUD had allocated $10.5 million dollars that would be spread among the city of San Diego, the county of San Diego, and a couple of other cities in San Diego County.

We thought, "What can we do to get these folks together so we create more of a regional approach to how we are going to handle the short-term homelessness prevention funding?" Because in many communities, and particularly in San Diego, prevention had never been part of the mix. We were always "plugging the hole, plugging the problem" but not really coming up with ideas to address prevention. It was always about serving the homeless but never about ending homelessness.

We convened our first meeting of those jurisdictions who were getting the HUD funding. At the first meeting there were about ten people around the table, and we talked about what we could do that would be different, and how we could address things in a new way. They were happy and surprised to be invited to the meeting. And one of the gentlemen at the table said, "You know, we've never really sat together; we've never had a discussion together, we've never talked about this together." He really expressed his appreciation that the funders had the foresight to bring everybody together. Otherwise they'd be working in their little silos thinking how they were going to spend this money in the same way they had always been spending it. In particular, we noticed this with the city of San Diego. We needed to do a bit of a paradigm shift because the city had been focused for so long on building a shelter for the homeless. We noticed when we had the summit that a light bulb went on everywhere when one of the speakers said, "It's not about shelters — it's about keeping people in their homes." It's like then "Oh, well if that's the case, then yeah we can get behind it." The concern about where we are going to put another shelter was just such an overwhelming prospect for most of the folks that they wanted to shy away from even talking about homelessness.

At our second collaboration meeting we had 25 people in the room and we thought, "Wow, this is really great! This is the place to be. People are really feeling like they want to be a part of this and that's why they are showing up!" It really blossomed into a discussion of how do we as a region address the issue, how do we make sure that those folks who are at risk of homelessness get what they need to prevent them from becoming homeless, and what developed collaboratively around the table was a model for doing this work.

For Grantmakers, our role was to convene the meeting, to bring information to the table. I got a call from the guy from HUD after I invited him but didn't hear back. But he said when he heard what was going on, "I want to be a part of this," after our first meeting. Well, for HUD to take this role was very unique in San Diego County. His desire to be much more engaged in the solutions, rather than just being the bureaucrat who oversaw the money, was just terrific.

This collaboration was evident in each of the funding applications everyone generated. Everyone was saying how much stronger they felt their jurisdiction would be to respond because they had been collaborating with the other cities. And they intended to continue to meet every quarter as a collaboration to assure connection and coordination among all the resources.

And then we learned that the state had received from HUD $44 million dollars that would be distributed throughout different regions. San Diego typically receives less money than other regions, so we decided to go for a larger piece of the pie. The Grantmakers started building a relationship with the head of the department of Housing and Community Development Agency in Sacramento — and telling him what we were doing in San Diego, and how we were picturing it, and what we were planning to do with the HUD money. He was really impressed, saying we were really ahead of the game, really talking to each other, and developing a strategy. He liked how we were really helping to guide some of the things the state was looking at — how to connect all the recourses together, what makes a competitive application, what makes things work better than others. We shared with him all of the best practices we had gotten from the National Alliance to End Homelessness.

Bottom line is, we've been able to bring down $13 million dollars. We continue to meet and discuss how to connect the dots between all the resources for families. We meet quarterly and are developing regional materials together so all the agencies will know who all the players are. But it wasn't that common an experience to have Health and Human Services — food stamps folks — sitting down and talking with housing and community development folks in the region, talking with the folks from north in Oceanside and Chula Vista down south about how to use existing resources. Folks are applying for food stamps who are at risk of homelessness, and how do we pull them all together so there is a smoother, fluid provision of services that will be more cost effective, that will significantly prevent people from losing their housing, and provide a higher level of care and service in their community?

And our next step, as a group of funders, we are working to pull together enough resources to develop a regional plan for family homelessness, in concert with the plan to end chronic homelessness. And we've already garnered 15K for that effort. And we hope at the conference we can get others to say, "Gee, that's a really compelling story, and we'd really like to join those efforts, because we see that leveraging that money will create something sustainable and long lasting."

Seeing that we can get a lot accomplished is very exciting. That the Grantmakers' funders have been able to garner the respect of folks throughout the community who see our value and ask for our expertise. One of our funding partners is taking the lead in contacting more members.

We've let people know that this is really about housing. Keeping people in their homes and making sure there's enough affordable housing. And when we talk about it in that way, people are really starting to listen. Because if you don't have a house, you cannot find a house. If you don't have a house, your children won't do well at school — they won't have a consistent school to go to or a place to do their homework, so their school success suffers. If you don't have a house, looking for a job is crazy because you are spending all your time worrying about where you are going to sleep. So you've got to keep people in their homes with short-term or medium-term rental assistance. How much more cost-effective is this? The average cost to have someone move in and out of a shelter is about $48,000 per year. The cost of providing even a $1,000 per month to keep them in their homes is significantly less than that — it's a fourth of that.

It's changing the perception in people's minds that it's about housing. The picture is not this grungy guy on the street. It's a picture of a family with kids who are struggling in this economy, about kids who are struggling in school because of losing their homes, and what are we doing to really support our families.

It has not happened before — this collaboration that's happened here. The Plan to End Chronic Homelessness really never had the buy-in that's needed. It's not like it came from the agencies, it came from the community, which the agencies ended up blessing. But in our example, it's the agencies that have gotten together to collaborate, which is outside of the norm. It happened because there was an opportunity for money — which is natural. The question is, "How do you hold it together after the money is in place?" So that is something Grantmakers will be pressing them on. How do we keep the dialog open, how do we make sure it's a meaningful dialogue, how do we keep everyone seeing the bigger picture? That is Grantmakers' role.

It is also being the glue — the convening, being their technical advisors has been our big role. It's been about the power of numbers. Yes, the philanthropy dollars are tiny compared to state money. So it's really about our commitment to the cause and leveraging Grantmakers' ability to provide technical assistance and technical expertise. A few of the cities have said that they would not have applied for this money if they hadn't had our support and assistance. We would not have bothered because we wouldn't have known about how to do it. You're looking at millions of dollars that have been brought to the community just because there has been a collaboration.

One of the things that was so interesting is that we kept asking the smaller cities who they needed to partner with to make this work. They would tell us, and we would then invite them to the table. So we got those folks together. Everyone showed up and that's what has made this work. It was that strength of ,"Okay, if we in the city don't have the capacity to immediate write the rent check if someone receives a three-day eviction notice, who does?" In some places it will be the city, in some places it will be a nonprofit, depending on the capacity of that particular jurisdiction.

Other benefits — I think it's energized the funders. Of seeing, "Hey, you know, it hasn't taken much but look at how far we are getting." Experiencing their political clout and looking toward the future and their next round of activity.

Six thousand two hundred kids have been identified by the homeless liaisons in the schools as being homeless or at risk of being homeless.

This experience showcases how a group of funders stepped into this new arena where funders hadn't been before and made something happen that would never have happened on its own, in terms of working with governments and agencies. So I think it speaks to the unique role philanthropy can play — in terms of breaking out of the box and doing something new. We talk about the power of philanthropy and grant-making, we talk about being innovative and taking risks that government agencies can't do — even though the money is so much bigger. And that's the point about why all of this did happen, why we did it this way.

If we were looking at just pooling Grantmakers' dollars and trying to do something then, that amount of money is going to be tiny. Versus saying by wading into this new arena and bringing different people to the table, we could bring significant dollars to the community. But a nonprofit alone couldn't have done it. And individual governments couldn't have done it because of the competition between organizations in both cases. So I think it really does showcase a very unique role where a group of funders did something that not only were they not meeting together on their own, individually any one of those components would not have been able to organize this collaboration on the fly. So I think that is a powerful story about what is unique about what funders can do.

Public-private partnership, leveraging dollars and resources, relationship building piece of it — key messages.

What I learned is that collaboration between funders can take many shapes. Sometimes the road has lots of bumps because of different priorities, resources, commitments, and needs:

✔ There is strength in numbers.

✔ What we do: Learn, demonstrate, advocate.

✔ Powerful: Ability to leverage our resources — please join us.

✔ Man at the corner panhandling, folks sleeping in Balboa Park.

✔ Economic crisis changed the picture — the new face was families.

✔ 6,200 children in schools identified as homeless or at risk.

✔ Families sleeping in their cars, in their friend's garage, in their parent's living room.

✔ Total for county: $13 million leveraged. *Used with permission. Copyright © 2009 by San Diego Grantmakers. Story collected from Project Lead Barbara Mandel and contributed by San Diego Grantmakers. All rights reserved.*

It's Not About Shelters: Version 2

By San Diego Grantmakers

What's always been the picture most people have about homeless people is those on the street panhandling, sleeping in a corner downtown, standing in the bread lines downtown — those that many people kind of fear — the chronic homeless. In San Diego, many of those people are chronically mentally ill individuals who are on the street because their resources run out on day 25 of the month and they are not able to manage their care for themselves.

It's been one of the goals of the HWG to support the plan and to create some long-term sustainability.

With the economic crisis we're starting to see a whole new group of people who are homeless — and we never really saw them before. But what's starting to happen is, with more people losing their jobs and homes, we're starting to see a lot of people in families, we are starting to see whole families who are homeless. And it's really apparent in the schools. The school homeless liaisons are the ones who have been instrumental in raising the red flag in a very quiet way. It's not until you ask them what's going on that they say, "Gee, we're seeing a lot more families coming for services, who are doubled up, or living in their car, or living in somebody's attic."

"Okay," agencies in San Diego were saying, "now that we've done what we can to launch the plan to end chronic homelessness, and we're supporting the Corporation for Supportive Housing to provide the appropriate resources for this group, how can we turn our attention to a rapidly growing group of folks?"

And we learned that the National Alliance to End Homelessness was going to have its national conference on family homelessness here in San Diego last February 2009. So we thought it would be a great opportunity for us to create greater public awareness — particularly among elected leaders — that there's a whole new group of people out here that we are not paying attention to. And as a community, cities focus on housing plans, while the county focuses on services. We decided to hold a summit and ask some nationally recognized speakers to present what the picture of family homelessness is around the country. We ended up with standing room only at the NTC Promenade at Liberty Station; those who attended were either elected leaders or their representatives. We were there to not only paint the picture about what the current situation is, but also to call attention to some stimulus money coming down the pike and this was a great opportunity to look at some short-term funding and solutions, and build them into some sustainable long-term kinds of results.

We did learn that in San Diego Country HUD had allocated $10.5 million dollars that would be spread among the city of San Diego, the county of San Diego, and a couple of other cities in San Diego County.

We thought, "What can we do to get these folks together so we create more of a regional approach to how we are going to handle the short-term homelessness prevention funding? Because in many communities, and particularly in San Diego, prevention had never been part of the mix. We were always "plugging the hole, plugging the problem" but not really coming up with ideas to address prevention. It was always about serving the homeless but never about ending homelessness.

At the first meeting there were about ten people around the table, and we talked about what we could do that would be different, and how we can address things in a new way. They were happy and surprised to be invited to the meeting. And one of the gentlemen at the table said, "You know, we've never really sat together; we've never had a discussion together, we've never talked about this together." He really expressed his appreciation that the funders had the foresight to bring everybody together. Otherwise they'd be working in their little silos thinking how they were going to spend this money in the same way they had always been spending it. We needed to do a bit of a paradigm shift because the city had been focused for so long on building a shelter for the homeless. We noticed when we had the summit that a light bulb went on everywhere when one of the speakers said, "It's not about shelters — it's about keeping people in their homes." It's like then "Oh, well if that's the case, then yeah we can get behind it."

Our second collaboration meeting we had 25 people in the room and we thought, "Wow, this is really great! This is the place to be. People are really feeling like they want to be a part of this and that's why they are showing up!"

For San Diego Grantmakers, our role was to convene the meeting, to bring information to the table. I got a call from a guy at HUD after I invited him but didn't hear back. But he said when he heard what was going on after our first meeting he said, "I want to be a part of this." Well for HUD to take this role was very unique in San Diego County.

This collaboration was evident in each of the funding applications everyone generated. Everyone was saying how much stronger they felt their jurisdiction would be to respond because they had been collaborating with the other cities. And they intended to continue to meet every quarter as a collaboration to assure connection and coordination among all the resources.

The Grantmakers started building a relationship with the head of the department of Housing and Community Development Agency in Sacramento — and telling him what we were doing in San Diego, and how we were picturing it, and what we were planning to do with the HUD money. He was really impressed, saying we were really ahead of the game, really talking to each other, and developing a strategy. He liked how we were really helping to guide some of the things the state was looking at — how to connect all the resources together, what makes a competitive application, what makes things work better than others. We shared with him all the best practices we had gotten from the National Alliance to End Homelessness.

Bottom line is, we've been able to bring $13 million in new government funding to San Diego County to help with prevention. It wasn't that common an experience, for instance, to have Health and Human Services — food stamps folks — sitting down and talking with housing and community development folks in the region, talking with the folks from north in Oceanside and Chula Vista down south about how to use existing resources.

And we hope we can get others to say, "Gee, that's a really compelling story, and we'd really like to join those efforts, because we see that leveraging that money will create something sustainable and long lasting."

We've let people know that this is really about housing. Keeping people in their homes and making sure there's enough affordable housing. And when we talk about it in that way, people are really starting to listen. If you don't have a house, your children won't do well at school — they won't have a consistent school to go to or a place to do their homework, so their school success suffers. If you don't have a house, looking for a job is crazy because you're spending all your time worrying about where you are going to sleep.

So you've got to keep people in their homes with short-term or medium-term rental assistance. The average cost to have someone move in and out of a shelter is about $48,000 per year. The cost of providing even a $1,000 per month to keep them in their homes is significantly less than that — it's a fourth of that.

It's changing the perception in people's minds that it's about housing. It's a picture of a family with kids who are struggling in this economy, about kids who are struggling in school because of losing their homes, and what are we doing to really support our families.

It hasn't happened before — this collaboration that's happened here. But in our example, it's the agencies that have gotten together to collaborate, which is outside of the norm. The question is, "After the money is in place, how do we keep the dialogue open, how do we make sure it's a meaningful dialogue, how do we keep everyone seeing the bigger picture?" That is San Diego Grantmakers' role.

It is also being the glue — convening meetings and being their technical advisors has been our big role. It's been about the power of numbers. A few of the cities have said that they wouldn't have applied for this money if they hadn't had our support and assistance. It was that strength of, "Okay, if we in the city don't have the capacity to immediately write the rent check if someone receives a three-day eviction notice, who does?" In some places it will be the city, in some places it will be a nonprofit, depending on the capacity of that particular jurisdiction.

Other benefits — I think it's energized the funders. They have been saying, "Hey, you know, it hasn't taken much but look at how far we are getting." They have been experiencing some political clout and looking toward the future and their next round of activity.

Six thousand two hundred kids have been identified by the homeless liaisons in the schools as being homeless or at risk of being homeless.

This experience showcases how a group of funders stepped into this new arena where funders hadn't been before and made something happen that would never have happened on its own, in terms of working with governments and agencies. So I think it speaks to the unique role philanthropy can play — in terms of breaking out of the box and doing something new. We talk about the power of philanthropy and grant-making, we talk about being innovative and taking risks that government agencies can't do — even though the money is so much bigger. And that's the point about why all of this did happen, why we did it this way.

So I think it really does showcase a very unique role where a group of funders did something that they could not have done if they were not already meeting together on their own. Individually any one of those components would not have been able to organize this collaboration on the fly. So I think that is a powerful story about what is unique about what funders can do when they come together. *"It's Not About Shelters" version 2 is used with permission. Copyright © 2009 San Diego Grantmakers. All rights reserved.*

When Failing Isn't an Option: Go For It

Told by Jan Pulvermacher-Ryan, crafted by Lori L. Silverman

In the mid-80s, I worked part-time at a branch of an independent bank in Madison, Wisconsin as a secretary and a teller. It was perfect because my daughter was still at home and I wanted to have a job. Eventually, it evolved into a full-time position, and in fact, I became the branch manager.

A couple years later, the president of the bank called one day and said, "Have you heard that our lending officer has given his notice and is leaving our bank?" I said, "Yes. It's too bad. He's a very intelligent young man and a very personable young individual and really did a lot for personal banking here." And the president said, "I want you to take that job. I want you to apply for it." I said, "I'm not going to apply for that job. I don't have any of the skills needed to be a lending officer at a bank the size of ours." He replied, "You're exactly the right person for this opportunity. We need you in it." And I said, "Well I'm going to have to think about it."

I went home that evening and my husband, Sylvester, and I had a very serious discussion over dinner. He said, "Do you want to continue to work? It's an opportunity to be in a professional position." We also included the kids in the discussion because their life was going to be affected by the fact that it was an officer position that required more than 40 hours a week. The bank was very community-related, and I'd need to belong to a service organization and participate in those activities, most of which were in the evening. I'd also have to represent the bank at a variety of events at the local schools. And there was Friday night and Saturday morning work as well.

At the time, Tami was seven and Scott was ten. I didn't want them to feel that I wasn't giving them the time that they needed. We all agreed that we'd think about it over the next day.

But, as you all know, there's the stuff you can talk about and then there's the stuff you can't. Personally, I didn't think I had the necessary skills or any knowledge about lending. And it scared me because in my whole life, I always had an opportunity to review the material before taking the test. Here I knew I was going to get thrown into the fray without having a lot of information and was really going to be learning on the job. I'd have to learn all the form documents and what was required by law — it's a huge area — and I was petrified that I was going to fail. That was something that's never happened before to me.

I graduated high school at the top of my class. Failure wasn't an option. And I was really concerned that I would fail. And not only fail, but fail miserably and lose my job entirely! I certainly didn't voice it to my children because I was always positive in front of them, for their sake, because they were achievers as well. I didn't want them to think that I didn't feel that I was capable of doing this.

On top of this, the job required collecting bad debts. That wasn't something I particularly liked to do or even wanted to do — calling people up and harassing them to make their payments. There were situations where I knew it could be traumatic. And this was also turning around in my brain. Plus I didn't know what the job really entailed so it was fraught with a lot of peril in my mind. I tell you: This made for a lot of stress in that 24-hour period!

The next night we had another discussion at dinner. I remember saying to Tami and Scott, "You were very supportive last night about the opportunity for mom. Are you still good with that? Have you had any other questions pop up in your mind? Or maybe you talked to some friends and said, 'Oh, I don't want my mom to work that bad. I thought it was okay but now I'm not okay with it?'" And they said, "No, we think you should do it." My husband was totally supportive, too, even after realizing the additional hours I was going to have to work.

So I figured if they were all comfortable with the job, I could find a way to stretch and get over my fear. I'm a quick study, so I knew every night I could take materials home to read and process. The educational piece of learning something new and different was a good challenge since I love to learn.

Because banking at that time was a male-dominated profession, there were very few female officers in my hometown. I felt the job would provide a platform to get more women involved in positions of authority in banking and other industries. Being an officer, I also felt I could do some things for women at our local bank as well. They really didn't have an opportunity to excel or to develop the skills needed to go beyond being a teller or a customer service rep opening up new accounts.

The next morning, I met with the president and accepted the position.

Two weeks later I was on the job. My boss promised me that the first Friday night that I had to work alone — you work alone as an officer — that he would work with me. That never happened. I just worked alone from the very first time that I was thrown into the fray. But, all in all, he was really very good to me. He helped me find a local instructor to complete my degree in finance from UW Platteville. While it took seven years, because I was working 60 to 70 hours a week, the bank paid for my education.

I was able to develop a full-fledged teller training process that put women in a much better position at the bank for future advancement and promotion. And, I know this might sound crazy but when I started at the main office I realized there were 35 women working in the bank with one bathroom and one toilet facility while five guys had the typical accoutrements in a man's bathroom plus a sit-down toilet. And I said to my boss, "You have to change this, like tomorrow," and he did.

While there were 7 people that reported to me initially, the job encompassed about 60 people after I was given personnel responsibilities. In many ways this allowed me to be a role model for my daughter. Being able to work and hold our personal life together and do the things for the family that I needed to do as well as doing it for my job — this was important. I think that she's developed into the type of a mother and professional woman she is today because I provided a roadmap for her to be able to that.

While I was initially fearful about taking the job, it taught me that you need to *stretch beyond your comfort zone* to reap the benefits you might not be able to see right away. This is no different than what the American Legion Auxiliary is going through today. Each and every one of us in this room — including me — will need to stretch beyond our comfort zone for our strategic plan to be a success over the next few years. Will you join me? I promise the benefits will be numerous to you and the Auxiliary. *Used with permission. Copyright © 2008 by Jan Pulvermacher-Ryan. All rights reserved.*

What's It Going to Take?

Told by Frank Sherwood, crafted by Lori L. Silverman

No sooner had Frank put down the phone than it rang again. She was calling from Toronto.

"Frank, this is Amy Royce. I represent an international consulting firm based in the U.S. Five and a half years ago, the firm leased 30,000 square feet of space in downtown Minneapolis that they're paying $11 a square foot net for. The lease is up in 18 months. I'm not licensed in the U.S. so I can't renegotiate the terms with the landlord. If my client can't get a lease renewal in the $8 range, they'll consider moving elsewhere in the Twin Cities, but it's not their preference. I've been told you can help us."

"Amy, you've come to the right guy. My company and I can do all the legwork for you here and get you exactly the deal your client deserves."

As soon as Frank hung up, he immediately dialed the listing agent for the property to set up a meeting — he knows everybody in the local corporate real estate market by first name. It's a talent that comes with 20 years of experience on the corporate side — and 14 more on the dark side acting as a mercenary on behalf of his clients.

There were three of them in that first meeting in June: Frank, his right-hand associate, and the most typical of typical listing agents — a man I'm sure you've met before — a wheeler-dealer type that gets his direction from on high. Frank spoke first. "As you know, Phil, we're representing Expert Consultants. With the downturn in the market, they're experiencing some cash flow issues. The only way they figure they can stay in your building and continue to lease 30,000 square feet is to renew their lease at $8 a square foot. Here's the RFP."

(Lots of laughter from Phil) "Frank, you know as well as I do that there's over a year remaining on that lease and in this market, not even Houdini could sublease that space." (Frank's internal dialogue) "Geez, what's this guy thinking . . . doesn't he know we have 'em by the balls?" (Frank's external dialogue) "Phil, thank you for your time." And with that, Frank and his right-hand man got up and left. Eight minutes had elapsed since they'd first walked in.

As soon as he got back to the office, Frank went to work doing what he does best: Getting tenants out of buildings owned by unresponsive landlords.

He went online to do a market survey. All the spaces that were vacant and 30,000 square feet in size popped up. But he'd only started. What Frank needed was somebody with deep pockets who was potentially in trouble — a guy who had $1.2 million dollars to buy out the remainder of this lease. So, he also researched the market. He figured out which landlords were approaching 50 percent vacancy in their buildings — a situation in which banks tend to call the loan. They have great incentive to work a deal. By the way, none of this stuff is readily apparent in the marketplace.

In the next sixty days, Frank found that guy — that guy with the deep pockets. It was a company that had vacated a building for a new headquarters office in downtown St. Paul. They desperately wanted to fill the old space. They offered an $8 net rate and a buyout of the entire remaining exposure on the old deal. Which meant Frank's client didn't have to suffer trying to sublease the old space. Though he knew his tenant wasn't all that fond of moving out of downtown Minneapolis, what was most important to him as a negotiator was that he had a bona fide offer that reduced his client's occupancy costs with no associated risk.

Frank also heard from Phil. The first time Phil responded, the offer was completely unacceptable. So Frank sent it back. The second time, it wasn't much better. So Frank sent it back again. (Frank's internal dialogue) "Thank goodness we have time on our side."

You'd think the third time would be a charm. But it wasn't. This last deal was definitely not as attractive as what Frank and his team had found. So, he set up another face-to-face meeting with the listing agent. "Phil, my client is ready to vacate 30,000 square feet in 60 days. We found them property in St. Paul for $8 a square foot net." (Phil's external dialogue) "C'mon, Frank, don't be so hasty, we can meet that deal!" (Frank's external dialogue) "Phil, the time to make that deal has long since passed. What are you willing to do to retain my client?"

(Phil's internal dialogue: "Ah, Frank, you just don't get it do you?") "Well, Frank, we're prepared to offer you an incentive if you can make that other deal go away." (Frank's external dialogue) "Phil, we work open book with our clients. They know how much we make — and that the landlord pays our fee. What else do you think you could do to retain our client?"

(Phil's internal dialogue): "Man, this guy is a nut case." "C'mon, Frank. You know as well as I do that the options are limited. What else do you think we should do?" (Frank's external dialogue) "Phil. Here's the situation. Overall our client likes the space they're in. They're willing to stay if you agree to rebate all the rent that's been paid year-to-date and do a renewal at $6 a square foot net." (Phil's external dialogue) "Frank, it's not likely to happen. But I'll present it to the owner and get back to you."

One week later, Frank got a fourth offer from Phil. He sent it back with a counter offer — restating exactly what he'd told him in the meeting — and attaching financials showing it was a good deal for the landlord. The next week, he got the fifth offer from Phil. Still not good enough. So he sent it back. The following week the same thing happened. Sixth offer? Better, but still not good enough. And the week after that? Improved but not good enough. The fifth week? Still no cigar.

Finally, 6 weeks after that second meeting, 155 days — more than 6 full months since the day that Amy first called Frank, he received the offer he'd be waiting for: One that saved his client more than $3 million dollars on a 10-year renewal to stay in the space the client loved. There was no need for them to even change their stationery!

Frank had done it. He'd made a deal happen where none existed. One that was infinitely better than his client had originally requested. As a highly experienced professional tenant rep, he'd leveled the playing field and gotten a win-win for all parties. But to make it happen, he'd been given the gift of time.

If you want me to do right by you then *give me time*. What do you want? Do you want these sorts of results or just some help? If you only want help, 90 days will do. Give me time to leverage my skills in this market. Make the decision now to move ahead. *Used with permission. Copyright © 2010 by Frank Sherwood. All rights reserved.*

Story Template

Here's a generic template to ensure you have all the pieces of a story in place.

Title of story

Don't give away the story's meaning through its title. Make it memorable.

Perspective

- ✓ Which side of the story needs to be heard?
- ✓ Which character needs to tell it?
- ✓ In which voice does it need to be told — first-, second-, or third-person?

Layers of meaning: Themes, key message

- ✓ Who are the potential audiences for the story?
- ✓ What are all the themes that the story brings forth?
- ✓ What's the key message? Make sure it conveys a universal message.
  - Use a full sentence — not a bullet point. Make it a concise and memorable statement, not a question. Confine it to a single point.
  - Craft it in the affirmative rather than in the negative.

Alert listeners before you launch the story

- ✓ Someone introduces you: Start with the first sentence of the story.
- ✓ The presentation or agenda is turned over to you with no formal introduction. You start with a setup phrase.
  - "Joe's comments remind me of a time when . . ."
  - "You've all heard Joe's experience. Something similar happened to me once . . ."
  - "As I was listening to Joe, his situation made me think about what happened when . . ."

✔ The story is one you've created from one or more books or news sources about a historical event in the company, in another organization, or the world at large. You say something like, "This is my take on . . ."

✔ You have permission to tell someone else's story. Find a way to provide attribution. Remember to actually get permission to use it!

Start the story

✔ How do you want to launch the story — its opening lines? Avoid a preamble. Give the audience an image to feast on.

✔ What do you need to say to set the stage — to paint the picture?

- What's the context?
- What's the setting?
- Who's the main character? Who are the other characters? What are their names?

Get clear on the core conflict

✔ How do the events in the *plot* unfold to reveal what the problem is?

✔ What's the *conflict* —problem/struggle/trouble — and what's at risk?

✔ How are the *characters* relating to the core conflict?

✔ How is the *story arc* shifting to reveal the awareness of the characters?

What to do about data

✔ What's the face behind the data?

✔ What dilemma do you want the data to illustrate or inform?

✔ What data is most important to achieving the outcome you're after?

✔ What's the frame for the data?

✔ What story structure helps in organizing the data and in relaying the story it tells?

- The deductive-argument-wrapped-in-a-story approach.
- The butler-did-it approach.
- The set-your-story-as-a-map approach.

✔ How can you break complex data into bite-sized chunks?

✔ How do you want to display the data?

✔ What's the key message in the data?

Get a story to pop!

✔ How can you bring characters to life? Have you included their inner and outer dialogue?

✔ How can you tap into the *language of the senses* (LOTS)?

✔ Where could you add stark contrast?

✔ What irony could you add to further embellish the story?

✔ Where can you add figures of speech (oxymorons, metaphors, similes, analogies, and aphorisms) to enhance contrast and visual language?

✔ How can you strengthen the emotions already resident in the story?

✔ What tension can you build into a story by waiting to reveal key pieces of information until the end?

✔ Where could you add humor, if it's appropriate for the story?

✔ What unexpected event or decisions could you embellish or add to the story to enhance drama and surprise?

✔ What surprising obstacles are standing in the way of the main character?

✔ Where could you add exaggeration or repetition?

End the story

✔ What's the resolution of the conflict or problem?

✔ What's the key message of the story?

- Do I as narrator want to deliver the key message or do I want my character to deliver it?

- Is there a question you can pose to your audience?

- Is there a quotation you can use to lead into the key message?

- Can you use a personal reflection to strengthen the key message?

✔ What's the transition to the action statement?

✔ What actions do you want others to take as a result of the story?

Determining story structure

Decide which structure your story follows and ensure all pieces are in it.

Hollywood storytelling structures

- I'm better off
- Highlight both loss and gain
- The Cinderella down-and-out story

Business storytelling structures

- SHARES: Setting, Hindrance, Action, Results, Evaluation, and Suggested actions
- PARLAS: Problem, Action, Result, Learning, Application, and Suggested actions
- CHARQES: Situation, Challenge, Action, Results Quantified, Evaluation, and Suggested actions
- CCARLS: Context, Challenge, Action, Result, Lesson, and Suggested actions

Other structures that serve specific purposes

- Open with an opportunity
- Speak to the why
- Leverage the underdog
- Present-future story structure

Tag line

A *tag line* is a phrase that's a memorable way to refer to your story. It might be the key message. It could also be an analogy, aphorism, or metaphor and may function as the story's theme or title — as long as you don't give away the core message in the title.

Index

• D •

Notes

About the Authors

Karen Dietz, PhD, is the owner of Just Story It! and a 25-year veteran in business, organizational, and leadership development. She works with leaders and companies in business storytelling so they're able to unite people together in achieving new goals. Karen draws on her experience with Fortune 500 companies, startups, and nonprofit organizations to provide practical experience, guidance, and tools in working with stories that can be put to work immediately.

Karen contributed the foreword and Chapter 6 in *Wake Me Up When the Data Is Over: How Organizations Use Stories to Drive Results* (Jossey-Bass, 2006) and is featured in Stephen Denning's book *The Leader's Guide To Storytelling: Mastering the Art and Discipline of the Business Narrative* (Jossey-Bass, 2011). She is also the top curator globally on business storytelling at www.scoop. it/t/just-story-it, sharing her reviews of the best material she can find so people can gain story knowledge, tools, and resources.

She received her doctorate in Folklore/Folklife from the University of Pennsylvania and is the former Executive Director of the National Storytelling Network. Karen is also a fiber artist, creating hand-dyed silk panels of the principles she employs that she then brings into her work with clients. She can be found at juststoryit@gmail.com and www.juststoryit.com.

Lori L. Silverman is the co-author of *Critical Shift: The Future of Quality in Organizational Performance* (Quality Press, 1999) and *Stories Trainers Tell: 55 Ready-to-Use Stories to Make Training Stick* (Jossey-Bass/Pfeiffer, 2003). Her book *Wake Me Up When the Data Is Over: How Organizations Use Stories to Drive Results* (Jossey-Bass, 2006) debuted in the top 100 books on Amazon. She's frequently asked to share her practical, results-driven, highly energized, and enthusiastic approach to business storytelling as a keynote presenter and in workshops to leaders and staff in recognized companies, nonprofits, and associations. She's also appeared on more than 70 radio and TV shows to share results from workplace story use.

As the owner of Partners for Progress®, for 25 years she's consulted on enterprise-wide change and strategic planning to organizations such as American Family Insurance, the American Legion Auxiliary, Bechtel, Chevron, Duquesne University, Valmet, and the U.S. Air Force Reserves.

Lori holds an MS degree in Counseling and Guidance from the University of Wisconsin-Madison, where she's an ad hoc instructor at the Fluno Center for Executive Education, and an MBA from Edgewood College. When she's not jetting between New York City and Phoenix or watching UW Badger football, catch her at lori@partnersforprogress.com or www.partners forprogress.com.

Dedication

To all those who are dedicated to and curious, learning, and passionate about the art and science of business storytelling for making a difference in the world.

Authors' Acknowledgments

A special call-out to Robert McIlree, Cristi Kanenwischer, Pam Stampen, David Brock, Barbara Mandel and the San Diego Grantmakers, Jan Pulvermacher-Ryan, Frank Sherwood, and Denise, for allowing us to showcase their compelling stories as teaching examples. Thank you to Rena Huber, Jean Peelen, Ari Weinsweig, and Carrie Severson for providing hip pocket story examples for Chapter 4, and Robyn Atkinson for her short story in Chapter 14.

Recognition also goes to colleagues who provided examples and assistance, including Madelyn Blair, Paul Furiga, David Hutchens, Thaler Pekar, Angela Prestil, Doug Stevenson, and Jo Tyler. We appreciate all the bloggers, writers, researchers, academics, and authors whose knowledge, insights, and examples we've referenced in the book, making business storytelling real and tangible.

To Michael Lewis, formerly of Wiley, for finding us. David Lutton, acquisitions editor, for guiding us through the process. Corbin Collins, editor for his expert eye; and Dave Awl, technical editor, for his helpful suggestions. And thanks to all the other staff at Wiley who have worked diligently to bring this book alive.

Many thanks to family, friends, and colleagues who encouraged, supported, helped, and cheered us on. Special appreciation from Karen goes to Tim Dietz, Alan Briskin, Doug Lipman, Annette Simmons, and Lorna Christiansen and from Lori to Marcy Fisher, Bruce Barney, Lisa Shlee, and Tony Dominguez.

Publisher's Acknowledgments

Acquisitions Editor: David Lutton

Editor: Corbin Collins

Technical Editor: Dave Awl

Project Coordinator: Sheree Montgomery

Cover Image: © iStockphoto.com/Andrew Rich